D

RULERS AND SUBJECTS

RULERS AND SUBJECTS

Government and people
in Russia 1801–1991

JOHN GOODING

Senior Lecturer in History, University of Edinburgh

A member of the Hodder Headline Group
LONDON • NEW YORK • SYDNEY • AUCKLAND

First published in Great Britain in 1996 by
Arnold, a member of the Hodder Headline Group
338 Euston Road, London NW1 3BH
175 Fifth Avenue, New York, NY 10010

Distributed exclusively in the USA by
St Martin's Press Inc.,
175 Fifth Avenue,
New York, NY 10010

British Library Cataloguing in Publication Data
A catalogue entry for this book is available from the British Library

Library of Congress Cataloging-in-Publication Data
Gooding. John
    Rulers and subjects: government and people in Russia 1801–1991/
John Gooding.
        p. cm.
    Includes bibliographical references and index.
    ISBN 0-340-66288-3.—ISBN 0-340-61405-6 (pbk.)
    1. Russia—History—1801–1917. 2. Russia—Politics and
government—1801–1917. 3. Soviet Union—History. 4. Soviet Union—
Politics and government. I. Title.
DK189.G66 1996
947.08—dc20   95-52847
                                                                CIP

ISBN 0 340 61405 6(Pb)
ISBN 0 340 66288 3(Hb)

Composition by Phoenix Photosetting, Chatham, Kent
Printed and bound in Great Britain by J W Arrowsmith Ltd, Bristol

For Katharine, Timothy and Christopher

Contents

Preface

Unjust and oppressive regimes have a gloomy fascination for many of us, and among unjust and repressive regimes Russian ones have been in a class of their own. When the adverse effects of a harsh climate, poor soil and foreign invasions are allowed for, much of the perennial misery of living in Russia must be put down to the country's own rulers. Throughout their history, Russians have been ruled by or on behalf of one person or no more than a very small group of persons. Government in Russia has never been by the people, and it is extremely doubtful whether it has ever been for the people. Nowhere else in Europe has the gulf between the powerful and the powerless been so yawning, and nowhere else have the fortunate few been so predatory towards their underlings. If Jeremy Bentham's device for measuring pleasure and pain, the felicific calculus, could be applied to Russia at any point in history, it would record a huge excess of pain; it would also find the pain and pleasure distributed extremely unevenly between the classes. It is no wonder that the songs of the Russian people sound so often like laments, and it is no wonder also that deep melancholy seems to mark the haggard faces which look out at us from photograph albums.

Yet however wretched their lives, most Russians have for most of the time accepted their lot and not tried or probably even wanted to rebel against it. When Russians or foreigners write about the ordinary people of Russia, what they highlight is their stoicism, passivity and simplicity. That Russia is a 'much-suffering' country was a recurring comment before 1917; and since the Soviet censors lost their grip, 'much-suffering' has been applied so frequently to the country that it has almost come to seem the natural qualifier. Just as France is '*belle*' and England is 'merry', so Russia, alas, is 'much-suffering'. Not only have the Russians suffered immensely; there is something peculiar to them, the description suggests, about the way they have put up with such inordinate misfortune. The author of a recent history of Russia called his book *Endurance and Endeavour*, and it perhaps says something about how we think of Russia that J. N. Westwood chose to put the 'endurance' first.

Why have Russians endured so much with so little protest? Partly of course because they have been kept in ignorance of conditions elsewhere. For this reason, Bentham's calculus would not be very useful for making national comparisons, since pains and pleasures other than the purely physical are culturally conditioned and depend upon custom and expectation. Isolation, lack of education, poor communications and unremitting censorship have made the rulers' task much easier in Russia by pitching expectations so very low. Russians have on the whole asked for little and received little. And yet this is not a complete explanation. Russians may not have been able to measure their living conditions against those of other nations, but they knew very well how badly they fared against the privileged of their own society. The sense of 'us' and 'them' was widespread and bred a deep resentment, though only in the early twentieth century was grievance translated into successful rebellion. Russians may have seen themselves as unfortunate and even as victims; only rarely, however, have they blamed their miseries on the ruler and his regime. It is hard to understand how a small ruling class could have held down so many people spread across so massive an area without the compliance if not the active support of very many of the ruled. Had a large number seen themselves as prisoners and their rulers as jailers, then the house of cards would have collapsed repeatedly. In the event, it collapsed only twice – at either end of the twentieth century. Tsars and commissars were very good at hiding (perhaps even from themselves) how effectively they exploited their subjects and how much they pulled the wool over their eyes, and until very recently these rulerly skills were still much in evidence.

The upheavals of 1917 should have seen at least a beginning of the end of the Russians' miseries. Revolution, Trotsky had predicted, would mean a final break with the Asiatic, with the seventeenth century, with Holy Russia, and with icons and cockroaches. But the Asiatic and the seventeenth century actually returned with a new vigour; the cockroaches remained; old icons were replaced by ones that were still more lurid and, for a time, more powerfully charismatic; while Trotsky himself changed from a would-be liberator into one of the principal makers and shapers of the new enslavement. The greatest experiment in social and cultural engineering that mankind had known turned into one of history's great disasters, and the regime which had launched it became an intensely repressive dictatorship with a Marxist–Leninist façade but an essence so Russian that at times it seemed to be summoning up all the furies of the country's past. To its subjects, the Soviet regime must have appeared as unending and as elemental and irresistible a force as Nicholas I's had seemed in the previous century. However, after seven decades, this regime which had become a travesty of the Bolsheviks' original hopes collapsed with a minimum of upheaval; and amidst the distress and confusion of Russia's troubled end of century, there are some signs at least that the ideals of a humane, just and democratic society may at last be beginning to be realized.

What follows comes close to being a general history of Russia in the nineteenth and twentieth centuries, though its main aim is to explore and to explain the relationship between the ruling few and the masses whom they ruled so little to the masses' benefit and so much to their own. It discusses rulers and the ruling class which served them, institutions of state, government policies and problems, the doctrines and myths which were the invisible chains binding subjects to rulers, the passivity of the many and the rebellions in thought and deed of the few. Economic policies and conditions, however, come into focus only where they seem directly relevant to the theme of rulers and subjects; and foreign policy and international affairs get little attention except when, as during the Second World War and the perestroika period, they cannot sensibly be separated from domestic affairs.

Now, two important notes. First, on the confusing subject of dates. Until February 1918, Russia used the Julian calendar, which was twelve days behind the Western calendar in the nineteenth century and thirteen days behind in the twentieth century. Rather than translate dates, I have used the ones that applied at the time; and so the Bolshevik capture of power took place, according to this book, not on 7 November (when the Soviet state would celebrate it) but, instead, on 25 October. The confusion ended in 1918, when the new government brought the Russian calendar into line with the Western one. As Trotsky put it, 'before overthrowing the Byzantine calendar, the revolution had to overthrow the institutions that clung to it'.

Second, please look out for the introductory sections at the beginning of each chapter (except, however, the scene-setting first chapter). You will see that the chapters are broken up into several numbered sections. The first section is an overview which discusses the main themes of the chapter and highlights any subjects that have been contentious among historians or particularly problematic for them.

Finally, I must say thank you to those who in various ways have helped me with *Rulers and Subjects*. I would like, first, to express my very great gratitude to Mary Buckley, Paul Dukes, Harry Rigby and David Saunders, who read sections of the manuscript. They are, of course, not in the least to blame for any errors and stupidities which the obstinate or obtuse author may have allowed to remain. I am most grateful, too, to the staffs of the National Library of Scotland and Edinburgh University Library, both of which provided fine facilities for research; and to the President and Fellows of St John's College, Oxford, who, by electing me to a visiting scholarship in the summer of 1993, gave me ideal conditions for a while in which to work. I owe many thanks to Gloria Ketchin, who not only typed the first four chapters of the book but helped me in various ways throughout. And I am deeply indebted to Christopher Wheeler, my editor, for his patience and understanding and for a flow of good advice. In addition, it would be ungrateful of me not to acknowledge some debts of longer standing: to Zhenya Lampert, who first stirred my interest in Russian ideas; to Maurice Larkin, for quiet encouragement and support over a number of years; and to John Roberts, who as my tutor helped me to see the wood for the trees and did more than either of us can have guessed at the time to shape my values.

Edinburgh, 1995

|1|

Russia at the beginning of the nineteenth century

1

In Russia the ruler was everything. There was general agreement that within the Christian world at least no other ruler could match the power of the tsar. Back in the sixteenth century, a visitor had written about the tsar:

> In the sway which he holds over his people, he surpasses all the monarchs of the whole world ... He uses his authority as much over ecclesiastics as laymen, and holds unlimited control over the lives and property of all his subjects: not one of his counsellors has sufficient authority to dare oppose him, or even differ from him, on any subject.[1]

When, three centuries later, Alexis de Tocqueville was writing his great book on democracy in America, the country he singled out as the polar opposite of America was Russia. While America relied on 'personal interest and gives free scope to the unguided strengths and common sense of individuals', Russia, he pointed out, 'concentrates the whole power of society in one man'. 'One', he argued, 'has freedom as the principal means of action; the other has servitude.'[2]

Far from being coy about their unlimited power, Russian rulers proudly proclaimed themselves as 'autocrats'. The title went back to the fifteenth century, when a Moscow prince had first used it as a way of asserting that he no longer owed any allegiance to his former overlord, the Mongol Khan. Once tsarism was under serious challenge in the early years of the twentieth century, those who defended Nicholas II's continued use of the title would argue that it meant nothing other than a ruler subject to no external control. But that was simply throwing dust in people's eyes, since the original meaning had long since been eclipsed by a quite different one. An autocrat, as everyone but these learned conservatives knew, was a ruler subject to no internal limitations; he shared his power with no other persons or institutions and every word of his had the force of an unconditional command.

A statute of 1716 had put the matter in a nutshell: 'His Majesty is an autocratic Monarch who is accountable to no one for his policies, but has power and authority to govern his states and lands as a Christian ruler according to his will and understanding.'[3] That would be reformulated in the early nineteenth century in article 1 of the Fundamental Laws of the Russian Empire. 'The All-Russian Emperor is an autocratic and unlimited monarch. God himself commands that his supreme power be obeyed, out of conscience as well as fear.'[4] But while absolute monarchy was acknowledged to be quite different from constitutional monarchy, Russia's rulers were anxious to distinguish themselves from Oriental despots, and Article 47 of the Fundamental Laws pointed out that 'The Russian Empire is governed on the firm basis of positive laws, statutes and regulations emanating from the autocratic power.'[5] The autocrat ruled, in other words, by law rather than simply caprice. He would also have claimed that, unlike a despot, he ruled on his people's behalf and he would have denied that his actions were prompted by personal ambition or interest.

But these two claims made in the Fundamental Laws – that the monarch had unlimited power and that he observed the rule of law – were not easy to reconcile. In theory the two were reconciled by the notion of self-limitation; a proper autocrat would choose to observe the laws established by his predecessors or himself and if he decided to change them he would do so in accordance with strictly laid down procedures. Self-limitation amounted to nothing more, however, than respect for legal formality. The words 'So be it' written in the ruler's own hand at the end of an official pronouncement were enough to make a law or to unmake one. The Emperor Paul (reigned 1796–1801) rather gave the game away when he struck himself on the chest and declared 'Here is the law!'[6] Whatever the formalities, the autocracy was simply an institutionalized form of arbitrary power (*proizvol* in Russian), and law was nothing other than what the autocrat chose to make it.

He ruled Russia very much as if the country and its inhabitants were his personal property, as if they comprised an enormous private estate which he could dispose of as the fancy took him. The inhabitants were *his* subjects rather than the subjects, still less the citizens, of the Russian state, and they owed him personal loyalty much as servants owe loyalty to a master. He looked after them in return for their obedience, but whereas he imposed strict obedience upon them, they had no way at all of making sure that he kept his side of the unwritten bargain – the only arbiter who might intervene on their behalf was God, and his intercession would come only in the afterlife. Elsewhere, people often had rights against the state as well as obligations towards it; the Russians, by contrast, had a heavy burden of obligations unrelieved by any rights whatever.

One approach to the relationship between ruler and subjects would be to say that in Russia, unlike the countries of Western Europe, there was a gross imbalance between an omnipotent and personalized state and a passive, defenceless and atomized society. Some would go further and say that in Russia there was no society, there were simply subjects – meaning that people were not allowed to combine except in ways that the state approved of, and even then it watched over them with an eagle eye. Virtually alone in Europe the country had no representative, law-making assembly – and since it had no such assembly it had no real laws at all, or so the early nineteenth-century constitutionalist Mikhail Speransky would argue. It had nothing similar either to the ancient corporations of nobles, lawyers and merchants which wielded great influence in Western Europe. Nor did Russia proper, as opposed to its western borderlands, have any old-established universities. Still less was there anything of the vigorous local government and the hum of grass-roots activity which so impressed Tocqueville as the essence of American democracy. Russia's evolution, the liberal historian and politician Paul Milyukov would argue, had been fundamentally different from that of the West. In the West society had made the state, but in Russia the process had been the other way round: the state had made society – and tailored it to its own special needs. 'The Russian state,' wrote Milyukov, 'not only did not have to fight against the rights and privileges of private persons and social groups, but itself ... tried to summon these social groups into existence and activity in order to make use of this activity for its own ends.'[7]

Russia was of course no exception to the general rule that the socio-economic 'base' influences the political 'superstructure'. But the point is that in Russia's case the extreme backwardness of the base had allowed the state to impose upon the people to a degree unparalleled elsewhere. In other countries there was a two-way relationship between state and society, an intricate pattern of give and take in which the state both shaped society and was in turn shaped by it. In Russia, however, the movement went solely in one direction. The state was the one dynamic force in the country and was constantly pushing, bullying and restructuring an inert society. There were two different and indeed contradictory reasons for this constant activity: rulers wanted to modernize the country since backwardness left it vulnerable to aggression, yet they were always on the alert to stifle anything that might have jeopardized their monopoly of power.

But how did the tsars get away with it? How was it possible for a ruler and a small number of officials to impose their will on forty million people spread across one-sixth of the earth's land surface? If we think of the tsar as a jailer and his subjects as prisoners, then tsarism's success seems incomprehensible: why did the prisoners simply not rebel and break their way out? The answer is that they, or at least the great majority of them, did not in the least see themselves as the tsar's prisoners and had no wish to escape. There are of course no opinion polls or election results to let us make the point with statistical precision. However, there can be no doubt that most people approved of the autocracy or at least did not question it and had positive feelings towards their 'little father' the tsar, even if they did not like all of the things done in his name. What most Russians wanted – and this would continue to be true long after the beginning of the nineteenth century – was good government rather than democratic government, security and material wellbeing rather than the freedom to arrange their lives independently of others. They tended to think of themselves not as individuals with careers to carve out and competitors to beat but rather as players in a team with its back to the wall, as members of a community beset with all sorts of hazards. What mattered, therefore, was not so much clearing away all the obstacles to self-fulfilment but maintaining solidarity within a community whose survival was vitally dependent on suppressing selfish impulses, avoiding risks and, above all, avoiding feuding. Members of the educated class, the nobility, were of course more likely to be influenced by Western ideals of individual liberty and self-realization. Yet most of them too (though there were, as we shall see, important exceptions) approved of the autocratic system of government, thought it better in principle than a constitutional system or at least more suited to Russia, and feared that without it the country would succumb to anarchy, disintegration and foreign invasion.

2

Why were the Russians, even educated ones, so ready to accept the absolutism of the tsars? Why was there so little confidence in the ability of ordinary people to run their own lives? Various answers can be given to this, but they all in one way or another come back to the basic fact of geography. The Russians had been unlucky in their location – they occupied a harsh expanse of land with a severe climate and a low level of fertility which lay, exposed to Asia, on the very margin of Europe. The area in which the Russian state had originated was in fact relatively favourable: around Kiev in the Dnieper valley in the far south-west of what would become the Russian empire, where there was considerable contact with European commerce and culture. The Kievan state was, however, destroyed by Mongol invaders in the thirteenth century, and after this disaster the focus of Russian life shifted hundreds of miles to the north-east. Isolated by distance, primitive communications and strong anti-Western prejudices, Muscovite Russia was left more or less untouched by the great movements which would transform Western Europe and make it an area of dynamic growth – the Renaissance, the Reformation, the scientific revolution, the burgeoning of capitalism. Not until the seventeenth and eighteenth centuries, and in particular the reign of Peter the Great (1682–1725), did Western ways of life and thought have much impact. Even then the state filtered the imports with extreme care, restricting them in the main to science and technology (especially military technology) and goods and pastimes for the upper class, and they had very little direct influence on the lives of ordinary people.

The Russians, then, belonged to the wide, open and inhospitable expanses between Europe proper and Asia, but there were no natural geographical features to say exactly where they belonged, to mark out and define a secure territory for them. No seas protected them, while major rivers such as the Volga, the Don and the Dnieper did not demarcate acceptable boundaries and were anyway easily passable, especially in winter. As for mountains, the Urals were relatively low and far to the east of the centres of Russian life, while the more formidable Caucasus were outside Russia proper. This lack of natural barriers left the Russians vulnerable to attack from all sides. In recent centuries invasion has come from the west, from Sweden, Poland, France and Germany, but much the most important invasion in terms of its shaping influence was the thirteenth-century Mongol one from the east, which led to more than two centuries of subjection of the Russians to pagan overlords. Much in later Russian life can be put down to the impact of this calamity: chronic insecurity; a tendency to keep the population mobilized as if for war even when no war was on the horizon; and a feeling that strong centralized leadership – precisely what the Kievans had not had – was vital if further disasters were to be avoided. That centralization of power is the price to be paid for survival is an assumption which few Russians have over the centuries felt able to challenge. The autocracy might be merciless towards internal critics, but at least it acted as a shield against external enemies – and the same thinking no doubt reconciled many later Russians to Stalin's modernized autocracy.

But not only had the Mongols rammed home the need for unity and strong centralized rule. They had also shown how an autocratic system should work, for the Mongol Khan had absolute control over the lives and property of his subjects. When an independent Moscow state emerged, its symbols – the ruler's title, his crown, the double-headed eagle – came from the Byzantine empire, the source of Russia's Christianity, which had fallen to the Turks in 1453. But if the public image of the tsar showed him as a Christian prince and the heir to Byzantium, in the practical business of government – levying taxes, imposing conscription, controlling and coercing his subjects – he owed far more to the infidel Khan.

The absolutism of the Russian state developed rapidly from the reign of Ivan III (1462–1505), and here again geography was important. The flatness and openness of Russia made centralization vital, but they also made it possible. 'Russia is made for unity', as an old Russian proverb has it. Mountains might have preserved local autonomies and the cultural and social differences which make people crave independence. A broad plain broken only by rivers provided no such barrier: the centralized power, once established, had little difficulty in imposing its writ over an enormous area. The plain which stretched from Moscow in all directions in fact offered an ambitious ruler almost limitless possibilities of expansion. Where, after all, should his armies stop? The states of Novgorod and Pskov were fair game, to start with, since they were Russian and Orthodox. In addition, they were an easy and tempting target since they lacked strong leadership and had a system of government which an autocrat could only regard as pernicious – the prince was accountable to an assembly, the *veche*, which elected and could dismiss him. But why stop with Novgorod and Pskov? On this borderless plain there was in fact no logical place to stop. Quite the contrary: the successful ruler was driven onwards by an irresistible logic which said that, since there were no natural frontiers, each conquest required a further one to protect it. The lack of a clearly defined Russian territory meant that 'Russia' was whatever its rulers chose and were able to make it. In bad times its territory would shrink considerably, but in good times a ruler would go from conquest to conquest without bothering too much about the race or culture of the conquered.

The insecurity created by unfavourable geography thus drove the state to expand – if the Russians were to be safe they needed a buffer of conquered and assimilated territories. By the end of the seventeenth century the Russians had acquired most of Siberia, adding a shore on the Pacific to the one they already had on the White Sea. By the end of the eighteenth century they had reached the far more valuable coastlines of the Baltic and the Black Sea. At the beginning of the nineteenth century they were about to begin the conquest of the ethnic patchwork quilt that was the Caucasus; and soon too they would turn their attention east of the Caspian to the lands of central Asia. Thus over the centuries the Russians built up a great colonial empire, though their empire differed in one important respect from the empires of Britain, France and Spain: the Russian imperialists did not cross any seas, merely the inland sea of the steppes, and the many peoples they overran inhabited territory close to what was properly Russian. Britain, it has been said, had an empire; Russia by contrast *was* an empire. There are no reliable figures for the ethnic composition of the country at the beginning of the nineteenth century, but the census of 1897 would show that the insatiable appetite for expansion had introduced something of a Trojan horse. For the Russians were no longer a majority of the population: they were a mere 44 per cent. For public relations purposes the figure could be presented as 70 per cent, though only by making the dubious assumption (increasingly resented by the 'Little Russians' or Ukrainians) that all the Slavs were Russians. In the end the task of assimilating or even controlling the non-Russians would prove too much: the empire would fall apart, be reassembled, and then collapse once more towards the end of the twentieth century. But building and maintaining an empire seen as vital for the Russians' security had had fundamental effects upon state and society. The task of governing a sprawling empire with a multitude of alien peoples was bound to strengthen the state's autocratic tendency. The Russians in fact paid a high price for the security and status empire gave them: the price, as liberals would discover, was freedom.

3

Geography, then, made Russia restless, insecure, and ever ready to mobilize its people for defence, though defence often took the form of attack against smaller peoples. But geography too explains its acceptance of Orthodox Christianity, and religion, as it turned out, would have a powerful influence upon politics. For Kiev was directly linked by river and sea to the Byzantine capital of Constantinople, and that made it natural that the early Russians should adopt Orthodox rather than Roman Christianity. In the early centuries they belonged very much to the wider world of Orthodoxy, and the head of their church, the metropolitan, was appointed in Constantinople, not Moscow. They came, however, to resent this dependence, and the sacking of Constantinople by the Turks in 1453 put an end to it. The collapse of the Byzantine empire at the very time when Muscovy was about to assert itself and shake off the power of the Mongols had a major impact on the country's political development. For Ivan III could now pass himself off as successor to the slaughtered emperor – and he substantiated the claim by taking the Byzantine title of 'tsar and autocrat', the symbols of Byzantine rule, and even a Byzantine wife. No longer a prince of merely local pretensions, he had become what the Byzantine ruler had been till now: the protector of the one true faith. 'The church of old Rome fell for its heresy', a monk wrote in the early sixteenth century. 'The gates of the second Rome, Constantinople, were hewn down by the axes of the infidel Turks; but the Church of Moscow, the new Rome, shines brighter than the sun over the whole universe ... Two Romes have fallen, but the third stands fast; a fourth there cannot be.'[8] This sense of being besieged spiritually as well as physically, of possessing a sacred truth which had to be preserved against enemies to east and west, fuelled the Russians' nationalism, but it also added to the charisma of their ruler – as protector of the new Rome he towered above any would-be domestic rival. Technically, state and church, tsar and patriarch, were co-equal powers, each supporting and complementing the other. In practice the state dominated; and the domination became complete and utter from the time of Peter the Great, who abolished the office of patriarch and turned the church into a department of state run in effect by a layman, the Procurator of the Holy Synod.

Why was the church so spineless? Why was it less able than any Western church to maintain a distinction between what was owed to Caesar and what to God? Part of the trouble was that, unlike Catholic churches, it had no external authority it could appeal to against aggression by the state. But there were more intrinsic reasons too. The church's basic teaching was submission – not only to the evils of life but to the secular power which had to cope with them. And what it asked of the peasants it practised itself; even when Peter flouted its beliefs and took away its last shreds of independence, the church made no protest. Passivity came naturally enough to an institution which did not, in principle, believe in asking questions. The Russian church had none of the intellectual vitality of its Catholic and Protestant counterparts and did nothing to stir curiosity, still less a critical spirit, among the faithful. This was a church which had founded no universities and had no Dominicans or Jesuits to ginger it, a church which had no custom of preaching or encouraging Bible-reading and which did nothing to stimulate thought about the relationship of man and God or the relationships between men on earth.

Social factors accentuated this tendency to passivity. Unlike its Western equivalents, the Russian church had no nobles or educated bourgeois entering its ranks. As a result the key positions in the church were not held by people whom the state had to treat with respect or who had the skills and the sense of their own dignity to defend and promote it. The clergy were in effect a closed caste and a rather lowly one: nobles were forbidden to join it and other laymen in practice rarely did. Priests had to marry; sons almost always, until the nineteenth century, followed their fathers into the church, and daughters equally invariably married priests. The village priest was generally uncultured if not illiterate, was scorned by his social superiors and enjoyed no special respect even from the peasants, ploughed the fields and in general lived a life little different from his neighbours' – except that on Sundays and feast days he dispensed the sacraments. Yet the clergy, however ignorant and despised, were a vital prop of the state. For the priest preached obedience to the tsar and was obliged by oath to do everything in his power to ensure that his flock acted accordingly.

4

While the clergy were essential to the machine of state, so too were the nobles. There were some 450,000 of them at the beginning of the nineteenth century, rather more than 1 per cent of the population, and they were the ruling class of the empire – if there was such a thing. The tsar, after all, could not rule 40 million people on his own: he needed civilian and military administrators, and that was precisely what the nobles were. Yet they were not a ruling class in the usual meaning of the term. In countries further west the ruling class in some degree or other shared power with the nominal ruler, who might be no more than first among equals, and in Britain at least it was nobles and gentry who ruled behind the façade of a largely ceremonial monarchy. In Russia, of course, there was no question whatever of the nobles vying for power with the ruler: they were a ruling class only in the sense that they ruled on his behalf over subjects even less free than they were. They were a managerial and officer elite, executives rather than in an important sense decision-takers, and until recently they had tended to think of themselves as the 'servants' or even 'slaves' (*kholopy*) of the monarch. True, they could sometimes get rid of an incompetent or unpopular monarch – hence a Frenchman's quip that the Russian government was 'an absolute monarchy tempered by assassination',[9] but that depended wholly upon accidents of personality. As of the beginning of the nineteenth century they had failed utterly to institutionalize their power, to turn themselves from a dominant class into a genuinely ruling one.

There had once been a much more independent nobility in Russia, but this had been eliminated in the fifteenth and sixteenth centuries with the rise of the Moscow princes to absolute power. The name by which the new nobles became known pointed to their weakness; they were the *dvoryane*, the people of the *dvor* or court, who served the tsar in the army or the administration. In return for loyal service they were given land, but the grant of land was strictly conditional. And here was the essence of what made them different from nobles in Western Europe. For by the early modern period Western nobles had gained an absolute property right to their land and land had become the source of their power: it gave both wealth and political clout. But the Russian noble was a mere lackey; there was no question of allowing him to develop a territorial power-base, and his right to his land remained precarious until Catherine the Great (reigned 1762–96) converted it into an absolute right in 1785. From the sixteenth to the late eighteenth century it was a deliberate policy not to let him settle. On the contrary, he was sent hither and thither and permitted to serve only in areas where he did *not* have land, which put him in entirely the opposite position from the Western noble, whose local power was the consequence of land ownership.

Not only was the land the Russian noble held not securely his; it was not the main source of his income – for that he had to look to the state; and it would anyway be frittered away among his heirs, since Russia had no tradition of passing property *en bloc* to the first-born. If we think of nobles as people who lived in castles or ancestral mansions, had titles, were wealthy, and did more or less whatever they wanted, then the Russian *dvoryane* hardly qualify as nobles at all. None lived in castles or in mansions that had been in the family for very long, nor were their ancestors remembered by splendid monuments in the local church. Few had titles – and titles, for those who had them, were never 'of' anywhere and so had no implications of territorial overlordship. A tiny number of them were very rich indeed and by the late eighteenth century some of these were indistinguishable from their European counterparts, though even they lacked the compact territorial base of English or French grandees. Most, however, lived modestly, without the inclination or the means for airs and graces, and some were no better off than peasants. As for freedom: till 1762 the nobles had been as much in harness to the state as everyone else, except that they served not by ploughing the soil or paying taxes but by entering the army or the administration.

Treatment of the nobility had been at its most draconian under Peter the

Great, who made all his nobles serve life-long in the armed forces or the bureaucracy from the age of fifteen. Peter's idea of the nobility was in fact almost wholly different from the Western one. People should be given status and privilege, he believed, not because of who they were but because of what they contributed. It was not status which should determine job but job which should determine status. The logical extension of Peter's position would have been to abolish hereditary nobility altogether. He was in fact too much a man of his time to do that, but he did insist that existing nobles should begin in the bottom executive positions and he combined this with a policy of encouraging talented non-nobles to enter the service. The new career structure was formulated in 1722 in the Table of Ranks: this had fourteen parallel civil service and army grades, 1 being the highest and 14 the lowest, and any commoner who reached grade 8 was automatically ennobled. The system was less meritocratic than it might sound since the upwardly mobile were drawn from a small pool of merchants', army officers' and priests' sons, and peasants were utterly excluded. An important factor in the resilience and longevity of tsarism was nevertheless that its ruling class was far from being a closed caste: clever and ambitious young men from outside the nobility were regularly recruited to it, and until the later part of the nineteenth century all non-peasant talent tended to flow towards it.

Members of old noble families who had resented being pushed around by Peter took a dim view of this semi-meritocratic Table of Ranks which allowed upstart bureaucrats and army officers to pass themselves off as nobles. But there was more here than snobbish disdain for the low-born – there was political calculation. For the old nobles saw clearly enough that a swollen nobility crowded with parvenus of no personal substance who owed everything to the ruler would inevitably be a pillar of the autocratic system. Grandees smarting because of Peter's treatment of them would have dearly liked to do away with the Table of Ranks and to establish a slimmed-down, genuine – as they thought – nobility of blood which would have become a real ruling class of the English kind. But an attempt to create an aristocratic regime under a figurehead monarch came to nothing in 1730, partly because it aroused fierce resistance from the noble rank and file; and in Catherine the Great's reign further pressures for aristocratic constitutionalism were thwarted by a *de facto* alliance of ruler and noble majority.

While the monarchy in its own interest maintained the principle of a service nobility, the terms on which the nobles had to serve became less onerous once Peter had gone, and in 1762 the compulsion to serve was abolished altogether. Despite this formal emancipation, however, the great majority of nobles continued to enter the service. In most cases they needed the income since their estates were so unlucrative; and even if not, they felt a moral obligation to serve – serving the state was, after all, what being a noble in Russia was all about. But now at least they could serve as and when they wished; and the well-do-do noble in particular often retired after a few years, provided that he had climbed high enough in the Table to be able to look his neighbours in the eye.

The result was that more and more nobles stayed on their estates and in their localities and lived the lives of country gentlemen. But was it safe to let the nobles put down roots in the countryside? Catherine the Great, a native of Germany, where the nobles were far from dangerous, thought that it was, and she set out to transform the nobles from uncultured lackeys into civilized, self-respecting and yet dutiful servants. That meant sending the upper crust abroad to get their education or at least their spit and polish, and during her reign there developed a gilded, French-speaking élite which had the tastes and something of the life-style of aristocrats in the West. These people constituted an élite within an élite, 1 per cent of a 1 per cent – the flavour of them and their salon society is caught in the opening chapter of Tolstoy's *War and Peace* (set in the year 1805). But at a lower level an educated middling nobility with something of the local associations, the rootedness in place, of a Western gentry began to emerge. Nobles of this kind lived on their estates at least in the summer and sometimes built themselves neo-classical mansions in the Western style. And a provincial social life came into being, centred on the local capitals, which nobles went to not only for pleasure but to take part in the work of the provincial noble institutions Catherine had founded. Getting these institutions off the ground was far from easy, as it happened, and so little of a threat did they present to the central power that Catherine had if anything to prod the nobles to interest themselves in them. For all that, the sea change which came over the nobility in the later eighteenth century did have threatening implications for the autocracy, at least in the long term. For the noble no longer necessarily thought of himself as above all someone who served the state. From now on in fact there would be two different sorts of nobles, and the distinction would become more marked as the nineteenth century advanced. On the one hand there were those who devoted themselves lifelong to the service: career bureaucrats, professionals, living most probably in St Petersburg and having little contact with the provinces or with the land. (For a vivid picture of such a man, see Anna's husband in Tolstoy's *Anna Karenina*.) On the other hand, there were those who, while they might dabble in the service, were no more than amateur bureaucrats: their real vocation lay in being estate owners and pillars of provincial society. These latter presented a potential problem. As the career bureaucrats took over, they were likely to resent their exclusion, and one way of getting their own back would be to turn the toothless institutions Catherine had created into something with real bite. One factor, however, made it most unlikely that the middling nobility of the provinces would mount any real challenge to the autocracy, and that was the nobles' privilege of privileges – serfdom.

5

The Muscovite rulers had rewarded their new servitor-nobles with land, but land was of little use on its own. In this sparsely populated and infertile country the human beings who inhabited the land mattered more, and it was the gift of 'souls' which made the nobles' loyalty to the ruler absolute. A man's standing was judged not by the area of land he owned – not by broad acres – but rather by the number of souls. One hundred or more male serfs was the sign of someone substantial, and 1,000 or more of a veritable Maecenas. The vast majority of lords, however, had fewer than one hundred serfs and about one-third had no more than ten; and these petty landlords, sometimes little different from peasants except in status, were notoriously the worst masters.

Owning serfs defined the noble as much as, or even more than, the moral obligation to serve. What after all was the noble? He might very well spend no more than a few years as a bureaucrat or army officer. He was most certainly not a gentleman farmer. But what he was, or at least had the right to be, was someone who had peasants at his beck and call. And there was a clear connection between his ingrained subservience to the ruler and the rights he enjoyed (in both senses of the word) over the serfs on his estate. Having been and perhaps still being something of a serf in regard to the autocrat, he was all the more likely to act the autocrat, perhaps benevolent, perhaps not, in his dealings with his own subjects, the serfs. Just as he grovelled before the tsar and grandees who represented the tsar, so his serfs grovelled before him – meeting him for the first time, for instance, they would usually fall on their knees and kiss his hands and even his feet. These rituals did not mean that they liked or even respected him – the lord, unlike the tsar, was in fact in the hazardous position of having power without charisma; but peasant subservience was at least a compensation to him for what he suffered at the hands of those above him.

Technically the serfs were not slaves, but the distinction was somewhat notional and would-be liberators understandably enough called them slaves. In practice they had no rights and were at best treated like children not old or wise enough to look after their own interests. What, to begin with, could the lord *not* do to his serfs? He could not kill or maim them, though he sometimes did and only the most grotesque cases of abuse (like that of a woman landowner found guilty of the death of seventy-five serfs) resulted in punishment. Selling serfs apart from the land was frowned upon because it led to the break-up of families and was reminiscent of the slave trade. Such sales, however, went on, and serfs were not only sold but given away as gifts, dowry, or in settlement of gambling debts. The Emperor Paul, who saw himself as something of a friend of the people, tried, though with little effect, to stop Sunday work and to restrict labour on the lord's behalf to three days a week. These notional limitations apart, the lord could do more or less as he wished. The punishments he could inflict including beating, chaining, making the guilty stand bare-foot in the snow, enrolment in the army, banishment to another estate and, in extreme cases, banishment to Siberia. The serf had no area of privacy which was safe from the lord's intrusions. The lord could, for instance, pair serfs off in marriage, or forbid couples to marry, or allow them to marry but forbid them to have children; and the sight of serf children who uncannily resembled the master sometimes made its own comment on how far his intrusions into the serfs' lives could go.

Not all lords of course were tyrants, still less sadists. Some adopted the role of paterfamilias and by their own lights did everything they could to make these grown-up children of theirs happy. But the crux of the relationship was the payment in labour or money which good and bad lords alike extracted from their serfs. There were some serfs, the so-called 'courtyard people', who actually lived under the lord's roof, working as footmen, butlers, coachmen, cooks, nannies, chambermaids, even in more exotic households as actors or musicians, and these were for good or ill totally exposed to his will. Most, however, lived in their own log cabins on the estate. In less fertile areas these generally paid the lord a money rent (*obrok*), supplemented usually by having to provide food for his table. This arrangement at least left them fairly unsupervised, and many were allowed to go off to the towns to earn the rent. Where the land was richer, however, and particularly in the Black Earth zone south of Moscow in which the greatest concentration of noble estates was found, serfs were usually required to pay a labour due (*barshchina*). Under this arrangement serfs worked several days a week and for up to twelve hours a day on the part of the estate – usually between a third and a quarter of the whole – which was set aside as the lord's personal area, his demesne. Both kinds of exaction were tending, moreover, to increase. The lords were under financial pressure, due partly to the expensive European tastes many had developed, and they reacted to this not by improving production methods but by trying to get still more out of their serfs. There was a considerable, perhaps fivefold, increase in the *obrok* demanded between the 1760s and the end of the century, while serfs on *barshchina* were squeezed by having to work longer and by having the area of their own holdings reduced. Never in fact had the serfs mattered more to their owners – for most lords, solvency and everyday life itself were unimaginable without them. Yet while the lords' title to the land had now become clear-cut, their right to the serfs had never been explicitly formulated and it still remained shaky and all too evidently revocable. The thought of what, were they to step out of line, they might lose was quite enough to bind most of them to the autocracy with hoops of steel.

The enserfing of the peasantry had begun, as we have seen, at the very time when the new class of servitor-nobles was being created, and it had been a vital element in the binding of the nobles to the autocrat. Serfdom was both a reward and a compensation for the nobles, and what it compensated was their lack of freedom. The serfs were all too obviously the lords' victims, and would-be liberators of the serfs from the late eighteenth century onwards would denounce their masters as inhuman and conscience-less oppressors. But another way of looking at the problem of lords and serfs was to regard both as victims, both in their different ways the captives of a mutual oppressor. Freedom for the serfs, Mikhail Speransky argued at the beginning of the nineteenth century, was a precondition of freedom for their masters. 'I would like someone', he wrote, 'to show the difference between the dependence of the peasants on the landowners and that of the nobles on the sovereign.' There was, he considered, none: the nobles were 'free' only in relation to the serfs, and both in essence were slaves.[10] That they were the victims of a 'divide and rule' policy was, however, lost on nobles and peasants alike. The nobles looked to the tsar to uphold and enforce their rights over the peasants, while the peasants on their side looked to the tsar to save them from maltreatment by the lords. Catherine the Great had admittedly taken away the peasants' right of petitioning the ruler about abuses; the distant tsar nevertheless lived on in the peasant's mind as a potential protector and benefactor rather than the source of his troubles.

Peasants made up more than 80 per cent of the population at the beginning of the nineteenth century, though by no means all of them were serfs. Almost half were 'state peasants', who lived in the less fertile and peripheral areas, such as northern European Russia and Siberia. There were no noble estates in these areas, and although the peasants who lived there were shackled to the state and its local officials their conditions were generally better than the serfs'. The fraught relationship between landowners and serfs in central European Russia was, however, to be crucial for the country's development. The serfs had understandably never reconciled themselves to the loss of their freedom, and during the eighteenth century resentment had increased. By coercing both classes Peter the Great had meted out a rough social justice – if the lord had to serve the tsar, why should the serf not serve the lord? – but any suggestion of even-handed treatment of the classes disappeared in 1762 when the lords were freed from their obligations but no corresponding gesture was made to the peasants. Within months of freeing the nobles Peter III had in fact been deposed and murdered, and it was widely rumoured among the peasants that it was precisely because he intended to take the logical next step of freeing them that the nobles had had him ousted. In the early years of her reign Catherine the Great, Peter's wife and successor, toyed with the idea of doing something for the peasants, but despite her commitment to Enlightenment principles her reign saw if anything a worsening of their conditions. The peasants did not, however, passively accept this breach of the unwritten contract whereby all had had to bear burdens on the state's behalf; and in 1773 a Cossack called Emilyan Pugachev began what became the greatest ever peasant rebellion in tsarist Russia. It said much about the peasant mentality that Pugachev did not pose as a revolutionary but instead passed himself off as the ousted would-be benefactor of the people, Peter III. His rebellion lasted a full year, led to the killing of some 1,500 lords, and implanted in the nobles a fear of peasant violence which would stalk them through the nineteenth century.

'We are yours', went a peasant saying, 'but the land is ours.' That did not imply acceptance by the peasant of his serf status – he resented the arbitrary powers of the master and in particular any interference with the life and work of the peasant community; but if he resented his dependent status, he felt still more bitter about being deprived of the land. The land-hunger of these people who scratched an inadequate living from an infertile soil was limitless, and this hunger would create enormous problems for any noble-inspired movement against the autocracy. There would never be popular support for such a movement unless it promised a wholesale transfer of the land into the hands of those who worked it.

What made rapport still more difficult to achieve was that lord and peasant did not meet as agriculturalists. Even in the Black Earth zone there was nothing resembling a 'gentry agriculture'. The peasants cultivated the lord's demesne with their own animals, used their own tools and their own traditional methods, and were supervised by the village headman rather than by the lord or his steward. The culture of contemporary Europe might be found in the manor house; but the agricultural practices of the estate, with its three-field system under which a third of the arable was left fallow and its shallow wooden plough, the *sokha*, smacked rather of the Middle Ages. The interested, still less the improving, landowner hardly existed outside the pages of Tolstoy (who happened to be one himself); and how difficult it was for the lord who wanted to get involved in the life and work of the village, *A Landowner's Morning* and other writings of Tolstoy would bear out. Agriculture in fact showed up the lord as a newcomer and an alien to the land, who consumed all too much and produced nothing whatever. He simply took the fruits of peasant labour as tribute, and this utter detachment of his from the land inevitably sharpened the peasants' sense of him as having stolen what should have been their own.

Thus lord and peasant lived cheek by jowl (except in the case of absentee aristocrats), yet they inhabited very different worlds and each knew little of the other's. 'Here and there is to be seen a country house', wrote the Marquis de Custine, 'to which an avenue of birch trees forms the approach. These are the manor-houses, or residences of the proprietors of the land; and the traveller welcomes them on the road as he would an oasis in the desert.'[11] But the Frenchman welcomed these 'oases' precisely because they had so little in common with the surrounding countryside. In this landscape the manor was not only incongruous; it was vulnerable – a 'nest', as Ivan Turgenev was to call it in the title of one of his novels, whose delicate contents needed protection from the elemental forces round about. Some nineteenth-century Russians would try to play down the estrangement. The Slavophiles, for instance, argued that until Peter the Great there had been a united rural community held together by shared values and a common national spirit, while some other conservatives believed that traces of that oneness lived on in the nineteenth century. But that was make-believe. The lords stuck out as unassimilable intruders, and stuck out all the more if they had been touched by the westernizing current of Catherine's reign, which had turned the upper crust among them into the wigged and powdered *grands seigneurs* who fill the salons of *War and Peace*. For such nobles Russian was the language of serfs; in Russia of the late eighteenth and early nineteenth centuries élite and people spoke different languages in the literal as well as the metaphorical sense. True, this extreme of derussification affected only a small minority of the nobles. Yet the class as a whole, even in its most coarse and impoverished representatives, remained irrevocably at odds with and excluded from the peasant world, at whose heart lay the village commune.

6

The commune – *mir* in Russian – served the state like every other institution in the country. It was the lowest rung in the administrative ladder, apportioning and collecting taxes and in general supervising its potentially troublesome members. Yet despite this, the commune was an authentic peasant institution which in its members' eyes belonged wholly to the world of 'us' rather than the world of 'them'. The lord was an outsider to it, and though he had formal power over it, he in practice rarely intervened directly in its affairs. In some shape or other the commune had existed since medieval times as a shield for its members against adversity and as the organizing mainspring of village life. In the nineteenth century dispute would rage about how desirable and how authentically national the commune was. To liberals it would seem depressingly hierarchical and authoritarian, while radicals would praise it as an egalitarian body which had reared the peasants in the spirit of socialism. There was a pinch of truth in both views. The commune was, to start with, undeniably patriarchal. Within the household the authority of the father (or in the case of a multiple family the oldest capable male) was unquestioned; he was the decision-taker and adult sons and others submitted to him. At the level of the commune as a whole the authority of the father was replicated by that of the elected headman, the *starosta*; his word too was final. And patriarchal attitudes which originated within the commune were projected on to the wider scene. The tsar was a 'little father' to his people, stern if need be yet at root benevolent; and above him there rose of course the father of fathers, God himself.

The patriarchal mentality was by no means, however, a slave mentality. Peasants did not submit to authority irrespective of where their own self-interest lay; patriarchalism prevailed because the world outside the commune seemed full of threats, and in a hostile environment unity was vital to survival. Younger deferred to older, yet the political culture of the village was far from high-handedly authoritarian. Major decisions were not simply imposed; they rose from a collective decision-making process which was finalized in the village assembly. All adults, even women, could attend the assemblies and speak at them, though the right to vote was limited to heads of household. The nineteenth-century Scottish observer of Russia, Donald Mackenzie Wallace, was deeply impressed by these assemblies. They were guided, he sensed, by an unwritten 'constitutionalism' and, much against the odds, had developed into 'capital specimens of representative constitutional government of the extreme democratic type'.[12] That was idealizing them a little, though no doubt Wallace was right to suggest that the assemblies' decisions by and large reflected the will of the community. There was, however, one feature of the assembly's decision-making process which was not at all in keeping with British notions of democracy. Debate could be uninhibited and passionate, but once a majority view had crystallized the minority would go along with rather than resist it and the decision taken would thus appear to be unanimous. This tendency of the community to pull together was understandable; solidarity was protective and factionalism a luxury the village could ill afford. The tradition of treating a majority decision, often arrived at after fierce debate, as if it were the decision of all and allowing, once it had been reached, no formal show of dissent from it would, however, in time help those who wanted to suppress the democratic impulse altogether and would do so by rejecting the majority principle in favour of a totalitarian counterfeit of democracy.

The egalitarian and collectivist aspect of village life was, like the patriarchal, undeniable. It could be sensed even from the look of the village. The houses were not, except in southern Russia, scattered in isolation among the fields but lined either side of a street; few were painted and the houses as a whole gave an impression of sombre uniformity. The egalitarianism of the Russian peasant was seen above all, however, in the distribution of land. There was nothing here resembling the peasant farming of Western Europe, where the better-off would have holdings of their own and the poor might well be landless. Here pasturage and meadow were for the use of all. As for arable land, that was divided up by the commune officials among individual households according to the number of adult members. What was crucial, however, was that households did not receive a single chunk of land, which they could have cultivated as they wished, but rather a large number of narrow and widely scattered strips – a practice not known in most parts of Western Europe since the Middle Ages. Such a division of the land made for very great inefficiency. The strips were often so narrow that there was no room to turn a plough; the uncultivated boundaries between them wasted much of the area; and in going from strip to strip – each household might have fifty or more of them – the peasant might have to walk for miles. The point of the strip system, however, was to ensure an equal division among

households of good, bad and indifferent land; and thus efficiency was sacrificed to fair shares for all.

But the most famously egalitarian feature of the communes was that
most of them periodically reapportioned strips in accordance with the
changing size of households. To socialists this periodic redistribution of the
land would be proof that the Russian peasant had a different character from
his Western counterpart: he was naturally communal in outlook, far less
prone to egoism and individualism, and potentially at least socialist.
Liberals would try to pour cold water on such claims by pointing out that
the practice of repartition had been unknown until the eighteenth century,
when it had developed largely because the state needed to ensure that all
members of the community were able to pay their share of taxes. What was
undeniable, however, was that the commune was pervaded by a general
feeling of fair shares for all – which merely stoked up the peasants' grievance
against those who flouted the fair shares principle, namely the lords.
Moreover, the commune's egalitarianism inevitably had collectivist implications. The scatter of narrow strips made it impractical for each household to
do its own thing; the commune as a whole decided what crops should be
sown and when, and each arable operation had to be identical. That admitted, the commune's agriculture fell well short of any socialist ideal of collectivism. There might be no private property; the peasant's strips were
nevertheless in a sense his own and he would give them up with much reluctance when the authorities made him do so. Most important of all, the commune did not farm as a single unit. Each household owned or hired its own
animals and implements; it had to observe a common rotation of crops, but
cultivation of its strips was otherwise under the guidance of its own head;
and what it produced was for itself rather than the property of the commune. It is impossible, therefore, to see any straight line pointing from the
agricultural practices of the tsarist Russian village to the collectivism of the
later Soviet kolkhoz. The practices of the village suggested rather that the
peasant had two very different possible destinies: he was a socialist in the
making, maybe, but he also had do-it-yourself and self-bettering instincts
which might in the end, if they were encouraged, make a full-blooded pro-
prietor of him.

For the moment, the impression left by village life on foreign observers at
least was of poverty, backwardness and isolation. These four-fifths of the
nation had received no education in citizenship, indeed in most cases no
education of any kind. Culturally and legally the peasants formed a nation
within a nation, and they reacted with fear and hostility to any external
authority other than that of tsar and church. The peasant had no personal
rights to protect him against the aggression of lords and officials; having no
rights, he had no sense of the law as anything other than the fiat of those
stronger than himself. That presented a major problem for anyone who saw
the development of a legal consciousness as vital if free institutions were
ever to be put on a firm footing. Against threats the peasant looked for

security not to the law and officialdom but to the commune; yet while that protected him it could do little to develop in him a sense of his own rights and dignity as an individual. Though he by no means blindly submitted to the will of a ruling élite, he saw clearly enough that safety for all lay in each being prepared to accept what the community as a whole, or at least a majority of its members, wanted. When the peasant spoke of 'freedom', what he had in mind was not civil liberties and living under the rule of law but, rather, throwing off the normal constraints and discipline of life and, most of all, seizing the land from the lords. And here was the factor which made the chances of a peaceful accommodation of the conflicting interests within Russian society look remote. In all pre-industrial societies the gulf between privileged and unprivileged was profound, but in Russia it took on a qualitatively different character from anywhere else. It was, as some saw it, the gulf between Europe and Asia, as others saw it the gulf between modern civilization and the Middle Ages; in any event it was a gulf so vast that no dialogue, still less conciliation, between the two communities seemed possible.

Yet despite sporadic uprisings and more frequent cases of passive resistance (including flight and suicide), the peasants on the whole accepted their lot. What reconciled them to the misery of their existence was, above all, religion. Peasant piety was intense. In pride of place in each peasant hut there was an icon portraying a saint, and no one entering the hut spoke before he had made obeisance to the saint and crossed himself. Religion comforted, restrained and uplifted the peasant, and if it did not explain away all the evils of his life it at least put them into a bearable perspective. The shrine in his hut formed in a sense the lowest tier in a structure of conformity whose intermediary tiers were the village church and the tsar's palace and which culminated with God on his lofty perch in heaven. Yet the peasant's loyalty to the beliefs and rituals which cemented the structure was conditional rather than absolute. They worked for him, giving him hope and comfort, and while they did he accepted them piously enough, but he accepted them for their efficacy rather than for their content. The 'beautiful corner' (*krasnyi ugolok* in Russian) in which the icon was kept would later be converted without much difficulty into a shrine to Bolshevism. For *krasnyi* meant not only 'beautiful' but 'red', the age-old colour of radicalism and in due course the colour of Bolshevism; and the 'beautiful corner' would live on in the apartments and institutions of Soviet Russia, except that now it would be decorated with red and a narrow-eyed but otherwise far from other-worldly saviour would stare out of it.

The church, like the commune, was both a state institution and something profoundly peasant, and Peter the Great's secularization of the nobility had increased its peasantness. How peasant it was can be seen by comparison with England, where something of the integrated rural society the Slavophiles yearned for actually existed. Not only did the squire play ritual games of cricket with his tenants on the village green; it was the gentry who went into the church, and they made it into an institution which communicated with some success between landowners and tenants. (Manufacturers and factory hands were a different matter, however.) But in Russia a deep wedge had been driven between the nobles, particularly the more educated ones, and their uncultured and obscurantist church; and the most striking badge of class difference from Peter's time on – a shaven chin – reflected the noble's rejection of religious traditionalism. One of Peter's actions after returning from Europe had been to go around the court shaving off his courtiers' beards. Beards were messy and unpractical but, worst of all, they were imposed by the church, which insisted that a man without a beard would be damned. For a ruler itching to rescue his country from stagnation and superstition, an assault on this particular piece of piety was irresistible, and soon he followed the assault up with a decree fining anyone other than a priest who entered a town bearded. But while the educated fell into line, even the autocrat could not make millions of peasants go cleanshaven. So the peasants kept their beards; and since a father-in-God would never commit sacrilege, many decided that the tsar must be a usurper, even Anti-Christ himself. From then on until well into the nineteenth century the chin of the adult male made a clear cultural statement. A smooth chin marked out an upper-class man, secular in outlook and oriented to the West, whereas the peasant's beard defiantly proclaimed his commitment to Orthodoxy and traditional Russianness. The church with its art and its sacraments would continue to comfort and restrain the peasant, feeding his monarchism and teaching him resignation. But what it could not do was reconcile him to the landowners, who not only by shaving but in a hundred and one other ways seemed to have put themselves outside the community altogether.

7

In more advanced parts of Europe, the driving force for change came from the towns, which dragged the rural areas along behind them. Vigorous towns in Russia, had there been any, might have had just the same modernizing effect. In addition, they might have softened the noble–peasant conflict by attracting both classes and dissolving some of their differences on neutral ground. But there were no vigorous towns in Russia. At the beginning of the nineteenth century, towns accounted for less that 5 per cent of the population; and over the vast expanses of the Russian empire there were only two towns of any significance – St Petersburg and Moscow, each with rather over 250,000 inhabitants. Most people who lived in the towns were, anyway, peasants – many of them serfs whose masters were happy for them to earn money there – rather than members of the official townsmen's estate.

Townsmen proper were subdivided into merchants, petty burghers and artisans, and the rivalries between these groups again suggested a 'divide and rule' policy at work. Of a middle class there was as yet no sign whatever. That said, there were some 200,000 merchants, who might have been expected to be a middle class in the making, yet Russian merchants had very little in common with the commercial and industrial entrepreneurs who would soon transform life in the West. With poor communications, little know-how, no significant urban markets and a tradition of trading by barter, Russia was still too backward for capitalist activity or the capitalist spirit. Its merchants were a profoundly conservative class and had more in common with the merchants of the Orient than with the emerging capitalists of the West. They were notoriously short of honesty, frugality and self-discipline. More important still, they were not driven by the desire to justify themselves by material success, which was what had given capitalism its dynamic. These Russian merchants were in fact profoundly traditionalist; like the peasants, they went bearded, though in their case the beard was a more conscious rejection of the West and its ways. Bright and ambitious merchants' sons did not set out to make fortunes by revamping their fathers' businesses. Quite the contrary, they turned their backs on the despised world of trade for the rewards and prestige offered by the state service. What Russia needed was a self-confident and aggressive middling element which was prepared to act independently of the state and might have formed something of a bridge between the extremes of nobles and peasants. But the merchants showed no sign whatever of becoming that; and the lack would not be made good throughout the tsarist period.

8

Such was the political and social landscape of Russia at the beginning of the nineteenth century. What, then, was the outlook for rulers and subjects? Most probably the autocratic system with its rigid control of the population would continue for some time to come; there might be zigzags in policy, but the political and social status quo would in essence remain. There were, however, other and not wholly implausible possibilities. One was that the long-threatened peasant revolution would indeed occur and would sweep the existing political and social structure away. A second alternative was liberal, or even possibly radical, revolution by members of the ruling class, partly in order to avert a revolution from below. A third, and probably the most likely, alternative was that the autocrat would more or less voluntarily push through major reforms, having decided that they would actually be in his own best interest.

Of these possibilities, peasant revolution was all too obviously on the cards. Pugachev in the 1770s had come closer to success than any previous peasant rebel and had badly scared the landowners. Still more recently the popular violence in France had been an uncomfortable reminder to them of how easily the masses could get out of hand. But if Russia was a high-risk location for peasant revolution, the chances of a revolution there by the privileged seemed remote. In the West the nineteenth century would prove to be the liberal century, and out of liberalism with its middle-class narrowness and restrictiveness would grow twentieth-century democracy. Liberalism would progress rapidly in the West because the socio-economic and cultural forces needed to propel it were now in place. The capitalist market economy was a liberalizing force, as was an expanding and prospering bourgeoisie. The ideals of tolerance, rationality and the rule of law had been widely disseminated, and in parts of the continent at least traditions of individual initiative and civil liberty long predated, and would now begin to nourish, a self-conscious liberalism. Russia, however, with its omnipotent, intolerant and monopolistic state and its passive and underdeveloped society had no liberalizing forces and attitudes for the would-be liberal to call upon. The values, institutions and ways of life Russian liberals admired and wanted to import were the product of factors almost wholly absent in Russia; bourgeois go-gettingness, urban civilization and an economy whose keynotes were enterprise and competition. By such tests as literacy, urbanization, communications, commercial activity and the existence of non-governmental pressure-groups and organizations, Russia offered a more or less barren terrain for liberal ambitions. The would-be Russian liberal in fact found himself in the polar-opposite position from his Western counterpart. In the West liberalism would develop and flourish as a result of conditions which naturally favoured it. In Russia, by contrast, the liberal had no chance of success except by reshaping conditions which, as things stood, looked almost wholly adverse to him.

Yet there were would-be liberals in eighteenth-century Russia. This was not surprising since nowhere else did the state so thoroughly crush anyone who thought of himself as an individual with certain inborn rights. And Catherine the Great herself had in the early years of her reign vigorously promoted Enlightenment ideas and encouraged free thought among the élite. Not only had she passed herself off as a *philosophe*; she had sent bright noble boys to study at the sources of enlightened thinking. Whereas Peter had hardly gone beyond importing technology and fashions, she took the more hazardous step of exposing her upper class to the Western experience in the round, and eventually this brought nemesis upon her. It was very hard, after all, to read Rousseau with any understanding and still believe in serfdom. Later in her reign Catherine herself saw the discrepancy and she banned many of the books she had once recommended. Some of her subjects, however, had by now decided that the gap between Russian realities and enlightened ideals should be closed not by rejecting those ideals but by carrying out fundamental social and political change.

The most outstanding of these radicals was Alexander Radishchev, the first in a long line of privileged Russians (Lenin would be one of the last) who would reject their privileges and throw in their lot with the exploited and oppressed. In 1790 Radishchev managed to get past the censorship with a travelogue, *A Journey from Petersburg to Moscow*, which would go down as a landmark in Russian history. 1790 was of course an unpromising year to publish a radical tract since by then revolution was well under way in the Enlightenment's birthplace, and Catherine was outraged by what she read. 'Worse than Pugachev!', she exploded in a margin – peasants might be expected to rebel, but whatever could she do if the ruling class turned against her?; and she had the miscreant sentenced to death, though as with Dostoevsky half a century later the sentence was in the end commuted to one of Siberian exile. Radishchev's offence was that he had used the device of the travelogue to depict the misery of the peasants seen *en route*, denounce their masters, make a plea for fundamental change, and in effect rebuke the empress for betraying the values of her youth. If maltreatment of the peasants continued, then the outcome could not be in doubt. 'We shall see around us sword and poison. Death and flames will be meted out to us for our harshness and inhumanity. And the slower and more reluctant we have been to loosen their bonds, the more violent they will be in their revenge.'[13]

Not only did Radishchev foresee a peasant revolution; he believed it would be justified and even that good would come from it. Yet he shrank from the revolution he himself predicted – he knew too much already about mutinous peasants after his own family had narrowly missed being slaughtered by followers of Pugachev. The hope that inspired his *Journey* was that, against the odds, the changes which would make any such uprising unnecessary would come about. Radishchev's ideal was civilized revolution as made by the Americans in the 1770s or the French in 1789: revolution made for philanthropic and libertarian purposes by men in wigs and knee-breeches. Yet the only people who could make such a revolution in Russia, his fellow nobles, were certainly not going to do anything on behalf of the serfs they treated so badly. And when 'civilized revolution' in France developed into the bloodletting and despotism of the Jacobins, Radishchev swung away from the very idea of revolution. The task, he now decided, was to spare Russia the horrors of revolution of any kind; and the only way of doing that was to turn the autocracy into a reforming and liberating force.

The idea was far-fetched, but not utterly implausible. Elsewhere liberal advances had been achieved by defying the government – in Russia could they not be achieved instead by a far-sighted ruler collaborating with his or her most enlightened subjects? The Russian monarchy had the advantage, after all, of not being a hostage to the privileged, and that made it potentially capable of acting on behalf of everyone. Peter and Catherine had already shown how a determined ruler could push the country forward. Their actions had of course been self-interested – they had wanted to make the state more effective and stronger, not to weaken it. And averting peasant revolution by abolishing serfdom was clearly enough in the ruler's interest. Liberal institutions were, admittedly, a different matter. Yet the autocrat might be persuaded to push through changes that were not obviously anti-autocratic, such as spreading education, and they in the long run at least would have a liberalizing effect. Thus Radishchev – and a line of Russian liberals after him – tried to clamber out of the apparently hopeless position they were in. They came up in fact with a saving paradox. Since society was too weak to generate liberal institutions by itself, the state would have to do the work instead. Other countries had got such institutions by way of revolution; in Russia they, or at least the conditions preliminary to them, would come as a gift from the autocracy.

That was asking a lot, however, of the autocrat. Any idea of the state doing society's work seemed wishful thinking when Catherine in her final years, elderly and frightened by events in France, had turned determinedly conservative. Prospects were still more dismal in the reign of Paul, an unstable martinet whose capricious behaviour showed just how great, in determined hands, the powers of the autocracy were. Terrified by the French upheaval, Paul unleashed a reign of terror against potential subversives in Russia and in effect against educated society as a whole. In Catherine's reign the nobles had had their rights and privileges enhanced and had been treated with something of the respect shown to Western nobles. Now the dignified and secure position they seemed to have achieved collapsed like a house of cards in the face of Paul's malice, whimsy, and outbursts of uncontrolled rage. If nobles were unlucky enough to meet the autocrat's carriage in the street, they had to get to the ground and bow or curtsy; and if they were more unlucky still they were taken from their beds and despatched into exile. Furthermore, they were again coerced into the service as if the 1762 emancipation had never taken place, and in general they were treated as if they were the 'slaves' their predecessors in a more primitive age had admitted to being. But while the autocracy itself was proof against assault, an individual autocrat who overstepped the unwritten rules was not, and Paul's reign of terror in the end produced a conspiracy against him. Peter III had, after all, been ousted by a smoothly executed palace coup; with careful planning Paul could be disposed of by something similar.

A further spur to action was that the heir, Alexander, was utterly different. Gentle, dreamy, idealistic and rather indecisive, he too had lived in fear of his father's despotism – which was a good reason to make him believe in limited rather that autocratic monarchy. The root of his attachment to constitutional principles went back, however, to his childhood: his grandmother, Catherine the Great, had given him a Swiss republican tutor, who had brought him up with the ideas of liberty and the rights of man. Unlike his father and grandmother, Alexander had welcomed the French Revolution in its moderate opening phase, and Paul's excesses had inevitably made him still more of a constitutionalist.

The coup went off without a hitch on 11 March 1801 – though Alexander, who had agreed to having his father deposed, was traumatized by the news that the conspirators had killed him. Paul's removal was greeted, however, with unalloyed joy by the privileged, who expected the new monarch to rule in an entirely different spirit. Other autocrats before and after him had or would have reforming intentions, but Alexander I (reigned 1801–25) was unique in coming to the throne with a widely known commitment to establishing the rule of law and a constitution. The general euphoria was caught for instance by Radishchev in a poem in which he greeted the new century as one in which 'peace, justice, truth and liberty from the throne shall flow' and Alexander as 'our guardian angel'.[14]

What had occurred had of course been a palace coup rather than a revolution, and Alexander inherited the full autocratic power. Many, however, assumed that he would not only undo his father's despotic actions – pardon political prisoners, abolish the secret police, open the frontiers, etc. – but put through fundamental changes which would make despotism impossible in the future. He might straightaway agree to limit his own power; and that seems to have been the hope of Major-General Peter von Pahlen, who had masterminded the conspiracy. Alternatively he might introduce constitutional reforms once he had fully established himself as a ruler. And even if he balked at direct limitation of his power, he might at the very least make social and institutional reforms whose long-term consequence would be to strengthen society at the monarchy's expense.

The first option was never very realistic. What made it still less likely was that Alexander had been left feeling conscience-stricken and highly insecure by his father's murder; and far from rewarding Pahlen with a constitution he soon packed him off into exile on his estate. Alexander's wish to move towards the rule of law was nevertheless sincere enough and was shown by the importance he attached to the Senate. This – officially the 'Governing Senate' but in practice a rubber stamp – was the highest administrative and judicial institution and the channel through which laws were issued. Alexander's apparent wish to turn it into a body with real substance was seized upon by the grandees who manned it: here, they reckoned, was their chance of creating an embryonic parliament. There was talk about electing senators, and in the autumn of 1802 the Senate gained two important new rights. It would have a 'right of remonstrance' with regard to proposed legislation – a right, that is, to criticize new laws; and ministers (another innovation of Alexander's) would have to make annual reports to it. The first seemed the germ from which the Senate might grow into a proper legislature; the second promised what was vital to any real parliament – ministerial accountability. Within a matter of months, however, both provisions had become dead letters, and in practice Alexander's rule was to be as unlimited as his predecessors'. The grandees could replace one autocrat by another; but even in circumstances as favourable as these, getting a formal, institutionalized share in power proved to be beyond them.

Would a genuinely 'governing' Senate anyway have done much for the nation? Alexander's friends Czartoryski, Stroganov, Kochubey and Novosiltsev, who with him formed what became known as the Unofficial Committee, were convinced that it would not, and they strongly opposed the idea of turning the Senate into a parliament. The way forward, these young radicals believed, was not for Alexander to shed his powers in favour of a self-seeking clique of nobles but rather to use them to the full against vested interests. Political reform had to come of course, but *social* reform needed to be at the top of the agenda, especially the emancipation of the serfs, which only an undiminished autocracy would be strong enough to push through against the noble veto. Underlying such arguments was the assumption that free institutions could only be based on a free and preferably educated society: if they were not, there would either be a rapid return to absolutism or, worse still, peasant uprisings and a slide into anarchy.

Radishchev in all probability thought much the same. He had been allowed back from Siberia by Paul, who had detested his mother and her doings even more than he detested radicalism; and the one-time unmentionable was now invited back to St Petersburg to join the reforming effort as a member of the commission to revise and codify the laws. Here, it seemed, was an opportunity to bring about real change within the system and Radishchev came to the job with high hopes that he would be allowed, even encouraged, to draft laws that would do something for the general good. The goals he set himself included equality before the law, open justice, a jury system and a ban on corporal punishment. But his hopes were short-lived, and before long the head of the commission was telling him that unless he changed his tune he might find himself back in Siberia. Rather than yield, Radishchev in September 1802 killed himself. His suicide seems to have been a despairing and yet defiant reaction to the realization that he would never achieve what he wanted through the legislative commission. But something else too may have contributed to his despair: the fear that any reforms his masters did concede would only scratch the surface of the country's problems, that liberal reforms would do little to help and might even hinder his dream of a free, humane and egalitarian Russia. The suicide of the first Russian democrat would in any event ring down through the nineteenth century, a warning to anyone else who believed in getting real change out of the autocracy.

Notes

1 Sigismund von Herberstein, *Notes upon Russia* (2 vols, London, 1851), vol. I, pp. 30 and 32.
2 Alexis de Tocqueville, *Democracy in America*, ed. J. P. Mayer and Max Lerner, (2 vols, London, 1968), vol. I, p. 511.
3 Cited from George Vernadsky, *Political and Diplomatic History of Russia* (Boston, 1936), p. 232.

4 Marc Szeftel, 'Forms of Government of the Russian Empire prior to the Constitutional Reforms of 1905–06', in John Sheldon Curtiss, ed., *Essays in Russian and Soviet History in Honor of Geroid Tanquary Robinson* (Leiden, 1963), p. 105.

5 *Ibid.*

6 Roderick E. McGrew, *Paul I of Russia 1754–1801* (Oxford, 1992), p. 220.

7 P. N. Milyukov, *Ocherki po istorii russkoi kultury*, 4th edn (2 vols, St Petersburg, 1900), vol. I, p. 125.

8 Nicolas Zernov, *Eastern Christendom* (London, 1961), p. 140.

9 Marquis de Custine, *Russia* (London, 1854), p. 73.

10 M. M. Speransky, *Proekty i zapiski*, ed. S. N. Valk (Moscow–Leningrad, 1961), p. 43.

11 Custine, *Russia*, p. 378.

12 D. Mackenzie Wallace, *Russia*, 9th edn (London, n.d.), p. 126.

13 A. N. Radishchev, *Puteshestvie iz Peterburga v Moskvu* (Moscow, 1973), p. 133.

14 Cited from David Marshall Lang, *The First Russian Radical: Alexander Radishchev 1749–1802* (London, 1959), p. 251.

|2|

Unreformed Russia,
1801–1855

1

Alexander I would go down as 'the Blessed', and he would be much the most popular of the nineteenth-century rulers. Women adored him; many of the officers who fought with him admired him almost to the point of idolatry; and peasant reverence for him would be reflected in a widespread myth that in 1825 he had not died but simply taken to the life of a wandering holy man. Those who had hoped that his commitment to liberty would lead to something concrete were, however, badly disappointed. The most likely explanation of Alexander's barren liberalism is that he was not really a liberal at all. What Alexander wanted was an orderly, civilized, enlightened and rule-of-law absolutism.[1] Of course, he was ashamed of his father's despotic regime. Ideally he would have acted upon the fine principles he had learned from his tutor. Yet sharing power with the nobles was more than could reasonably be expected of someone who had inherited unlimited power. There was, as it happened, a genuine liberal at the court: Mikhail Speransky, who for several years was Alexander's closest friend and chief adviser. But Speransky was tragically in advance of his time; and his ideas for quietly dismantling an absolutism from within would have to wait almost two centuries until they were tried out, no doubt quite unwittingly, by Mikhail Gorbachev.

The hinge between Alexander's reign and that of Nicholas I (1825–55) was the uprising of the Decembrists, who were called this because they made their attempt in December 1825. The Decembrists in some ways looked back to the tradition of palace conspiracy; Lenin nevertheless rightly enough saw them as beginning the revolutionary movement. Yet, with one important possible exception, the Decembrists would have detested the movement's Bolshevik denouement. They were liberals like Speransky, though army officers rather than courtiers, and they had been deeply wounded by Alexander's apparent betrayal of his former principles. A liberal Russia could, however, no more be created by armed force than it could by Speransky's attempts to persuade and beguile Alexander. The effect was in fact counter-productive: the uprising precipitated 30 years of harsh repression, in reaction to which the opposition movement became far more radical than almost any of the Decembrists would have wanted. Yet when Boris Yeltsin and his supporters resisted a would-be authoritarian coup in August 1991, there was a sense of a circle at long last being closed. What the Decembrists had begun in 1825 with their bungled uprising, the barricaded democrats seemed to have brought within sight of a conclusion.

Nicholas I was brave and good-looking, but he lacked Alexander's charm and soft mystical appeal and was all too obviously a son of the martinet, Paul. Since his father and grandfather had been murdered and he himself had all but been ousted on the first day of his reign, he had good reason for taking his own and the regime's security very seriously. He was harsh, unimaginative and inordinately suspicious, and for most educated Russians life under him must have been depressing or at least dreary in the extreme. However, seen in the gallery of Russian autocrats, he has his merits. He was not an unstable tyrant, unlike Paul. He did not have the bottomless cruelty and cynicism of Stalin. He was repressive, though not in any crazy or sadistic way, and what drove him was a sense of duty, however misguided, towards his subjects. Here in fact was the patriarch of Russian patriarchs, tirelessly doing what was best for people who did not know what was best for themselves. Doing what was best meant staving off revolution and keeping society in a straitjacket. Conservative and apparently stagnant periods have tended, we shall see, to alternate in Russian history with turbulent ones. Nicholas's reign illustrates the point. Beginning under Decembrism's shadow, it soon acquired a feeling of timelessness. Nothing was changing, it seemed, and nothing ever would change. (The sense of statis, of a society suspended outside time, is marvellously captured in Turgenev's short novel *Rudin*, written at the very beginning of the next reign.) But the impression was misleading. Strong currents were flowing beneath the surface, and Alexander II would be welcomed as fervently as Alexander I had once been.

2

Alexander I's record as a reformer can be summarized quickly. Little came of the constitutional ideas which he had played with while heir to the throne. The Senate was, as we have seen, denied any independence, while two apparently promising new bodies, the Committee of Ministers and the Council of State, proved to be equally tied to the ruler's apron strings. The colleges or boards which till now had administered the country were replaced in 1802 by ministries headed by a single person, and the ministers met regularly in a committee. But the Committee of Ministers had none of the collective rights or responsibilities of a British cabinet. Alexander had all the power; the ministers, being simply his appointees, were helpless to resist him, and they tended to see one another as rivals for his favour rather than as colleagues who should present a joint programme and if necessary stand up to him. The Council of State was intended to vet all proposed legislation, and had it done its job properly might have done something to establish a distinction between laws and mere decrees. But a body which was a puppet of the ruler and could look to no support in society was in no position whatever to establish such a distinction; Alexander could simply disregard what his wise men thought, even if they were unanimous, and in practice many laws were implemented without ever coming before the Council.

Social changes were hardly any more radical than institutional ones, despite the pressure from Alexander's friends on the Unofficial Committee for something to be done about serfdom. The Law of Free Landworkers (1803) gave serfs the right to buy freedom and land from their masters, but did no more than nibble at the problem. Serfs were too poor on the whole to be able to pay what their masters demanded, while the masters were, with a few liberal exceptions (who became heartily unpopular with their colleagues), unwilling to let them go. During the whole reign no more than 37,000 serfs out of some six million were freed under this law's provisions. Many more serfs benefited from a general emancipation carried out later in the reign in the Baltic provinces, where the landlords were more liberal-minded and thought it worthwhile giving up their rights in order to end peasant unrest. The Baltic deal, however, gave the peasants freedom but no land and left them in the position of having either to rent land or to work as hired labourers. Hopes that it would act as an inspiration to the rest of the empire came to nothing. Russian landlords hung on determinedly to their rights, while the Baltic peasants, far from gratefully accepting the new arrangement, became increasingly restless as their economic situation worsened. Within a few years the Baltic approach came to seem exactly the wrong one; if the Russian serfs were to be freed, somehow or other they would have to be provided with land.

Alexander had a better record in education, especially higher education. Before his reign Russia had had only one university, that of Moscow, founded in 1755, and it had been so insignificant that anyone seriously interested in university education had gone abroad. Russian higher education began in effect with Alexander, who founded new universities at Kazan, Kharkov and St Petersburg and re-founded universities in the western borderlands at Vilnius and Dorpat (the modern Tartu). His work was driven by practical need rather than cultural aspiration: the country was under-administered and badly needed more educated manpower. Starting higher education virtually from scratch was not at all easy. At first the universities were staffed almost entirely by Germans, but once nobles saw the linkage between educational attainment and success in the service they made eagerly for the universities and before long a genuinely Russian higher education would develop. Russian universities were of course quite different from Western and especially British ones. Far from being independent bodies dedicated to the self-development of the individual, they had been created by the state and strictly for the purposes of the state. Their aim was to turn out men whose minds were trained and well-stocked but essentially unquestioning – capable bureaucrats, in fact. But squaring the circle of educating people without giving them ideas of their own would not be easy, and even before the end of Alexander's reign purges of the universities had begun. Alexander had wanted to create administrative staff colleges; without realizing it, however, he had laid the foundation of dissenting seminaries.

All in all it was a poor harvest for those who had hoped that Alexander would set the country on the path towards free institutions and a society dominated by an enterprising middle class. Perhaps the most disappointed was Mikhail Speransky, a priest's son of outstanding talent and firm liberal opinions who rose to become Alexander's chief adviser and close personal friend from 1808 until 1812. Speransky was all too aware of the obstacles to what he wanted – Russia could hardly have a constitutional monarchy while most Russians were ignorant and enserfed. Yet he believed that institutional change did not have to keep strictly in step with general social change; it could go somewhat ahead and by doing so would speed up the process of general change. The vital thing was to establish a parliament, however inadequate; and once a public opinion and a free peasantry existed, the parliament could be transformed into a proper one. And in 1809, with Alexander's apparent approval, Speransky drew up a plan of institutional reform whose centre-piece was to be an elected parliament, the State Duma, which would have the right to reject laws.

The Duma's rights would at first, in fact, have been purely nominal. It would have been at Alexander's mercy and its continued existence would have depended entirely upon his good will. But if only it could continue the Duma would soon grow in authority and self-confidence; people would get used to the notion of power being located outside the monarchy; and eventually a point would come when Alexander or his successor would no longer be able to bludgeon or abolish it. A peaceful, gradual and stealthy revolution from within would thus in time convert a sham parliament into a real one. 'When the time is ripe', Speransky predicted, '... then almost without any changes a new structure will be put into this very same, so to speak, frame, and this will be based not on appearances but on something intrinsic and real.'[2] What had begun as within-system reform would become reform of the system itself. The ruler, like some sorcerer's apprentice who had lost control of his own work, would face a moment of truth; and if he were sensible he would bow to the inevitable and accept the role of constitutional monarch.

Speransky had shown remarkable insight into the means by which absolutism could be dismantled in Russia, and when Mikhail Gorbachev eventually did the job it would almost be as if he had Speransky's writings at his elbow. But the chance of any such outcome in the early nineteenth century was remote. However could Speransky persuade his friend even to begin the reform process? In the event he tried diplomacy – muffling, for instance, the ticklish matter of the Duma's legislative veto. He cajoled and flattered. Above all, he used blackmail. There was, he insisted, no alternative. Russia was on the brink of revolution. Either Alexander reformed or he would go the way of the Bourbons.

But would he?

The French Revolution had been brought about by a large, wealthy and ambitious middle class which had been embittered by social and political exclusion. Russia had no equivalent whatever to this. The revolution had been helped too by the anger of the town poor and the peasants. Russia, however, had nothing resembling the *sans-culottes*; its town poor – artisans, traders, domestic servants – were docile and the towns would remain quiet for decades to come. The peasants were a different matter, of course. After relative quiescence in the final years of Catherine's reign, there had been a rash of disturbances under Paul, despite or perhaps because of his pro-peasant stance, and official statistics would show almost 300 uprisings under Alexander. Yet the uprisings were widely scattered and none was sufficiently threatening to galvanize the government into action. The brute fact was that, despite Speransky's claims, there was no crisis. Alexander could safely ignore his friend's warnings.

Speransky in fact was out on his own – his only supporter, ironically enough, was the idealistic emperor. Not only was he alone, he had stirred up immense hostility within the élite. Many men in high places detested him for his humble origins, his cold, ingratiating character, his radicalism, and above all for his apparent success in captivating the gullible autocrat. To the inner circle of nobles, Speransky was in fact a dangerous subversive: he had to be stopped at all costs. A campaign against him gathered force and came to a head in 1811, when Nikolai Karamzin wrote a memorandum for Alexander which very powerfully put the case for preserving the autocracy unchanged.

Autocracy, Karamzin argued, was essential to Russia. The country's safety and wellbeing depended upon it and the loss of it would lead to disaster. There should, he insisted, be no limitation upon the autocrat – except this: 'You may do everything, but you may not limit your authority by law.' The danger of autocracy was that the autocrat might, like Paul, turn out to be a tyrant, and tyranny would occasionally have to be suffered like 'a plague or some other dreadful but uncommon occurrence'.[3] Despite that risk, however, autocracy was a far better option for Russia than the alternative of oligarchy, the rule of the few.

That sounded strange, coming from someone who would presumably have belonged to the ruling few, but what lay behind this apparent self-abasement was a shrewd defence of the noble interest. Liberalism after all posed a mortal threat to the nobles' privilege of serfdom, which only an unreformed autocracy would be able to preserve. But while the nobles needed the autocracy, the autocracy in its turn was dependent upon the nobility; and to make the point that they stood or fell together Karamzin quoted Montesquieu's aphorism 'No monarchy – no nobility; no nobility – no monarchy'. His view of the noble–autocrat relationship was in fact very far from a servile one. The nobles might not air their opinions in a parliament; they were nevertheless a ruling class in that they together with the autocrat ran the country, he taking the decisions at the centre and they exercising more or less unlimited authority in the provinces. This unstated contract Karamzin saw as the basis of Russian government, and it explains how proud, educated and Westernized nobles could happily defend the autocratic principle. For absolute power at the centre was, or seemed to be, indispensable to the nobles' absolute power in the provinces, and that made it something well worth putting up with. If there were no tsar in Petersburg, there could be no little tsars in the provinces.

It was not only nineteenth-century aristocrats, incidentally, who thought that their position as a ruling class required absolutism at the centre – the belief would jump the October Revolution and re-emerge among the proletarian rulers of Stalin's Russia. The two ruling classes would have something else in common too: both would play the patriotic card against liberal-minded rivals, lambasting them as pro-Western renegades. 'Russia', Karamzin protested, 'has been in existence for a thousand years, and not as a savage horde but as a great state. Yet we are constantly being told of new constitutions and of new laws, as if we had just emerged from the dark American forest.'[4] The 'constitutions' and 'laws' he wanted to kill off were indeed inspired by the West. Such things could hardly have Russian roots (though the Decembrists would soon try to invent Russian precedents for constitutionalism). And now that Napoleon, who was both a Westerner and a radical, was casting an ominous shadow over Russia, Karamzin's patriotic fulminations on behalf of the status quo were not at all easy to rebut.

Mounting opposition at home and the threat of Napoleon abroad had in fact made Speransky's position untenable. In March 1812 Alexander in effect called his bluff: he dismissed him and sent him into internal exile. Had Speransky's predictions been correct, his dismissal should have provoked protests and even a revolt. The only reaction as it turned out came from his enemies, who rejoiced. Speransky's disgrace meant of course the end of Speranskyism – his papers were placed under seal and public discussion of his ideas would be stifled for almost a century. Any lingering hopes of Western-inspired change were then finally put paid to in June, when Napoleon invaded Russia with his Grand Army of 600,000 men.

3

Hostility to Napoleon had persisted through the years when Alexander was trying to live in peace with him, and the patriotic bluster masked a deep-rooted insecurity among the nobles. For the wars the French had been fighting since the 1790s were by no means traditional state-to-state ones: wherever the revolutionary armies went they had taken with them the principles of 1789, and they had appealed to the masses in the countries they invaded to support them against their masters. Napoleon had continued in the same spirit, combining old-fashioned imperialism with new-fangled radical talk. Noble attacks on Napoleon therefore reflected an understandable dread of him as a revolutionary propagandist and enemy of feudalism. And no country, one might have thought, was more likely to be receptive to his propaganda than Russia.

The reality, however, turned out very differently. The nation – nobles, townsmen and peasants – united in patriotic fervour against the invader, and only the Spaniards equalled the Russians in their single-minded rejection of him. The Russian armies found themselves outnumbered three to one; Napoleon, however, had against him not only regiments but an aroused people. After fighting an inconclusive battle at Borodino on 26 August he went on to occupy Moscow, but far from being met by a submissive population he found the city almost empty – a quarter of a million inhabitants of all classes had simply left the city to him. For more than a month he camped out in the deserted and partly gutted ancient capital. But it was clear now that he could not beat the Russians or even come to terms with them, and when he began the inevitable retreat his army was harried relentlessly by partisans.

Why did the nobles' fears turn out to be groundless? The material for social revolution certainly existed. Coincidentally or otherwise, 1812 proved to be a particularly bad year for peasant uprisings. Why, then, did revolutionary doctrine and peasant discontent not produce a conflagration? One reason is that Napoleon had no wish to kindle any such thing. When the French occupied Moscow their proclamations to the inhabitants urged the need for order and a return to normal living and trading; they said nothing whatever about abolishing serfdom or any kind of social restructuring. Part of the problem for the French was that, unlike in Italy and Germany, there were no radical intellectuals willing to collaborate with them (and rumours about would-be collaborators, for example the exiled Speransky, were almost certainly malicious slander put out by the conservatives). As for turning the peasants against their masters, that was out of the question for them. To the French, the peasants seemed more beasts than humans; it was only the educated, who after all spoke French, with whom they felt any rapport. And when the whole disastrous expedition was over, Napoleon admitted that he had been deterred from exploiting the serfs' discontents by his fear that the outcome would have been a massacre of the educated. The peasants on their side could hardly have any sympathy for this raggle-taggle army of foreigners who looted, killed and destroyed. The idea of ideological solidarity between them and these invaders was nothing other than a book-ish fantasy. Hating the invader did not make them like the nobles any more, and outbursts of class hatred did, as we have seen, continue: but the trauma of the invasion made them rally in defence of Russia and its symbol, the tsar. A Pugachev, who could have appealed both to peasant hatreds and to peas-ant pieties, might perhaps have done well in these circumstances, but the 'Anti-Christ' Napoleon was in no position whatever to exploit them.

Napoleon's disaster was, of course, Alexander's triumph. Russian armies under Alexander marched westwards to complete Napoleon's rout, and in March 1814 the tsar led his victorious troops into Paris. Russia was acknowledged as the liberator of Europe as well as the greatest land-power; its ruler became a hero to many in the West and, all the more so, to many of his own subjects. The glory Alexander acquired between 1812 and 1815 never entirely rubbed off: to the end he had something of a halo, even to those he would disappoint. The cult of Alexander created in these years attracted, however, two very different kinds of people. On the one hand were the Karamzins, who idealized Alexander for having helped liquidate a disastrous quarter-of-a-century-long revolutionary experiment and looked to him as a pillar of the post-revolutionary order. On the other, there were those who admired him as a liberator, as the man who had conquered a tyrant and helped set up a constitutional monarchy in the tyrant's home.

Both groups came from the small world of the well-educated nobility. Members of the second group, however, were younger, in their teens or at most their twenties, and for them the war had been a watershed. They in fact were the generation of 1812. Many had had a bloody induction into adulthood on the battlefield of Borodino, in some cases as volunteers who were still technically too young to serve. They had then gone with the Russian armies across Europe to Paris and had returned in 1814 or 1815 as battle-scarred veterans, sometimes as medalled and wounded ones. Such young officers had idealized Alexander for his achievements in war and peace, had seen him as a military and moral giant. Yet they had revered Alexander as a leader rather than as an autocrat, and above all as someone who was dedicated to the good of Russia. War had made ardent patriots of the generation of 1812. The historian Klyuchevsky wrote of them: 'The fathers were Russians who passionately wanted to become Frenchmen. The sons were Frenchmen by education who passionately wanted to become Russians.'[5] But how exactly were they 'to become Russians'?

First of all, by rediscovering the language. In the kind of household in which the generation of 1812 grew up Russian had largely been displaced by French. But talking French while the French were invading Russia and killing Russians could hardly have been more unpatriotic. It was also dan-gerous, and there were incidents of stones being thrown at nobles heard speaking the enemy's language in the street. Suddenly it became *comme il faut* to speak Russian, and those who could not hurried to take lessons. The change could not be accomplished overnight of course, and the élite would remain at home in French (and usually German and often English as well) until the empire fell. But the trauma of 1812 began a distinct and irreversible shift towards Russian. The language of peasants and provincials became the language of everybody; the language of the kitchen and the ploughfield became also the language of art and thought. For instance, the early poems of Alexander Pushkin, born in 1799, were written in French, but all Pushkin's mature work would be in Russian. The change was vital. The Russians had to lay hold of their language before they could lay hold of their history. Karamzin's great achievement would be a multi-volume *History of the Russian State* in which he sang the praises of the autocracy. But the history of Russia as opposed to the Russian state – the history in other words of Russians trying to take their country's destiny into their own hands – begins in effect with the generation of 1812.

Rediscovering the language was part of rediscovering those who used it. In *War and Peace* Pierre Bezukhov, observing the horrors and the heroism of Borodino as a civilian outsider, undergoes a moral rebirth as a result of seeing those he has somehow never noticed before – the common people, *them*. They, he decides, are Russia. There was perhaps an element of anachronism in this – not till somewhat later did intellectuals begin to idealize the people and see in them good qualities which they themselves lacked. But while the men of 1812 did not compare themselves unfavourably with ordinary Russians, they did recognize their bravery and devotion and come away from the wars with a strong feeling that their lives should be made more bearable. That feeling was confirmed by service in Western Europe, where peasants were not serfs and had far better living conditions. The generation of 1812 had been reared on Western, especially French, thought; they knew Voltaire, Diderot and Rousseau as well as fashionable contemporary thinkers such as Benjamin Constant and Mme de Staël. But it was one thing to know Western ideals through books; it was quite another to see them embodied in everyday life. Service in the West was in a sense a school for the men of 1812. They left Russia wanting to liberate Europe; they came back wanting to liberate their own country. All the signs, moreover, were that Alexander wanted to do the same. He had after all done much to get rid of a tyrant and replace him on the throne of France with a constitutional monarch. More important still, he had given the Polish territories he acquired at the peace settlement a constitution and their inhabitants freedom of press, habeas corpus and other civil liberties. Alexander would rule in Poland as king in conjunction with an elected parliament which had to meet every two years. Finland too kept its elected parliament and basic liberties, and here too Alexander ruled not as an autocrat but in accordance with local tradition – in this case as grand duke. Surely, once the war and the restructuring of Europe were put behind him, he would act in a

similar spirit in Russia and give the people what, as it seemed to these liberal-minded officers, they wanted: freedom for the serfs and a parliament
for the propertied.

But Alexander did not. 1812 had had a traumatic effect on him also, but
the trauma had pushed him in a quite different direction. The main problem
for him from now on was how to achieve stability in society and to make
sure that revolution never again endangered it. The answer did not lie in liberal teachings – they indeed had been part of the problem; it lay rather in
religion, which provided society with essential moral ballast, and in firm
support by rulers of the existing social and political order. In a sense
Alexander accepted Karamzin's criticisms and the implicit deal he had
offered. The nobles would be left to rule at the grass-roots, while he would
rule at the centre without tampering with existing structures. In practice,
however, he withdrew more and more from domestic affairs and left the
everyday running of the country to a henchman, Aleksei Arakcheev, who
was an uneducated martinet and the antithesis of his former favourite, the
mild and civilized Speransky.

4

Alexander's failure to live up to the hopes he had aroused in the end made
revolutionaries of many of the men of 1812. The history of the Russian liberal movement begins with them; so too does the history of Russian socialism. Most, however, were reluctant revolutionaries who would have much
preferred Alexander to do the job for them. For 'revolution' still had dreadful associations of bloodletting, egalitarianism and dictatorship – in a word,
of Jacobinism – to any member of the propertied class. The wish not to go
from the frying pan into the fire was a good reason for giving Alexander
every possible chance. Occasional flickers suggested that his reformism
might anyway not be entirely extinguished – in 1818, for instance, he commissioned Nikolai Novosiltsev, who had been a member of the Unofficial
Committee, to prepare a draft constitution. Some of the 1812 men believed
too, as had the Committee, that only an unlimited monarchy would be
strong enough to push emancipation through. And was it not, Nikolai
Turgenev argued, immoral for landowners to hanker after a parliament
when most Russians did not even enjoy basic freedom?

By 1820, however, impatience was getting the better of such scruples and
the arguments against revolution were looking less convincing than those in
its favour. For one thing, it was now perfectly clear that Alexander had set
his face against reforms of any kind. Either, therefore, changes would have
to be imposed on him or there would be no changes at all. Equally important was that events elsewhere in Europe, and especially in Spain, had done

much to dispel doubts about revolution. The Spanish revolution of March 1820 had been carried out by men similar in type to the generation of 1812 – middling and junior army officers, intellectuals in uniform. It suggested that liberal ideas could very well triumph without any of the bloodshed and chaos till now associated with revolution and it had all the more of a tonic effect in that Spain too was a backward country on the margin of Europe. Here was a revolution entirely free of the savagery and social convulsions of the French. Might not something similar in Russia actually avert a French-style bloodbath?

The Spanish parallel was in reality misleading. The Spanish revolutionaries had appealed for popular support, had obtained it from the considerable middle class and at least not run into trouble from the peasants. The Russians, however, had no equivalent middle class to appeal to, nor could they safely assume that the serfs would remain passive and not take the law into their own hands. Liberal revolution had triumphed in Spain thanks to the combination of middle-class support and peasant passivity, but neither could be counted upon in Russia. That was why, one Russian liberal argued, it would be better *not* to imitate the Spaniards: their example was 'seductive' and, if followed, might trigger an uprising of the masses.[6] The real choice, Prince Vyazemsky believed, was between popular revolution with all its hazards and no revolution at all. But most of the liberal malcontents refused to accept that there was no safe way between these extremes. The dangers could be avoided, they argued, by 'military revolution' – which sounded Spanish but would in fact be a variation upon the theme of the traditional Russian palace coup. Like the conspirators who had deposed Peter III in 1762 and Paul in 1801, they would mobilize the guards regiments and seize power, though unlike them they would change not only the ruler but the political system as well. In this way they hoped to get the best of all worlds: they would destroy absolutism without stirring up trouble and thus keep the one undoubted advantage of change via the autocrat – the change would be tightly controlled and order and property would not be put in danger.

Thus was born the idea of a 'safe' liberal revolution. Despite this agreement on tactics, however, the conspirators were seriously divided in their aims. The movement had been got going by a core of high-born and wealthy guards officers who wanted no more than moderate changes. One of them, Nikita Muravev, wrote draft proposals for the new Russia which advocated equality before the law, the abolition of serfdom and the setting-up of a representative government and a federal state, but which would have left the landowners with their land and would have denied most adult males the vote by making it subject to a wealth criterion. That may sound rather illiberal, though it must be remembered that liberalism (and the name 'liberal' dates from this very time) began as a reaction against the French Revolution's radical excesses. Most liberals were opposed to one man one vote because they associated it with Jacobin dictatorship – only the educated and the propertied, they believed, could be trusted to use the vote properly. Some, however, argued more radically that to reject democracy just because the revolution had degenerated into dictatorship was to reject its most valuable legacy. These liberals opposed political privileges for the landed classes and challenged the fashionable *laissez-faire* belief by arguing that some state intervention in socio-economic affairs was essential if the poor were to be protected. Among the conspirators it was moderates who made the running in the early stages, but by 1825 the Northern Society, the conspirators' organization in the capital, had a radical majority. The radicals, led by a poet, Kondratii Ryleev, were republicans and regicides rather than constitutional monarchists, and they favoured a broad franchise and giving the serfs not only freedom but some land. The Decembrist movement, as it became known, was thus a broad church in which paternalistic liberals rubbed shoulders with democrats whose views anticipated socialism. The coalition nevertheless held together; what cemented it was not only the common commitment to revolution and a common revulsion against the autocracy and the complacent conservatism of the ruling class but a shared assumption that the revolution's main purpose was to establish freedom by overthrowing the autocracy. Once that had been done, it would be for the nation's representatives, and not simply a handful of revolutionaries, to decide the country's future.

There was, however, one conspirator who rejected this assumption: Pavel Pestel, the leader of the Ukrainian-based Southern Society. In this respect he was on his own, but Pestel matters because in intellect and personality he towered above the other Decembrists – indeed he was the most impressive Russian revolutionary till Lenin. He matters even more because with his radical and authoritarian vision it was he rather than the liberals who anticipated the eventual Russian revolution. Many of them rejected the autocracy with contempt as un-Russian and immoral, but he saw that a revamped absolutism was essential for the revolution's purposes. They would have made Russia a society of free and increasingly unequal individuals dominated by its middle class; he by contrast fervently defended the collectivist and egalitarian features of Russian society. Their plans for transforming Russia seemed far less draconian than his, yet he was more sensitive than they to the living tissue of Russian tradition and to the country's political and social realities.

'It seemed to me', Pestel would tell his interrogators, 'that the chief tendency of the present century is to be found in the struggle between the masses of the people and the aristocracies of all kinds, whether based on wealth or hereditary rights.'[7] Pestel himself was an aristocrat educated within the precincts of the Winter Palace, yet in this struggle he plunged in passionately on the people's behalf. Whereas liberals wanted to redistribute and limit power so as to create a maximum of freedom, Pestel's very different aim was to concentrate and use power so as to create a maximum of wellbeing. He was quite prepared to take drastic measures to achieve his aim – and was

not in the least upset when opponents accused him of being a Jacobin. For
instance, abolishing the nobles' privileges would not be enough: noble status, he insisted, should be abolished altogether. All Russians would simply
be citizens; all would be enrolled in a commune (*volost*), which would be an
amplified version of the existing *mir*, and there each would be able to rent
the land he needed from a common land fund. Under the umbrella of a
paternalistic commune and a state which embodied the general will, social
differences would to all intents and purposes disappear. The sorely divided
Russia of the tsars would turn into a united and homogeneous society in
which all pulled together for the common good. National divisions too
would be eliminated. Non-Russians would simply be turned into Russians,
except for the Poles, who would be allowed to form a satellite state of their
own, and the Jews, who would probably have to be expelled from the new
Russia altogether.

That was an ambitious programme, to say the least, and it went together
with a highly distinctive view of the revolution and the role of the revolutionary. For liberals, the revolution would be short-lived and essentially
negative; its job was to knock out the autocracy and release the creative
energy of the people, in particular the enlightened minority. But for Pestel
this strike was no more than a preliminary. The real revolution would consist in using the captured power to change Russia; it would be a lengthy
transformative process, and its success would depend crucially on the skill
and discipline of the men who directed it.

Discipline was the keyword. In his regiment Pestel was a feared and
highly effective commander, and he believed in treating revolutionaries as if
they were soldiers. Like an army, the revolutionary society should be strictly
hierarchical; the lower ranks should swear unconditional obedience to those
above them and be punished severely if they broke their oath. That made
sense in a spy-ridden and autocratic country – unless the leaders made their
followers tight-lipped and blindly obedient the conspiracy would be in danger. Pestel insisted, however, that even after power had been seized the society would still have to be the strictly disciplined instrument of its leaders'
will: without that the Russian revolution would squander its potential,
much as the French had. Russia in fact would either have to have a tightly
controlled revolution or else it would have no revolution worthy of the
name at all, and two safeguards were vital if the French débâcle was not to
be repeated. First, until the new order had been completely established
Russia would have to be ruled by a provisional government of three members of the secret society, which would wield absolute power. This revolutionary dictatorship would eventually give way to democratic institutions
elected by universal male suffrage; but it would have to hold power for ten
years at the very least, would itself decide when its task was completed, and
while it ruled the society would monopolize all significant civilian and military positions. Thus a century before the October Revolution Pestel thought
up the one-party state as the means of achieving happiness in Russia. His

second safeguard was to insist that the government would have to implement to the letter the society's programme, which laid down in meticulous detail the features of the new order and how they were to be attained. The programme was called *Russian Justice*, and it had been written by Pestel himself.

Yet for all his radicalism Pestel lined up in one respect with the liberal moderates: like them he believed that the autocracy should be got rid of by a coup in the capital, a lightning strike which would present the country with a *fait accompli*. This, however, was old-fashioned thinking for someone so self-consciously modern, and it riled Sergei Muravev-Apostol and some other Southerners. Why could they not start the revolution rather than wait for the lacklustre Northerners? Why should it not begin in the south and move towards St Petersburg, gathering support like a snowball as it went? But Pestel strongly opposed this: like the Northerners he was afraid that mass involvement would result in anarchy. This common aversion to popular revolution sprang, however, from very different sources. The liberals feared that the masses, once let off the leash, would run amok and butcher the landed classes. Pestel by contrast was against popular revolution simply because he saw it as messy and uncontrollable. His support for the lightning strike and his unwillingness to give popular spontaneity its head seemed to hark back to an older age; but it also looked forward to later ideas of the revolution carefully guided by an élite. The debate between Pestel and his more adventurous Southern Society colleagues touched in fact on issues that would preoccupy Russian revolutionaries for almost a century. Pestel rightly enough saw that undirected peasants would never make the revolution-to-blueprint which he considered the only revolution worth having. His opponents equally rightly sensed that without popular participation there would be no revolution at all. The problem of how to make a popular revolution yet guide it to predetermined goals would not be solved until much later – and then by someone whom Pestel in many ways anticipated: Lenin.

5

The dispute was for the time being cut short by news which came like a bolt from the blue: Alexander had died quite unexpectedly on 19 November 1825 at the early age of forty-seven. His death jolted the Northerners into action since they had been assuming all along that a vacancy on the throne would give them the ideal opportunity. The pressure to act was made all the more difficult to resist by confusion as to which of Alexander's brothers, Constantine or Nicholas, would succeed him. The Northern Society found itself, however, at a low ebb in numbers and morale, and to make matters worse the conspirators had not yet solved the problem of how to get their soldiers to join them in the uprising. There had been no such problem for their 'predecessors' in the palace coup tradition – as commanding officers *they* had simply ordered their regiments to march and had explained nothing. But the members of the Northern Society, captains rather than generals, could hardly rely on the traditional blind obedience when the order to mutiny might well be countermanded by their superiors. Yet they were most reluctant to do the one thing that would have ensured the men's support – to reveal their intentions. And in the end they took the cautious course of appealing not to the radicalism of the soldiers but rather to their traditional peasant pietism. Once it became clear that Constantine, the elder brother, would not accept the throne they decided to pose as his supporters and to ask their men to rally to the cause of the 'true tsar' against the unpopular and, as they alleged, usurping Nicholas.

This monarchist figleaf would stop the revolution getting out of hand, they hoped, but it put them at a serious tactical disadvantage. If they were pretending to stop a usurper, they could do nothing until he had begun the act of usurpation. The timing of the uprising would therefore be decided by Nicholas and in particular by the moment at which he chose to have the oath of allegiance to himself taken. And it was the oath, administered in the early morning of 14 December, which provoked the uprising. The conspirators urged their soldiers to refuse it and then march to the Senate, which they meant to coerce into issuing a manifesto endorsing the coup carried out in Constantine's name. The revolt was, however, almost fatally flawed from the start by the fact that its military commander and other key personnel lost their nerves and failed to appear; and the outcome was that only about half of the 6,000 troops the conspirators had hoped for gathered in front of the Senate, whose members had anyway long since taken the oath to Nicholas and dispersed.

Yet the Decembrists might still have saved themselves if they had been willing to exploit the wave of sympathy which ran through the huge crowd milling around the square and which affected some even of the loyal troops drawn up against them. People in the crowd made their feelings very plain by hurling abuse and missiles at the loyalists. Some of them, moreover, knew perfectly well what was at stake, to judge by the shouts for a constitution and the injuries done to a man who had betrayed the society's plans to the new ruler. There were even those who demanded arms. 'In half an hour', some are reported to have said, 'we will turn all Petersburg upside down for you.'[8] But if there were those in the crowd who understood the issues, this was because the society's intentions had been leaked rather than because they had been deliberately spread. Indeed, the leaders had carefully excluded such words as 'constitution', 'law' and 'freedom' from their slogans and had concentrated wholly on the cause of the 'true tsar'. It was precisely because they feared the turning of all Petersburg – and all Russia – upside down that they were determined to exclude any popular involvement, and they could not bring themselves to appeal for it even when it might have saved them.

The hoped-for 'safe' revolution proved to be a chimera, and the would-be liberators found themselves trapped between the forces of the autocracy on the one hand and those of popular revolt on the other. Faced with that choice, they preferred the autocracy – and the decision pointed forward to the early twentieth century, when Russian liberals would revive the idea of the safe revolution and again have their fingers burnt by it. For the implacably conservative Nicholas was less alarming to them than the prospect of an unleashed populace. What bound them to their 'enemies' in the square was far more substantial than what linked them to their 'friends', from whose anger they several times rescued loyal officers. When the great radical Alexander Herzen commented that 'the people remained indifferent spectators of the 14th December' he would be right enough in pointing to isolation from the people as a factor underlying the Decembrists' defeat, yet quite wrong to suggest that the indifferences lay on the side of the people.[9] The rebels' isolation was in reality self-imposed, and it was symbolized by those among them who continuously drove members of the crowd back from the soldiers' lines. The Decembrists would be defeated in the end by their fear of anarchy, by the ghost as it were of Pugachev; and before darkness fell that short midwinter day the hoped-for revolution had been put down by cannon-shot, a victim not so much of popular indifference as of its own fearful exclusiveness.

The disaster in the Senate Square disposed for three-quarters of a century of the idea of a safe liberal revolution. Vyazemsky had evidently been right. There could be no revolution without the people – revolutions were popular or they were nothing. And when news of what had happened reached the south, an attempt at a more popular uprising was made by the conspirator least attuned to the *coup d'état* approach, Sergei Muravev-Apostol. What he attempted had more in common with what the Spaniards called a *pronunciamiento* than with what had been tried in St Petersburg. Like the Spanish liberals, Muravev-Apostol *pronounced* in public – he asked his troops to pledge their support for the uprising and explained its purpose in a Spanish-inspired manifesto which denounced the tsars and extolled the ideas of freedom and equality. Yet even he was uneasy about breaching the Decembrists' taboo against proselytizing among the masses, and once he sensed that the argument against the autocracy was making little headway he reverted to the cause of Constantine instead. Whatever his approach, however, he had little chance with only 800-odd men and no fixed plan of campaign, and within a few days his desperate attempt to save the liberal cause had been crushed.

Could the Decembrists have won? Could there have been a liberal revolution in the Russia of the time? Liberal-inclined historians have often seen modern Russian history as punctuated by a series of might-have-beens – possible turning-points when the country's history might have taken, but narrowly failed to take, a liberal direction. The first of these is 14 December 1825. And had the Decembrists succeeded, then Russia's development might well have been very different. The liberal victory could have helped the emergence of an urban, entrepreneurial and middle-class society which was open to Western values and increasingly respectful of civil liberties – the society which Speransky for one had regarded as sooner or later inevitable in Russia. In the revolution's immediate aftermath the country would of course have been dominated by the major landowners, who would have become a genuine ruling class rather than simply the ruler's privileged agents; but in Russia as elsewhere the rule of the few would probably have proved to be a preliminary to the rule of the many. The problem for the liberal democrats of the early twentieth century would be that they had to make the country pass from autocracy to democracy in a single leap: the transition from oligarchy of some sort to democracy, from an unrepresentative parliament to a popularly elected one, would have been much less difficult. The consequence of a Decembrist victory might therefore have been that Russia would have followed, belatedly and with something of a zigzagging step, a Western-type path of development rather than the highly distinctive one it was in fact to follow.

Yet it is hard to take this might-have-been very seriously. The reality is that the Decembrists faced inevitable defeat. True, they could hardly have bungled their attempt more completely: with more competence and a little more luck they could very well have ousted Nicholas in St Petersburg on 14 December 1825. Yet if the coup could well have succeeded, the revolution was most unlikely to; and a successful coup would in all probability have ushered in a period of confusion and lawlessness which would have been cut short by a reassertion of autocratic power as the only alternative to total system-collapse. For the conspirators were, as we have seen, united by little more than the negative aims of getting rid of the autocracy and serfdom. Once they had won, the deep division between oligarchic and radical liberals over such issues as land and suffrage (with Pestel and his followers complicating the matter by making demands unacceptable even to the most radical liberals) would have made solidarity between them very hard to maintain. Those who had taken power would, moreover, have represented only a tiny minority of the nobility. As in 1730, the class as a whole would have fiercely resisted the would-be oligarchs. The new rulers would by no means have been helped, in addition, by the blatant westernism of their thinking and of the institutions they wanted to set up. They had taken their ideas above all from France, yet they wholly lacked the middle-class support which in France and elsewhere was turning liberal aspiration into institutional reality. What they would have faced instead was a nobility whose vested interests they had threatened and whose national feeling they had outraged; and beyond these hostile nobles the dark masses, whose alienness and potential for violence they were deeply afraid of. This was hardly the landscape for liberal revolution.

6

The Decembrist uprising put an end to the monarchy's pussy-footing. Since the first day of his reign had so nearly been his last, Nicholas I was going to safeguard himself at all costs, and the result was a reign marked by severe repression and a rigorous filtering of ideas and innovations from the West. Nicholas began naturally enough by dealing with the conspirators. Arrests began within hours of the revolt and almost 600 suspects were eventually brought in. Many the new ruler interrogated himself; and having browbeaten them he sent them off to the Peter-Paul Fortress with a chit in his own hand stipulating exactly how they were to be treated – whether chained hand and foot, for instance, or only by the foot. After an exhaustive investigation, 121 were eventually put through a carefully stage-managed trial. Five, including Pestel, Ryleev and Muravev-Apostol, were sentenced to be hung and quartered (though as a clemency they were to be spared the quartering), and more than a hundred others were sentenced to what, for most, proved to be life-long exile in Siberia. The impact upon high society was devastating: for every person punished, many others who shared the same cast of mind now sank into silence and inertia. A burgeoning public opinion had been cut off, a generation's most talented spokesmen had been eliminated. It would be three decades before another public opinion was able to form, and then the dominant voices in it would no longer be liberal ones.

Much about the formidable Nicholas was reminiscent of Peter the Great, who in his time had also been merciless towards rebels. In his poem *The Bronze Horseman* (1833), Pushkin would describe a poor clerk being pursued through the streets of the capital and driven to his death by the equestrian statue which Catherine the Great had had erected to Peter – and erected in the very square where the Decembrists would be crushed. But the autocrat who had executed and exiled Pushkin's Decembrist friends and whose menace hung constantly over the poet himself was of course Nicholas. Pushkin's eliding of these two personifications of autocratic might and invincibility was understandable enough. Both were tall, awesome and overbearing; both were convinced of their own rightness on all occasions; both showed scant mercy towards any opponent. Yet Peter had been a root-and-branch reformer, and Speransky for one thought that Nicholas too had the making of a reformer. One way, after all, of ensuring that 14 December would never be repeated was to tackle the grievances which had provoked it, to cut the Gordian knots which Nicholas's indecisive brother had shied away from; and in the early part of the reign it seemed that Nicholas might do just that. The hated Arakcheev disappeared, while leading liberal lights were given high positions. Viktor Kochubey, one-time member of the Unofficial Committee, headed a committee whose task was to examine legislative projects left over from the previous reign and to make reform proposals; General Pavel Kiselev, who had moved in Decembrist circles and favoured freeing the serfs, became chief adviser on peasant affairs and minister with responsibility for the state peasants; while Speransky himself, who more than anyone embodied Alexandrine liberalism, was put on various committees and given the job of codifying Russian law.

But it turned out that there was little Petrine about Nicholas apart from his manner and his love for the parade ground. Kochubey's committee toiled for five years, but at the end had nothing to show for its labours. Kiselev did something for the educational and physical welfare of the state peasants, but on the crucial question of serfdom he failed to achieve even what had been given to the Baltic serfs – an emancipation without land. It was Speransky, however, who cut the most pitiful figure. Nicholas had seen him as the evil genius behind the uprising, but lacking proof of his direct part in it he had hit upon a subtle way of punishing him – he would be the chief judge of these young men who had tried to bring about the changes he believed in. Speransky emerged broken-spirited from the ordeal, and from then on tried to redeem himself and prove his loyalty by doing unstintingly what Nicholas asked of him. His multi-volume *Digest of the Laws of the Russian Empire* was a major achievement of its kind: now at last the laws were set out in a clear and orderly way. But he had begun his career by wanting to change the laws; he finished by simply spelling them out. He began by wanting to use an autocrat for liberal ends; he finished by being used by an autocrat for autocratic ends. He began by wanting to replace arbitrariness by the rule of law; he finished by devising rule-of-law trappings to cover up unlimited power that was still more arbitrary and pervasive than Alexander's.

None of the problems, then, were tackled. Nicholas mulled over the conspirators' ideas and aims, but the chief lesson he drew from Decembrism was not that the country needed change but rather that it needed a proper intelligence-gathering and security force. He met the need by setting up, in July 1826, a so-called 'higher police', the Third Department of His Majesty's Own Chancery, which would prove to be a forerunner of the later Okhrana, Cheka, NKVD and KGB. The new body was made part of his own private office, his chancery, rather than a separate ministry because he no longer trusted the ruling class. The appointment of a close friend, General Alexander Benckendorff, as the Third Department's head was an additional guarantee that it would be utterly compliant. Nicholas nevertheless minutely supervised its work himself, and since it was known to be the direct instrument of his will the Department had *carte blanche* to act as and where it wanted. The Department's public functions were carried out by uniformed gendarmes, but they were helped by a vast army of incognito agents, who infiltrated all the activities of educated society.

The Third Department had arisen in response to a political crisis, and its prime and immediate task was to root out subversion. But subversives were few (though Nicholas exaggerated their number) and by no means its only concern; the Department did battle in addition with a far more widespread evil – corruption. Nicholas saw himself as a crusader against this, and quite how determined a one was shown by the licence he allowed to the writer Nikolai Gogol. Gogol's play *The Inspector-General* caused a huge stir in 1836 by satirizing the dishonest, money-grubbing and ignorant officials of a provincial town. This exposé of the squalid morality of grass-roots official-dom was too close to the bone for the censor, but Nicholas not only insisted that the play should be staged, he went to the first performance. A few years later Gogol was allowed to make an equally savage exposé in his novel *Dead Souls*, which depicted provincial Russia as a den of rogues, cheats and hypocrites.

But if this rogues' gallery was indeed representative, how were honesty and decency to get the upper hand? If officials great and small were unfailingly corrupt, who could protect the ordinary Russian against them? No one other than the tsar himself. But since he could not be everywhere, the Third Department had to act on his behalf; it had to be his eyes, ears and arms in all the nooks and corners of Russia, redressing injustice, smiting offenders, and reporting all serious transgressions back to him. The 'philanthropic aim' of the Department, in Benckendorff's pious words, was to 'bring the voice of suffering mankind to the throne of the Tsars'.[10] As a result, petitions against injustice and abuse poured in in their thousands to the Department; so too did reports by its spies and denunciations written by malevolent or self-righteous freelances. The Department did not only intervene between officials and subjects; it kept an equally sharp eye on subject–subject relationships and intervened in, for instance, personal quarrels, business disputes, and cases of sexual wrongdoing. In fact almost no friction or deviation from normality was too small for its attention The decree founding the Department had required it to provide 'information and reports on all events without exception'; that almost literally it tried to do, and the result was that its officials and the autocrat himself were overwhelmed by a mass of paper.[11]

This tidal wave of paper afflicted the government as a whole – in 1850, for instance, the Ministry of the Interior processed no less than 31 million documents. Every document received had to be recorded in a ledger, many were copied out in a prim copperplate hand, and all were then filed or passed on to another office. The sheer number of transactions and the complex regulations governing them clogged the machine of government and made for huge delays. By any criterion of efficiency Nicholas's administration would have failed dismally: it was not capable of keeping business turning over properly, still less of coming up with solutions to problems, and its forte was simply to generate documents, endlessly pass them round, and devise ever more complex and bizarre procedures for handling them. Here was bureaucratism gone mad, one might have thought, yet there was method in the madness – doing everything by the book protected the official from his superiors, and the more intricate the regulations the more protective they seemed to be. The climate of fear, in which every official feared or was at least wary of those at the level above him and took it out on those beneath him, resulted inevitably in a government machine in which caution was at a premium, initiative and risk-taking were out of the question, and self-protection by means of procrastination and Byzantine ritualization became the order of the day. But such a machine served the interests of nobody except the pen-pushers within it. Ordinary Russians suffered from the delays and the inhuman bureaucratism, while Nicholas suffered from its sheer ineffectiveness as an instrument of government. Unless he intervened, officials fiddled and nothing got done. That was why the Third Department, his pet creation, had a better record for achievement than the ministries. Yet even that proved incapable of delivering the changes he wanted.

At the root of this malaise of government lay the fact that absolute power was in the hands of a single person, who was feared with good reason and who considered himself infallible. The assumption of infallibility was crucial. The autocrat was the absolute judge of what was right and wrong for the Russian people; *he* knew what was best for them. This moral absolutism was deeply ingrained, incidentally, in Russian thinking and was found on the left as well as the right; Pestel too knew what was best, and so in time would Lenin. Moral absolutism went together with an oppressive paternalism. Thus when Pushkin had made a clean breast of his political sins, Nicholas rewarded his candour by saying that he himself would act as his censor. He then took the poet by the hand and introduced him to an assembly of courtiers with the words: 'Gentlemen, here is the new Pushkin for you; let us forget about the old Pushkin.'[12] So, ideally, he would have turned all his black sheep into white ones.

But did Nicholas know best? He set out to establish order and legality, yet the body he created to uphold the laws became a byword for its arbitrary actions. 'Laws are written for subordinates and not for those who make them', Benckendorff is alleged to have said; and the saying was certainly in character since the Third Department cut every legal and moral corner.[13] Nicholas's aims were admirable enough – bribery, arbitrariness, bullying, cheating and sycophancy were rampant and cried out to be eradicated. But not only did he fail to achieve his goals; thanks to his methods, the goals receded still further from reach. Life at the base of the social pyramid, which Gogol, despite some embroidery, faithfully enough portrayed, merely reflected life at the apex. People bribed, bullied, cheated, grovelled, etc. at the bottom because people bribed, bullied, cheated, grovelled, etc. at the top – and at all the intermediate levels as well. The paradox which doomed Nicholas to failure was that the vices he railed against were an inevitable result of the system he so fervently defended, and his inquisitorial methods merely drove them deeper into the woodwork. Spies, censors and gendarmes could not eradicate the Gogolesque vices; only free speech and accountable government could do that, and the autocrat rejected *them* in principle.

Nicholas took it for granted that normal people would think as he did, welcome his efforts, and do everything to assist him. But people turned out to be by no means as grateful as he expected. Visitors to Russia tended to be particularly ungrateful for the Third Department's attentions and often wrote scathingly about it when safely back home. Russians could not express themselves so freely. Their reaction to surveillance was often a sense of weariness or humiliation rather than indignation – similar, if less extreme, conditions had after all existed in their country for ages. Even hardened free-thinkers found it difficult not to bend the knee to this all-seeing and all-knowing autocracy. Pushkin for one seemed at times almost mesmerized by the autocrat who had deigned to be his personal captor; in *The Bronze Horseman* he sympathizes with the poor clerk who perishes, yet regards his attempt to assert himself against the might of the state as futile. Helplessness did not, however, make the subject love the police state any more. When Pushkin's fellow poet Mikhail Lermontov was about to be sent into exile, he wrote in a farewell to Russia:

> Perhaps, beyond the Caucasian hills
> I shall conceal myself from thy tsars,
> From their all-seeing eye,
> From their all-hearing ears.[14]

7

The police state needed to do more, however, than watch people and punish them whenever they stepped out of line. Equally important was to create or to preserve conditions which minimized the very likelihood of misbehaviour. Backwardness helped in this respect, and poor communications were an especial asset. Roads, for instance, remained appalling, even though a hard-surfaced road linking the two capitals did open in 1834. In the West the railway train was beginning a revolution in communications, but the attitude of the Russian ruling class to railways was almost unremittingly hostile. Railways would ruin the country's finances. They would deplete the forests. They would certainly damage agriculture. Behind such arguments lay the realization that peasant mobility was dangerous. Once the peasant started travelling, serfdom and even the autocracy itself would be in jeopardy. Count Kankrin, the finance minster, was a fierce opponent of railways, and not only on financial grounds: they were a danger to public morals, he believed, since they fostered 'the restless spirit of the age'. Count Toll, another adviser, warned Nicholas that railways were 'the most democratic institution which one could devise for the transformation of society'.[15] Much safer, Toll believed, to develop the waterways. Nicholas, as it happened, was not wholly convinced by the general hostility to railways. He

allowed a short line to be built in 1837 to the summer residence of Tsarskoe
Selo; and in 1842 he gave the go-ahead for a line between the two capitals,
which was completed in 1851. Yet this still left Russia with a smaller railway mileage at his death than any major European country other than Italy
and Spain. Conservatives could comfort themselves that the country was
very far from having a rail network. No line went south or east of Moscow;
and, what mattered more, no line yet linked Russia with the West.

For the days when Russians were sent cap in hand to the West to solve
their country's problems were past. The West was now seen as a source of
sedition rather than enlightenment, and limiting access to it had become
important for state security. Something of an 'iron curtain' now made foreign travel difficult. Such travel was not actually forbidden, except that
those under eighteen were required to be educated at home, and the adult
noble could in theory live abroad for up to five years. But the heavy tax now
levied on passports often made foreign travel in practice impossible. Even if
the Russian did manage to cross the frontier he was still not safe from the
regime; he would be closely observed by the Third Department's agents, and
if he did anything suspicious he would be ordered home at once.

Quite how dangerous the West was had emerged from a searching
enquiry into what the Decembrists had read. What books, they had been
asked, had influenced their 'criminal behaviour'? The books they admitted
as influences were nearly all Western and overwhelmingly French. If proof
were needed that France was a threat to all that right-thinking Russians held
dear, the Decembrists' confessions amply provided it. French and Western
ideas in general (though with an exception, as we shall see, for German
ones) now fell into deep official disfavour. But 'negative repression' – stopping people saying, writing, reading and doing what they wanted – was
clearly not enough. Something more positive had to supplement this. Ways
had to be found of ensuring that people did not even *want* to act disloyally
in the first place – and here Nicholas left traditional conservatism behind
and took a first step towards later Russian totalitarianism. The problem was
that people had come to assume that Western ideas and attitudes were
superior; kowtowing to the West had become second nature. If the regime
were to be safe, pro-westernism had to be replaced by the conviction that
Russia and things Russian were far better. Beating the radicals, in short,
required a vigorous offensive which bombarded people with conservative
and nationalist ideas.

Nicholas's break with his country's subservience to the West was not,
however, the isolated act of a man made paranoid by near disaster.
Nationalism was in full flood in early nineteenth-century Europe, and by
using nationalist language Nicholas was moving with the current rather
than against it. The Decembrists, as we know, had been ardent patriots; and
it helped Nicholas that his cultural reorientation looked like the act of someone who wanted to rescue the country from a humiliating dependency.
Nationalism elsewhere, however, was very largely a movement of liberals

who demanded the same right of self-determination for the nation as for the individual. Nicholas, by contrast, took up nationalism for the very different reason that he wanted to stifle individual self-assertion, and nationalism at his hands became a means of defending – not assaulting – an endangered fortress. It was this mixture of nationalism and conservatism which drew him to the Germans. At home russified Germans such as Benckendorff and Kankrin became his main henchmen – after his betrayal by the Russian nobility in 1825, they alone seemed trustworthy. And the Germans in their native land complemented this practical good work by the moral and intellectual example they set. It was the Germans, led by Johann Gottfried Herder, who had first challenged the cultural supremacy of the French. More recently, the philosopher Hegel had identified German nationalism with the highly traditionalist monarchy of Prussia. All Nicholas needed was to have this conservative and monarchist nationalism transplanted to the apparently receptive soil of Russia, in which cosmopolitanism was now deeply discredited and political radicalism had been dealt a devastating rebuff.

The new ideology, largely the work of Nicholas's education minister, Sergei Uvarov, was launched in the early 1830s and preached hard for the rest of the reign. The ideology had three main components: Orthodoxy, autocracy and nationality. In unambiguous terms it told educated Russians what to think and how to behave: they were required to be faithful to the church, devoted servants of the autocracy, and zealous upholders of the spirit and traditions of Russia. All of which was a direct riposte to the Decembrists, who had been free-thinking, anti-autocratic, and cosmopolitan despite their patriotism. 'There is certainly no country in Europe', wrote someone who knew what was now expected, 'which can boast of such a harmonious political existence as our fatherland. Almost everywhere in the West dissension as to principles has been recognised as a law of life, and the entire existence of peoples transpires in heavy struggle. Only in our land the tsar and the people compose one unbreakable whole, not tolerating any obstacle between them.'[16] Anyone who challenged such gush was likely to be exposed as an enemy of Russia.

By hijacking nationalism Nicholas made life still more difficult for the beleaguered community of intellectuals. The plight of the liberals was particularly pitiful. They had staked all on revolution and revolution had failed them. Most now swung back to belief in change via the ruler, but Nicholas not only denied them change: by his nationalism he exposed them to taunts of not being Russian enough and put them in the position of having to choose, or so it seemed, between their ideals and their country. The extremism of Nicholas in fact cut the ground from beneath the feet of the moderate opposition. A desperate situation required desperate remedies rather than milk-and-water ones. And the main intellectual resistance to Nicholas – any other resistance being out of the question – came not from liberals but from groups to the right and left of them: from religious-minded conservatives and from radicals who took up the new doctrine of socialism. Both, unlike most liberals, were at home with nationalism; and both by implication rejected Nicholas's identification of Russia and Russianness with the policies of his regime.

The conservatives were the Slavophiles, a group of Moscow-based landowners who saw Peter the Great as a disaster and refused to accept his westernized, bureaucratic state as a proper Russian autocracy. The new absolutism had subjugated the church; it had cut itself off from the people and ruled without any regard to their opinions; and it had worsened the conditions in which an unjustly enserfed peasantry lived. That amounted to a major indictment. Yet despite such beliefs the Slavophiles were strongly opposed to anything that smacked of Western constitutionalism. Power, they insisted, was an evil; therefore the fewer people who were contaminated by it the better. The autocracy as it once had been and should again become was the ideal form of government precisely because it put the whole burden of power on a single pair of shoulders. In a proper autocracy the ruler would do what the people wanted without being made to do so by constitutional limitations or electoral mechanisms; and while he carried out his unenviable duties the people would be left free to follow their spiritual vocation.

Thus a powerful assault on the policies of tsarism petered out in a form of mysticism. Something similar happened with the Slavophiles' social criticism. They deplored the gulf between the classes. They were wholly against serfdom. They idealized the peasants as the finest members of the community. They regarded a *rapprochement* between peasants and the educated as vital. Yet what the Slavophiles saw in the peasants was above all something spiritual. The peasant commune was an expression in everyday life of Orthodoxy's distinguishing feature of communality (*sobornost*), and it showed the peasant as someone who, unlike his counterpart in the West, had renounced his egoism and his individuality and given himself in brotherly love to his fellow men.

The Slavophiles were not alone in regarding the peasants and their commune as special. In 1847 a German conservative, Baron August von Haxthausen, caused a considerable stir by publishing a book in which he praised the commune as a unique national institution whose patriarchal and collectivist principles would save Russia from the upheavals afflicting the West. The revolutions which broke out in the West the following year gave his message a much deeper resonance. From then on the commune would fascinate educated Russians. For conservatives, whether secular or religious, its 'discovery' had obvious advantages. For liberals, by contrast, the commune became almost as much of an embarrassment as nationalism itself. Most instinctively recoiled from it, since it seemed to thwart that cultivation of individuality which they saw as Russia's only salvation; a few managed somehow to come to terms with it. But while the discovery of the commune created further difficulties for a demoralized liberalism, it proved to be the starting-point of a radical movement which would dominate the opposition for most of the second half of the century. The movement was Populism or Russian socialism; its founder was a publicist of genius, Alexander Herzen.

Herzen had all the makings, one would have thought, of a liberal. He came from a wealthy noble background. Nearly all his friends were from the liberal cultural élite. As a youngster he had dedicated himself to avenging the Decembrists, and he would revere them as martyrs for freedom all his life. If we compare him, moreover, with the great radical of his youth, Pavel Pestel, his convictions come out as through-and-through libertarian. 'The liberty of the individual', Herzen believed, 'is the greatest thing of all'; and that belief would underpin all that he wrote and did.[17] He left Russia in 1847 for what proved to be life-long exile in the West in order to campaign more effectively for freedom in Russia, and he vowed never to return until the worth of the individual had been recognized there.

Yet for all that, Herzen became not a great liberal but a scourge of liberalism. He respected his liberal friends as well-meaning people who acted out of conscience, but became convinced that the institutions they believed in could never solve Russia's problems. Did the liberals but know it, they were simply laying down pontoons over which people would one day walk from patriarchal oppression to the promised land of socialism. The 1848 revolutions in the West had shown him just how wrong-headed the liberals were. The Western liberals had played with the idea of revolution until revolution had actually happened. Then they had taken fright, swallowed their words about freedom and equality, and resorted to 'the bayonets of martial law so as to save civilization and order'.[18] Herzen had disliked the bourgeois society he found in France in 1847 and denounced it in letters to his friends at home. The 1848 events then made him break, seemingly for good, with the bourgeois world and its liberalism, now damned in his eyes as a creed of self-serving hypocrites. This civilization the liberals had saved by force was a civilization of the minority, incompatible with real freedom and equality. Parliaments, law courts and reform programmes would not deliver justice to the people, nor would any kid-glove, purely political revolution. The structures the liberals had managed to prop up in 1848 were in fact beyond salvation and their doom was inevitable. Herzen no more welcomed the coming upheaval than had Radishchev, since he guessed that much that was precious to him, as a child of the doomed civilization, would be swept away by it. But the alternatives were clear: 'either monarchy or socialism'. And which would win? On that he had no doubt – 'Myself, I back socialism'.[19]

Karl Marx, who had watched the 1848 events as keenly as Herzen, assumed that socialism would first come in a developed country such as Britain or Germany. Herzen thought otherwise. He looked instead with rising hope towards his own country, which not long before he had left in despair. The Western workers would, no doubt, one day establish socialism, yet the obstacles put in their way by bourgeois civilization were immense. And what Herzen now saw – and the perception would inspire Russian revolutionaries for the rest of the century – was that in backward Russia the task of creating a socialist society would actually be easier. The country's very backwardness, for so long a source of shame to Russians, would help. Having no towns of note would help. Having no middle class would help. Having no traditions of private property would help. That Russia would choose the delusory 'freedom' offered by liberalism was out of the question. There liberalism was an 'exotic flower' which would never take root – hence Nicholas's persecution of the liberals was quite superfluous. Russia would never take the liberal way because its people remained untouched by Western civilization; and what had saved them from that was the commune.

Here Herzen was on common ground of course with the Slavophiles. Not that he saw in the commune what they did. For them the commune pointed towards an idealized past; for him it pointed instead towards an ideal but realizable future. For them the commune expressed the essence of Russian spirituality; for him it indicated that the Russians were 'primarily a socialist people'. As a libertarian, moreover, he had fears that the commune might stifle the development of individuality. These fears had indeed led him while he still lived in Russia to reject the commune altogether. From abroad, however, he saw the commune in a more favourable light. The very fact that it had kept the redistributive principle and rejected private property made it the source of Russia's future regeneration. Out of it would come, he fervently hoped, a socialism that reconciled communalism with the freedom of the individual.

8

That required revolution, of course. Herzen believed that popular revolution was not far off. Many conservatives feared that it might not be far off. In its 1830 report to the tsar, the Third Department listed among opposition elements 'all the serf class, which considers itself oppressed and yearns for an alteration in its condition'.[20] A few years later Benckendorff put the matter more starkly: 'Serfdom', he warned Nicholas, 'is a powder barrel beneath the state'.[21] And Ministry of the Interior statistics showed a steadily rising graph of serf discontent: there were 148 recorded disturbances between 1826 and 1834, 216 between 1835 and 1844, and 348 between 1845 and 1854. But Nicholas, while admitting that disorders were on the increase, thought that for the time being at least the peasants could be contained. They might rebel against officials or landlords, but they still believed in *him*; and twice he gave striking proof of his power over ordinary Russians, and his courage, by haranguing and calming mobs which had been on the rampage.

These were urban riots, triggered by fear of the dreaded new disease of cholera and by the draconian way in which the authorities had tried to deal with it. Yet despite such outbreaks urban Russian was generally quiet. Even St Petersburg, the country's largest and most westernized town, was far less combustible that its European counterparts. By the 1840s its population had risen to more than 400,000, but the rise had not been dramatic and was not the result of rapid economic development. This was still a capital of the traditional kind, and in the first place a city of courtiers and nobles: out of 443,000 inhabitants in 1843, no less than 50,000 – one in six – were nobles.[22] It was also a city of bureaucrats and army officers, greater and lesser, and to one observer at least it seemed that half the people in the streets wore uniform. Many of its inhabitants were admittedly poor and badly housed and fed, but they were not a proletariat – their poverty, in other words, was not crushing and they had not become utterly alienated from those they served. A German visitor reported that St Petersburg had no scenes of wretched squalor such as in London or Paris. Its working-class areas were desolate and uninviting, yet they were not repulsive and disgusting.[23] Many of these Petersburg workers were of course serfs, whose owners had every incentive to keep them alive and healthy. And the largest single group consisted of domestic servants – 114,000 of the 1843 population, and thus more than one quarter of the total. Of all the categories of workers, these were the least likely to cause trouble. Paris at the same time with more than twice the population had a mere 50,000 domestic servants. Complaints by middle-class Parisians and others that servants could no longer be got were a sure sign of industrial advance and of deteriorating class-relationships. But in Petersburg servants were still two a penny; and the same applied to Moscow. Recalling his childhood in Nicolaevan Moscow, the anarchist Peter Kropotkin would remember that fifty servants 'were considered not one too many. Four coachmen to attend a dozen horses, three cooks for the masters and two more for the servants, a dozen men to wait upon us at dinner-time (one man, plate in hand, standing behind each person seated at the table), and girls innumerable in the maid-servants' room'.[24] While such people outnumbered factory workers, the tsar, or at least tsarism, would be safe.

Yet Nicholas did not feel safe – the fear of revolution, planted in him at the very start of his reign, haunted him unceasingly. The fear was exacerbated in 1830, when the July Revolution in France toppled the conservative Charles X and replaced him by a liberal monarch. The July Revolution had knock-on effects, moreover, within Nicholas's own realm: the Poles broke into revolt, deposed Nicholas and declared themselves independent with Czartoryski, Alexander's old liberal friend, as their president. After some months Russian troops crushed the revolt; the 1815 constitution, which Nicholas had always disliked, was revoked, and a harsh regime of repression and russification imposed on the Poles. From then on Nicholas saw an immediate threat to himself in any disturbance beyond his dominions, and when in 1848 much of Europe erupted in revolution his reaction was thunderous. He issued a manifesto denouncing revolution, offered a six-million-rouble loan to the tottering Habsburg empire, and then in 1848 sent an army of 200,000 men to put down the revolt of the Hungarians against their Austrian overlords. The Hungarian uprising, indeed the whole European-wide revolution, was nothing other, he decided, than a conspiracy directed against Russia and in particular against himself. It had come to a conflict to the death between revolution and the sacred principles which he alone now firmly upheld.

This time, as it happened, there were no knock-on effects: Poland, St Petersburg and Russia as a whole remained quiet. Yet Nicholas was not deceived. There were bound to be traitors at home, and in April 1849 the Ministry of the Interior (not, to its mortification, the Third Department) unearthed some. Forty Petersburg intellectuals, members of a discussion group headed by M. V. Petrashevsky, a Foreign Ministry official, were then arrested for treasonable activities. Petrashevsky had been one of the authors of a *Pocket Dictionary of Foreign Words*, in which radical and socialist ideas were discreetly discussed, and he and his friends had gone in for some rather wild talk and even proposed setting up a secret printing press. For this they were sent to the Peter-Paul Fortress, and twenty-one of them, including the writer Dostoevsky, were condemned to death by firing-squad. At the very last moment, however, when the first three had already been blindfolded and tied to the firing-posts, a messenger broke in with the news that they had been reprieved, and they were instead sent to Siberia.

In these final years of Nicholas's reign repression reached new heights, and the position of intellectuals became pitiful. His regime was utterly secure; he nevertheless acted like someone surrounded on all sides by enemies who were closing in for the kill. Yet while Nicholas fought off these phantoms, a real threat was appearing on the horizon. In 1853 Russia became involved in a war with Turkey, ostensibly over the rights of the Christian denominations in the Holy Land. It was an unequal contest and in November 1853 the Turks suffered a crushing naval defeat. Early in 1854, however, Britain and France entered the war on Turkey's side. Nicholas had not expected this, and soon his troops were being besieged in the fortress of Sevastopol in the Crimean peninsula. He died in February 1855 several months before Sevastopol surrendered, but by the time of his death the outcome of the Crimean War was not in doubt. Russia, since 1814 the strongest military power in continental Europe, was about to be humbled on its own territory. Nicholas's brother had thrashed the great Napoleon; now his troops were on their way to defeat at the hands of the much lesser Napoleon III.

What had gone wrong? Why had Russia lost its supremacy? In a nutshell, because of the very policies which had seemed to make Nicholas secure – repression and keeping the country isolated and backward. Russia lacked the economic, cultural and technological base to remain a great power in the mid-nineteenth century, and was relatively more backward now than at the beginning of the century. In the intervening years Western Europe had developed by leaps and bounds – the triumphs of its new technology and its middle-class civilization would be celebrated at the great exhibitions of the 1850s. Russia, however, had neither, having fallen behind by the deliberate choice of its ruler and ruling class. The Crimean disaster resulted in the first place from technological weakness; there were no railways to transport troops and supplies to the distant Crimea, and the army lacked up-to-date artillery and equipment. Thinking Russians saw, however, that the débâcle in the Crimean was the inevitable outcome of short-sighted conservatism in general. Nicholas had barricaded himself against the illusory threat of revolution by policies which left the country externally vulnerable and unable to compete with the West in the arts of either war or peace. The poor performance of the armed forces in the Crimea pointed in fact to much more than technological weakness. The armed forces would not again become an effective shield without all-round modernization of Russian life, and that in turn was incompatible with crude repression. If the country was to remain a great power it could not depend solely upon its own resources and its supposed innate virtues; it would have to open itself once more to the West, to learn not only the techniques but something of the ways of life and thought which had found reflection in the armed superiority of Britain and France.

In London the news of Nicholas's death was received with joy by Alexander Herzen. He had seen Nicholas only once – at the coronation, when as a boy of fourteen he had beheld the imperial hands 'still red with the blood of the Decembrists' – but the autocrat had dominated the next thirty years of his life. On hearing the news of his and Russia's release he summoned in his *émigré* friends, uncorked champagne, and threw pieces of silver at the urchins who gaped through the garden gates, calling them to shout through the streets: 'Hurrah! Hurrah! Impernickel is dead! Impernickel is dead!'[25]

Herzen expected that life in Russia would be quite different from now on, and he would not be mistaken.

Notes

1 See, for instance, Marc Raeff, *Michael Speransky: Statesman of Imperial Russia 1772–1839* (The Hague, 1957), pp. 37–46.
2 M. M. Speransky, *Proekty i zapiski*, ed. S. N. Valk (Moscow–Leningrad, 1961), p. 132.
3 Richard Pipes, *Karamzin's Memoir on Ancient and Modern Russia: A Translation and Analysis* (New York, 1966), pp. 139 and 137.
4 *Ibid.*, p. 155.
5 V. O. Klyuchevsky, *Kurs russkoi istorii* (8 vols, Moscow, 1956–59), vol. V, p. 249.

6 P. A. Vyazemsky, *Zapisnye knizhki (1813–1848)*, ed. V. S. Nechaeva (Moscow, 1963), p. 60.
7 M. N. Pokrovsky and M. V. Nechkina, eds, *Vosstanie dekabristov* (17 vols, Moscow, 1925–80), vol. V, p. 91.
8 D. I. Zavalishin, *Zapiski dekabrista* (2 vols, Munich, 1904), vol. I, p. 347.
9 A. I. Gertsen, *Sochineniya v devyati tomakh* (9 vols, Moscow, 1955–8), vol. III, p. 461.
10 P. S. Squire, *The Third Department: The Political Police in the Russia of Nicholas I* (Cambridge, 1968), p. 243.
11 *Ibid.*, p. 241.
12 Ernest J. Simmons, *Pushkin* (London, 1937), p. 253.
13 Squire, *The Third Department*, p. 103.
14 *Ibid.*, pp. 234–5.
15 Richard Haywood, *The Beginnings of Railway Development in Russia in the Reign of Nicholas I, 1835–1842* (Durham, N.C., 1969), p. 180.
16 S. P. Shevyrev, cited in Nicholas V. Riasanovsky, *Nicholas I and Official Nationality in Russia, 1825–1855* (Berkeley, Calif., 1959), pp. 75–6.
17 Gertsen, *Sochineniya*, vol. III, p. 240.
18 *Ibid.*, p. 60.
19 *Ibid.*, p. 285.
20 Squire, *The Third Department*, p. 204.
21 Jerome Blum, *Lord and Peasant in Russia from the Ninth to the Nineteenth Century* (Princeton, N.J., 1961), p. 547.
22 J.-H. Schnitzler, *L'Empire des Tsars* (3 vols, Paris–Strasbourg, 1862–6), vol. II, p. 294.
23 J. G. Kohl, *Russia* (London, 1842), pp. 3–4.
24 Peter Kropotkin, *Memoirs of a Revolutionist* (New York, 1962), p. 21.
25 Martin Malia, *Alexander Herzen and the Birth of Russian Socialism, 1812–1855* (London, 1961), p. 426.

|3|

Modernized Russia,
1855–1900

1

The period 1855–1900 in Russia looks remarkably similar in its general pattern to the first part of the century. This period too began with a mild, reform-minded ruler, Alexander II (reigned 1855–81), who aroused wild hopes among the educated and after a while dashed them. Once again, a ruler who had disappointed but never quite lost his reformist aura would be succeeded by an implacable conservative – in this case, by Alexander III (reigned 1881–94). Moreover, the hinge between the reigns was, yet again, a revolutionary outburst: the assassination of Alexander II in 1881 by terrorists aiming to create a socialist Russia. True to form, Alexander III not only rejected the reformist spirit of the previous reign but did his best to tear up organized opposition by the roots.

Yet beyond these superficial similarities there were important differences. Unlike Alexander I, Alexander II was from the outset wholly committed to the autocratic principle. He was never in the least tempted by constitution-mongering, and no Speransky figured among his advisers. Admittedly, his reforms had a liberal element, but that was a reluctant tribute to all-conquering Britain and France. Russia had been brought to defeat and the verge of ruin, Alexander saw clearly enough, by isolationist conservatism. It had to learn from the victor countries; and what had given them their dynamic was liberal-capitalist civilization, which had created the wealth, technology and *élan* that had proved unbeatable in the Crimea. The point, however, was to borrow selectively rather than to imitate; and Alexander would be constantly on the alert for any borrowings that might prove subversive. Thus when the minister of war, Dimitrii Milyutin, wrote in a draft statute extending military service to all classes that 'the defence of the homeland against foreign enemies is the sacred duty of every Russian', Alexander, scenting danger, corrected the draft to read that 'the defence of the throne

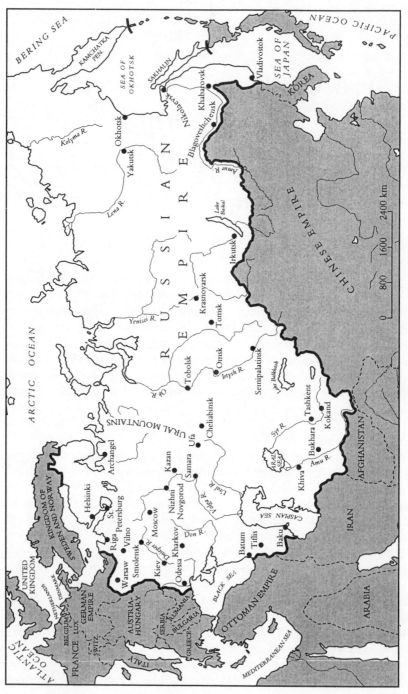

The Russian empire in the late nineteenth century.

and homeland' was the duty of 'every Russian subject'.[1] Russia might be modernized; it would nevertheless remain a patriarchal society and its people would be subjects of the tsar rather the citizens of the state. Yet Alexander could not achieve the changes he wanted simply by issuing orders. Even Peter the Great had lamented that he could not drag millions of Russians after him; all the more so, Alexander II could not. People would have to be *persuaded* by the good sense of his plans to give active help in implementing them.

Alexander's 'Great Reforms' in the event touched almost all aspects of life. They freed the peasants, rescuing them from legal limbo and giving them clearly defined, if still inadequate, rights. They established elected local councils. They replaced an archaic legal system by a modern, Western-type one. They transformed the general climate of opinion and granted people very much more scope to say and do what they wanted. Underlying them was a belief in what might be called unequal partnership. Ex-serfs and landowners, nobles and the autocrat, would join hands as partners, though not as equals; and just as Alexander was the first noble of the realm, so the landowner on his estate would be the first peasant. Yet Alexander's attempt to create a sense of community, in which discipline and coercion were complemented by persuasion and a carefully circumscribed freedom, inevitably ran into trouble. Half-hearted reforms, which gleamed with a liberal potential he would never allow to be realized, sooner or later displeased almost all shades of educated opinion. Conservatives were alarmed by the implications of what had been conceded, while liberals became disenchanted because all too little had been conceded. As for the growing body of radicals, the moral they drew from Alexander's reforms was that liberalism of any kind was a cheat and that nothing other than revolution would create happiness and justice in Russia.

Alexander III, getting off to a more traumatic start even than Nicholas I, soon showed how irresistible a determined autocrat could be. Revolutionaries might create sound and fury, but a strong-minded ruler could still crush them utterly. Even before his father's murder, Alexander had decided that liberalization and softness were a mistake. He would impose what was necessary irrespective of public opinion, and the machinery of repression which enabled him to do this was tightened and refined considerably. 'Politics', Alexander made it clear, would not be tolerated: society would have no say, formal or otherwise, in the decision-making process. Yet this unabashed political reactionary turned out to be a radical in one vital policy area: the economic. Like his father, Alexander saw that modernization was essential if Russia was to keep its great-power position. However, the modernization he believed in did not entail tinkering with institutions, lowering class barriers or allowing a limited freedom – all of that only made the task more difficult. The modernization that mattered was economic; and, throwing his father's caution in this respect to the winds, Alexander went for rapid economic growth and the creation of a heavy-industrial base.

Nicholas II (reigned 1894–1917), the first nineteenth-century ruler not to begin with an about-turn, continued Alexander III's mixture of political antediluvianism and economic progressivism. An inevitable by-product of the bid for economic growth by these last two rulers was dramatic social change – in particular, the development of an urban working class and drastically deteriorating conditions in the countryside. By the end of the century the drive for economic modernization had had a seriously destabilizing effect. Policies intended to shore up the autocracy had instead undermined it; and the pressure to complete Alexander II's reforms and give society a real say in affairs was by now very hard to resist.

2

The most important of Alexander's reforms, and a watershed in Russian history, had been the emancipation of the serfs of 1861 (followed by similar, though more generous, provision for the state peasants in 1866), which went some way towards meeting, at least on paper, the basic liberal demand that all members of society should be free and equal in civil status. The Crimean humiliation had made emancipation seem vital. The question from then on was when and upon what terms the serfs should be freed, and here Alexander's hands were tied by the nobles' determination to keep their losses to an absolute minimum. The least contentious issue, as it turned out was serf-ownership itself. There was wide agreement that this was anachronistic and inhuman – the serfs simply had to be given their freedom.

Yet the freedom the serfs gained at the emancipation was far from clear-cut. The manifesto of 3 March 1861, which in due course was read out in churches throughout the land, announced that the serfs would 'receive in time the full rights of free rural inhabitants'.[2] But they remained in practice a segregated and disadvantaged group, and their freedom when it came would be so circumscribed that to many Europeans it might not have seemed like freedom at all. True, they were to enjoy the rights of free persons – to own property, for example, and to marry without permission, and in general to shape their lives without regard to the landowners. But these rights were only for the future. For the next two years the existing order would remain: the ex-serfs would have to be 'obedient towards their nobles and scrupulously fulfil their former obligations', and the lords would keep their police powers over them. Even when the transition period had finished there would be no dramatic change in the peasant's position: he would then become what was called 'temporarily obligated' to the landowner, and would have to continue paying him in cash or labour for the land he used until he had completed the lengthy and expensive process of purchasing the land. Whether sale of the land went ahead at all depended, moreover, on the lord. He had the right not to sell and, if he decided against it, the peasant would either have to stay 'temporarily obligated' for ever or else accept what was called a 'beggar's allotment', in which case he was freed from his obligations in return for a holding a mere quarter of the maximum area he was entitled to.

A further limitation of the peasant's 'freedom' was that the land transferred from the lord would be allotted not to him but to the community as a whole. As a result he could not farm independently even if he wanted to, and the communal agricultural system would continue as before. There had been a debate within the government on the merits of the commune, but those who were against it and wanted to set up individual peasant farming on the Western model had lost the argument. The victors pointed out that the peasants themselves were strongly wedded to the commune (though quite how strongly would not become clear till half a century later when the government tried to dissolve it), and argued that in this case peasant inclination and the interests of society as a whole coincided. The commune, they were convinced, was vital. Someone or something would have to do what the lords had always done – collect taxes, find recruits for the army, administer justice, in general impose order on this potentially troublesome body – and only the peasants' own institutions could do this. The commune, its elder and officials, would in fact have to replace the lord, even to the extent of having his police powers and his right of exiling members to Siberia. And the emancipation legislation supplied a higher level of peasant government as well: several communes were grouped together in a canton (*volost*), which had its own elder and officials, its own assembly of representatives from the communes, and its own court. 'Free' though they were, peasants would not be able to escape from the clutches of commune and canton. They could not even leave the village temporarily unless the canton authorities granted them an internal passport; and the conditions governing permanent withdrawal from the commune were so difficult to fulfil that in practice it was impossible. One of the lessons the government had learned from 1848 in the West was that the migration of peasants into the towns was dangerous, and not until the 1880s would it change its mind and decide that wandering peasants and the risk of a proletariat were a price worth paying for a modern industrial economy.

The strengthened commune perpetuated the traditional way of doing things. Land was still to be parcelled out in strips; a third would lie fallow every year; there would be a common rotation of crops; most communes would periodically reallocate the strips; and the peasants would set their sights on getting more land rather than on making better use of the land they already had. Peasant living standards after the emancipation have been hotly debated by historians, but the view that the standards for most peasants deteriorated is hard to resist. Those who framed the emancipation no doubt wanted to improve things for the peasant; the communal structure, alas, made that impossible.

Yet the peasants did not rail against the commune and its officials – their anger was reserved for the lords, since it was they who were denying them freedom. Freedom to the peasants meant land. The land was rightfully theirs; therefore it should pass to them for nothing. An emancipation that provided for anything else was not freedom at all, simply a cheat. And the manifesto they heard in church in March 1861 had nothing to do with the freedom they longed for since at the very outset it declared that the nobles would retain full property rights and later it stated that any land the peasants did acquire would have to be paid for.

Peasant hopes were, of course, unrealistic. Alexander had enough difficulty in persuading the lords to give up control of the serfs' persons; to get them to sacrifice their land as well was out of the question. On the other hand, at the end of the whole massive reorganization the peasants had to find themselves with enough land to live off. Between the nobles' wish to keep all their land and the peasants' urge to get it all for nothing a compromise had to be found. The legislation laid down maximum and minimum areas which the lords had to make available to their peasants and the way in which, with the lord's permission, the peasants could buy the land allocated to them. Since the peasants would be unable to pay, the government would forward 80 per cent of the price on their behalf and then reclaim the amount from them over forty-nine years in the form of annual 'redemption' payments. The remaining 20 per cent the peasants had to pay to the landowner direct unless, as often happened, he made the commune enter into the purchase against its will, in which case he forfeited the remainder.

But why ever should the lords *impose* purchase? Why should they want to sell and the peasants not want to buy? Partly because any price would in the peasants' eyes have been too high – they, after all, regarded the land as theirs by right. What, however, sharpened peasant reluctance was that these particular prices and conditions seemed outrageous. As the legislation went through the committee stages, the lords' compliance had in fact been bought by tilting the settlement very much in their favour. In the less fertile areas the land rental, on which purchase prices would be based, was highly inflated, giving the lords in effect a hidden compensation for the loss of their rights over the peasants. In the richer Black Earth area the lords had a different priority – not so much to get the maximum for their land as to relinquish the minimum amount of it. Here the land made over to the peasants was about 25 per cent less in area than that which they had been allowed the use of under serfdom. These 'cut-offs' infuriated the peasants; and their sense of grievance was increased by the fact that forests and meadows, which they had previously had free access to, were now in most cases declared to be the landowner's property.

The government knew very well that this was not the emancipation the peasants had expected, as references in the manifesto to peasant 'misunderstandings' made clear. It was so worried about the likely reaction that on the day of the announcement large numbers of troops patrolled the capital.

Moreover, publication of the manifesto had been held back a couple of weeks until Lent in the hope that, without alcohol to fuel their grievance, the peasants would react less badly. And once the peasants had grasped what lay behind the manifesto's opaque prose, they vented their anger and frustration in a widespread scatter of disturbances. Some assumed that this was a mere preliminary: the real emancipation was yet to come – a rumour which the government tried to scotch with a statement that 'there will be no emancipation other than that which has been granted'. Others put a darker gloss on what had happened. The tsar, they believed, had been the victim of grasping landowners and officials, who had forced him to issue a false manifesto. There were even rumours that he had fled abroad or to the Crimea with the 'golden charter' of freedom he had meant for his people and that from exile he had ordered them to rise up against their masters. Such beliefs fuelled the biggest of the 1861 disturbances, that at Bezdna near Kazan, which was put down with the loss of some 200 lives. Two years before, a Russian radical had written: 'Remember that for hundreds of years faith in the good intentions of the tsar has ruined our land.'[3] That faith survived the emancipation by putting a special gloss upon it, yet peasants reconciled their belief in the tsar with the injustice of what had happened only by assuming that a second and truer emancipation would come along very shortly. Four decades later, worsening conditions would drive many of them to seize for themselves the land which, they believed, the tsar had wanted but been unable to give them in 1861.

3

The emancipation was followed in January 1864 by the second of the 'Great Reforms': the reform of local government. This was needed because local government had largely been carried out by the nobles through their powers over the serfs. It had been clear for some time that the country had too little local government, that some more formal structure was called for, and the prospect of abolishing the nobles' powers had made the need for a replacement acute. But what should the replacement be? Most bureaucrats and authoritarians in general wanted simply to increase the role of central government in the localities: to expand the powers of provincial governors and to send Ministry of the Interior officials closer to the grass roots. The alternative was to follow the European example, set up elected institutions, and give the tsar's subjects at least some scope to run their own local affairs. Doing that would obviously mean a radical departure from Russian tradition. Till now all power had flown from the centre; executive authority was simply delegated from the tsar, who had the right to override any action by those to whom he had delegated it. Representative institutions, were they to be set up, could not be so easily controlled, since there would be at least an implicit suggestion that the elected derived their mandate not from the tsar but from those who had elected them. Yet the representative principle won because in the climate of the early 1860s it appealed to two different groups with an influential voice. It had the support of liberals and liberalizing bureaucrats, who thought that elected institutions would make for efficiency and would help establish respect for the law. But it also had the support of many nobles, who believed that the new system, which they seemed certain to dominate, would give them back in a 'democratic' guise some of their lost powers over the peasants.

The local government act of 1 January 1864 set up local councils called zemstvos in most parts of Russia at two levels, province and district. Landed proprietors, town dwellers and peasant representatives voted separately for members of the district zemstvos, and these in turn elected to membership of the provincial zemstvo. Zemstvos were instructed to involve themselves in local economic affairs; they also had a role in medical care, agriculture, education, provisioning, and the building and upkeep of roads. They were allowed to levy a tax to finance their activities, and they recruited many trained specialists to work for them.

But how much scope would the zemstvos be given? The representative principle after all made a clear, if implicit, challenge to the notion that all power in Russia derived from the tsar. The zemstvos also embodied a subversive social principle – equality of the classes. Not only were members of all classes eligible to elect; all had the right to be elected; and peasants and nobles, sometimes ex-serfs and their former masters, could and would sit side by side as elected zemstvo members. All of this made the zemstvos potentially dangerous, and the government boxed them in accordingly. Chairmen of their executive boards had to be officially approved. Collaboration between zemstvos was forbidden, or else they might have turned into a formidable pressure-group. Moreover, zemstvos were allowed only at the level of province and district. There were none at the grass-roots, only the exclusively peasant commune and canton. Similarly there was no all-class representative institution at the top; and the demand for 'completing the edifice of liberty' with a national assembly was, as we shall see, firmly slapped down. The government had in fact conceded the representative principle only at the relatively harmless, as it must have judged, middle level, and it fiercely rebuffed any suggestion that, having allowed elected assemblies in the localities, it was in logic committed to allowing an assembly at the national level as well. As for equality, that was largely nullified by the electoral system: segregation of voters according to class achieved the intended result that nobles dominated both the provincial and, to a rather lesser extent, the district zemstvos. Segregated voting, noble domination, and the absence of any equivalent at the cantonal level (which the nobles would probably not have dominated) soon killed off hopes that these nominally all-class institutions might act as an integrating force between nobles and peasants. From the peasants' point of view the zemstvos were landowners' bodies which imposed taxes they could ill afford to pay, and after a brief initial interest they turned their backs on them.

The government, then, seemed to have neutered the new institutions fairly effectively. Liberal-minded nobles were attracted to them, but were unable to broaden the narrow bounds within which they were allowed to act, and the scope of zemstvo action was if anything narrowed further as the reign went on. In establishing the zemstvos the government had nevertheless given a hostage to fortune which it would later have reason to regret. For it had conceded, and would never be able to retract, a political principle that was highly dangerous to it; it had also broken its own monopoly of public life and created a parallel and potentially rival administrative structure to the official one. As a high-ranking enemy of the zemstvos would point out at the end of the century: 'Opposition between local self-government and the central administration or supreme power is inevitable. The latter is based upon the principle of the single and undivided will of the monarch, while local self-government ... is based upon the independent activity of representatives elected by the people.'[4] By this time a highly discontented landed nobility was prepared to use the zemstvos to fight for its rights. There was trouble brewing too from the specialists who worked for the zemstvos – teachers, doctors, statisticians, agronomists, etc. These zemstvo employees, scattered through the 350 towns with zemstvos, represented a new force in Russian life. Neither nobles nor bureaucrats, socially humble and often radical in outlook, they did their utmost to improve the quality of life for ordinary people, and their special position was reflected in the name they acquired around the turn of the century – 'the third element'. During Alexander II's reign they concentrated largely on their professional work, but in the closing years of the century they would help radicalize the emergent liberal movement.

4

The most far-reaching of the 'Great Reforms' was the reform of judicial procedures of 20 November 1864, which set out, in the words of the preamble, 'to establish in Russia courts of justice that are swift, equitable, merciful, and equal for all subjects'.[5] Such words could certainly not have been applied to the existing judicial system: trials were behind closed doors, the accused was assumed guilty unless proved otherwise, there were no juries and lawyers, and the judges acted simply as government functionaries. The reform, however, marked a radical departure by establishing a Western-type system of courts that were separated entirely from the state administration. Judges were to be appointed for life, not at the emperor's pleasure, and so would be in a position to be impartial. Trials were to be held in public and would be adversarial, with public prosecutors representing the state and an independent bar providing lawyers for the defence. Criminal cases were to be decided by juries, who would be drawn from all sections of the population. And minor disputes and infringements were to come before justices of the peace (JPs), who would be appointed not by the government but by district zemstvos.

It was of course too much to expect an overnight transition to Western-style legality. There was still no right of habeas corpus to protect the individual; and a serious limitation was that the new system did not extend to the peasants, who in cases affecting only themselves were tried by separate courts in accordance with separate laws. Those who worked within the new system did their utmost, however, to make it live up to its professed ideals, and from the government's point of view they overdid it. Judges of no known liberal sympathies proved all too impartial; at the bar there appeared a horde of eloquent defence advocates who used their right of free speech to the full, while juries similarly insisted on an unfettered freedom of decision. The consequences for the government were unfortunate. At the trial of the alleged accomplices of the revolutionary Sergei Nechaev, fifty-four out of eighty-seven were acquitted. At the political show-trial of 193 revolutionaries, ninety were acquitted. And when the woman terrorist Vera Zasulich was on trial for a crime – shooting and gravely wounding the governor-general of St Petersburg – to which she had already confessed, the jury caused a sensation by finding her not guilty.

The government had hoped that judges, juries and lawyers would regard what it wanted as necessary for the public good. With nominally independent courts that did its bidding, the government could then have prided itself on having established what the Germans called a *Rechtsstaat*. Its basic assumption, however, came badly unstuck, and in trial after trial during the 1870s the courts failed to endorse its case to the full. In reaction the government began whittling judicial independence away. The investigation of political crimes was transferred from the courts back to the Third Department. Political trials were moved to a special supreme criminal court or to the Senate. And after the Vera Zasulich fiasco the government stopped using the courts at all in political cases, since the risk of getting a wrong verdict was no longer even compensated by public sympathy (which had been overwhelmingly on the side of Zasulich). From now on the regime's enemies were dealt with by 'administrative methods' – arrest for an indefinite period followed usually by banishment to some remote corner of the empire. This onslaught on the reformed system came to a head in August 1881, shortly after Alexander II's murder, when the government established emergency powers which formalized its existing arbitrary practices and extended them still further.

The fate of the legal reform pointed to the fallacy which underlay the 'Great Reforms' as a whole. Independent courts and guaranteed rights were incompatible with the autocratic system because untrammelled arbitrary power was of the system's essence. The reforms had either to be taken much further or reduced to something purely formal and decorative; and since, despite the convulsions which marked Alexander II's final years, the social force to push the reforms further did not yet exist, the likelihood was that they would be cut back or even withdrawn altogether. Given an inch, people had been unable to resist taking an ell. At the outset the government had been confident that it could manage public opinion. People would be grateful to be consulted, and they would leave the actual decision-making where it always had been. That, however, proved to be a misjudgement, and the reign which had begun with euphoria finished with bitterness and bloodshed.

5

Winter, it seemed when Nicholas died, had suddenly given way to spring, an unending nightmare to a happy awakening. The happiness of the liberals in particular was understandable: here at last, it seemed, was a ruler who would give them the changes that would make revolution unnecessary. The last thirty years would be wiped out, the agenda of Alexander I's reign would be reinstated; and one sign of leftover business being looked at again was that the twenty-nine Decembrists still alive in Siberia were amnestied and allowed to return to European Russia, where their reappearance as if from the dead caused a sensation. It seemed, too, that liberals and radicals might get together again as they had in the Decembrist era. For it was not only the liberal who welcomed the ruler's reforming intentions; so did many to their left, notably Alexander Herzen, who was so carried away by the turn of events that he greeted Alexander as the heir to the Decembrists and gave him the title of 'tsar liberator'.

At the heart of the loose liberal–radical coalition were radical liberals from the province of Tver, north-west of Moscow. The Tver liberals pressed Alexander for an emancipation that was as rapid and as generous to the serfs as possible; but they also called for other noble privileges to be abolished and for the creation of a 'legally unified citizenry'. After the disappointment of the emancipation they went further, announcing that only a 'complete fusion' of the classes would eliminate antagonisms between them. The liberals' aims were by no means as radical as this might suggest: they did not envisage giving up their status as nobles and still less their land. But they saw that the noble–peasant antagonisms and the immense gulf separating the classes presented an almost insuperable obstacle to the creation of a liberal Russia, and they were ready to make major sacrifices – of their tax immunity, for instance – in order to narrow the difference.

This self-denial put the Tver liberals at odds with the majority of nobles, who had found the emancipation too radical rather than disappointingly half-hearted. But on one issue many nobles agreed with the Tver men: they too wanted a parliament or at least a consultative national assembly, and something of a constitutionalist fever was whipped up in the wake of the emancipation. The Tver reasoning was that if the government could not reform effectively on its own, then society through its elected representatives would have to do the job instead, and they therefore called for an assembly elected by all classes. Rather different thinking lay behind the parliamentarism of more conservative nobles. Having lost their serfs they no longer felt any reason to be grateful or subservient to the autocracy, and their hope was that an assembly elected on a property franchise and hence dominated by their own sort would protect noble interests better than the autocracy had. Others to left and right added to the pressure. On the left, Herzen in London and the home-based radical Nikolai Chernyshevsky endorsed the parliamentary campaign as a desirable first step, even if inadequate in itself. On the right, a number of people in Alexander's entourage, including his brother the Grand Duke Constantine and the minister of the interior, P. A. Valuev, believed that some move towards a national representative institution was now necessary.

Alexander, however, snapped his fingers at the constitutionalists, and a number of the Tver campaigners were put in prison. His 'no' marked another of those moments when Russia's development might have taken a decisive liberal turn but failed to. Just as the attempt to achieve a constitution by force had been thwarted in 1825, so an attempt at more modest constitutional advance by peaceful means came to nothing in the early 1860s. The pressure had simply been inadequate and the ruler had brushed it contemptuously aside. The failure of the constitutionalist campaign left the liberals in a difficult position. From 1865 the zemstvos would provide something of an outlet for their energies. The reality, however, was that liberalism had been pushed to the sidelines, and the liberals would be no more than spectators of the fierce battle which now developed between an increasingly conservative government and a burgeoning revolutionary movement.

How low the liberals' stock had fallen could be judged by the derogatory verb 'to play at being a liberal' (*liberalnichat*), which was widely bandied about. A liberal, went a definition of the time, is 'a man who loves liberty, generally a noble ... These men like looking at liberty from windows and doing nothing, and then go for a stroll and on to theatres and balls.'[6] Liberals, then, were frivolous, unprincipled and feeble – no wonder many of the liberal-minded shunned the label. That the literary giants of the reign were fierce enemies of liberalism only made its plight worse. Like Herzen, Tolstoy had broken decisively with his liberal friends and the civilization they stood for. *War and Peace* (1869), his epic of the Napoleonic wars, was inspired by more than anti-French venom; it was a sustained attack on progress and the fifth column of Russians who wanted to import it, a hymn of praise to the national traits of simplicity, non-intellectuality and passivity, and a defence of the traditional Russia of landowners and peasants against those in the government and the intelligentsia who wanted to destroy it. Tolstoy did not hesitate to pillory living liberals, nor did Dostoevsky. The prominent liberal Boris Chicherin appears as the inadequate and over-cerebral Koznyshev in *Anna Karenina* (1877), while Ivan Turgenev is the wordy Karmazinov in Dostoevsky's *The Devils* (1871). The liberals in Dostoevsky are feeble, vain and pathetic, but they are also worse than that: as rationalists and individualists they are, whether they know it or not, in league with the forces of revolution. In his most famous novel Turgenev had presented the liberal 'fathers' and the radical 'sons' as opposite types: Dostoevsky replied to this by insisting that the two were equally degenerate and genetically linked, that the liberals had fathered revolutionaries and terrorists.

Such mud-slinging reflected panic on the right at radicalism's advance. The radical cause had been given an enormous fillip by the bitterness and disillusionment created by the emancipation. Herzen for one, deluded for so long by the 'tsar liberator', now denounced his former idol as a deceiver and his government as 'a gang of scoundrels'. Disturbances broke out among St Petersburg students in the autumn of 1861, and after some bloody clashes with the police the university was closed. 'To the people!', Herzen from his London exile urged the excluded students. An underground manifesto that autumn declared that 'if we have to slaughter 100,000 landowners in order to realize our aspirations – the distribution of the land among the common people – we would not be afraid of that'.[7] But not for a decade would there be a serious attempt at popular revolution. The rebellion of the moment was in words rather than deeds, and its catch-word was not socialism but nihilism.

Nihilists were angry young men and women, generally non-noble, who rejected with contempt the society they lived in and the state which policed them. The word was made voguish by Ivan Turgenev with his novel *Fathers and Sons* (1862), in which the central character was a self-proclaimed nihilist. Bazarov was a man against, and his immediate aim was to smash rather than to create. He prided himself on being a man of the people, rejected even liberal members of the upper class, yet treated the peasants with almost as much contempt as the privileged. Contempt for others was matched by unlimited belief in himself. So far there were only a few men like him in Russia – new men, rationalists and materialists, men who understood the essence of things, moral giants amidst the pygmies; but everything about him exuded the conviction that in time he and his like would create a new Russia.

Not surprisingly many real radicals were touched to the quick by this portrait of radical arrogance and contempt, and what incensed them all the more was that by the end of the book Bazarov had become a broken man who believed so little in his cause that he threw his life away. But the next year they were given exactly the book they wanted by Nikolai Chernyshevsky with his *What Is To Be Done?* Chernyshevsky was a priest's son from the provinces whose radicalism was harder and less wavering than that of the genteel and moneyed Herzen, and he had only briefly succumbed to Alexander's blandishments. Arrested in 1862, he managed to write his novel in prison and get it published and at once it became the bible of the radical young – all the more so because the authorities, realizing their mistake, quickly banned the book. Two generations of Russian radicals would be reared on *What Is To Be Done?*, for here, woodenly but piously portrayed, were the new men and women they dreamt of, people who were free of the vices of ignorance, prejudice and passion and were rationally self-determining. Here too was a vision of the new society: for Vera Pavlovna's co-operative of seamstresses pointed towards the day when all production in Russia would be co-operative, when there would no longer be employers and employees, exploiters and exploited, when all would work and all would have equal access to the fruits of society's labour.

Among the book's worthy but nevertheless run-of-the-mill characters one, however, stood out as absolutely different. This was Rakhmetov, an almost Christ-like figure, who had renounced not only his noble status and privileges but all the pleasures of the flesh. 'I will not touch a drop of wine', he vowed. 'I will not touch a woman.' His self-denial went further, however. One day his landlady was horrified to see his shirt covered with blood – as a trial of will he had lain all night on a bed covered with one-inch nails. 'They', Chernyshevsky said of Rakhmetov and those like him, 'are the best among the best, they are the movers of the movers, they are the salt of the salt of the earth.'[8] Such examples of moral strength and purity would not be other than rare exceptions, and Chernyshevsky introduced Rakhmetov, or so he explained, just to set in relief the achievable moral qualities of his other new men and women, to persuade people that they could at least raise themselves to the level of *them*. But there would be some who would brush Chernyshevsky's disclaimer aside, whose role-model would be not the salt-of-the-earth Vera Pavlovna and her menfolk but the inhumanly perfect Rakhmetov. It was no accident that Lenin took *What Is To Be Done?* as the title for his first major work on political strategy. After his brother, a Populist revolutionary, had been executed, he had turned to Chernyshevsky's novel. 'It captivated my brother', he said of the novel, 'and it captivated me. It bowled me over completely … It's one of those books that give you ammunition for the rest of your life.'[9]

But while Chernyshevsky could inspire (and how the sixteen-year-old Lenin, grieving for his brother, must have responded to that image of total commitment), he had not been able to give a detailed answer to his own implied question – how was revolution to be brought about? Once the post-emancipation troubles had died down, it seemed that there was little point in looking to the masses. The only hope lay with the regime's opponents among the tiny educated élite – with those who now become known as the 'intelligentsia'. Their duty was to decide and act on the masses' behalf; and since there were very few of them and they would be watched at every step, strict discipline and conspiratorial methods seemed their only hope of success. The authors of the manifesto *Young Russia* argued in 1862 that 'the party must seize dictatorial power and stop at nothing'. There was a Jacobin tendency too in the organization 'Hell', one of whose members tried to shoot Alexander II in 1866; and the tendency was taken still further in Sergei Nechaev's organization 'The People's Vengeance'. It was Nechaev who established the image of the Russian revolutionary as a person totally committed and living a life utterly apart. The revolutionary, he laid it down in his *Catechism of a Revolutionary*, would have no private life, no material or emotional attachments, no interests other than the single obsessing one, not even a name; he would devote himself to the revolution – to all-encompassing destruction – to the exclusion of everything else. Whereas Chernyshevsky's Rakhmetov had had a touch of saintly selflessness, Nechaev's revolutionary would be nothing other than a fanatic. His morality had to be that the end justified the means, whatever the means might be, and he would destroy with his own hands anything that stood in his way. This precept Nechaev carried out to the letter in November 1869 when he decreed and took part in the murder of a colleague whom he regarded as a threat to his own authority. The trial in 1870 of Nechaev's accomplices caused a sensation, since the accused were not merely unscrupulous conspirators who had murdered in the name of high principle but in effect the radical opposition as a whole. Dostoevsky, a one-time radical who had seen the light, used the Nechaev affair as a peg on which to hang – in *The Devils* – a blistering denunciation of revolution and revolutionaries in general. If there was no God and no heaven, there could be no basis for morality and everything became permissible. The inevitable outcome of that was Nechaev.

6

Many young radicals, however, refused to accept that God and the existing order were the only alternative to Nechaev. They were determined to show that radicalism – real radicalism – was on a higher rather than a lower moral plane than the society it fought against. The lesson of Nechaevism, for them, was that only ordinary people could make the revolution, and the job of the educated minority was simply to help them. The antidote to Nechaev was in fact not God, still less the slavish Orthodox Church, but the simplicity, humility, wisdom and instinctive socialism of the Russian masses, the *narod*.

Thus Herzen's 'To the people!' appeal of 1861 at last found a response, and the 1870s saw a 'movement to the people' in which thousands of young radicals, women as well as men, landowners' children mingling with those of priests and former serfs, scattered among the villages of Russia. Not only did the people badly need a revolution; they were capable of making one now or at least in the very near future. Fervently the Populists (*narodniki*), as they became known, latched on to Herzen's belief that Russia's backwardness – its lack of towns, a middle class and private-property consciousness – was an advantage which would allow the country to go quickly and by its own special path to socialism. Not only did Russia lack the various things that got in the way of socialism in the West; its village commune was an inestimable asset. Thanks to the commune, the Russian people were innately socialist, and consciously or otherwise they willed the creation of socialism. Thus the Populists turned Marxism on its head – socialist revolution would come in Russia as a result not of development but of backwardness, not of economic advance and urbanization but of peasant misery and pre-capitalist communalism. Marx himself they greatly respected, and *Das Kapital* was published to acclaim in Russian translation in 1872 (the censor had passed it on the reasonable enough ground that it was not relevant to Russian conditions). But its readers were not persuaded that capitalism was either progressive or inevitable. On the contrary, the horrors of capitalist society as Marx depicted them made them all the more determined that Russia should not be dragged along that particular path.

Revulsion against capitalism and its evils was understandable. But in rejecting capitalism the young radicals rejected something else as well – political freedom and all the rights conferred by the liberal-capitalist state. They too wanted to be free of course, they too wanted to be able to say, write, read and do what they wanted. Nowhere else in Europe was freedom so conspicuously absent; nowhere else, one might have expected, would the educated so clamour for a parliament and civil liberties. Yet consciously and willingly the Populists rejected such objectives as an unworthy temptation. For political freedom would merely encourage the obstacles to socialism from which Russia had so far been saved, and its result would be a society run for and by the middle class. The autocracy, detestable though it was, was a lesser evil, since its very conservatism and ineffectiveness retarded developments that could only make the creation of socialism more difficult. Parliamentarism, by contrast, would be a disaster for people who needed bread and decent living conditions far more than they needed a constitution. Better, then, if Russia could go straight from absolutism to democracy, skipping the liberal stage. The country would be free before long, but Russian freedom would owe nothing to so-called 'free institutions' and the rule of law, which were simply devices for perpetuating middle-class domination.

Guilt towards the people and prejudice against the West helped muddle thinking on this vital issue of freedom. Was freedom for the individual bad because in the short term it was likely to harm the peasants? Or was there something intrinsically undesirable about it? Few Populists made the distinction. Most wanted to live in free conditions but felt that to try to institutionalize freedom at the moment would be immoral. Mikhailovsky spoke for these when he said that 'We renounce the increase of our rights and our freedom, since we see these rights as instruments for the exploitation of the people and the multiplication of our sins.'[10] The sins of the possessing could be expiated only if they shed not only their privileges but some of the refined tastes and cultural needs they had developed as a result of privilege. So young radicals put on peasant smocks and went to the villages and tried to live and work like peasants. Personal *rapprochement* had to come first. But they hoped in time for a fusion of outlooks: their freedom and the peasants' equality, their individualism and the peasants' communalism, would somehow or other be synthesized.

Some radicals, however, pooh-poohed such thinking – notably a former associate of Nechaev's, Peter Tkachev. The whole idea of peasant revolution was absurd, Tkachev thought. The revolution could only be made by an élite, a small group of professionals acting through a militant and highly centralized organization. Equally firmly Tkachev nailed the belief that in a socialist Russia freedom and equality could somehow be reconciled. That was sentimental twaddle: the two were antagonistic, a choice had to be made, and Tkachev himself opted without hesitation for thoroughgoing equality and for a regime in which the individual was utterly subordinated to the social whole.

Tkachev had few followers, and from 1873 he lived abroad. Yet Russian Jacobinism was stronger than its small following suggested because of what it had in common with traditional practice and thinking. What after all had the autocracy done but make its subjects subordinate their individuality within a collective whole? The church was strongly collectivist, while the *mir* had done nothing to make its members think of themselves as individuals whose prime loyalty was to themselves. Many Slavophiles agreed with Tkachev in rejecting the cultivation of individuality. Developments in the West were meanwhile spurring on the anti-individualists of the left and right in Russia. The German sociologist Ferdinand Tönnies would soon give the anti-individualists more ammunition by distinguishing between the traditional *Gemeinschaft* of the peasant and artisan world and the new *Gesellschaft* of the cities, in which people led unhappy lives locked in competition with others and without the bonds of community to support them. To Jacobin and conservative alike it seemed madness to let this atomized, joyless and conflict-ridden way of life triumph in Russia, where it had so far not got a foothold, and many Populists who did take individual freedom seriously could not help sympathizing with them. At times the extremes even seemed to link hands in conscious defence of the national values they both cherished. The conservative Constantine Leontiev consoled himself that if the socialists did win in Russia they would at least crush the liberals. The victors, he prophesied, would prove more Russian than socialist, would

exploit the natural humility and obedience of the people and when necessary use terror to discipline them. Leontiev even dreamt of the tsar putting
himself at the head of the socialist movement – an idea which Pestel on
the far left had also played with. A still darker prefiguring came from
Dostoevsky with his legend of the Grand Inquisitor in *The Brothers
Karamazov* (1880). The Inquisitor rebukes Christ for wanting to give men
freedom. What they need, he insists, is not freedom but bread, something
they can worship, and an authoritarian regime which will order every detail
of their lives as if they were children.

Dostoevsky feared rather than relished the regime he foresaw, and few at
this stage would have wanted to replace the tsarist state by a new Leviathan
which reduced people to childlike dependence in return for material wellbeing. Yet in one respect Tkachev and those who thought like him were
right – the idea of peasant revolution was a will-o'-the-wisp. The movement
to the people peaked in the summer of 1874 but proved a fiasco: the peasants failed to respond and often regarded the agitators with bewilderment
and suspicion, if not outright hostility. To the young radicals the peasants
were their separated brothers; to the peasants, however, they were unwelcome visitors from the world of 'them'. A second movement to the people in
1877–8 proved equally unsuccessful. But an exception to the general picture
of failure came in Kiev province, where a certain Jakov Stefanovich managed to recruit more than 1,000 peasants into a secret society pledged to rise
up against officialdom and the nobility. Stefanovich, however, took a highly
distinctive line. Far from attacking the tsar and tsarism, he passed himself
off as the tsar's agent, and the secret of his success was a fabricated imperial charter in which Alexander, pleading that he was bound hand and foot
by the nobles, ostensibly urged the peasants 'to free yourselves from griev-
ous oppression and excessive exactions' and 'to rise as one man with
weapons in your hands against your hated enemies and take possession of
all the land'.[11] There was something of Pugachev about Stefanovich but
something too of the Decembrists, who had also claimed to be acting on
behalf of a maltreated ruler; and the success of his primitive tactics showed
how great the mental gulf still was between the radicals and those they
idealized as would-be socialists. The peasants were a potential revolutionary
force, certainly; but the problem of how and in the name of what to arouse
them was for the time being unsolvable.

This rebuff by the peasants forced the Populists to rethink their strategy,
and between 1876 and 1879 they thrashed out a new one. A minority led by
Georgii Plekhanov, the future 'father' of Russian Marxism, came to the conclusion that Russia was simply not ready yet for revolution. Most, however,
swung to a position closer to that of Nechaev and Tkachev: revolution was
perfectly possible, and would be less difficult now than when capitalism had
got a grip (so there should be no delay), but only dedicated professionals
could bring it about. Those who thought like this founded, in October
1879, a revolutionary organization called The People's Will, which aimed to

make a frontal assault on the state by terrorism and, in particular, by regicide.

Faced in the late 1870s with mounting terrorism and a threat to his life, Alexander II had good reason to rethink. The fanaticism of a few terrorists was but the tip of an iceberg of disenchantment which had spread through educated society as a whole and had affected the young especially. After the attempt on his life in 1866 he had given up trying to cultivate even moderate opinion, and his education minister, Count Dimitrii Tolstoy, had cracked down on those seedbeds of subversion, the secondary schools and universities. The rapid spread of the revolutionary movement suggested, however, that repression simply increased the number of the disaffected and drove them to extremes. Something else had to be tried, and in 1880 Alexander signalled a return to the spirit of his first decade by dismissing the hated Tolstoy and replacing him by a moderate. He also set up a Supreme Executive Commission with the task of countering the revolutionary movement and examining its causes. The commission's head, Count Loris-Melikov, was convinced that conciliation was the only possible effective counter, and he drew up proposals which would have given persons elected by the zemstvos and city councils a certain limited role in legislation. Alexander approved the proposals; on the morning of 1 March 1881 he signed a decree summoning the Council of Ministers to consider (i.e. rubber-stamp) them; and had it not been for The People's Will, the proposals would sooner or later have been implemented.

But it was not to be. The People's Will had so far pursued its quarry determinedly but without success. They had fired at him and missed outside the Winter Palace. They had blown up the imperial train. They had set off a bomb inside the Winter Palace. And on 1 March 1881 they at last achieved their aim with a bomb thrown in a St Petersburg street.

The bomb that killed the tsar would, they hoped, bring down the coping stone which held the whole structure of tsarism in place. The outcome, however, proved to be very different. They could kill a tsar, but tsarism as a regime and as a myth remained vigorously alive and their efforts had the short-term effect of strengthening both. Others tsars had died violently, but they had been discreetly disposed of by or on behalf of high-born palace conspirators; never before had a ruler been killed in the street by his rank-and-file subjects, and this murder of the Lord's anointed caused almost universal revulsion. Within days most leading members of The People's Will had been arrested. On 3 April 1881 five regicides, including one woman, were hung.

The terrorists' bomb, some have believed, cheated Russia of another possible 'turning-point' – but for it, Alexander II would have set Russia on the path towards a constitution. That was certainly the reaction of his successor, who heaved a sigh of relief that 'this criminal and hasty step towards a constitution was not taken'.[12] But Alexander III had little understanding of constitutionalism, and the proposals which frightened him would not have

limited the autocratic power in the least. What the terrorists' bomb did do
was vindicate, and clear the way for, people who believed that Alexander
had got the country into a mess from which neither reform nor mild repression would save it.

7

Alexander III would have been a conservative ruler in any circumstances; his
father's murder merely made him more so. He had been wholly out of sympathy with his father's reformism, and ministers who after the murder
denied that there had been any causal connection between the reforms and
the revolutionary movement cut no ice whatever with him. His father,
Alexander was convinced, had embarked on a fatally mistaken policy in trying to appease the liberals and kowtow to fashionable political thinking.
The advice *he* most readily listened to came from a former law professor
who had once been his tutor, Constantine Pobedonostsev, whose dominant
passion was hatred of liberalism and all its works. The people did not want
a constitution, indeed hated the idea of it, Pobedonostsev had kept telling
him, and were one to be imposed it would have more terrible effects even
than a revolution. A revolution could at least be quickly overcome, whereas
a constitution would poison the nation. Alexander fell deeply under the
influence of his fanatical former tutor. He would be a traditional tsar, a tsar
of the people as Pobedonostsev described the part – Orthodox and strong
and an unswerving defender of the national interest. During his father's final
years he, Pobedonostsev and some other conservatives had formed an
unconcealed opposition. Once his father was dead, reformism and its supporters were doomed. The reformers were 'flabby eunuchs and tricksters',
Pobedonostsev told him, and Loris-Melikov, were he to be kept on, 'will
lead you and Russia to destruction'. Within a couple of months all the leading reformers had been purged. This was the time, Pobedonostsev again
urged the new tsar, 'to put an end, once and for all, to all talk about freedom of the press, freedom of assembly and a representative assembly'.[13]
There would be no partnership, not even a highly unequal one, between the
government and society. Any attempt by private persons to interfere in government affairs would be treated as a criminal offence. Everything would
flow from the tsar and his officials. That was what the people wanted, or so
Pobedonostsev believed; and it was most certainly what they would get.

The first task was to crush the revolutionary movement so thoroughly
that it never raised its head again. An Act of August 1881 allowed the government to declare a state of emergency wherever trouble threatened; within
the designated area its officials were given almost unlimited powers. At the
same time an élite political police, the Okhrana, was created. This soon-to-

be notorious organization worked through a combination of plain-clothed sleuths and secret agents; its tentacles also reached abroad – nowhere could the revolutionary feel safe from it. But making the police state more effective than before was not in itself enough: the root problem lay in reforms that had put wide areas of activity beyond the government's immediate control and had embodied a pernicious principle of equality. Given his way, Pobedonostsev would have wiped the slate clean altogether, abolishing the zemstvos and the judicial reform and perhaps even restoring serfdom. Alexander could not go that far, though a sign of what he might have liked to do came in 1886 when celebration of the emancipation's twenty-fifth anniversary was banned. Something of serfdom was, however, re-established in 1889 by the institution of Land Captains, government-appointed noblemen who were given a wide remit to regulate the lives of the peasants and to ride roughshod over the decisions of canton and commune. Moreover, the peasants' slim influence in the zemstvos was reduced by an Act of 1890 which cut down their zemstvo representation and gave provincial governors the final say in choosing peasant members. The government did its best, too, to curb social mobility by restoring the old principle that children should be educated according to their status rather than their talents. Children of 'coachmen, servants, cooks, washerwomen, small shopkeepers, and persons of similar type', according to a circular of 1887, were to be kept out of secondary schools and hence from universities. Education, being potentially harmful, could only be safely entrusted to the church, and so the number of church elementary schools increased considerably.

Professionals and all who worked in the non-government sector suffered as well. Press freedom was crippled; zemstvo activities were further restricted; the universities lost their autonomy; and what remained of legal independence was steadily eroded – for instance, the position of JP was abolished in all but a few urban areas. Militant conservatism went hand in hand, moreover, with militant Russian nationalism. Orthodoxy and Russian culture were now seen as vital to loyalty, and where they were missing disloyalty was assumed or at least suspected. Jews were treated as a particular problem. Rumours that 'the Jews' had killed the tsar (one of the regicides happened to be Jewish) triggered numerous 'pogroms' – assaults on Jews and their property – which the authorities did little to stop and may in some cases have connived in. After 1881 the violence died down and did not return till the early twentieth century; but the reign of Alexander, a notorious anti-Semite, saw steadily increasing discrimination against the country's five million Jews, with restrictions being placed on where they could live, which schools, universities and professions they could enter, and even which names they could use. With most other non-Russian groups, the government's aim was not so much to harass as to assimilate. Keeping their heads down was no longer enough; the non-Russians had to *prove* that they were reliable subjects by becoming Russian in faith and language. The Poles suffered particularly, and almost all primary teaching in Poland now had to be done in Russian. They at least did have a record of disloyalty, but there was no such justification for the russifying measures against the loyal Baltic Germans, Finns and Armenians. The government's belief that without cultural homogeneity the empire would sooner or later fall apart was no doubt correct, yet by its high-handed actions it merely stoked up the fires of nationalism and revolution and so brought nearer the very thing it wanted to avert.

In the short run, however, Pobedonostsev's blood and iron approach seemed to work. Order was rapidly restored throughout the country, and an uncanny calm fell upon the biggest trouble-spots, St Petersburg and Moscow. The quiescence lasted until 1891 and gave a special quality to the 1880s, marking the decade off from those to either side of it. For the atmosphere of the 1880s one has only to read the stories and plays of Anton Chekhov. Chekhov began his medical studies at Moscow University in the turbulent conditions at the end of Alexander II's reign, but he was shaped as a writer by the very different conditions in which he completed his training. Though he lived on till the eve of the 1905 revolution, he remained until the end a quintessential 1880s' man, and his central characters – decent, sensitive and striving for the good, like Chekhov himself – were all crippled by deep pessimism, apathy, and a sense of helplessness before the might of the autocratic state and the enormity of the country's problems. 'If only the workers could be educated', says Vershinin in *Three Sisters* (1901), 'and if only the educated could learn to work.' The convergence would come one day, but it was still far off; meanwhile there was no chance of happiness for either sort.

8

Yet the quiescence would not last long because this reactionary tsar, this pupil of Pobedonostsev, was also in his own way a radical and a modernizer; and it was during his reign and partly at his instigation that the country was set on the course which would lead to tsarism's early twentieth-century collapse. Alexander II, for all his reformism, had been keenly aware of the dangers of industrializing, and his wish to avoid a proletariat had done much to shape the emancipation. The son, however, reversed the priorities of the father. Firmly rejecting conciliation and institutional modernization, he nevertheless gave the go-head for a crash industrialization policy which by the end of the century had equipped Russia with a heavy-industrial base and a proletariat.

Good reasons lay behind Russia's late nineteenth-century dash for economic modernization. The country now had on its doorstep a united Germany, whose military strength was clearly underpinned by industrial and technological achievement. Bismarck had followed up Sedan – the Prussian victory over the French in 1870 – with an industrial Sedan: or so said Sergei Witte, Russia's minister of finance from 1892 to 1903. The danger was not only that Russia would cease to be a great power; it might even, unless it cast off its backwardness, become dangerously dependent upon the great powers and a victim of their political and economic aggression. Russia had fallen 200 years behind, Witte believed, and unless the lost ground were made up very soon it never would be. The country was at a cross-roads. Either it went the way of China – i.e. lapsed into being a semi-colonial appendage of the great powers – or it struck out determinedly along the German road. For Germany too had been a backwater and in the first half of the nineteenth century it had lagged woefully behind Britain and north-western Europe. But Germany had caught up – more than caught up – and Russia if it took the right decisions could do the same.

That was how progressive members of the ruling class reasoned towards the century's end. Their thinking gave a new meaning to the term 'industrial revolution'. In Britain, where it began, industrialization had been an almost wholly spontaneous process, which the government had merely somewhat belatedly reacted to. In France and in particular in Germany it had been a more conscious process with a considerable amount of state guidance. But in Russia the process would be wholly state-inspired and directed and not in the least the result of grass-roots initiative. End-of-the-century Russia in fact set an example which would be followed in the twentieth century by many a developing country: it tried to modernize in a hurry, to 'catch up' in accordance with a government blueprint. Five-year plans would be introduced by Stalin, but the idea of a rapid and imposed transformation of the national economy to timetable originated in the final years of the nineteenth century.

The dash for economic growth is associated above all with Witte, but it began in the 1880s under his predecessors Bunge and Vyshnegradsky. The problem faced by successive finance ministers was to create or maintain a favourable trade balance and so attract foreign investment. That meant steadily increasing tariffs against imports, which inevitably hurt domestic consumers. It meant increasing revenue from taxation, which was bad news for ordinary people, since there was no income tax to spread the burden justly and tax revenue came overwhelmingly from items of everyday use such as alcohol, tobacco, sugar, oil and matches. And it meant exporting ever more grain irrespective of the needs of people at home. 'We may not eat enough,' Vyshnegradsky said in 1887, 'but we will export.' The 'we' did not, needless to say, include Vyshnegradsky and his sort; and when famine struck many of the provinces of central Russia in 1891, grain continued to be exported.

That was the trouble with industrialization-to-blueprint: it heaped enormous and at times unendurable burdens upon the unprivileged. This was an abstract design created by men who were themselves sheltered against

everyday privations and were not in the least accountable to those who had
to put up with them. 'Suffering today in return for jam tomorrow' sounded,
as things looked from a ministerial window, an eminently sensible motto.
Yet many in the ruling class, including successive ministers of the interior
(who had to deal with the policy's consequences), thought that this rapid
economic transformation was madness. Why throw Alexander II's caution
to the winds? Backwardness was what had preserved tsarism; and if Russia
had to become an urban and industrial society, could the change not at least
come about more slowly? Ordinary people had heavy enough burdens:
increasing them because of some hare-brained modernizing fancy simply
risked an explosion. Did the tsar not see that this pell-mell change threatened to undo all his other good work?

Yet to all such objections Sergei Witte, who masterminded the modernization programme, had an answer. First, the belief that tsarism could be
saved by continued backwardness was an illusion. Change was vital and
had to be comprehensive, to embrace not only economic life but all aspects
of life – with the important exception of the political. Second, it was useless
for the government to impose change upon an inert people, as Peter the
Great had done. Most Russians did not live, they simply vegetated, and until
they shook off their inertia and became active and enterprising Russia
would never draw abreast of its rivals. The government's immediate task
was therefore to inject life and vitality into the slumbering masses. They
would have to be educated at least to primary level (the census of 1897
showed that 72 per cent of peasants were illiterate), given the normal civil
freedoms of speech, conscience, movement, etc., and allowed to pursue their
careers without discrimination on grounds of class or race.

Such changes, Witte argued, would present no threat whatever to the
autocratic system. He was no liberal, indeed, he became something of a *bête
noire* to liberals because he saw the zemstvos as dangerous and wanted them
curbed, and he justified the changes he wanted as likely to save Russia from
liberalism rather than deliver it into the liberals' hands. Yet the conservative
belief that political trouble could be avoided only by repression and changing nothing he rejected as absurd. 'The full and all-round development of
social forces is not only not irreconcilable with the principle of absolute
monarchy,' he argued, 'but, on the contrary, gives it life and strength.' The
power of the state in fact depended directly on the amount of self-activity its
people achieved; the more individual initiative flourished, the more stable
the social and political order would be. 'I am deeply convinced', he wrote,
'that only with a population capable of self-activity can there be a powerful
state, and that a sound policy for the autocratic empire must inculcate the
widest possible social activity in the sphere of private-legal interests and
must react trustingly to all public activity not directly concerned with the
state structure or its internal and external administration.'[14]

The proviso was of course vital – the subjects/citizens of the transformed
state would have to keep well clear of politics. But would they? Was it real-

istic to think that people, once unshackled, educated and given civil liberties, would restrict themselves to 'private-legal' affairs? Would the unleashed energies not inevitably be drawn to politics? Witte's opponents certainly thought so. But since Witte was never given the comprehensive reform he wanted, his strategy would never be put to a proper test. Alexander III might be a progressive in economic policy, but he remained a pupil of Pobedonostsev, and in general outlook Nicholas II would be as adamantine a conservative as his father. Giving Witte the extra-economic changes he wanted was out of the question. The result was an incoherent and downright contradictory government programme in which economic radicalism co-existed with traditionalism and repressiveness in other areas of life. To many it seemed as if tsarism's right hand did not know what its left hand was doing, and vice versa.

Yet Witte did at least get what he wanted on the economic front, and the result was a dramatic transformation. The 1890s proved to be boom years in which Russia's industrial growth rate approached 10 per cent a year. During the decade railway mileage almost doubled; and a triumphant coda to Witte's career, which had begun in railway management, would be provided by the completion of the Trans-Siberian railway in 1904. Textiles were the largest industry, but due to the demands of the railways metallurgy and mining (coal and iron ore in southern Ukraine, oil extraction in the Caspian) were catching up fast. Industrializing late had its advantages: factories tended to have the latest equipment and were unusually large – at the century's end half the labour force worked in factories with over 1,000 employees. So far the development affected only the two great cities plus areas of Poland and Ukraine, which stood out as islands of modernity amidst the backwardness. But factories, railway stations and stock exchanges were proof that, whatever conservatives and many radicals might have hoped, Russia had moved decisively down the capitalist path; and the ornate railway stations ringing inner Moscow were in their way a jubilant assertion of the capitalist case. The 1897 census showed that European Russia had an urban population of 12.5 million, twice what it had been forty years before and 13 per cent of the total. St Petersburg and Moscow had become modern European metropolises, each with more than one million inhabitants and a large working class. The census showed more than two million factory workers; and manufacturing, mining and the railways taken together probably employed more than three million people by the century's end.

The working class was overwhelmingly peasant in background and its members were still officially considered peasants, even though more than a third had by the end of the century been born in the towns. These worker–peasants, driven into the industrializing towns by overpopulation, brought with them the grievances and the mentality of the village. In the towns, however, new grievances were added and quickly eroded what remained of traditional deference. Labour conditions were appalling, despite a nominal labour code and a factory inspectorate, and price rises

which outstripped wage rises during the 1890s added to the harshness of
life. But if there were new grievances, there was also a new and effective way
of tackling them – the strike. According to official estimates, which were
probably underestimates, there were 17,000 strikers in 1894, 60,000 in
1897 and as many as 97,000 in 1899. The first major strike, which broke
out among St Petersburg textile workers in 1896, eventually forced the government to limit the working day to 11.5 hours. In the wake of that it looked very much as if hasty industrialization had done exactly what its critics
had warned that it would: created for the regime a problem of working-class
discontent that was all the more menacing for being close to the citadel of
power.

Nor did the peasant three-quarters of the population look likely to provide the regime with a bulwark. The peasants of Russia were in fact stirring
from their slumbers, though by no means in the way Witte would have
wanted. For most, life had worsened since the emancipation and conditions
were by the end of the century becoming intolerable. True, the peasants now
owned most of the country's land – almost 60 per cent as against little more
than 20 per cent owned by the nobility. True too that the Russian peasant
owned a lot more land than his counterpart in Western countries.
Nevertheless, the peasant still did not have enough land for his needs, and
the average area of peasant landholdings had actually halved between 1861
and the century's end. The root cause of peasant land-hunger was a massive
and unprecedented population increase, which had doubled the number of
Russians between 1850 and 1900. Had there been a corresponding increase
in productivity of the land this might not have mattered, but since there had
not been, living standards inevitably suffered. With his commune, his primitive implements and his three-field system, the Russian peasant achieved
only a quarter or at most a third of the productivity of his Western equivalents, and without a complete reconstruction of the agricultural system there
seemed no hope of saving him from impoverishment.

Witte for one saw this. The commune, he came to realize, was a mill-
stone; only a private-property agriculture would rescue the peasantry. But
such thinking was still the mark of a maverick: conservatives, like most radicals, saw the commune as indispensable, and its critics were ruled out of
court. Meanwhile, government policies were making things worse for the
peasants. The emancipation had already burdened them with heavy debts,
and the industrialization policy now added to the burden by imposing pun-
itive levels of taxation on articles they could not do without. The yield from
indirect taxation, only 16.5 million roubles in 1881, jumped to a startling
109.5 million roubles in 1895. The rapid industrialization was in fact being
paid for by the peasants and was bleeding them white. Not surprisingly,
peasant Russia began to rebel. It had been quiescent in the 1870s – the
1890s would be a different story. In 1891 famine afflicted twenty of the
most fertile provinces of European Russia and tens of thousands of peasants
died from it. 'A bad harvest comes from God', went the peasant saying, 'but

famine comes from the tsar.' The government was not of course to blame for the weather; but it had made a bad situation worse by trying to pretend it did not exist and continuing to export grain.

Yet for the peasants it was still the landowners, rather than the tsar and his advisers, who were the main villains. They had always submitted reluctantly to their 'betters', but never had they been less inclined to turn the other cheek than now. The increase in peasant bitterness was caused above all by land-hunger and land-envy. Noble landholding had admittedly shrunk considerably since 1861. What, however, made it hard for the peasants to accept even a reduced noble land-share was the size of noble estates, which now averaged 1,350 acres as against seven acres for the average peasant holding. A small-scale noble agriculture might have been bearable, but for a pauperized peasantry these latifundia were a gross provocation. Institutional developments only added to peasant rancour. The zemstvos had done nothing in three decades to build bridges between the communities; peasant representation had anyway now almost disappeared from them; and a form of serfdom, as it seemed to many peasants, had been restored with the appointment of local noblemen as Land Captains with sweeping powers over them. As a result of these various circumstances a showdown between peasants and landowners was now looming. Disorders began in 1899 when peasants in some southern provinces seized landowners' cattle and attacked manors and outbuildings. Impoverished and bitter, peasant Russia was slumbering no longer and would soon declare war on the landowners.

Workers and peasants were not alone; the educated too were becoming combative. For them the watershed had been the famine of 1891. The government had at first tried to deny that anything was wrong and refused to let the word 'famine' appear in the press, and only when the reality that thousands of peasants in central Russia were dying of hunger and disease could no longer be hidden did it back down and allow public participation in famine relief. Committees of aid were then rapidly set up throughout Russia: 'To the famine' became the rallying cry of progressive Russians, who had been outraged both by the tragedy and by the attempted cover-up. The depressed and apathetic mood of the 1880s had been broken, and public opposition to a government which seemed both callous and incompetent would mount from now on until in 1905 it reached a crescendo. The zemstvos became more active and renewed their demand to be allowed to organize nationally. Professional men (the 1897 census showed almost half a million of them) became increasingly outspoken, and their meetings and conferences often turned into thinly veiled political forums. The idea was even floated of joint action between liberals and revolutionaries, of a broad-based party of the intelligentsia with cells throughout the country. The fledgling party was soon smashed, but the idea would resurface successfully a decade later. Most liberals, however, and especially zemstvo nobles, clung to the hope that the autocracy could yet be persuaded to change, and hopes soared when Alexander was succeeded in October 1894 by his twenty-six-year-old son, Nicholas.

9

The last tsar, as he turned out, was charming, good-natured, and not unintelligent, but he was no more willing than his father to adapt to the demands of a changing society. Though it was obvious from the start that he was not a liberal, reform-minded people nevertheless took heart from the fact that he was young, brought a fresh mind to the task, and was known not to have his father's iron will. A number of zemstvos, including the traditionally liberal Tver one, even sent loyal addresses to him in which they suggested that the new government should pay attention to the will of the people. Hopes that Nicholas might begin his reign by making a conciliatory gesture to public opinion were, however, shattered in January 1895 by a speech in which he dismissed 'senseless dreams' of zemstvo representatives participating in government and asserted that 'I shall maintain the principle of autocracy just as firmly and unflinchingly as did my unforgettable father.'[15] Many suspected that the speech had been written by Pobedonostsev; it most certainly had the smack of him. Nothing anyway would change and the strategy crafted by those incompatibles, Pobedonostsev and Witte, would continue, except that the ruler implementing the strategy would be weaker and circumstances increasingly adverse to him.

'You have begun the struggle', an indignant radical wrote in an open letter to Nicholas, 'and the struggle will not be long in coming.'[16] The rebuff to hopes of peaceful change could only boost radicalism, and the revolutionary movement now developed rapidly. After more than a decade in the doldrums Populists reappeared in considerable numbers, though under the new name of socialist revolutionaries. Their predecessors' hope that Russia would avoid the capitalist path had not been borne out, but these neo-Populists were convinced that the country would not go far along it: capitalism was weak and unnatural in Russia, they argued, and its traces would soon be swept away by the socialist revolution. They were ready to collaborate with more radical liberals in the immediate task of getting rid of the autocracy, and they saw the new industrial working class as a vital ally, but they looked above all to the peasants, to peasant anger and innate peasant socialism, as the guarantees of the revolution's success. Like the Populists of the late 1870s, they had no qualms about terror. Yet terrorist actions, while important, were subsidiary to their main task of propaganda. Their message was that after the revolution the land would be socialized – turned over, that is, to the communes, which would divide it equitably among their members. The autocratic state would be destroyed as an unqualified evil; in the new society there would be a minimum of centralized authority and absolutely no bureaucratism. With such ideas, a group of revolutionaries met in Kharkov in 1900 and founded the Socialist Revolutionary (SR) Party, which they hoped would shortly overthrow the autocracy and establish socialism in Russia.

The SRs, however, had a rival: the Marxists. In the 1870s there had been no Marxists in Russia because the conditions Marx considered as essential to revolution simply did not exist there. (Marx himself had towards the end of his life had the intuition that this backward country, which he had previously scorned, might indeed get to socialism without taking the painful capitalist route, but this insight seemed a blatant contradiction of his own teaching.) In the 1880s and 1890s, however, circumstances began to favour the Marxist approach. The Populists had, after all, got it wrong: the peasants had turned out to be by no means a revolutionary force, while the Populists' attempt to act on their behalf had failed disastrously and landed the revolutionary movement in a cul-de-sac. The advance of industrial capitalism had, moreover, put a serious question mark against the idea of the 'special path'. It had also brought into being the essential instrument of Marxist revolution – a proletariat.

Not surprisingly, Marxism began to make converts. Plekhanov and some other *émigrés* had gone over in the 1880s, and in the 1890s Marxism gained something of a cult following among Russian-based intellectuals. Whereas Populism seemed simple-minded and homespun, Marxism had foreign chic and claimed the exactness of a science. And whereas Populism was discredited by failure, Marxism promised, indeed guaranteed, success. Marxists did not simply dream of revolution as something likely or desirable: the science of Marx assured them that revolution was bound to happen, could not *not* happen. This assurance of ultimate success, this absence of 'ifs' and 'buts', was an important psychological resource and helped Marxists ride out adversity better than their rivals. Of course, the Marxists did not know exactly when the revolution would occur in Russia, nor did they know how it would occur. What they did know was that developed countries such as Britain and Germany would get to socialism first. Not only was Russia behind such countries; its development was by no means exactly duplicating what had happened in the West. For instance, the country now had a sizeable and highly discontented working class, but it had not yet got a middle class that looked capable of taking the first step towards socialism – making the bourgeois revolution. Yet, as against that, certain factors suggested that Russia might not lag far behind the West – the massive size of its factories, the militancy of its working class, the radical commitment of very many of the intelligentsia. And even the timid and puny bourgeoisie was not necessarily a disadvantage since experience elsewhere suggested that when the bourgeois had set up their own regime they would defend it sturdily against assault. The Russian Marxists would at least not face that problem.

The outcome would anyway not be decided by impersonal forces alone.

Socialism's triumph in Russia might be inevitable, but whether it triumphed sooner or later depended very much on the Russian Marxists. Breakneck industrialization gave them a real chance of a popular following, and they tried to make the best of it. In 1895 the Fighting Union for the Liberation of the Working Class was founded in St Petersburg, and it took a major part in fomenting the textile workers' strike there. Three years later the first congress of the Russian Social-Democratic Labour Party met in Minsk. The transition from theory, at which the Marxists excelled, to achieving something in practice was, however, by no means easy. Within a few months the leading figures in the Fighting Union, Lenin and Martov, had been arrested and sent to Siberia. The delegates to the Minsk congress were rounded up by the police even more rapidly. In fact at the turn of the century the Marxists' prospects seemed far from rosy. There were not many of them and as revolutionaries they seemed no match at all for the police. Their 'the worse the better' attitude – the more workers suffer, the more responsive they will be to socialism – had caused revulsion among more traditional revolutionaries, who saw it as utterly unfeeling and un-Russian. In addition, they were seriously divided among themselves over whether their main emphasis should be on bread-and-butter questions or on the struggle against the autocracy. These squabbling Marxists were far less threatening to the regime, one might have guessed, than the SRs or the liberals. For the SRs by now had behind them what the Populists had never had: an aroused peasantry that was about to go on to the offensive. As for the liberals, they still had no mass following, yet they were by no means the onlookers in the political battle that they had been in Alexander II's reign. By the century's end a third option, neither autocratic nor revolutionary, seemed to be opening up before the country, and many now took it for granted that a liberal regime was tsarism's natural successor, even if it proved to be only a staging-post to something else.

The question of the succession was meanwhile becoming acute. At the time of Nicholas II's 'senseless dreams' speech the historian Klyuchevsky had predicted that the Romanov dynasty would end with him. This was not wishful thinking by Klyuchevsky, who was far from being radical: the writing was on the wall, at least for the sharp-eyed to see, though few could have foreseen how soon the country would be in the throes of revolution. The autocracy had been safe as long as it presided over an inert, classically simple, two-tier society of lords and peasants, as the opponents of modernization had rightly enough sensed. That society had, however, now vanished. New social elements, professionals and proletarians, had begun to organize themselves and exert pressure on the centre, while the peasants were about to break into open revolt. People were refusing to be pushed around any more, and the mystique on which the coercive power of the monarchy ultimately rested was fading fast. Tsarism's reputation had not been helped by a disaster which had darkened Nicholas's coronation celebrations: a stampede had developed amidst a huge crowd gathered near

Moscow to receive small gifts from the tsar and some 1,300 people had been trampled to death. A reputation for indifference to its people's welfare was bad enough; but worrying too was that the regime was now meeting resistance from within the heart of the traditional ruling class, the landed nobility. Suffering economic decline, excluded from influence at the centre by a landless bureaucracy and even having their local – zemstvo – power severely restricted, the landed nobles of provincial Russia were in a back-to-the-wall mood. They had begun indeed to fight this government which treated them so badly, and their voices were being added to the chorus of liberal demands arising from professionals and intellectuals.

Faced with this formidable array of opponents, the regime had little room for manoeuvre. After the Crimean War it had tried to work with educated opinion, but its reforms had not had the intended result; far from enabling it to manage opinion, the reforms brought a revolutionary movement into existence. The response to this mistake had been a return to full-blooded repressiveness, though that had been combined with a policy of rapid economic modernization. The modernization had, however, destroyed the social basis of stability by completing the ruin of the peasantry, creating a proletariat, increasing the number of educated malcontents, and furthering the alienation from the regime of its traditional backbone, the landed nobility. As a result the regime was left dangerously isolated, and the political structure it clung to had begun to look out of date even in the Russian context. What options remained as the twentieth century approached? There was Witte's as yet untried idea of turning subjects into citizens and hoping that their unleashed energies would be devoted to business rather than politics. Concessions to the modernizing Witte would, however, only infuriate the landed nobility and were anyway contrary to the inclination of Nicholas and his intimates, who were determined to leave things as far as possible unchanged. Russia would enter the new century as a divine-right monarchy without even a consultative elected assembly, ruled by a highly conservative if weak-willed patriarch who believed that he was answerable only to God and in practice answered only to his family and a handful of courtiers.

Notes

1 W. Bruce Lincoln, *The Great Reforms: Autocracy, Bureaucracy and the Politics of Change in Imperial Russia* (Dekalb, Ill., 1990), p. 175.
2 Basil Dmytryshyn, ed., *Imperial Russia: A Source Book 1700–1917*, 2nd edn (Hinsdale, Ill., 1974), p. 272.
3 Probably Nikolai Chernyshevsky. Cited from Lincoln, *The Great Reforms*, p. 59.
4 Sergei Witte. Cited from N. M. Pirumova, *Zemskoe liberalnoe dvizhenie: Sotsialnye korni i evolyutsiya do nachala XX veka* (Moscow, 1977), p. 31.

5 G. Vernadsky, R. T. Fisher, A. D. Ferguson, A. Lossky, S. Pushkarev, eds, *A Source Book for Russian History from Early Times to 1917* (3 vols, New Haven and London, 1972), vol. III, p. 614.

6 Franco Venturi, *Roots of Revolution: A History of the Populist and Socialist Movements in Nineteenth-Century Russia*, tr. by Francis Haskell (London, 1960), p. 299.

7 Vernadsky *et al.*, *A Source Book*, vol. III, p. 639.

8 N. G. Chernyshevsky, *What Is To Be Done?*, tr. by Benjamin R. Tucker (New York, 1961), pp. 220 and 241.

9 N. Valentinov, *Vstrechi s Leninym* (New York, 1953), p. 103.

10 Andrzej Walicki, *Legal Philosophies of Russian Liberalism* (Oxford, 1987), p. 63.

11 Daniel Field, *Rebels in the Name of the Tsar* (Boston, 1989), p. 173.

12 Leonard Schapiro, *Rationalism and Nationalism in Russian Nineteenth-Century Political Thought* (New Haven and London, 1967), p. 126.

13 Vernadsky *et al.*, *A Source Book*, vol. III, pp. 673 and 672.

14 Sergei Witte, *Samoderzhavie i zemstvo: Konfidentsialnaya zapiska ministra finansov stats-sekretarya S. Yu. Witte* (Stuttgart, 1903), pp. 209 and 16.

15 P. B. Struve, 'My Contacts with Rodichev', *Slavonic and East European Review*, vol. 12 (1933–4), p. 350.

16 *Ibid.*

4

Saving tsarism, 1900–1914

1

A far-sighted observer in 1900 might have seen three possible outcomes to the power struggle now getting under way in earnest in Russia. First, tsarism would survive and indeed revive, though only if it cast off its bunker mentality and made fundamental changes. The landed nobility would have to be bought off and given a formal stake in power; some *modus vivendi* would have to be reached, too, with the professionals; and, most vital of all, a basis of popular support would have to be found, perhaps by creating a property-owning sector among the peasantry.

Second, tsarism would be ousted by a revolution in which radical liberals and moderate revolutionaries worked together. The revolution would be more political than social and its main achievement would be to establish democratic institutions. The new government would of course have to take social reform seriously, but it could not afford to be so radical that it alienated its supporters among the privileged. For this would be a dual-power regime, a regime of inter-class collaboration, and to survive it would have to create common loyalties and a sense of common citizenship among people who up till the revolution had been deeply divided.

Third, tsarism – or the moderate revolution – might be swept away by a radical revolution, a revolution that was as much social as political and whose slogan was class war rather than class collaboration. Though they might have majority support, the radical rulers would have little time for constitutional niceties: the violent resistance they aroused and the traditionalist Russian culture they embodied would encourage strong-armed methods and a contempt for democracy. In the resulting convulsion there would be massive destruction of life and property. Amidst the ruins, fundamental social, economic and political restructuring would be attempted, inspired by a mixture of Marxism and the age-old demands and perceptions of the village; and while all this was happening the country would turn in upon itself, rejecting not only its westernized class but the West itself at least until socialism had triumphed there.

All three possibilities would be tried in the opening decades of the twentieth century. This chapter will highlight the first. Chapter 5 will give special attention to the attempt to replace tsarism by a dual-power regime. And radical revolution will be discussed in the chapters which follow that.

Tsarism had first of all to go to the brink before it made a serious attempt to save itself. Witte was dismissed in 1903, but no one of similar calibre replaced him: it would take the revolution of 1905 to throw up a successor. His dismissal was no surprise since he had alienated almost everybody. The part of his strategy that had been tried had simply caused trouble, or so it seemed, and the part which might have lessened the trouble had been ignored. By now it was too late, however, to escape the consequences of Witte's work; and the feints by which the authorities tried to divert people's attention from their miseries only made things worse. The storm which broke in 1905 did not result in a revolution, though that had seemed so inevitable that the events would always be known as 'the 1905 revolution'. The autocracy had by now lost the respect of most unprivileged Russians, and what remained of its mystique was laid to rest amidst the bloodshed and chaos of 1905. It survived because its opponents were divided and because the loyalty of the armed forces on the whole held. But it survived only by granting many of its liberal opponents' demands – from October 1905 Russia had the constitutional dualism that Speransky for one had wanted a century earlier. The outcome was not, however, the smooth transition to full and undiluted constitutionalism that Speransky had hoped for. On the contrary, autocrat and parliament became locked in bitter conflict, and it took tsarism's last statesman, Peter Stolypin, to find a way out of the conflict.

Stolypin was, like Witte, a tough, realistic and yet visionary modernizer with a comprehensive plan for transforming Russia. His main concern, however, was not economic progress but creating a stable social foundation for the regime, and he did not in the least share Witte's objection to parliamentary institutions. His reformist ideas ran into opposition, however, from the major landowners, who from 1907 were the dominant force in Russian political life. These happily accepted his aim of a property-owning peasantry, but his broader ambitions on behalf of unprivileged Russia provoked their fierce resistance. This apparent conservative was more likely to subvert the regime, many nobles came to feel, than to save it. Nicholas and his circle decided the same; and as a result, Stolypinism had been killed off well before Stolypin himself was murdered in 1911.

The rejection of Stolypin's master plan for survival left tsarism without a strategy: tsar and nobles had retreated into a fortress, from which they looked out at the massed ranks of repressed but disaffected Russians. By the eve of the First World War, the question of the succession was again becoming acute. If tsarism would neither step down nor regenerate itself, revolution was inevitable – but what sort of one? Those who saw Russia following the West counted on a moderate, inter-class revolution. Whether their aim was a liberal or a socialist Russia, such people took it for granted that a moderate revolution was the inevitable next step. Two factors, however, lessened the chances of a moderate outcome. First, many liberals had lost their nerve and now feared that they might themselves become the victims of popular violence. Second, there was the challenge of the Bolsheviks, who though Marxists had something of the SRs' impatience and were vehemently against any compromise with the privileged. The issue would be decided of course by the masses and in particular by the urban workers. Would they follow the moderates? Or would they instead go for a total revolution?

2

Trouble had erupted on 9 January 1905, and for the rest of that year Russia had been convulsed. The background to the revolution was smouldering discontent in almost all sections of society: workers, peasants, minor nationalities, intellectuals and professionals, even landed nobles. Protest took a variety of forms: strikes, rural uprisings, the assassination of more than a hundred leading officials, including the hard-line minister of the interior, V. K. Plehve, in July 1904, and, towards the end of 1904, a campaign of protest banquets and meetings organized by liberals. The revolution's cause lay in the discrepancy between an archaic political structure and a society subject to all the pressures and deformations caused by intensive modernization. But the immediate catalyst came from the tactics with which the government tried to divert people's attention from their miseries. Against Witte's advice but at the urging of his rival, Plehve, Russia had become drawn into a war with Japan. 'A small victorious war', Plehve had believed, was what would save the country from revolution. But the war against this distant and despised power turned out to be a disaster; and the news that on 19 December 1904 Russia's Far Eastern stronghold of Port Arthur had fallen to the Japanese, together with thousands of sailors and most of Russia's Pacific fleet, did much to precipitate what Plehve had wanted to avert.

This foreign policy feint had had a domestic counterpart: the experiment in 'police socialism', pioneered by an Okhrana official, Sergei Zubatov, who believed that the government should fight subversion of the working class not by forbidding labour organizations but by setting up its own and trying to satisfy some of the workers' non-political demands. But this too created problems rather than solved them – Zubatov's organization got out of hand, directed strikes, and far from increasing loyalty to the regime, opened up new channels for the revolutionizing of the workforce. As a result, Zubatov was dismissed from his Moscow post in 1903. However, a former associate of his, Georgii Gapon, a priest who moved somewhat ambiguously between the secret police and the workers, set up a similar body with official approval in St Petersburg. Gapon directed a strike which broke out among workers at the Putilov metallurgical plant at the end of 1904 and soon spread to workers elsewhere, and on 9 January 1905 he led a column of the striking workers to the Winter Palace to present a petition to the tsar. The petition listed the men's immediate grievances but also made political demands – for an end to the war, civil liberties and a constituent assembly. The march was peaceful despite the huge number of participants, and icons, portraits of the tsar and hymn-singing gave it a piously religious air. Amidst the brutalities of this industrialized metropolis, the culture of the village still seemed alive; and its voice could be clearly heard in the petition, which was an appeal to the tsar 'directly and frankly as to a father' by people who saw no other hope than to cut through all the layers that separated him from them and put their miseries with total candour before him. 'Tear down the walls between Thyself and Thy people and let them rule together with Thee. Hast Thou not been placed on the throne for the happiness of the people, and has not this happiness been denied to us by the bureaucrats?'[1] But what if the tsar refused to listen to his people? 'Then for us', said Gapon, 'there is no tsar'; and so it would prove to be.

As the column approached the palace, soldiers opened fire. Official figures would put the dead at 130, though the number killed or badly wounded was probably nearer 1,000. With 'Bloody Sunday', as it became known, the Russian revolution had begun.

It was not Nicholas, who was safely out of Petersburg at Tsarskoe Selo, who had ordered the shooting. The massacre nevertheless destroyed what remained of the charisma which had made tsarism invincible. A benevolent father could not even be indirectly responsible for the slaughter of his children. When later in the year peasants became galvanized by rumours that the nobles' land was at long last about to be given to them, it was no longer 'the little father' they looked to as their would-be benefactor but rather an elected parliament. Benevolence and protective care were, however, only part of the tsar's paternal image; the obverse was awesome strength and invincibility. But that part, too, was destroyed in 1905, for the events which unrolled from the shooting brought the monarchy to its knees.

Between Bloody Sunday and December 1905, the country was in a continuous state of upheaval. The immediate response to the massacre was a general strike, which soon spread to other big cities. Disturbances began, too, among peasants. But the disaffection spread beyond workers and peasants into the urban, white-collar classes. Professional unions – of lawyers, doctors, engineers, etc. – now sprang up with overtly political aims: and in

May these federated with a number of blue-collar unions into a powerful pressure group, the Union of Unions. Even more ominous for the regime was disaffection in the armed forces, most notably in June when the crew of the battleship *Potemkin* mutinied in the Black Sea (the Soviet film director Sergei Eisenstein would celebrate the mutiny in a famous film). Victory over the Japanese might perhaps still have saved the regime, but instead there were defeats on land and at sea and these were followed by peace negotiations which could hardly have a happy outcome. In February, shocked by the murder of his uncle, the Grand Duke Sergei, Nicholas had come up with the offer of a consultative representative assembly. The details were published in August: the assembly would be elected on a narrow franchise which would exclude the whole working class and many professionals, and its only right would be to *suggest* measures for consideration as laws. A year before, many liberals would have welcomed such an assembly. Now it bought off very few of the regime's opponents.

During the summer, peasant disturbances increased in number and violence. Mutinies occurred among troops returning from the Far East. And in October the opposition came to a climax with a general strike which covered much of the country. Trains stood still in sidings. Gas and electricity were cut off. Telegraph and telephone services no longer worked. Not only did factories close down; so too did shops, schools, hospitals, law courts and government offices, and in St Petersburg even the corps of the imperial ballet walked out. Urban life came to a halt; city centres were deserted and unlit; and Nicholas himself was virtually isolated by the strike at his summer residence of Peterhof. To make matters worse for him, urban and peasant Russia seemed to be speaking with one voice, and disorders in the countryside were intensifying.

Faced with near-universal resistance, the government had lost its grip, was paralysed and helpless. What could save it? In desperation Nicholas turned to the only man who seemed equal to the task: Witte. During the summer he had sent him to America to make peace with the Japanese; now he needed Witte's help to escape from a still more disastrous situation. What should be done? Either grant freedom, Witte said, or install a military dictatorship. Nicholas's own preference was for a dictatorship. Witte, however, made it clear that he would have nothing to do with such a regime, whereas he was prepared to act as prime minister of a constitutional government. That foreclosed Nicholas's options, and on 17 October he signed what became known as the October Manifesto. The manifesto granted basic civil liberties, 'including real personal inviolability, freedom of conscience, speech, assembly and association'; announced that 'participation in the Duma will be granted to those classes of the population which are at present deprived of voting powers'; and laid it down 'that no law can come into force without its approval by the state Duma', thus converting the previously offered consultative assembly into a legislature.[2] Another manifesto gave the Council of Ministers power to co-ordinate the work of the separate ministries and Witte, its chairman, something of the position of a Western prime minister.

The autocracy, it seemed, had at last surrendered; a divine-right monarchy which had lived on into the twentieth century had belatedly adjusted to modern realities. Yet this was far from the scenario envisaged by Speransky, who had seen the autocrat graciously and far-sightedly agreeing to share power with his subjects. There was nothing gracious or far-sighted about Nicholas's concessions. Rather than being the wise, pre-emptive act of a ruler with a Speransky at his side, the October Manifesto had been granted only under extreme duress, without premeditation and as a gesture of desperation by a ruler who was still deeply committed to the autocratic principle and felt humiliated by the concession which had been dragged out of him. As a constitutionalist, Witte too was no more than a reluctant johnny-come-lately, though that did not stop Nicholas's dislike of him turning to detestation. For Witte was indelibly associated with the enforced sacrifice of principles that Nicholas regarded as sacred; and as prime minister he now posed an obvious threat to whatever remained of the autocratic prerogative.

What Nicholas had conceded, however, was no more than broad principles. The details of the new order still had to be worked out, and the details were vital. Exactly how much power had he sacrificed? Thanks to the manifesto, this would be decided in much calmer conditions than those which had produced the original concession, and the more peaceful the country was, the more say Nicholas himself would have in deciding the extent of his own loss. But, in adjudicating, he would of course be subject to enormous pressures. For one change was absolute and could never be taken back. Over the centuries only one official voice had been heard in Russia – that of the tsar. From now on there would be a cacophony of voices claiming the right to speak for Russia. One of the most striking results of the October Manifesto was in fact the emergence into the open of a wide spectrum of political parties and groupings. Russia, and Nicholas, would have to learn to live with politics.

3

To a Western reader it may seem astonishing, but by no means everyone in Russia welcomed the gain of freedom. During 1905, various groups had sprung up in defence of the autocracy and Russian traditionalism, and they were aided by gangs of thugs known as Black Hundreds who beat up Jews and leftist intellectuals. The right's nucleus consisted of nobles and priests, but it picked up enough support from small traders, minor officials and others who felt threatened by working-class assertiveness to be able to claim that it was a popular movement. The right appealed to Russian nationalism,

Orthodoxy and loyalty to the throne; it was anti-Western, anti-intellectual, and, above all, fiercely anti-Jewish. But like movements to its left, the right became split over the October Manifesto. Its instinct was to reject whole-heartedly anything that smacked of constitutionalism as an anti-Russian device foisted upon an unwilling people by a conspiracy of Jews and liberals. But since the tsar himself had decreed the change, the gut reaction of the right was at odds with its cardinal tenet: obedience to the autocrat. The largest party of the right, the Union of the Russian People, founded in late October under the leadership of Dr Alexander Dubrovin, got around the problem by accepting the manifesto's concessions but insisting that the Duma should be no more than an advisory body which left the autocracy intact. The Union had high hopes that by playing its nationalist and anti-Semitic cards it would emerge as a strong force in the Duma. But it had one serious electoral disadvantage: the tsar and autocrat had ceased to be an icon for most Russians.

Next in the political spectrum came the Union of 17 October, the Octobrists for short, who were the most rightist of the two liberal parties. The Octobrists were heirs to those zemstvo nobles who had resented being excluded from central decision-making by the bureaucrats and who fiercely opposed Witte's industrializing policy. Their predecessors had wanted to replace bureaucrats and industrializers as tsarism's policy-makers; they had wanted in fact to become the ruling class, with or without a representative assembly. As the monarchy's crisis deepened, the liberal movement had become more radical and the influence upon it of intellectuals, urban professionals and the third element had increased. Reluctantly, the zemstvo liberals too had yielded to the radical influence, until in the end they had accepted the idea of a constitution, universal male suffrage and even a limited transfer of land to the peasants. But the autumn 1905 disturbances put an end to the zemstvo nobles' leftward movement. The Octobrists took their stand on the October Manifesto. Unlike the more radical liberals, the Octobrists were committed monarchists; and unlike the radicals they strongly upheld law and order, opposing anything that smacked of revolution and pledging themselves to peaceful change by negotiation. Their leader, Alexander Guchkov, was an industrialist, and they attracted some following among the nascent business class. Yet despite democratic language, the Octobrists had essentially oligarchic instincts, and their oligarchic tendency would be strengthened by the swing to the right among the provincial nobility from the late autumn of 1905. The Octobrists wanted the landed nobility and its business allies to become the country's power-brokers. In the West, absolutism had given way to the rule of the landed, and they believed this to be the natural sequence in Russia also. What they did not take into account, however, was that in the West the landed had not had to face the fierce hostility of peasants and workers. Russian nobles had failed in their power bids in 1825 and the 1860s when the lower classes would have given them a clear run. The question now was whether they had not left it too late.

The more radical Russian liberals had in October 1905 formed the Constitutional-Democratic – for short, the Kadet – Party. The Kadets too had their roots in nineteenth-century zemstvo liberalism, though their predecessors had been nobles of the Tver type. As the monarchy's crisis deepened, the radical liberals became the central element in a broad anti-autocratic coalition, flanked by libertarian socialists on one side and zemstvo moderates on the other. The journal *Liberation*, published abroad from 1902, voiced the radicals' demands, and from January 1904 they were organized within Russia as the Union of Liberation. The Liberationists tried to avoid the 'liberal' label because of its association with *laissez-faire* policies and the pursuit of bourgeois self-interest. They wanted an interventionist state, a state actively committed to the welfare of *all*; and Peter Struve, *Liberation*'s editor, saw no contradiction in calling himself both a liberal and a socialist. Their immediate aims were a constitutional and democratic regime and 'four-tail' – universal, equal, secret and direct – suffrage; and early in 1905 they added expropriation of noble land to their basic demands.

But the more radical the Liberationists became, the more unlikely it seemed that the government would voluntarily accept what they wanted, and the more tempting therefore became the idea of revolution. The need for a tactical working alliance of liberals and revolutionaries was urged by Struve. He was admittedly a former Marxist, but the revolutionary tactic was supported too by Paul Milyukov, the Kadets' future leader, who had no socialist background whatever. The difficulty of collaborating with revolutionaries was shown in September 1904 when Liberationists and SRs, meeting in Paris, agreed to work together for the autocracy's overthrow but failed to agree either on how they should do it or on a socio-economic programme. The Liberationists nevertheless dismissed fears that revolutionaries were dangerous bedfellows. There were, they insisted, no enemies to the left – the only danger lay rightwards. Struve for one believed that the removal of the autocracy would bring the revolutionaries to their senses, while ordinary Russians, once they had the vote, would behave responsibly 'and learn to understand what is possible and what is not'.[3] Milyukov had the same belief in the civilizing effect of free institutions. The radical liberals' optimism was reflected in these words of his to an American audience: 'there is no ground for apprehension that the first Russian parliament will be a "Parliament of Saints and Levellers", and that it will end in the dictatorship of a new Cromwell. On the contrary, one may hope that the actual practice of general suffrage will ... disillusionize [*sic*] the socialists and free them from one more of those utopias preserved by their theoreticians from the earlier stage of their political education.'[4]

But would it really be easy to introduce democracy to a largely illiterate peasant people which had no tradition of it? Of course not. That was no argument, however, for sitting back and waiting till the necessary conditions for democracy had somehow created themselves. On the contrary, Milyukov argued, 'there never was a people that was "ripe" for a constitution when that constitution was first introduced'.[5] Later, Lenin would argue similarly that in Russia political revolution had to precede and prepare the ground for cultural revolution. 'If a definite level of culture is required for the building of socialism (although nobody can say just what that definite "level of culture" is, for it differs in every West-European country), why cannot we begin by first achieving the prerequisites for that definite level of culture in a revolutionary way?'[6] Substitute 'democracy' for 'socialism' and the reasoning could have been Milyukov's. The moral was clear – politicians had to seize the initiative from the autocrat and themselves create the conditions for democracy.

1905 seemed to provide the opportunity. The Kadets' first congress met in St Petersburg during the week when the October general strike was at its height. The party had a more radical programme, Milyukov claimed, than any similar grouping in Western Europe. He and his colleagues expressed their solidarity with the strikers and a more qualified approval of the revolutionaries, with whom they hoped 'to march together to a common goal'. That goal could not be achieved by the October Manifesto. 'Nothing has changed', was Milyukov's response to it. 'The struggle goes on.' The Kadets were not prepared to share power with the autocracy on these or any other terms. The bitter experience of Russian liberalism had taught them that they simply had to wrest power from it – nothing else would do.

But if the Kadets were revolutionaries, they were reluctant and highly conditional ones. They did not like violence or conspiracy. The revolution they wanted would be a largely spontaneous mass movement, one so broad that the regime would put up no resistance and disruption of everyday life would therefore be minimal. Better still, they hoped that the very prospect of revolution would be enough, that they could, as Milyukov put it, combine 'liberal tactics with the threat of revolution'.[7] The phrase spoke volumes about the Kadets' ambivalence towards revolution.

Of the revolutionary groupings proper, two had something in common with the Kadets: the SRs and the Mensheviks. The SRs had already parleyed with the Kadets' predecessors, were quite prepared for a bourgeois regime to take over from tsarism, and had a strong commitment to civil liberties. But as against that, they would fight determinedly for socialism, and far from being held back by any belief that Russia was not yet ripe for it they would be driven on by their conviction that the people were already innately socialist. Moreover, the intellectuals of the SR leadership loathed the privileged class and had in this respect taken on the attitudes of the village. And their belief in terrorism, and a string of assassinations, made them look like barbarians in the eyes of men who wanted to create a stable parliamentary democracy of the Western type.

With the Mensheviks, the prospects for mutual understanding seemed better. The Mensheviks were one of the two factions into which the Russian Social Democrats – the Marxists – had become split in 1903. Their name meant 'minoritarians' or 'people of the minority', which in itself put them at a disadvantage, and was hardly deserved since they often proved to be a majority within the Social-Democratic movement. At the heart of what divided them from their Bolshevik ('majoritarian') rivals was the question of how quickly Russia could advance towards socialism. Both agreed that Russia would have to go through the bourgeois revolution first – that alone could lay the foundations for socialism. Both agreed that since the Russian bourgeois were few and feeble, the workers would largely if not wholly have to make the revolution for them. From here on, however, their views diverged. The Mensheviks insisted that once tsarism had been toppled, power would have to be taken by a bourgeois parliamentary regime – the kind of regime the Kadets aimed at and hoped would in time tame the re-volutionaries. The Social Democrats would then become an opposition and exert pressure upon the government. But they would resist any attempt to take, power – that would be futile until the necessary economic, social and cultural preconditions for socialism had been created. How long this would take, the Mensheviks were unable to predict; they steeled themselves, how-ever, for a fairly long wait, during which they would not only act as an opposition but educate the working class for its future role as ruler of the country.

The Mensheviks' readiness to tolerate bourgeois rule and their belief that Russia needed to progress a great deal before it was ripe for socialism made them natural partners for the Kadets, the one party that looked capable of providing the dynamic liberal-capitalist government which would clear away the obstacles to socialism. Beyond this, there were similarities in cast of mind and personality type. The Menshevik leadership included a galaxy of talented, westernized and often highly erudite intellectuals – Plekhanov, Martov, Dan and Axelrod, to name a few. Such men attacked constitutional democracy as a political system which masked the gross exploitation of the many by the few. They nevertheless believed in individual liberty as a good in itself, wanted a socialist Russia to make liberty a reality for everyone, and were reluctant to impose limits upon it for the sake of other needs. They were Marxists first and revolutionaries second, and their faithful and some-what pedantic Marxism exposed them to criticisms of being un-Russian – Western Europe, went the cruellest and most damning jibe, begins with the Mensheviks. That could most certainly not have been said of their rivals, the Bolsheviks.

Whereas the Mensheviks had a variety of dazzling but ill-assorted talents, the Bolsheviks had a single and utterly dominant star: Vladimir Ulyanov, born into the provincial upper-middle class in 1870, who in 1901 had taken the pseudonym of Lenin. He was first and foremost a revolutionary, and once a Marxist he focused on problems which Marx himself had given little attention to – how exactly was the revolution to be brought about and how in particular was it to be brought about in Russia? In temperament and out-look Lenin had much in common with the SRs. Like them he was a revolu-tionary zealot; like them he had an instinctive feel for the peculiarities of Russia; and even more than they he rebelled against any idea of playing sec-ond fiddle to the liberals.

But how could this backward country draw close to socialism in the near future when not even the advanced countries had yet got there? Was there any chance of it making rapid progress despite being backward? Lenin was convinced that there was, that the problems created by a feeble bourgeoisie and the lack of a mature and class-conscious working class could be over-come. Human contrivance could make up for what was missing, and the contrivance that would do it was the party. By 'party' he meant a small, con-spiratorial, tightly disciplined and highly professional elite of revolutionar-ies who would guide, inspire and mould the masses. Left to themselves, he had argued in *What Is To Be Done?* (1902), the workers were capable only of developing a 'trade-union consciousness' – would concern themselves, in other words, only with problems of everyday living and not look beyond them to the causes of their misery and the means of eradicating them. Therefore, they should not be left to themselves: spontaneity – the natural process of development – was simply not enough. Nature had to be given a hefty push by trained revolutionaries, who would educate the workers, turn their trade-union consciousness into revolutionary consciousness, and so make them an instrument of revolution. 'Give us an organization of revolu-tionaries', he had proclaimed, 'and we will overturn Russia.'[8]

This idea of the party as a tightly disciplined and guiding nucleus – of the party as a vanguard – was Lenin's vital contribution to Russia's political development. He would cling to it through thick and thin; without it, the Bolsheviks could hardly have won power in 1917 and certainly not have held on to power after 1917. The Mensheviks, too, saw the need for the party to be a guiding nucleus. In a police state a clandestine organizing cen-tre was indispensable, and there was no denying that the workforce badly needed instruction and guidance from those who understood socialism. But a balance had to be found between direction from above and freedom for those below. The revolution the Mensheviks wanted would get rid not only of poverty and exploitation but of that passivity and slavishness before power which they thought of as Russia's 'Asiatic heritage'. Lenin was sec-ond to none as an opponent of poverty and exploitation, yet with his ruth-lessness and authoritarianism he seemed more likely to perpetuate the Asiatic heritage than to get rid of it. The Mensheviks aimed at a looser, broader party, a party that was less leader-centred, less hierarchical, and more responsive to its rank and file – in a word, at a more democratic party. Lenin's party smacked to them of what Russian Marxism had begun as a protest against – The People's Will with its attempt to force the pace of change beyond what objective conditions would allow. But such criticism left Lenin, the brother of an executed Populist, unmoved. Let them call him a Populist, a Jacobin, or whatever they wanted: his was the only path to socialism in Russia.

Party and proletariat could not, however, make the revolution on their own. Where could they look for help? Certainly not to the bourgeois – they were neither willing nor able to play a revolutionary role. And here came the second of Lenin's insights into how, despite its deficiencies, Russia could advance rapidly towards socialism. The country might lack a militant bourgeoisie, but what it did have was a revolutionary peasantry. Workers and peasants together would overthrow tsarism in an alliance which the workers would dominate but which would depend for its success on the peasants' overwhelming numbers. There was nothing un-Marxist, he insisted, about such an alliance. Workers and peasants would merely make the *bourgeois* revolution; their alliance would be no more than temporary; and before the socialist revolution, there would have to be a showdown in which workers and rural proletariat fought it out with the property-owning peasants. But this was a very different view of the bourgeois revolution from the Mensheviks', and it led on to a very different view of what would happen *after* the revolution. For the workers and peasants to hand over power to the liberals was, in Lenin's eyes, out of the question. Having won power they should keep it, and they should set up not a parliamentary democracy but a revolutionary dictatorship. For this too he claimed Marx's authority – had Marx not written of 'the dictatorship of the proletariat'? But despite such genuflections, what was striking was Lenin's debt to the *Russian* revolutionary movement and his sharp eye for the realities of *Russia*.

During 1905, those realities were changing fast. In the early months there had been no more than 15,000 Social Democrats of both sorts in Russia. Their leaders were nearly all in exile – Lenin for one would not return to Russia till November. The upheaval owed nothing whatever to the Social Democrats. From October, however, they would begin to influence events. Once they did, the rank and file would press hard for the leaders to put their differences aside, and they would be rewarded in 1906 with a reunion of the factions. Yet the unity would be no more than formal, and the real effect of 1905 would be to drive a still deeper wedge between Menshevik caution and the fiery aggressiveness of the Bolsheviks.

4

The October Manifesto had aroused widespread rejoicing, but it had not brought peace to the country and in particular it had not brought peace to the countryside. There was nothing in the manifesto for the peasants; far from being pacified, they had simply interpreted its promised liberties as a licence to settle scores with their enemies. Over a wide area, and especially in the classic zone of landlordism, the Black Earth, the peasants, directed by their communes, moved to 'smoke out' the nobles, and when the eruption petered out in late November more than 2,000 manor houses lay in charred ruins. 'You are a gentleman', one bunch of peasant insurrectionaries said to a landlord. 'We don't need masters, it is necessary to destroy all of you and then we will be able to live.'[9] For the time being the peasants did not try to seize the land, since they assumed that it would be given to them very soon: their aim was, rather, to evict the owners, very many of whom now fled to the safety of the towns. Liberal landowners did not get off any more lightly, and perhaps because they were regarded as soft touches the Kadets seem to have suffered even more than their conservative counterparts.

In the towns, there was little violence, but passive resistance to the regime continued despite the manifesto and the subsequent collapse of the general strike. On 13 October, forty factory delegates in St Petersburg had founded a 'soviet' or council of workers' deputies. Soon there would be soviets in fifty-odd towns and the foundation would have been laid of the soviet movement in whose name Russia would be ruled from 1917 to 1991. Workers rather than revolutionaries created the St Petersburg soviet, and its immediate task was to act as co-ordinating committee for the strike. But as the soviet's size and influence grew – the number of delegates would rise to more than 600 – it turned increasingly to broad political issues, demanding not only an eight-hour day but a constituent assembly and a democratic republic. A body so large needed an executive, and this very soon became dominated by revolutionaries. The Bolsheviks had initially been uneasy about the soviet as a product of worker spontaneity, whereas the Mensheviks had welcomed it as evidence of the workers' growing maturity and ability to organize themselves; and it was a Menshevik with exceptional gifts as an orator and organizer, Leon Trotsky, who became the soviet's leading member. Despite the collapse of the strike, the soviet continued into December as a powerful influence and rival authority to the government. For the workers, this was 'their government'; they listened to it when they would not have obeyed the authorities. The government for its part suffered the humiliation of having no control over wide areas of the capital and of having to negotiate with the workers through the soviet. By 3 December, however, it had sufficiently recovered its nerve to send troops to the soviet headquarters and have all the deputies there arrested. But this was not the end of the soviets – within days a counterblast had come from Moscow. The soviet there had appeared only in late November; unlike the St Petersburg one, it was a revolutionary creation and it was dominated throughout by Bolsheviks. On 9 December the soviet decided, at Bolshevik instigation, to turn the general strike in the city into an armed insurrection. For the next few days proletarian Moscow was the scene of desperate and bloody battles, and not till 15 December was the insurrection finally put down.

There would be more flare-ups, especially in outlying parts of the empire, but with the crushing of the Moscow revolt the revolution had in effect been defeated. That did not mean of course that things could go back to where they had been before October. For the tsar had given promises which he would now have to honour. And important changes in attitude had resulted from the struggle.

The peasant insurrection had had a decisive impact upon the landowners. They now swung sharply away from the radical liberalism of the Kadets whose influence in the zemstvo movement would from now on be negligible. The period of noble frondeurism – of discreet skirmishing with the monarchy – was over. Now monarchy and nobility would stand shoulder to shoulder against a common enemy: popular revolution. Noble support would go to the Octobrists, who had advocated martial law against the rebels and were having second thoughts about universal suffrage, and also to parties and movements that were overtly conservative; as for the Kadets, they were rejected as traitors to their class.

Even without the insurrection, the Kadets would have parted company with the landed nobility, for in a democratic Russia the fate of political parties would be largely decided by the peasants and the peasants were clamouring for the nobles' land. At the October congress Milyukov had hedged on expropriation, but after the insurrection it was clear that the Kadets would have to come out unequivocally in its favour. Yet it would not be easy for them to frame an expropriation policy that would satisfy the peasants without alienating the party's nucleus of landowners and professionals. Events in the towns too had emphasized the difficulties and dangers of radicalism and set a question mark against the Kadets' hopes that in a democratic Russia they would emerge as the party of the people. The Moscow uprising in particular had been a moment of truth, ending any illusion that an aroused working class was likely to go to the barricades for liberal purposes. From now on the Kadets would be wary of the revolutionary parties and the ambiguity in their attitude towards violence would disappear. There would be no more talk of combining 'liberal tactics with the threat of revolution'; the Kadets' challenge to the regime would henceforth be strictly constitutional.

The two Social-Democratic factions reacted very differently to the events of 1905. The Mensheviks had been encouraged by the Kadets' refusal to be bought off by the October Manifesto and still more by the St Petersburg soviet, which had shown how effectively socialist intellectuals and the advanced sector of the working class could collaborate. But the Moscow uprising had in their eyes been premature and hence an inevitable disaster. The 1905 experience simply confirmed the Mensheviks in their belief that Russia was not yet capitalist or cultured enough for revolution and made them still more averse to the conspiratorial politics and gung-ho posturing of the Bolsheviks. Lenin, by contrast, had despite the Moscow bloodbath ended the year on a militant high. For the Moscow events had provided the Bolsheviks with a legend; they had also given solid proof of the revolutionary capacity of the proletariat, while the rural disturbances had underlined his point that the peasants too were a revolutionary force. 1905 had emphatically *not* been a failure, *not* proved that the workers were too immature and undisciplined for revolution. Quite the opposite: the message of 1905 was that Russia now had a class-conscious working class which was straining at the leash for action. The insurrection might have been put down but the revolution lived on, and a boundlessly aggressive Lenin now called for further uprisings in the belief that they would ignite nationwide civil war.

The truth, however, was that physical resistance was at an end, and victory then shaped the way in which Nicholas and his advisers implemented the October Manifesto's promises. Even before the Moscow uprising was put down, the electoral system had been decided. The system of voting would be indirect – voters would be divided into separate categories of nobles, burghers, peasants and workers in a complicated mechanism which was heavily biased towards those thought most likely to favour the government. One noble vote would have the weight of three burgher votes, fifteen peasant votes and at least forty-five worker votes. The conservative trend was continued by a decree of 20 February 1906 which announced that the legislature would consist not of one chamber, as had been expected, but of two. The Duma would be flanked by an upper house, the Council of State, half of whose members would be elected by privileged bodies (the Church, the zemstvos, the nobility, the universities and chambers of commerce) and the remainder of whom would be government appointees. The Council of State's purpose, all too clearly, was to act as a restraint upon the Duma.

By this time, elections to the Duma were under way after a general election campaign – the first in Russia's history – which had been dominated by the Kadets. Using the slogan 'Political Freedom and Social Justice', they had campaigned with a verve and professionalism shown by none of their rivals and had attracted to their ranks a galaxy of talent from the professions and the intelligentsia. By election time, the Kadets had a network of some 200 branches; and their drive to win votes across the board was reflected in a brochure specially written for peasants, of which they circulated 100,000 copies. (In another gesture to the masses, the Kadets called themselves 'the Party of the People's Freedom', dropping the unfamiliar and Western-sounding 'constitutional' and 'democratic'.) The results put them deservedly first: of 478 deputies elected to the first Duma, 179 were or soon became Kadets. Otherwise, there were seventeen Octobrists, seventy-odd representatives of the national minorities, a few Social Democrats, and some 230 unattached peasant deputies. The right, then, had been soundly defeated; and in the absence of the left, which had decided to boycott the elections (though a few Georgian Mensheviks got elected), peasants and Kadets had swept the board. The government took comfort from the large number of peasants – they would surely, it reckoned, be loyal. The Kadets were nevertheless euphoric. They might not have an overall majority, but they had won an undoubted moral victory, and by dint of numbers, eloquence, learning and parliamentary know-how, they would in fact dominate the Duma. They had been very considerably helped of course by the decision of their revolutionary rivals to boycott the elections. That had given them a clear run as the only radicals; they would never enjoy such favourable conditions again. And despite the lack of left-wing rivals, their claim to represent *all* classes was hardly borne out by the results, which showed them to be the party of the professional classes and of some of the petty bourgeoisie – of educated, newspaper-reading, westernized and westernizing Russia. That Russia, however, was now very much on the march, and it had high hopes of carrying some workers and a lot of peasants with it.

But would the government accept that the Kadets had a popular mandate and so give way to them? Would it allow a democratic resolution of the country's crisis? That seemed most unlikely, given its conservative interpretation of the October Manifesto; and the Kadets received a further body blow within days of the opening of the Duma when a new version of the Fundamental Laws was issued. The new version put paid to any lingering hopes that Russia would make a smooth transition to constitutional democracy. Nicholas was determined to stand firm on his autocratic power and he rejected any suggestion that the October Manifesto had implied a limitation of it. He did very reluctantly concede, under pressure from his advisers, that he could no longer describe the autocratic power as 'unlimited', but in the new version he still laid claim to 'supreme autocratic power', and he justified the formula by arguing that this was what the people wanted. Criticism would admittedly come from 'the so-called educated element' and the proletariat – 'But I am confident that 80 per cent of the Russian people will be with me, will support me, and will be grateful to me for such a decision.'[10] This was not entirely wishful thinking on Nicholas's part: right-wing pressure groups had bombarded him with pleas to resist constitutionalism as an attempt by Jews and traitors to impose something that went counter to the wishes and the spirit of the people.

Since Russia would continue to be an autocracy, there could be no responsible government. Ministers would be accountable to the autocrat alone; he could keep them in office irrespective of votes in the Duma; and he could dissolve the Duma whenever he wanted, though the dissolution decree would have to name the dates for the new election. Getting his own way would of course be more difficult than before. Deputies had the rights of free speech and immunity from prosecution; they could question ministers; they could propose new laws; most important of all, they could refuse assent to the government's legislative proposals. That had been a vital concession in October. Speransky's attempt to insert a legislative veto into his reform was what, remember, had led to his breach with Alexander and subsequent downfall. Now what Speransky had wanted, the regime had reluctantly accepted – bills would not become law unless the representatives of the people approved them. But having conceded this issue of principle, Nicholas and his advisers then clawed back some of what they had lost by Article 87 of the Fundamental Laws, which provided that when the Duma was not in session the government could issue emergency laws – giving it in effect a back door method of returning to rule by decree.

Had there, then, been a real constitutional change? Could Russia now be said to have a constitutional monarchy? The government for its part refused to use the word 'constitution' since that would have implied a limitation of the autocrat's power. The autocrat, according to its version, had freely granted the changes; he could equally freely amend or even withdraw them; and they could not be touched by the Duma. Liberal critics of the government claimed that what Russia now had was no more than 'false constitutionalism', a sham which merely provided a screen for the continuation of autocracy. But whether or not Russia had a proper constitution, what was certain was that it lacked a workable political system. The system would not work because two wholly opposed political cultures vied within it: a traditional culture, whose defenders deeply resented the constitution they had had to accept, and a modern one whose advocates saw the traditional culture as a detestable anachronism. At its extreme, this was a confrontation between people who did not want a constitution at all since they rejected the very idea of limiting the autocrat's power and those who would accept nothing less than a constitution establishing fully responsible government and rejected with scorn the counterfeit they had been fobbed off with. The modernizers dominated the Duma, though not the Council of State, and they were led of course by the Kadets. Milyukov regarded the new Fundamental Laws as a violation of the October Manifesto and 'a conspiracy against the people'; and buoyed up by their electoral victory and apparent popular mandate, he and his colleagues decided upon fierce opposition to a regime whose illegitimacy was now, they believed, clear for all to see.

The first Russian parliament had a short and stormy life. The government's assumption that the peasant deputies would be loyal turned out to be a bad mistake – the peasant deputies on the contrary voiced the anger and land-hunger of the villages. More than a hundred of them soon united as the Trudoviks (Labour Group), and these joined the Kadets in demanding a responsible government and expropriation of estates. Peasant intransigence left a deal with the Kadets as the government's only hope of achieving an amenable Duma, and two sets of secret negotiations with the Kadets took place. The negotiations came to nothing, however, and as a result the government continued to face acrimonious opposition from most deputies. The Kadet leadership would later be strongly criticized for its stiff-necked, 'all or nothing' attitude towards a coalition. There was something in the criticism: the Kadets seemed to be on course for victory, they were anxious to keep to their principles and not to succumb too easily to the temptation of office. Milyukov and his colleagues were nevertheless not against a coalition in principle; but they were against the particular terms offered, and the sticking-point was the government's refusal to expropriate land.

Towards the end of 1905 Witte had, as it happened, come round to the idea that the peasants had to be granted a limited expropriation, and so had his agriculture minister, N. N. Kutler. But the landed nobles, shell-shocked by the peasant rebellion, were not prepared to yield an inch of their land. Once the country was pacified, they exerted great pressure on Nicholas to uphold the right of private property, and before the Duma met Kutler and Witte himself had been dismissed and the government had swung back to an uncompromising stand on the issue. This, however, was the one issue on which the Kadets could not back down. They had accepted an undemocratic electoral system and a toothless parliament, but if they gave up expropria-tion, their claim to be the party of the people – which, after all, meant the peasants – would be threadbare. In addition, their domination of the Duma depended upon keeping the support of peasant deputies. And in May, forty-two Kadets went so far as to propose that all land currently rented by peas-ants from landowners should be expropriated, plus all estates of more than fifty desyatins (about 135 acres). That was going too far for some of their colleagues, but it did not go far enough for the Trudoviks, who came up with a counter-proposal that *all* private land should be expropriated with-out compensation.

The land issue was one in fact on which the Kadets could not win, and it showed how impossible the moderate radical position had become. The need for support from peasants and peasant deputies made them demand expropriation, which put paid to the idea of a coalition ministry. But while the Kadets could not do a deal with the government, neither could they achieve any stable alliance with the Trudoviks, who denounced their insist-ence that expropriated landowners should be compensated. The collapse of the negotiation for a coalition ministry came in fact at the time when the Kadets' fundamental tactic – determined constitutional resistance to the government – was running into trouble. For its success depended upon the credibility of their claim to represent the nation. Dissolution of the Duma, they persuaded themselves, would provoke a nationwide uprising. The sour-ing of the Kadets' relationship with the Trudoviks suggested, however, that their claim to be *vox populi* was a hollow one. The government saw its chance and on 9 July 1906, after a mere seventy-two days, it dissolved the Duma.

The Kadets' bluff had been called: how should they respond? Some 180, led by Milyukov, crossed the border to Vyborg in semi-independent Finland. There they issued an appeal urging people to put up passive resist-ance to the government – to refuse to pay taxes or send recruits to the army. The appeal, however, fell upon deaf ears. The failure of the populace to react devastated the Kadets. It destroyed the belief which till now had had the effect of oxygen upon them – that ordinary Russians had taken to the cause of constitutional democracy. The Kadets had reached out across the massive social, cultural and psychological gulf which divided educated Russians from the masses. Their policies had pushed liberalism to a radical extreme. Yet they had still not reached far enough; indelibly 'gentlemen', they had been unable to establish any real contact with the masses. And the only result of the Vyborg appeal was that its signatories were briefly imprisoned and lost their political rights for life, which deprived the Duma of many of its best parliamentarians.

The Kadets had failed because they had been unable to find either a viable tactic or a strategy with broad appeal. There was no such thing, they now saw, as a safe revolution. They were more likely to be the victims than the beneficiaries of popular violence, and some even foresaw that revolutionary radicalism plus popular hostility to 'gentlemen' might result in a holocaust of educated and westernized Russians. Yet for all that, they knew perfectly well that any negotiation with the regime that was not backed by strong popular pressure was likely to be futile; and this left them without a tactic. There were problems, too, with their strategy. They had wanted a *political* revolution, a complete break with the autocratic system and the creation of a modern constitutional democracy; but their social programme, while radical by the standards of European liberalism, would have been far less than workers and peasants demanded. Their formula of political revolution and essential, if unstated, social continuity had little appeal outside the country's islands of modernity. A decade later, power would fall to a party which turned the Kadet formula on its head: instead of political revolution and *de facto* social continuity, the Bolsheviks would offer *social* revolution and a political order which exploited traditional Russian statism to the full. The Kadets' claim to be an 'all-class' party and the party of the people turned out to be an empty boast. They had support in the larger cities, especially St Petersburg and Moscow, but they faced the indifference if not the hostility of the bulk of the people, peasants and workers.

After the October Revolution, controversy would rage about the Kadets' performance. Russia was not yet ready in 1905, critics of the leadership argued, for full constitutionalism; the Kadets should have been more conciliatory, collaborated with the government, and so weaned the country away from violence and turned the regime by stages into a constitutional monarchy. To this, the leadership's defenders replied that collaboration would certainly not have led to social harmony or constitutional democracy. Both negative claims were justified; and this double negative had tragic implications for the fate of liberalism in Russia.

5

The Vyborg fiasco marked the end, then, of a chapter. The regime had warded off the threat of revolution, and the Kadets would never seriously challenge it again. But repressing its enemies was clearly not enough, and in July 1906 Nicholas had appointed an energetic and imaginative new prime minister. Peter Stolypin had first come to attention as a strong law-and-order conservative, and in the first months of his premiership he enhanced this reputation by vigorously putting down a wave of terrorism. Yet Stolypin was more than a mere hang 'em and flog 'em conservative. He was Witte's heir in that he saw that only a positive strategy could save the regime. Reform, modernization and elimination of the ills which had produced the 1905 upheaval were indispensable. Unlike Witte, however, Stolypin welcomed the new political structure and was anxious to make it work. And his priority, unlike Witte's, was not rapid economic change but social reform and in particular a profound reshaping of rural life along lines that Witte himself had anticipated. Given twenty years – or so his ambition ran – he would transform the country and leave a remodelled regime with a secure social base. Yet even before this remarkable politician was assassinated, his hopes had been destroyed. What went wrong? Was Stolypin's failure to turn the country around a personal failure? Or was tsarism incapable of regenerating itself?

The first obstacle Stolypin faced was deadlock in the parliament. Kadet representation in the second Duma fell to ninety-nine deputies – little more than half their previous tally. But the revolutionary parties had given up their boycott and they and the peasants together had some 200 deputies. While the left had increased its strength, so had the right: the Octobrists had gone up to fifty-four, and there were in addition sixty-odd members of the extreme right. The result was a profoundly polarized Duma dominated by extremes which had nothing in common except a shared belief that democratic institutions were not the way to realize their ambitions. Meanwhile Stolypin's reform programme was in danger because legislation could not be got through except under Article 87. What should be done?

Dissolve the Duma, clamoured many on the right. But another dissolution might produce an even less co-operative Duma. And many court reactionaries wanted to go further still – to abolish this turbulent legislature altogether and return to the pre-October situation. To Stolypin that was out of the question. Yet something needed to be done and dissolving the Duma was clearly not enough. And this time, the dissolution (2 June 1907) was followed the next day by a decree changing the ground rules which determined the Duma's composition. The change violated the Fundamental Laws and the Kadets protested vigorously, though in vain, against what they saw as a *coup d'état*. The new electoral law was biased still more in favour of the landed classes and reduced the representation of peasants (who had let the government down so badly), industrial workers, and those other malcontents, the national minorities. Under the new system, 1 per cent of the population would control some 300 of the Duma's 442 seats. Thirty thousand landowners would become in effect the country's power-brokers. Thus the 3rd of June System, as it became known, cemented the alliance between monarchy and landed nobility which had emerged from the fires of 1905. The final victors of the upheaval turned out to be not the professionals but the landed nobles. For they would now dominate the Duma and the State Council, as well as exerting enormous influence through a variety of extra-parliamentary bodies. Instead of unlimited autocracy, there was now insti-tutionalized power-sharing between monarch and major landowners, who for the first time became a ruling class proper.

Which way would the new regime go? Would the magnates who shared power with the ruler ease the country along the road of reform and allow a gradual broadening of the political base? That was what Stolypin intended. He had put through the coup with reluctance, and his aim was not to shore up the privileges of the élite but rather to enlist their support for policies that would change Russia. For this he needed a moderate and co-operative mid-dle ground of deputies who would become in a sense his partners in gov-ernment. And the elections to the third Duma gave him exactly what he wanted – a Duma that was right-of-centre, as well as overwhelmingly Great Russian; and despite periodic frictions the Duma would be in essence co-operative and would run its full five-year term. The socialists were cut down to thirty-two deputies and the Kadets to fifty-four; there were some 150 out-right conservatives; but the dominant force was a phalanx of 154 Octobrists.

The Octobrists were natural partners for Stolypin and they were happy to adjust their not very firm liberal principles in order to accommodate him. To them, he was a potential Bismarck – someone who would combine a strong arm with creative statesmanship, integrate an authoritarian mon-archy and parliamentary institutions, and achieve a broad national con-sensus through policies that were modernizing yet patriotic. The alliance was helped by their intense loyalty to the monarchy and also by a common nationalism and reluctance to make concessions to the minor nationalities. But what perhaps above all made the Octobrists Stolypin's natural partners was that their roots, like his, lay among the landed nobility, whose members he had turned into the country's power-brokers.

Thus Stolypin depended upon the Octobrists and they in turn upon the landed nobility in order to realize a programme of modernizing and, by implication, liberalizing reforms. The arrangement proved to be unwork-able, but at the beginning it worked very well because the Octobrists and their followers were at one with Stolypin on the question of agrarian reform. The clear lesson of 1905 was that something had to be done about the peasantry. And Stolypin had grasped the nettle in this respect with an ambitious plan, already under way, to transform peasant life and end the peasants' age-old disaffection.

The heart of the matter was of course the land. He and the nobles rejected outright the expropriation solution – Russia's 130,000 large and medium estates would remain inviolate. Extra acreage would still not give the peasants decent living standards: only improved productivity could do that, and this required a system of agriculture that encouraged individual initiative. His counter to demands for expropriation was therefore dissolution of the commune, which conservative opinion had now come to see as a socialist institution and a source of sedition. He was making, he told the Duma, 'a wager not on the needy or drunken but on the strong and sturdy', and he hoped that his wager would in time bring into being a new class of independent and modestly prosperous peasant farmers. Once the peasants had property of their own, they would become hard-working, or so the thinking went; they would also be more likely to respect the property rights of others.

Yet the commune could not be abolished outright. It could only be removed in stages, and the first stage was to enable those peasants who wanted to farm privately to withdraw from it and set up on their own. That required two changes, one juridical and the other practical. First, the peasant's right to his land allotment had to be converted into a private-property right. Second, his scattered strips had to be consolidated into a compact, enclosed farm. In both respects, however, the results would disappoint those who had had high hopes of the reform. During the decade 1906–16, little more than 20 per cent of households with communal tenure asked to be given private-property rights. Those anxious to take advantage of the legislation tended, moreover, to be not the 'strong and sturdy' but poorer peasants, who wanted simply to sell their strips and get off the land altogether. And those who did want to become independent farmers very often found that the commune authorities refused to let them consolidate their strips. When the February 1917 revolution brought the whole development to a halt, the face of Russian agriculture remained essentially unchanged: this was still a country of strip farming and only 10 per cent of peasant households had set up independently.

Stolypin's solution to the peasant problem was thus rejected by the great majority of peasants. The very fact that the reform stemmed from the nobility no doubt damned it from the outset as another attempt to exploit and deceive, and most peasants held unwaveringly to the belief that expropriation and nothing else would solve their problems. In troubled times the commune became all the more a needed bulwark, a source of material and personal support without which life for most was unimaginable. As for those peasants who did split off from the commune, they were generally greeted as renegades. When law and order collapsed in 1917, their holdings would be among the first to be seized by peasant militants and reincorporated into the communal lands. Thus peasant Russia would write the epitaph to Stolypin's experiment, doing on a large scale what it had often before done on a smaller one: defying the interference, even if well intended, of its 'betters'.

While Stolypin achieved little in the way of agrarian reform, his attempt did at least have the wholehearted support of the nobles since they saw their best interests being served by it. His wider programme of reform was, however, a different matter. To convert the peasants, or at least a fair proportion of them, from an embittered and anarchic element into a stable foundation for the regime required far more, he realized, than simply phasing out the commune. If the peasants were to play a constructive social part, they would have to be educated at least to primary level. Health and welfare services would have to be improved. And it would not be enough to talk about civil rights: they would have to be made a reality. That meant protecting people against arbitrary arrest, giving full recognition to trade unions, and removing the disabilities suffered by religious and ethnic minorities. Most contentious of all, making the peasants citizens required a thorough overhaul of local government, which was still based on the principle of class discrimination. Cantons would have to be given powers over *everyone* who lived within their area. Above them, the zemstvos would have to become proper organs of self-government and a genuine reflection of what the community wanted. Their powers would have to be increased; they would have to be freed from bureaucratic interference; most vital of all, they would have to be elected on a fully democratic franchise.

But to ask such changes of a political system dominated so completely by the nobility as was the 3rd of June System was to ask for the moon. Stolypin found himself opposed by increasing numbers of Octobrists, not to mention the Duma's unconcealed rightists. He was opposed within the highly conservative Council of State. He was opposed by the Council of the United Nobility, which had emerged after 1905 as a powerful pressure-group for the nobility. He was opposed even by the hierarchs of the Orthodox Church. The Establishment, in short, closed its ranks firmly against him, and as a result none of his proposed reforms apart from the agrarian ones passed into law; on all other issues he was frustrated.

The seeds of his defeat lay in the 3rd of June System itself. In order to escape a deadlocked Duma, he had given a decisive voice to the landed nobility, but his tactic of boosting noble power plainly contradicted his strategy of modernizing and creating a popular base for tsarism. Ends and means were impossibly mismatched. In effect he was asking the nobles to use their power in ways that would undermine rather than consolidate the influence of the nobility. Noble power at the centre would weaken noble power and status in the provinces and help improve the conditions of the masses at the nobles' expense. Not surprisingly, the noble power-brokers balked at this, and as a result Stolypin found himself hoist with his own petard. Like Speransky and Witte, he had been defeated in his bid for reform by the magnates, though there was a special pathos about his defeat since, unlike his predecessors, he himself came from the landed nobility and he had allowed his own kind a dominant political role in the hope that they would respond to his reforming vision.

Against the hostility of the right, Stolypin could look for support only to the liberals. But he could expect little help from the Kadets and even his relationship with the Octobrists became increasingly strained. His brand of peasant monarchism made him at once too radical and too conservative for them, and within fifteen months his Octobrist-based majority was disintegrating. While the country gentlemen deserted, a minority of more radical Octobrists, led by Alexander Guchkov, remained faithful to him: but in March 1911 even Guchkov's group broke with him. An intransigent upper class was not, however, the only problem – Stolypin fell victim also to an increasingly hostile monarch and court circle. He had begun as a resource-ful and strong-armed champion of the regime, but soon the court came to see him as less of a protector than an enemy. There was something in the suspicion. Stolypin was very far from being a second Speransky – this was no closet liberal who had infiltrated the power-house with ideas of sabotag-ing it. Quite the contrary, he was a traditionalist, a natural preserver, who saw the monarchy as the lynchpin of the social order and was determined to save it from the reactionary element which was dragging it down. Yet this traditionalist came to see transformation as the essential condition of preservation. It was not enough to save the monarchy from court reac-tionaries only to deliver it instead into the hands of a declining but increas-ingly fractious nobility: if the monarchy was to survive, only a free and tolerably prosperous peasantry could provide the support needed. The task ahead was therefore intensive, all-round modernization, which would leave the monarchy as a powerful symbol and focus for unity but hardly, despite Stolypin's own claims and even convictions, as the prime moving force in Russian politics.

Those who saw Stolypin as a threat to the autocracy perhaps read him better than he read himself. Blind to the implications of his own pro-gramme, Stolypin had something in common with that later revolutionary-from-within, Mikhail Gorbachev. Both came to power when an ossified regime was dying; both saw the need for fundamental change; both hoped to save much of the old order by reforming it; and both met fierce resistance from conservatives who sensed that disintegration rather than preservation was the reforms' likely outcome. Of the two, Gorbachev got further: he was able to push his changes through by enfranchizing ordinary citizens and in particular by mobilizing the intelligentsia against his opponents. Stolypin by contrast had been forced to move in the opposite direction: he had nar-rowed, not widened, the political nation and had as a result put himself at the mercy of the landed oligarchy. And even if he had not eliminated the peasants as a parliamentary force, they were hardly likely to have rallied to him. Stolypin's tragic plight was that despite his brand of peasant mon-archism he found himself without the support of either peasants or mon-archists; in addition, he was deserted even by those moderate liberals who had shared his vision of gradual change towards a socially integrated Russia but had finally lost faith if not in his sincerity at least in his ability to deliver. By his blend of conservatism and radicalism he had managed to appear, in the words of Alexander Solzhenitsyn, 'a reactionary to all on the Left, yet practically a Kadet to the true Right'.[11] Abandoned by his original support-ers and never finding support outside the ruling class, he had been mortally wounded politically months before he was assassinated at the Kiev Opera

House in September 1911 by a revolutionary who doubled as a secret police agent; and had he not been killed, he would almost certainly have been dismissed.

Stolypin's attempt was doomed, then – monarch and landowners had not fought off the Kadets only to succumb to a more insidious radicalism from inside the government itself. No one of the same calibre would follow him as prime minister, and even an able and determined successor would have failed to deflect the regime from its course. Monarch and supporters had retreated into the 3rd of June fortress, immune from constitutional attack, and there they intended to stay. Some historians would portray Stolypin and the Octobrists as 'true liberals' who, had they got their way, would have guided Russia into the safe harbour of constitutional democracy. 1907 on their reading was a potential turning-point comparable in importance to 1825 and the early 1860s. But this 'chance' was no less illusory than the previous ones. There was no question of Stolypin and the more genuinely liberal Octobrists getting their way. In the early twentieth century Russia was not yet ready for democratic liberalism, but had already passed the stage when it might have had a liberalizing oligarchy. Oligarchy had come too late to be a force for progress. Faced with a mutinous peasantry and proletariat, the landowner-oligarchs were in no mood to bring about a gradual transition to democracy and instead used their powers to make a last-ditch defence of privilege. Their rejection of Stolypin's lifeline was understandable – he might have saved them from violence, but he would not after all have saved their privileges. And so there would be no positive strategy, no blueprint which might have saved tsarism from the burning. There would just be repression, the grim defence of an endangered redoubt by a government that was bereft of ideas but still had soldiers, sailors and policemen.

6

Without the First World War, would there have been a Russian revolution? Almost certainly, though it would not have happened when it did nor followed the exact course that it did. Since tsarism no longer had a strategy for survival yet was determined not to abdicate, the question was not whether it would be toppled but when and by whom it would be toppled.

The liberals made a poor showing in these final years of peace, even though the fourth Duma (1912–17) had a lot of them: eighty-five Octobrists, fifty-seven Kadets, plus forty-one members of a new party representing the commercial–industrial élite, the Progressists, giving the liberals as a whole almost 50 per cent of the deputies. Liberal effectiveness was undermined by deep divisions not only between the various parties but within them. The Octobrists split in 1913, and while the Kadets avoided a formal schism they too were deeply divided over tactics. Most liberals clung to the hope that moderate and responsible behaviour might yet be rewarded by concessions, though a minority wanted to go back to the more radical tactics of 1905. The radicals were encouraged by developments in the revolutionary movement. Among the SRs, a right wing had appeared which urged the need for *lawful* activity and was chary of revolution even as a long-term prospect. As for the Mensheviks, they too had reacted to the 1905 defeat by stressing the need for above-ground and piecemeal activity rather than conspiracy and insurrection. The most urgent need, as they saw it, was to develop the trade unions and make them schools of democratic politics for the workers, thus preparing the ground for socialism. The Mensheviks set great store on building up a core of informed and responsible workers. These would become the unions' leaders and would guide, educate and restrain less mature workers, instilling democratic and socialist values into them and teaching them to distinguish what was possible from what was not. This worker-intelligentsia would, Mensheviks believed, be a vital element in the inter-class coalition, bonded by a common commitment to democratic institutions, which would sooner or later overthrow tsarism and set up a bourgeois-democratic regime.

However, the Menshevik who had had most impact in 1905, Leon Trotsky, came out against this approach. Perhaps because he had been in the thick of the events, he now saw the idea of wholly separate bourgeois and socialist revolutions as bookish and unrealistic. Once the workers had won power, they were not going to hand it over to bourgeois who had been incapable of making the revolution themselves. Despite the country's backwardness and their own minority situation, they would hold on to power and start the drive for socialism straightaway. Trotsky's idea of revolution as an uninterrupted process – the theory of 'permanent revolution', as it would become known – showed real insight into what would happen in 1917, when he would join the Bolsheviks and spearhead their capture of power from the moderates. Until 1917, however, he would stand alone because he did not accept Lenin's two master ideas for making good the country's backwardness: the vanguard party and the proletariat–peasant alliance.

Lenin's idea of the party guiding an immature workforce had of course not tallied at all with what had actually happened in 1905 – workers had gone on strike and organized themselves in soviets with very little guidance by revolutionaries. This unexpected creativity at the grass-roots presented him with a problem. He stood out, after all, as a Marxist who believed in the guiding role of professional revolutionaries, and this disciplinarian and centralizing self would never disappear. Yet the lesson of 1905 was not lost on him. From now on there would be a second Lenin, who co-existed rather uneasily with the authoritarian – a Lenin who believed in the creativity of the masses and saw the revolutionaries as simply having to unleash a mass spontaneity which would very largely direct itself. But how did he manage to believe at one and the same time in a vanguard party *and* in popular self-government? Partly by pretending, perhaps even to himself, that there was no contradiction between the two beliefs. Thus, the post-revolutionary dictatorship would, he insisted, be 'democratic': it would be a dictatorship *of* the people rather than *over* the people. Ordinary Russians would cease to be the passive objects of government and begin to exercise power themselves, as had happened in the soviets. The soviets had in fact given him a first inkling of what this revolutionary dictatorship would be like, though the workers involved in them had been a mere minority of the proletarian minority and not by any means a government *of* most people. His attempt to dress up the rule of the few as the rule of all, to present dictatorship as something democratic, to substitute smaller bodies for larger ones, disturbed many of his rivals. Trotsky for one had warned even before 1905 of the likely outcome: 'the party organization is substituted for the party, the Central Committee is substituted for the party organization, and finally the "dictator" is substituted for the Central Committee.'[12]

After 1905, Lenin's savage militancy and his complete refusal to collaborate with the liberals isolated him still further from the other leading Social Democrats. How, someone once asked the Menshevik Pavel Axelrod, could one man be so effective and so dangerous? 'Because', Axelrod replied, 'there is not another man who for twenty-four hours of the day is taken up with the revolution, who has no other thoughts but thoughts of revolution, and who even in his sleep dreams of nothing but revolution.'[13] Till 1907, Lenin continued to call for an armed uprising, and his fury against the liberals rose to fever pitch. Liberals were craven and grovelling; they were dirty and repulsive pigs; they were vile, foul and brutal. And in his rage against the 'pigs', he became a positive carnivore: 'we must', he told his followers, 'be Kadet-eaters as a matter of principle.'[14] Such language might displease the Mensheviks but it expressed the emotions of the village, the pent-up rage of ordinary Russians against their 'betters'. Nor did Lenin change his tune once it became clear beyond doubt that tsarism had for the time being triumphed. His anger had hidden a fear that the liberal con trick might succeed, that gullible people might actually swallow the liberals' democratic pretensions. Now with some justification he claimed that events had vindicated him – the liberals had been shown to be both ineffectual and hypocrites. Parliamentary pratings and manoeuvrings had achieved nothing. The liberals had turned out to be mere windbags; not only had they put up no opposition to tsarism, they had as he predicted rolled over and sided with it against the forces of democracy. All of which merely confirmed his view that armed struggle alone would produce results. And the struggle when it began would start from a much higher point than in 1905. For the workers now felt their position as an oppressed class more strongly than before, and proletarian class consciousness had been reinforced by the emergence of the bourgeois as an organized political force. This growth of political awareness on both sides of the class divide made the politics of compromise and class collaboration more futile even than before.

In the years immediately before the war, Lenin added one more group to the forces he had arrayed, on paper, against the regime – the national minorities of the empire. This was a natural follow-up to his 'recruitment' of the peasants. Just as the peasants formed a majority of the population, so did the national minorities – admittedly a smaller majority, but out of 170 millions a full 100 millions, he calculated, were non-Russians. Just as peasant indignation had spilled over in 1905, so the passions of the minorities were reaching boiling-point now. And just as his recruitment of the peasants had upset Marxist purists, so too his encouragement of the minorities scented to many of heresy. Marx, after all, had argued that 'the worker has no country' and had looked to an internationalist future. Lenin nevertheless wholeheartedly supported the minorities' right to self-determination. Giving them the right to secede was not the same, he pointed out, as encouraging them to use it, and he hoped that most would stay within a socialist Russia, but he saw it as vital that they should feel free to leave if they wished. Lenin had no more become a nationalist than peasant socialist; he was simply determined to muster all the support he could get.

While peasants and national minorities would help, the decisive blow would have to be struck by the workers; and an upsurge of worker discontent after several years of sullen quiescence gave the Bolsheviks a boost in the immediate pre-war years. From 1909 the Russian economy showed a marked return to buoyancy after a period of depression, and renewed growth brought large numbers of peasants to seek work in the large towns. There had been 158,000 factory workers in St Petersburg in 1908; five years later the influx from the countryside had brought the number to 216,000. The dramatic increase in numbers made already bad living conditions worse, and worker grievance was reflected in a rising graph of strikes. In 1910 and 1911, strikes were numbered in the hundreds. In 1912, however, there was an escalation to over 2,000, prompted by the shooting of striking miners at the Lena goldfield in Siberia; and in the first half of 1914, 3,534 strikes were recorded.

As the country moved once more towards a revolutionary situation, Bolsheviks and Mensheviks fought for influence over the aggrieved. Not only did the two factions have different policies and attitudes; a snapshot of the two taken in the pre-war years would have shown distinct differences in personnel. At the leadership level, the Mensheviks came mainly from the national minorities, especially the Jews and Georgians, whereas the Bolshevik leadership was overwhelmingly Russian. Difference of background explained differences in attitude. Coming from minority cultures, the Mensheviks were more naturally receptive to democracy and decentralization and less marked by the 'Asiatic heritage'. The rank and file too showed distinct geographical and social differences. The Mensheviks did particularly well in Ukraine and the Caucasus, while the Bolsheviks were strongest in Russia proper, especially the large towns. And where the two competed, they attracted a different following. The Mensheviks appealed successfully to the more skilled, educated and better-paid workers, but their message of compromise and temporary collaboration with the bourgeois got little response from the mass of raw, unskilled and uneducated peasants now pouring into St Petersburg from the overpopulated central provinces. Had the gulf between the classes been narrowing, as revisionist socialists in the West argued that it would, then the Mensheviks might have done better: but if anything the gulf was widening. Peasant immigrants suffering in a capital whose streets were far from paved with gold had no reason for warm feelings towards their bosses or the well-to-do in general. As living conditions worsened, the mood of the swelling semi-peasant proletariat became increasingly confrontational.

With circumstances turning in his favour, Lenin tried hard to oust the Mensheviks from their entrenched position in the labour movement. His aim was a Bolshevik party cell in every union branch, which would then be able to direct strike action and at the right time organize an uprising. In 1910 there had been no more than 600 Bolsheviks in St Petersburg; by the eve of the war the number had grown to 6,000. Party members were still a drop in the ocean, yet each could influence dozens of 'average workers', who in turn could spread the word among the mass of 'backward workers'. Thus one party activist might directly or indirectly influence thousands. A sign that it was Lenin who was telling the workers what they wanted to hear was that *Pravda* and other Bolshevik papers considerably outsold their Menshevik counterparts. The strength of the rival factions was most clearly shown, however, in the struggle for control of union organizations, which the Bolsheviks were winning hands down. In August 1913 they took control of the most important Petersburg union, the Union of Metalworkers; and by July 1914 they dominated fourteen out of eighteen unions in the capital and ten out of thirteen in Moscow. Taunted as 'liquidators', the Mensheviks were being chased out of union after union as a wave of anger and belligerency swept workers towards the Bolsheviks.

How much militancy had got the better of moderation was shown in July 1914, when the working-class areas of the capital erupted in a general strike under Bolshevik slogans. Barricades were thrown up, as in 1905, and all the signs were that a major uprising was close. Perhaps too close, the local Bolshevik leaders decided – a premature attempt would damage the movement – and after a few days they called the strike off. The Petersburg proletariat was not easily restrained, however, and it was a full week before peace returned to the industrial suburbs.

The Bolsheviks need not have worried, as it happened: restraint was about to be applied from a quite different source. On 15 July Russia mobilized against Austria–Hungary, which had declared war against the small Slav state of Serbia. On 19 July (1 August in the Western calendar) Germany, Austria's ally, declared war on Russia. The tsarist regime thus became drawn into the very thing that some of its advisers had warned might destroy it – a major war. Immediately, the war created a mood of patriotic euphoria and defiance, and differences seemed forgotten in a surge of unity around the tsar, who once more symbolized the nation. Lenin for one, however, was not displeased by what had happened. He had written in 1913 that a war between Russia and Austria would be 'a very helpful thing for the revolution'.[15] Now, somewhat unexpectedly, he had been given what he wanted.

Notes

1 Sidney Harcave, *First Blood: The Russian Revolution of 1905* (London, 1965), p. 287.
2 Martin McCauley, *Octobrists to Bolsheviks: Imperial Russia 1905–1917* (London, 1984), pp. 13–14.
3 Richard Pipes, *Struve: Liberal on the Left 1870–1905* (Cambridge, Mass., 1970), p. 382.
4 P. N. Miliukov, *Russia and Its Crisis* (New York, 1962), p. 522.
5 *Ibid.*
6 V. I. Lenin, *Collected Works* (45 vols, Moscow 1960-70), vol. XXXIII, pp. 478–9.
7 P. N. Milyukov, *Vospominaniya (1858–1917)* (2 vols, New York, 1955), vol. I, p. 316.
8 Lenin, *Collected Works*, vol. V, p. 467.
9 Roberta Thompson Manning, *The Crisis of the Old Order in Russia: Gentry and Government* (Princeton, N.J., 1982), p. 169.
10 George Vernadsky *et al.*, *A Source Book for Russian History from Early Times to 1917* (3 vols, New Haven and London, 1972), vol. III, p. 771.
11 Aleksandr Solzhenitsyn, *The Red Wheel: A Narrative in Discrete Periods of Time* (London, 1989), p. 552.
12 Baruch Knei-Paz, *The Social and Political Thought of Leon Trotsky* (Oxford, 1978), p. 199.
13 Bertram D. Wolfe, *Three Who Made a Revolution* (London, 1956), p. 249.
14 Lenin, *Collected Works*, vol. XVIII, p. 297.
15 V. I. Lenin, *Polnoe sobranie sochinenii*, 5th edn (55 vols, Moscow 1958–65), vol. XLVIII, p. 155.

|5|

Dual power and the Bolsheviks, 1914–1917

1

The Bolshevik revolution of October 1917 was not foreseen until shortly before it happened, even by the Bolsheviks themselves. As late as January that year, a despondent Lenin had seemed to think that he might not live to see the revolution he believed in, little knowing that tsarism was already on its deathbed. The unity around the ruler created by the outbreak of war had long since evaporated. The war had proved to be longer, more awful and more far-reaching in its consequences than almost anyone had envisaged, and of all the participants tsarist Russia had been least able to take the strain. It was not only soldiers at the front who suffered; so did millions of people behind the lines whose lives had been devastated by the war's indirect effects. A short successful war might have boosted the regime, but the long-drawn-out agony of this particular war had by the beginning of 1917 destroyed whatever popular support it still had. Like most great revolutions, the Russian revolution of February 1917 took most people by surprise in the sense that few expected the regime to be toppled at that particular moment. Tsarism's fall after a few days of unorganized disturbances in the capital was nevertheless no more of an accident than the fall of an apparently sturdy but rotten oak which is brought down by a sudden gust of wind.

Liberals now formed a caretaker government, though in conditions of chaos and social breakdown which made its task very difficult. The liberals were in fact in the peculiar position that they had gained power as the result of a revolution which they themselves had taken no part in. Yet in the aftermath of the crash few people challenged their view of themselves as tsarism's natural heirs. They had a near monopoly, or so it seemed, of the skills and talents necessary for governing the country and steering it towards a new life based on conciliation and democracy. They could count on the conditional support, or at least the forbearance, of most Mensheviks and

SRs and of anyone else who thought that the war effort was the most urgent necessity of the moment. Moreover, it was clear that, with the tsar swept away, most people had no stomach for further upheavals. At this stage there was almost no demand for radical revolution. The mood of the country was, on the contrary, for unity and pulling together. The Mensheviks and SRs of the Petrograd Soviet would put up with liberal ministers, while workers would rub along with managers, soldiers with officers and even peasants with estate-owners. The assumption underlying this precarious peace – or at least suspension of hostilities – between the classes was, however, that the war would be brought to an end soon and that a democratically elected parliament, the Constituent Assembly, would set about solving the country's problems: of which the most pressing was the peasants' need, as they saw it, for the landowners' land.

'Dual power' worked well enough at the top, and liberals and moderate socialists, in formal coalition from May, governed the country right through, in different combinations, until the Bolshevik take-over in October. But at the level of workers, soldiers and peasants, it proved unworkable and broke down very quickly: there simply was no democratic middle ground between them and their respective masters. Animosities which had hardly cooled flared up powerfully once more, and now of course there was no autocratic state to hold them in check. The renewed hatred of 'them' turned people away from the moderate socialists, now badly compromised by their willingness to deal with 'them', and towards the one party which had almost always preached class war and the destruction of privileged Russia and whose leader had insisted throughout that the idea of a peaceful middle way was a snare and a delusion.

The change in the Bolsheviks' fortunes was remarkable. In February they had been isolated, out of touch with the popular mood and apparently wrong-footed by events; eight months later they would be swept to power in the capital on a wave of popular enthusiasm. The Bolsheviks' victory owed much to Lenin, who returned to Russia in early April when the honeymoon of dual power was already ending and from then on guided them almost unerringly. Their programme captured two vital popular impulses, which surged to the fore as the dual-power idea crumbled. The first was the desire to smash (Lenin talked of 'smashing' a great deal in 1917) and to get rid of 'them' once and for all. The second, equally fierce but positive rather than negative, was the drive to make an entirely new order of things. The Bolsheviks alone satisfied both cravings: they would destroy the old society and in its place build one with no state and no classes and hence no bossing and no injustice.

These aims and the ruthlessness with which they pursued them set the Bolsheviks utterly apart from their moderate socialist rivals. The clash between the two echoed that between Pestel and the mainstream Decembrists almost a century earlier. The moderates, like most of the Decembrists, wanted to tame and liberalize the overmighty Russian state and thus to make a complete break with the country's political tradition. The Bolsheviks had the more dizzying ambition of transforming the human condition altogether, but in order to do this they would have to use state power far more decisively than the tsars ever had. The danger, which their rivals had already protested vigorously about, was that they might perpetuate and even exacerbate the very evils they had been fighting against. Yet it was they rather than the moderates whose message caught the imagination and stirred the emotions of the ordinary people of Petrograd between April and October 1917. 'Smash the old world!' 'Build a new world!' was a message which, amidst the distress and chaos of 1917, many Russians found irresistible. It was a message to which people had been made receptive by the gross injustices and inequalities of Russian life. In that sense the Bolsheviks' victory in October was no fluke: the ground had been all too thoroughly prepared for them by tsarism. But there were of course elements of luck in their success; and one was that in Lenin they had a leader of unequalled flair whose prime of life came at the very time when the tsarist regime, already undermined, got drawn into a war of unprecedented destructiveness.

2

Some 15 million men served in the Russian army during the three years of the war. Of these, about half were either killed or wounded or captured. No other army suffered that terribly. Why did the Russians manage the war effort so badly?

The reasons were essentially the same as in previous wars, though this war was fought closer to home, in a more extensive theatre and over a much longer time, and the consequences of failure were therefore more devastating. In the first place, the Russians did badly because of economic and technological backwardness. Superior manpower was no substitute for lack of firepower, and when the war broke out the Russian armaments industry was not up to the demands that would be made of it. By the fifth month of the war supplies were running out: soldiers found themselves without bullets for their rifles or shells for their field-guns. The problem was not only of quantity but of quality. The Russian armaments were not equal to German ones, and soldiers became demoralized by being exposed to the fire of much heavier and more accurate guns. Supplies did in fact improve, and by 1916 the army had the guns, shells, hand-grenades and most other things it needed. But if the Russian soldier had been let down at the outset by poor supplies, he was let down still more badly – and in this case, consistently – by those who commanded him. He himself fought with the dogged courage the peasant-in-arms had always shown, or did so at least until his will to fight had been eroded by complete demoralization or disaffection. But the officers corps could not compare with their German equivalents in terms of professionalism, technical expertise or dedication. The leadership was hampered by out-dated attitudes and riven by animosities. The human failure, moreover, went right to the top. The commander-in-chief, Grand Duke Nikolai, was not up to his job, nor were his chief assistants up to theirs; the emperor, who took over as commander-in-chief in August 1915, was wholly unsuitable for the position, while few of the generals rose above mediocrity.

It did not take the soldiers long to realize that with such a high command all their effforts were likely to be in vain. A shattering blow to morale had come at the very beginning of the war when the army had been routed with some 300,000 losses in East Prussia. Whatever belief remained in the competence of their officers and high command did not survive the great retreat of 1915. An offensive into Galicia in the spring turned out to be a mistake since the army did not have the firepower to keep it going. The supposed Russian steamroller then retreated throughout the summer of 1915, and by the end of the retreat it had lost a million dead or wounded and another million taken prisoner. In this case the high command's conduct had a direct effect upon civilians as well as soldiers. The only way to stop the German advance, the command decided, was to apply the scorched earth policy which had been used against Napoleon: and so the countryside was systematically wasted and millions of people were expelled from their homes and sent as a tidal wave of refugees eastwards, many of them dying on the road.

'A fish begins to stink from the head', was one soldier's reaction to the misery inflicted upon the people by the army in 1915. 'What kind of tsar is it who surrounds himself with thieves?'[1] Once the tsar had become commander-in-chief, there was nothing to shield him against the unpopularity incurred by his commanders: he simply became chief of the 'thieves'. But if there was despair at the bottom, there was disarray and something approaching panic at the top. Minister of war Polivanov's reaction to the 1915 retreat was that he relied upon 'immeasurable distances, impassable roads, and the mercy of St Nicholas, patron of Holy Russia' to save the country: he had clearly given up hope of the army or the government making any real contribution.[2]

This colossal mismanagement of the war effort could only help the regime's opponents, and it had a tonic effect upon the liberals. Here, it seemed, was a chance for them to complete the unfinished business of 1905 under the impeccable pretext of doing what they could for the nation's defence. Zemstvos banded together in a nation-wide organization to make good gaps in official health and welfare services; so too did the municipalities; and in November 1915 the two fused into a single powerful body, *Zemgor*. Equally influential were the War Industries' Committees (WICs), headed by the Octobrist, Guchkov; and a network of these spread throughout the country in 1915 to try to ensure that industry supplied the army with its requirements. But having a minor say in running the country was not enough: liberal ambitions would not be satisfied until they controlled the government or at least had a decisive voice in it. And in the summer of 1915 some 300 Duma deputies – out of a total 430 – joined together in a liberal-inspired 'Progressive Bloc' with the aim of making the government change its course.

The Bloc's basic plea was for a government that would win the nation's confidence; its more specific objectives included the restoration of trade union activity, the extension of peasants' rights, an amnesty for political detainees, and more lenient treatment of ethnic minorities and non-Orthodox religious believers. There was good reason to think that Nicholas would agree to much that they asked for. The country was after all in crisis, and the disasters of the war were almost universally laid at the government's door. It would surely not be easy for Nicholas to reject a programme supported by most members of a Duma elected on a highly restrictive franchise and even by some normally conservative Nationalists. Not only did parliament and the press give strong support to the Progressive Bloc; nearly all ministers, with the exception of Goremykin, the elderly prime minister, believed it vital to negotiate with the Bloc and concede some at least of its demands.

Yet Nicholas dug his heels in against the pressure from the capital's political circles, its legislators, its journalists, its intellectuals. He would continue to rule as *he* wanted, and he had already made the point by deciding to take personal control of the army against the advice of almost all his ministers. Not only did he flatly reject the Bloc's programme; he punished the impertinent politicians by giving instructions that the Duma should be prorogued.

Thus tsarism once again defied the liberal windbags, safe in the knowledge that, as in 1906 and 1907, they would do no more than talk. What else could they do? The only alternative to impotent parliamentary protest was to take to the streets – but that was the last thing most of them wanted. The *raison d'être* of the Progressive Bloc, as one member put it, was to calm passions rather than inflame them, 'to replace the discontent of the masses, which might easily turn into revolution, with the discontent of the Duma'.[3] The Duma would thus act as a kind of lightning conductor: by its loyal opposition it would take the edge off popular hostility to the regime. Nicholas, however, disdained such help, and the Bloc's leaders would not come into their own until the popular wrath from which they had hoped to save the regime had already swept it away. Nicholas's instinct seems to have been that the politicians, experts and literati formed an isolated and exotic coterie which he could safely ignore since its members' views meant nothing to the masses. That was true enough. What was unwise of him was to assume that the support withheld from the coterie would be given to the monarchy instead.

The liberals too sensed their own isolation, and behind their unwillingness to confront the government lay an uneasy awareness that not only had the tsar lost the nation's confidence – so had they. The Octobrists had almost no grass-roots following left; and the Kadets' support was now limited to the largest cities – 'a Kadet archipelago', as one historian put it, amidst the immensities of Russia.[4] The 'all-class' claim of the Kadets hid the depressing reality that they had no significant support in any class: certainly not from workers and peasants, certainly not from the landed nobility, not even from what there was of a commercial and industrial class; and the often outstanding talents of the intellectuals and professionals who stayed true to them could hardly compensate for the lack of a mass following. The number of liberals in the Duma therefore misled, and the leftward swing in public opinion during the war years suggested that, come the fifth Duma, there would be pitifully few liberal deputies.

Most liberals understandably, then, put the idea of ousting the government on one side and instead did their best to save it from blundering so badly that it ignited a social explosion. Yet they were far from agreed about what would happen if, despite all, a revolution did break out. Milyukov, the Kadet leader, for one remained unwaveringly confident that Russian liberalism would emerge victorious. The revolution might well lead to a period of disorder, during which the liberals would be well advised to 'stand aside': but soon they would have to form a government since only they had the necessary know-how and experience. Nothing in the war years had dented Milyukov's underlying optimism. Russia's destiny was liberal, and its whole history, or so this distinguished former history professor believed, pointed towards a liberal denouement.

Other liberals, however, doubted whether history was necessarily on the liberals' side and whether the leaders of a popular revolution would inevitably defer to them. Among the doubters was Guchkov, who believed, on the contrary, 'that those who make the revolution will themselves head the revolution'.[5] It was therefore vital to avert popular revolution, since once it had occurred the game would from the liberal point of view already have been lost. But how, with rapidly worsening conditions in Petrograd (as the capital had been renamed instead of the German-sounding 'St Petersburg'), could revolution be avoided? Only, Guchkov decided, by a pre-emptive strike which rescued the monarchy from its current discredit. He clutched in fact at the old liberal belief in a palace coup, and in the summer of 1916 began preparations for one. So much had liberal optimism faded since 1905–6. The natural tendency of events had then seemed to be carrying the liberals to victory. Now some at least believed that their cause could be saved only by intervention against a natural tendency which, if left to itself, would result in anarchy and socialism. The coup against Nicholas was planned for March 1917. It would never of course take place because the disaster it should have staved off had already occurred.

There were, however, some liberals, among them the left-wing Kadet Nikolai Nekrasov and the Progressist leader Alexander Konovalov, who read the signs very differently. Rejecting the majority-liberal assumption that it was vital not to rock the boat, they wanted to recreate the broad coalition which had existed briefly in 1905, to collaborate with the moderate revolutionaries and to dislodge the autocracy by pressure of public opinion or even by force. A political revolution, if it occurred, would be held in check, they believed, by the level-headed revolutionaries they intended to ally with. As for social or socialist revolution, that lay well beyond the horizon, as even sensible socialists admitted.

Two developments since the war began had made a liberal-revolutionary coalition look increasingly viable. First, Mensheviks and SRs who supported the war effort had in effect come together in a tactical alliance dominated by the Mensheviks. Second, the issue of the war had so deepened the split between moderate and radical revolutionaries as to make reconciliation between the two seem impossible. Most home-based Mensheviks, and a lot of SRs as well, regarded defence of the fatherland as their first priority, and 'defensism' had by its very nature made them collaborate with other classes in the overriding common cause. In theory they were still committed to the class struggle; in practice, while the war lasted there had to be class peace. Hard-nosed defensism, moreover, pushed them towards positive collaboration with the liberals, since installing a competent bourgeois regime seemed the only way of making the war effort effective.

The convergence of liberal left and revolutionary right was seen in similar thinking about the working class. Both believed in cultivating a worker élite and saw it as performing two tasks: it would pressurize the government but also exert a restraining influence on the worker rank and file. The liberals had a real success in this direction when they persuaded a reluctant government to allow worker representation on the War Industries Committees, and by the spring of 1916 there were workers elected from the factory floor on the Petrograd, Moscow and Kiev WICs, on some hundred provincial ones, and also on the central WIC organization. These worker representatives were Mensheviks or SRs who were willing to use 'bourgeois' channels to protect the workers' interests and to air their grievances. The demands they made went well beyond liberal ones, and yet they were prepared, the Petrograd representatives declared, 'to back every genuine effort by bourgeois circles towards a gradual liberation of the country'.[6] 'Gradual liberation' was not, however, an easy idea to sell to workers suffering from wartime conditions. The workers' representatives might not be stooges of the bosses, but it needed little flair to persuade people that they were. Non-defensist Mensheviks warned the workers not to be deceived by them; and the Bolsheviks still more thunderously repudiated them as 'traitors and renegades'.

Lenin too believed in a worker élite, but certainly not the 'worker aristocracy' of the WICs, which he saw as capitalism's lackeys. *His* élite would make every effort to fan the class war. It would most definitely *not* mediate between the classes, not mark out a democratic common ground, nor create a labour movement which would teach parliamentary methods. Instead, it would deepen the class consciousness of the more backward, push them from economic to political demands, teach them that only destruction of the whole existing order would benefit them, and so convert them into shock troops capable when the time was ripe of seizing power in Russia.

It had not needed the war to show Lenin that Menshevik conciliatory policies were a gross betrayal of socialism. The war had, however, put the opportunist evil in a new perspective, exposing it as a disease which had all but rotted the world-wide socialist movement. For when the war broke out virtually every social-democratic party in Europe reneged on its internationalist professions and backed its own country's war efforts. True, patriotism had not to the same degree afflicted the Russian Social Democrats, whose eleven Duma deputies had all refused to vote war credits. 'Internationalist' Social Democrats – Martov, Dan and Trotsky, for instance – opposed the war and demanded a 'democratic peace' without annexations or indemnities. Yet even this did not go far enough for Lenin. The internationalists' mistake was to demand an end to the war, when what was needed was not to end it (Lenin loathed pacifism) but rather to make use of and to transform it. If transforming the war meant that tsarist Russia had to be defeated, then Lenin for one was not ashamed to call himself a 'defeatist': in the circumstances defeat, he argued, would be the least of evils. What mattered was that soldiers should stop fighting their brother workers and turn their guns instead against their own governments and bosses. The war, in short, should be turned from an inter-state into an inter-class one, from an imperialist war into a civil war.

This was the ultimate in anti-war extremism. Among leading European socialists, no one else publicly took such an out-and-out defeatist line; and when a conference of anti-war socialists met at Zimmerwald in Switzerland in September 1915, a mere half-dozen of the delegates supported Lenin's civil war policy. Among Russian Social Democrats there was, as we have seen, a widespread rejection of defensism, yet only a handful of Bolsheviks immediately adopted their leader's stance. To many Bolsheviks, facing not only near-destruction of their party's organization but an upsurge of patriotic feeling among ordinary Russians, Lenin's attitude seemed little short of suicidal.

Yet Lenin had never been more confident – now he *knew* that capitalism was about to be destroyed not only in Russia but throughout the world. For the war proved that capitalism had reached its ultimate phase, imperialism. Once it had been a progressive and liberating force, but that was now far behind. Competition, the life-blood of the old capitalism, had been replaced by monopoly as capital became concentrated in fewer and fewer hands and as economic activity came to be dominated by a few giant corporations. The decay of political liberalism was additional proof of this trend towards monopoly. Late-capitalist regimes were increasingly repressive towards their own citizens; but they had also become externally aggressive as the ruling élites were driven by their greed for profits and their need for markets to fight the élites of other countries for the control of colonies. The war, therefore, was the inevitable outcome of the contradictions of late capitalism's final phase.

But it would also prove to be capitalism's death spasm, since the imperialist states were suffering fierce internal opposition on two fronts: from national liberation movements in the colonies and from the proletariat at home. These anti-imperialist thrusts threatened the tsarist regime as well, though Russia's position was, as it happened, peculiar. The country was a great colonial power which oppressed 100 million non-Russians, yet it was also on capitalism's periphery and itself exploited by the more advanced nations. Looking to both West and East, Russia linked the two worlds of imperialism, but as the link it was the weakest and most vulnerable point in the system. Sooner or later the system would burst apart there. When that happened the Russian proletariat would begin capitalism's world-wide destruction by overthrowing the autocracy and then launching a revolutionary war which would liberate both the Western proletariat and the oppressed peoples of the East.

3

Was this the fantasy of an exile living in comfortable Switzerland far from the pulse of events? Perhaps. Yet Lenin was certainly not wrong in thinking that the war had rekindled a revolutionary situation in Russia and that the situation was becoming more acute by the day. The government's mismanagement of the war was now having dire effects upon civilians – most obviously upon evacuees, but also upon the living conditions of those far behind the lines. The effects were particularly severe in Petrograd, whose labour force had increased by more than half during the war years as peasants flooded in to work in its defence industries. The influx worsened the housing shortage, but a still more drastic deterioration occurred in the food supply. This city, with two and a half million inhabitants by 1917, was like an island needing to be supplied from overseas in that it was dependent for its food supplies on agricultural areas hundreds of miles to the south. Peasants, however, were increasingly reluctant to part with their produce because there was little they could buy with the money they got for it. Even when they were ready to sell, a collapsing railway system was less and less capable of delivering produce to the capital. Scarcity of goods was reflected in price rises that outstripped wage rises, and by the end of 1916 the shortage of grain in particular, and hence of bread, had become critical. Not only were basic foodstuffs being priced out of reach; the same was happening to that other staple of life in Russia – fuel for heating. Coal no longer came from

Britain via the Baltic, and by the unusually cold winter of 1916–17 the over-stretched railways were by no means making good the loss with domestic coal and timber.

Workers' readiness to put up with the privations of war was not helped by severe curbs on the liberties they had known before the war – trade unions were suspended, workers' publications and meetings banned. Nor was civilian morale helped by a thickening flurry of rumours. There were lurid stories about the empress and her confidant, the notorious Rasputin, who were widely thought to be running the country while the emperor was away at army headquarters. More damaging still were accusations, aimed particularly at the German-born empress, that the war effort was being undermined by treason in high places.

As the mood soured, strike activity resumed. 1915 saw some 900 strikes, and in 1916 the number rose to 1,400. The strikes, moreover, followed the pattern Lenin for one had hoped for and predicted. At first they were pre-dominantly economic in their demands: but as the conditions of life worsened and the influence of the minority of advanced workers increased, so the strikes more and more took on a political colouring. In 1916 the strikes lasted longer and attracted wider support. A sign of the changing temper of the workers was that in January 1916 only 67,000 in Petrograd responded to a call to strike in commemoration of Bloody Sunday. In January 1917 a similar appeal brought out 145,000 Petrograders – virtually half the industrial labour force. Those to left and right who had predicted that a war would destroy tsarism might well, it began to look, have been prophetic.

One sign of the deepening crisis was that the left liberal/moderate revolutionary tactic seemed to be failing. This could be seen in the fate of the WICs' Workers' Groups, which had tried hard to create an atmosphere conducive to all-class action against the government. They had hoped to improve worker-employer relations by introducing conciliation boards into factories. They had hoped, too, to improve workers' conditions by setting up public canteens and to do something about the food supply by convening an All-Russian Congress of Food Supply on which all classes would be represented. But these and other such ideas were all vetoed by government and industrialists alike. The workers were meanwhile becoming impossible to hold. The Workers' Groups had warned against isolated strike action and argued for a common anti-governmental front with other classes, and they had opposed the strike called in 1916 to commemorate Bloody Sunday. A year later, their tactic in ruins, they had no alternative but to endorse the summons to strike on 9 January 1917.

More radical factions were now making the running in the labour movement. Among them were the Interregionalists, anti-war Social Democrats who aimed to reunite the Bolsheviks and Mensheviks; anti-war Mensheviks and SRs; and, above all, the Bolsheviks. Crushed after the outbreak of the war, when their Petrograd membership had fallen to about a hundred, the Bolsheviks had sprung back, reorganized and recruited, and by the end of

1916 there were almost 3,000 of them in Petrograd. Numbers were still tiny – on the eve of the February Revolution no more than 2 per cent of Petrograd workers were active members of revolutionary parties. Yet even without direct revolutionary guidance, the workers were moving in the direction the most radical revolutionaries wanted. The police might repeatedly decapitate the Petrograd revolutionary leadership by arresting its members and closing its printing presses, yet they were helpless to stop the deepening of the crisis and the approach of that Rubicon at which a revolutionary situation crosses over into a revolution.

4

Events were now moving so rapidly that Lenin for one found it hard to keep pace with them. He had written in 1915: 'no socialist has ever guaranteed that this war (and not the next one), that today's revolutionary situation (and not tomorrow's) will produce a revolution'. And as late as January 1917, speaking in Zurich, he had admitted his doubts as to whether people of his generation would 'live to see the decisive battles of this coming revolution'.[7] Little did he guess that in three months he would be back in Russia and in nine months its effective ruler. For 'this war' was, as it happened, doing the Bolsheviks' business more thoroughly than he could have imagined.

In Petrograd in January 1917, flour was so short that some bakeries had closed altogether; others were selling no more than one-tenth of their pre-war output of bread. Meat and sausage had disappeared from the shops and milk become unaffordable. Boots and medicines were among other vital commodities no longer found, while firewood had become so expensive that the poor were having to choose between eating and keeping warm. That food and fuel were still available to the rich of course made the poor even less willing to accept their own deprivation of them. Observing people's misery and desperation, a secret police agent predicted 'The underground revolutionary parties are preparing a revolution, but revolution, if it takes place, will be quite spontaneous, quite likely a hunger riot.'[8]

The strike movement intensified through January and into February, reaching workers, in textile mills for instance, who had not been involved before. The distinction between economic and political demands was becoming obliterated. People were striking against catastrophic living conditions, and the government was now universally blamed for these. Getting rid of the government therefore seemed the only solution, but that required more than strike action. Marches and demonstrations multiplied, and as the workers took their protests from the suburbs into the city centre the revolutionary situation turned into a revolution.

The change came on 23 February, International Women's Day, when women textile workers marched into the streets with cries of 'Bread!' and called on other workers to join them. The next day strikes and demonstrations occurred throughout the city, but together with the cries for 'Bread!' there was an insistent chanting of 'Down with the autocracy!' The first was the cry of the masses, the second until recently the cry of no more than a minority, but now in Petrograd both had come to the fore of popular consciousness; and crowds driven by these two demands, and seeing the second as the condition of achieving the first, were about to destroy tsarism.

On 25 February the city became virtually paralysed by a general strike involving more than 200,000 workers. That day Nicholas, who had just returned to army headquarters, sent orders to the Petrograd military commander to end the disorders. In normal circumstances this should have been easy enough, since the authorities had no less than three levels of defence against trouble-makers – police, mounted Cossacks with their whips, and finally a huge army garrison with its rifles and machine-guns. But circumstances were no longer normal. The police were a mere 3,000 and cordially hated; and ominous signs for the authorities had appeared that the Cossacks and the troops might no longer be wholly reliable.

The Cossacks had seemed reluctant to disperse the demonstrators and had let some pass between and even under their horses – the revolution, as Trotsky would put it, 'made its first step towards victory under the belly of a Cossack's horse'.[9] The crucial factor, however, was the attitude of the soldiers, some of whom had already shown their sympathies by mingling with the crowds. On 14 December 1825, remember, the prospect of popular passions infecting the soldiers had terrified the Decembrists, who had chosen defeat as a lesser evil than victory achieved with the help of an unleashed populace and soldiery. Now the fusion of peasant soldiers and people which the radicals of 1825 had dreaded was about to be accomplished. Had the Petrograd garrison with its perhaps 400,000 men consisted of the well-seasoned and disciplined soldiers who guarded the capital in peacetime, then the authorities' task would not have been difficult. These, however, were raw recruits, some even strikers conscripted as a punishment, and they had by no means been insulated against the emotions now driving the civilian population. On 26 February they were for the first time ordered to shoot at demonstrators. The next day the mutiny began when soldiers of the Volynsky regiment refused to march against a demonstration and killed their commander instead. The mutiny then spread like wildfire. By the evening of the 28th the revolution was in effect over: no loyal detachments were holding out any longer and almost all high functionaries of the tsarist regime had been arrested or killed or had fled. The capital was awash with jubilant crowds; there was a lot of looting and much killing, especially of policemen and army officers. Tsarism had proved to be so rotten that after a mere five days of rioting it had collapsed, and something which 'society' had dreaded ever since Pugachev had come to pass. The masses, whom the state had failed to educate or to draw into civil society and whom even the best of the privileged had failed to find a common language with, were off the leash and in danger of going on the rampage.

Right and left have tended to agree on one thing at least: that this revolution which toppled tsarism in February 1917 was not 'spontaneous'. Thus for the *émigré* historian, George Katkov, the regime did not so much collapse as was pushed (the main pushers being liberals and agents of imperial Germany), while for Leon Trotsky the revolution's guiding force was provided by 'conscious and tempered workers educated for the most part by the party of Lenin'.[10] In fact the overthrow of tsarism was largely the work of the unguided and unorganized masses in a city where acute and rapidly worsening privation created an irresistible groundswell of feeling that ordinary people would never have wellbeing unless they destroyed this government and the existing social system.

True, conspirators had done their utmost to ram this message home. Much the most important of these were, as we have seen, the Bolsheviks, whose slogans spoke to the feelings of ordinary Petrograders more than any others. Yet this would not be a contrived revolution, and on 23 February the Petrograd Bolsheviks had no more inkling of the epoch-making events about to unfold than had Lenin in faraway Zurich. The Bolsheviks had done nothing to create and little to canalize the seething discontents (though they would soon begin to manipulate them very dexterously); and the reshaping of popular consciousness had been the result not so much of Bolshevik agitation as of spontaneous processes which the Bolsheviks had gratefully taken advantage of.

The loathing ordinary Russians felt for 'them' went far back, as we know, but it had become more intense in the late nineteenth and the opening years of the twentieth century. What had saved the old order was that the tsar was untouched by this loathing, indeed was seen as a semi-divine protector of his people against the evils and injustices of life. Between 1905 and 1917, however, this immunity was finally destroyed. No longer a protector, the tsar crossed over in the popular perception to being the leader of 'them', the chief of the 'thieves'; and the sense of his betrayal was heightened by wartime rumours that he and his family were in league with the enemy. The discrediting of the tsar removed any lingering shred of legitimacy that the government apparatus might have had in peasant eyes – but it also undermined the regime's ultimate sanction, the army. For the peasant who got conscripted was expected to give blind obedience to someone who was a landlord in uniform and might well recall the master or the master's son at home. Fear of the consequences of not obeying was a powerful enough reason for doing what you were told, but in the army there was an additional reason for obedience: the soldier might see the officer not so much as a landlord but as the servant of the tsar, the instrument of his will and thus indirectly at least of the will of God. However, by the time the soldier was exposed to the carnage of the First World War that perception had either vanished or could do nothing whatever for discipline. When the soldiers were sent out into the turbulent streets of Petrograd in February 1917, there was nothing but their fear to hold them.

And set against that were the faces, the shouts, the appeals of men and even more tellingly perhaps of women who pleaded with them to disobey the orders of the landlords in uniform and to risk death themselves rather than inflict it on them, their brothers and sisters in the street. Here and there a brave decision was made, the fetters of fear were snapped: and once a few had snapped they were all snapping in a headlong rush as the soldiers shed their fear of the officer-landlords and did to them what, had the mutiny failed, they would have done to the soldiers. Red, the age-old colour of peasant rebellion, the colour of fire, of blood, of courage, and now, they discovered, of socialism, was everywhere in the streets; and the images and emblems of a once-revered tsarism were rapidly toppled from plinths and stripped from buildings. What Radishchev and Herzen had feared but many other radicals had longed for had at last come to pass. Russia had had its revolution.

5

The February Revolution gave power to the liberals; to be more exact, it allowed them to fulfil their ambition of forming a government. But this was a strange outcome. For the people who had made the revolution and were now drunk (often literally) with its success were certainly not liberals, and the red festooning the streets was certainly not a liberal colour. Equally certainly, these were not the circumstances in which the liberals had expected or wanted to form a government. They had envisaged an orderly transfer of power with the monarchy remaining in a purely symbolic role yet by its very presence acting as a force for stability. They had assumed that their takeover would stave off the disaster of revolution; but in fact it was 'the disaster' which had precipitated them into government. Why, then, did these unrevolutionary liberals with the pince-nezed, all too bourgeois Milyukov at their head, emerge as the apparent victors of the February Revolution? Simply because this revolution, unlike the October one to come, had had no organizers: it was, as we have seen, an unprompted and unguided convulsion, and there were no revolutionaries waiting in the wings, blueprint in hand, to take over. As tsarism tottered only the Petrograd liberals, who were numerous, self-confident, knowledgeable and mentally prepared for the task, could take on the awesome responsibility of filling the power vacuum and saving the country from anarchy. On 27 February a provisional committee of the Duma was set up to try to take control of the situation. The next day this announced that it had assumed the functions of government.

Then on 1 March a Provisional Government was established with the respected zemstvo leader Prince G. E. Lvov as prime minister and Milyukov as foreign minister and power behind the throne.

But by what right had the liberals taken over? Till a few days before they could have given a clear-cut answer: they had been appointed by the tsar in response to the wishes of the people. But now tsarism had gone and the monarchy itself was hanging by a thread. The only hope of saving it was for Nicholas, who had ridden out the revolution at army headquarters, to abdicate speedily in favour of his son and then appoint his brother, Grand Duke Michael, to act as regent. This would have been the ideal solution for the liberals; they would have had a free hand yet could still have called on the traditional reflex of obedience to authority. But the solution did not work because Nicholas, unable to bear parting with his son, abdicated instead on behalf of Michael, who then refused the offer. The refusal came on 3 March at the end of a tense encounter with the new cabinet at which Milyukov had made an impassioned plea to him to accept. If the new government was to be strong, Milyukov had urged, the familiar symbol of the monarchy was vital, and without it the government was unlikely to survive. Most of his colleagues, however, argued against – the intense unpopularity of the monarchy had made them reluctant republicans. They felt unable to guarantee the new monarch's safety, and that decided the issue. After some minutes of private reflection Michael rejected the throne, adding, however, that he would accept it if the Constituent Assembly chose to offer it to him. The Constituent Assembly never did. Michael's 'no' had, to Milyukov's despair, put an end to the centuries-old Russian monarchy.

The monarchy's unexpected demise left the new government naked, unprotected by the veil of charismatic authority which had assured obedience to its predecessors. For the first time the Russians had a government which could not claim to express the will of a tsar and therefore could make no claim to being the voice of God. Whose will, then, did it express? And why should anyone obey it?

The liberal lawyers who drew up Michael's abdication statement described the Provisional Government as having come into existence 'On the initiative of the State Duma'.[11] But giving it legitimacy via the Duma was far from easy. There was a technical problem – the Duma had been prorogued on 27 February and would never officially meet again. The Provisional Government was therefore the illegitimate offspring of a body which had already passed into history. But a more serious objection was that the Duma had no authority whatever in the eyes of the masses – being its offshoot would as a result do the Provisional Government no good at all. The disagreeable but unavoidable fact was that this was a revolutionary government, at least in its origin. Asked 'Who chose you?', Milyukov, who of all the ministers had most wanted the protection of the monarchy, was forced to reply: 'We were chosen by the Russian revolution.'[12] That was the truthful answer; it was also the only possible one while turbulence still raged in the streets. Having been brought to power by revolution, the new government would have to answer to those who had made the revolution. And in reality it had shared power with revolutionaries from the outset.

6

The day of tsarism's fall, 27 February, had seen the creation not only of the Provisional Government but also of the Petrograd Soviet of Workers' (and soon of Soldiers') Deputies. The two bodies were camped in the very same building, the Tauride Palace, home of the Duma, the government taking the right wing and the Soviet appropriately enough the left. In this stately setting the two Russias came face to face and jostled uncomfortably in the corridors. By the evening of 27 February the Duma deputies had already become a minority in their own building. Nikolai Sukhanov, the revolution's Menshevik chronicler, noticed how the palace 'was obviously filling up with an alien population, in fur coats, working-class caps, or army greatcoats', while the deputies 'looked like masters of the house rather shocked by the roistering of their uninvited guests'.[13]

The two bodies were obvious rivals, yet they did not fight and in fact they had every reason to collaborate. The immediate bonding factor was fear. Both were worried by the marauding troops and workers outside; and both feared that loyal troops might yet restore the autocracy, in which case their members would finish on the gallows. The immediate need, therefore, was to impose order on the mutinous troops outside and shape them into a fighting force which could defend the revolution. But even when fear for their own survival had passed, there was still good reason for the two sides to collaborate. The ministers knew all too well that they owed their positions to the supporters of the Soviet. Without the Soviet they were helpless. Only the Soviet could control the mutinous troops. Only the Soviet could get the factories working again. Only the Soviet could get the trams running and the printing presses rolling. Once normality was restored the old habit of obedience to the government would with luck return. But for the moment people were in shock after the collapse of everything familiar and they would listen only to their own leaders. The liberals were not, however, going to defer to the Soviet any longer than necessary; and they hoped that the practice of democracy would soon puncture the more unrealistic expectations of the masses and make them accept the good sense of what the government told them.

But why was the Soviet so ready to co-operate with these powerless liberals? Why did collaboration between the two Russias come so easily? In the months leading up to the revolution class antagonisms had, after all, been becoming more acute. A strong current had been pushing the workers towards the Bolsheviks; there had been next to no popular support for the Duma; the Workers' Groups' efforts at class collaboration had been a dismal failure; and the Menshevik and SR defensists who preached collaboration and the necessity of a bourgeois regime had appeared to be a defeated and dwindling minority. Yet now things could not have been more different: it was the Bolsheviks who to their dismay found themselves isolated and going against the current. They might have expected to have a majority at least among the 850-odd worker delegates to the Soviet; in fact they were in a small minority. When on 28 February the Bolshevik Bonch-Bruevich published a manifesto calling for a revolutionary government and a 'merciless struggle' against the possessing classes, he won almost no support. It was not surprising that when two more senior Bolsheviks, Stalin and Kamenev, arrived in Petrograd in mid-March they decided upon an altogether more moderate line. But why had the Bolsheviks been wrong-footed? Why had the conciliators come out on top?

The reason was that people were for the moment happy, even euphoric; and at the same time they were sated. Overthrowing the tsar and tsarism had been a mighty achievement, and for now it was quite enough. A social revolution was certainly implicit in the political revolution; more distantly an economic revolution could be discerned in it as well. But the new social and economic relationships could be worked out over time and, it was hoped, without violence. Meanwhile, success created a mood for unity and conciliation. Only unity, it was felt, could guarantee the defeat of any attempted counter-revolution, and the inclination towards conciliation was strengthened by the apparent rallying of many of the privileged to the new order. There was, too, a certain nervousness among the workers and their leaders at the prospect of having to manage everything themselves. How, overnight, could they acquire the skills necessary to running a modern government and economy? The workers were in fact sobered in their moment of victory by realizing how enormous the country's problems were and how incapable they were of solving them on their own. They needed the skills and know-how of the privileged – they would therefore have to try to live in peace with them.

In this atmosphere it had not been hard for the Duma committee and the Soviet to agree on a government and a programme. The government, the Soviet executive commttee decided, should be a purely bourgeois body and no Soviet member should join it. That was basic Menshevik doctrine: the bourgeois had to govern after the bourgeois revolution. The Soviet would exert pressure from the sidelines; it would offer the government conditional support – and it set up a committee to ensure that its conditions were complied with; but it would do no more than that. The liberals would have preferred to have Soviet members inside the government, and they offered places to Nikolai Chkeidze, the Soviet's Menshevik chairman, and to Alexander Kerensky, a lawyer who had led the Labour Group in the Duma and was now the Soviet's deputy chairman. Chkeidze properly enough declined, but Kerensky, who as a non-Marxist had more freedom of manoeuvre, defied the Soviet and became minister of justice. As a result there was a direct link between the two bodies in the person of this eloquent lawyer, who acted as a reminder to his liberal colleagues of the government's revolutionary origins and as a reminder to the Soviet of the difficulties and responsibilities of government.

The agreement between the two sides called for full civil liberties and democratic rights, an amnesty for political prisoners, new police and local government administrations and, vitally, for the calling in the very near future of a Constituent Assembly elected on a democratic franchise. The Soviet's social and economic demands did not, however, enter into the agreement. The two were hardly likely to agree on them, and fundamental issues were anyway to be left to the Constituent Assembly. That alone could decide whether Russia became a republic or returned to a form of monarchy. That alone could adjudicate the question of nationalities. Above all, that alone could decide the burning question of the land.

The government promised to convene the assembly as soon as possible, though there would have to be a delay, Prince Lvov explained, of between three and six months. A commission would first have to decide on the system for electing the assembly. Organizing the elections would be difficult, given that millions of voters were away at the front and that the old administrative structures were breaking down. Practical problems were not, however, the only reason for the delay. Liberal ministers had little incentive to hurry when an assembly elected on Russia's first ever democratic franchise would most likely have a socialist majority. Meanwhile, the government promised that even before the assembly met it would provide the country 'with laws safeguarding civil liberty and equality to enable all citizens to apply freely their spiritual forces to creative work for the benefit of the country'.[14] These lofty phrases glossed over – for a while successfully – the reality that the government could offer the newly enfranchised very little of what mattered to them.

The cohabitation of Provisional Government and Soviet had got off to an auspicious start, but the dual-power formula would not be so easy to apply at the bottom of society – to the relationship between workers and bosses, soldiers and officers, peasants and landowners.The workers, for instance, were not prepared to have 'democracy' limited to public life: it had to enter their own working lives. Now that the autocracy of the tsar had been removed, the autocracy of those little tsars, the factory bosses and managers, had to go as well. In a democratic Russia, workers had to be treated as human beings – paid properly, not made to work more than eight hours a day, and given citizens' rights within the factory as well as outside it. There were violent outbursts against detested bosses, some of whom suffered the humiliation of being carted out of their factories in a wheelbarrow with sacks over their heads and dumped in the street outside. Yet this revolt against factory autocrats was not a revolt against capitalism or the capital-

ist classes as such. The workers did not demand socialism or even nationalization of industry; they simply demanded better conditions and some control over factory management. The bosses willy-nilly conceded both: an
eight-hour day without any lowering of wages and the right of workers to
form their own factory committees. The committees spread rapidly and
made the radical-sounding demand for 'workers' control'. What that meant,
however, was not that the workers should take over, but rather that their
representatives should exercise the same close control over the management
that the Petrograd Soviet exercised over the Provisional Government and
that they should press it for change as unremittingly as the Soviet, or so they
assumed, was pressing the government.

Thus the accommodation between government and Soviet at the top was
mirrored in the new relationship which emerged between management and
workers. The managers would go on managing, but now they would be
closely monitored by and answerable to the workers' representatives. It was
much the same in the army. Soldiers had felt the same alienation from officers
that workers had felt from managers and peasants from estate owners. The
officers were 'masters', often arbitrary and brutal ones, and the autocratic
regime within the army put the soldiers completely at their mercy. After
February, however, the officer-autocrat was no more tolerable than the tsar-
autocrat or the manager-autocrat. From now on ways would have to be
found that safeguarded the soldiers' rights and dignity without destroying the
operational efficiency of the army. Order Number 1, issued on 1 March to the
local garrison by the Petrograd Soviet, set out to do this. The Order author-
ized each company to elect a soldiers' committee and also to send a representative to the Soviet; laid it down that soldiers should not obey any orders that
conflicted with those from the Soviet; put weapons under the control of committees rather than officers; imposed strict military discipline on soldiers yet
insisted that outside the service they should have full citizens' rights; forbade
rudeness towards soldiers and in particular use of the demeaning 'thou' ('ty',
the form of address used by adults towards children); and replaced the old
officers' titles by 'Mr Lieutenant', 'Mr Colonel', and so on.

The Order, intended for the Petrograd garrison, rapidly transformed
relationships throughout the Russian army. It affirmed the soldiers' dignity
and seemed to give them some power. Yet it stopped short of turning everything upside down, and rumours that it had given the soldiers the right to
elect their officers were promptly discounted by the Soviet. Like the workers, the soldiers would, however, now have the right to humane treatment
and to exercise 'control' over – i.e. to supervise – their superiors. The change
was enough to prevent any widespread revolt against the officers. Nor did
the soldiers desert in any numbers and go back to their villages. Bolshevik
anti-war propaganda at this stage cut very little ice with them. They wanted
to finish the war and beat the Germans, but they wanted as rapid and pain-
less a completion as possible and they expected the Soviet to make sure that
the government did not drag the war out.

In the countryside, news of the revolution provoked a few attacks on estates, but on the whole it was received calmly. The news did of course have a profound impact: it removed whatever justification noble landholding still had in peasant eyes. If there was no tsar, then there certainly could be no landowner. However, the peasants made no immediate attempt to evict their enemies. Rather than seize the land, they waited to be given it by the new government. Meanwhile, they, like workers and soldiers, set up their own local executive committees.

The honeymoon of the dual-power regime did not, however, last long either at the top or at the bottom. At the top, the problem was that the relationship between Provisional Government and Petrograd Soviet was intrinsically unstable. While formal power lay with the government, it could in reality do little without the Soviet's agreement, since ordinary Russians looked to that as the only body from which they would accept orders. The result, as Prince Lvov put it, was a government which had 'authority without power' and a Soviet with 'power without authority'. It would have been easier if the two had agreed on what they wanted to do, but the common commitment to democracy and civil rights was by no means enough to bond them. Democracy in the broad sense mattered little to the Soviet's constituents: they were concerned with everyday living conditions and the question of control or ownership of industry, the army and the land. But industry and the land were issues which only the Constituent Assembly could decide upon, and on these the liberal ministers had very different ideas from the Soviet.

There was, however, one issue on which the two parties did seem to agree: both wanted to continue the war to a successful conclusion. Yet even here there were fundamental differences behind the apparent consensus. The ministers most responsible for the war, Milyukov at Foreign Affairs and Guchkov, the armed forces' minister, wanted to continue the war until 'complete victory' and in particular until the Allies had honoured their promise of giving Russia Constantinople and the Straits. But that turned the war into a flagrantly imperialist one, something no decent socialist could stomach. What the Soviet and its supporters hoped was that the war would be brought to a rapid end as a result of revolution in Germany; until that happened, they stood for a war of revolutionary defence. But if they were hostile to Milyukov's imperialism, they were even more disturbed by what seemed to lie behind it. For the conviction was growing in liberal circles that a glorious conclusion to the war – such as the capture of Constantinople – was the one thing, in an otherwise hopeless situation, which might tilt the internal balance of power decisively in liberalism's favour. That made the war a burningly contentious issue; and large-scale demonstrations on 20–21 April against Milyukov's policy, which were countered by middle-class ones in the foreign minister's favour, suggested that the fragile class peace established in the wake of the February Revolution was beginning to collapse under the pressure of unresolvable internal contradictions.

But how could the relationship between these two reluctant partners be recast? An obvious solution was for the partner with power, the Soviet, to take over formal authority as well. In the Menshevik view, however, it was far too early for that. An alternative was for the soviets to withdraw into uncompromising opposition. But that too ran inadmissible risks. The liberal house of cards might collapse all too soon, leaving the soviets with no option but to take over; or else the army command and the propertied might attempt a counter-revolution, which if it succeeded would bury all February's gains. And by early May a majority of the Soviet executive felt that they had only one choice. 'Power' had to be fully and formally united with 'authority'; socialists had to join liberals, representatives of the people, those of the propertied classes, in a coalition government. The ambiguity of supporting the government yet refusing to take responsibility for what it did was no longer tolerable. Only a government with broad popular support could do what was urgently needed – stop the country falling to pieces and bring the war to a speedy and proper conclusion.

The decision had been difficult since it flouted a fundamental belief – that the socialists' task after the bourgeois revolution was to act as a strong, though peaceful, opposition. By May 1917 such standoffishness looked absurd and Kerensky's insistence on joining the government had been vindicated. When a new cabinet was announced on 5 May, Milyukov, the Soviet's prime bogy, and his ally Guchkov were no longer in it, while six of its members were socialists. Kerensky had taken over the Ministry of War, and among the newcomers V. M. Chernov, the SR leader, was minister of agriculture, I. G. Tsereteli, the most prominent Menshevik, was minister of posts and telegraphs, and another Menshevik, M. I. Skobelev, was minister of labour. To the Soviet's supporters it seemed that this influx of socialists into the government would lead to decisively different policies. Now the bourgeois ministers would have to submit to the Soviet's will, the war would be conducted properly, and the interests of workers, soldiers and peasants would be protected at the highest level.

The coalition of liberals and socialists lasted until the Bolshevik take-over, apart from three weeks in September when Kerensky ruled without a cabinet. It was, however, reconstructed in July, when Kerensky replaced the ineffectual Lvov as prime minister (while keeping the War Ministry), and it was reconstructed again in late September. But the socialist ministers did not achieve what their followers hoped for – they did not impose socialist policies and soon began to look less like men of power than the liberals' hostages. Even had they wanted to act decisively on the vital issues of land, peace and the economy, they would have been unable to: for they had to keep in with the liberals and the liberals' increasingly right-wing supporters, and they had of course to tread water until the still remote Constituent Assembly. But the root problem was that the ministers saw socialist policies as belonging for the moment to the realm of fantasy. The task for now was simply to consolidate the gains of February: to keep the alliance with the bourgeois alive and to prevent a break-down of order, which could only boost the hardline right. The inevitable result, however, of these very different views of what the socialist ministers should do was that an increasing wedge was driven between them and their supporters. By early summer the dual-power arrangement at the top no longer mirrored anything similar at the bottom. It assumed the existence of a middle road. But, alas, there was no such road, only the illusion of one, and lower down even the illusion had disappeared. While class collaboration continued at the level of government, a vicious class polarization had set in down below. The result was to leave the dual-power arrangement suspended in the air and to turn popular support more and more towards those who refused any compromise with 'them'.

At the bottom, hopes of inter-class co-operation had been short-lived. In the factories, employers were ready to make concessions on conditions of work, but they were unwilling to pay wage increases that kept up with or exceeded inflation. And they bitterly resented the new factory committees as an encroachment on their right of management. When workers went on strike over wages, they responded by dismissals or even wholesale lock-outs. By May the atmosphere in industry had become one of sharp confrontation. The employers' determination to show who were the bosses produced an increasing feeling among the workers that supervision of management was not enough. The dual-power arrangement mark one, as it were, simply would not work in the factories, just as it had not worked at the level of high politics. But the solution the politicians had then turned to – much closer collaboration, involving a full sharing of responsibility – was obviously not available to those who worked in the factories. Liberal and socialist intellectuals might rub along well enough; however, between factory managers and factory hands (the Dickensian term fully applies) the chasm was enormous and developments since February had if anything made it more unbridgeable. Employers waged war against employees by cutting production and scaring them with the spectre of mass employment. Employees replied by demanding state economic regulation in order to stop this economic sabotage by the bourgeois. They tried, too, to protect themselves and their plants by setting up armed units of 'Red Guards'. And since 'control' was clearly not enough, the factory committees increasingly demanded worker self-management. These men were not far removed, after all, from the villages. They wanted to reclaim the factories from owners and managers much as the peasants wanted to reclaim the land from owners and stewards. And they wanted to run them rather as the peasants wanted to run their communities: collectively and democratically, making each self-governing and as far as possible self-sufficing.

Among soldiers, too, hopes that a new deal might be worked out with their masters faded rapidly. Order Number 1 had assumed a radical transformation of army relationships, but it had also assumed that a stable *modus vivendi* would emerge from the restructuring: officers would keep undisputed operational control, while non-operational relationships would be humanized and democratized. The Order had suggested in addition that soldiers could look to the Soviet leadership to protect them and veto anything undesirable proposed by the government. This alternative source of authority over the army was, however, removed by the creation of the coalition: soldiers no longer had powerful friends outside the government to whom they could look for protection.To rub salt in the wound, it was a socialist minister of war, Alexander Kerensky, who now tried to stiffen the officers' authority and to impose discipline upon the ranks. The officers for their part had responded to Order Number 1 and the new self-assertiveness of the soldiers as bitterly as had industrialists to factory committees and wage demands. Here too there could be no easy cohabitation as between liberal and socialist intellectuals. Here too the relations between the two sides degenerated into acrimony. The disappearance of the hope of a transformed and more human army increased the soldiers' reluctance to serve. From the spring, desertions became rife. And when in June Kerensky ordered a new and large-scale offensive, the result was a rapid collapse of morale: desertions reached massive proportions and there were outbreaks of fraternizing with the enemy. To the government, reviving the war effort appeared vital. Only if Russia kept the eastern front alive and helped defeat the Germans could it have any influence on the eventual peace talks. But these high strategic considerations meant nothing to war-weary soldiers, who by now felt badly let down by their own leaders. They wanted peace and they wanted it straightaway. For these peasants-in-arms, peace meant not only an end to carnage and to abuse by officers. It meant freedom to go back to the villages, to settle scores with the officers' civilian counterparts, and to fulfil their age-old dream of getting the land.

For in the countryside, too, whatever honeymoon there had been – and it had never been more than an absence of hostilities – had ended. The government had prevaricated on the land issue. Only the Constituent Assembly, it had declared, could resolve this; meanwhile the law had to be upheld and property respected. It set up a Central Land Committee and a network of provincial committees to consider the issue, but to peasants this simply seemed a way of staving off a decision in their favour. The issue was particularly cruel for the SRs, and it highlighted how great a sacrifice class collaboration exacted from the radical parties. They after all were the peasant party; expropriation and socialization of private land was their basic policy, and there can be no doubt that this reflected the wishes of most peasants. Yet the SRs were for the time being stymied on this by the commitment which, as democrats, they had made to the Constituent Assembly. Their room for manoeuvre was further limited by the fact that they were minor partners in a coalition which, though headed from July by a nominal SR (Kerensky had joined the party in March), was dominated by liberals and Mensheviks who opposed any immediate expropriation. The issue was especially tormenting for the SR leader, Chernov, who was agriculture minister from May until August. He accepted that the final decision on the land had to be made by the Assembly, but in the interim he tried to head off peasant indignation by urging that land should be provisionally transferred from private ownership to the control of the Land Committees. Here, however, he came up against a veto from both his Kadet and his Menshevik colleagues, who insisted that tampering with land ownership prior to the Assembly would only increase anarchy in the countryside. It was no wonder that strains within the SR party, torn between loyalty to its coalition partners and commitment to its own followers, became acute and that increasing numbers sided with the dissident left SR faction, which in October would break away from the main party altogether. It was no wonder also that the peasants, despairing of their leaders, started taking matters into their own hands. The waves of violence began in April and were particularly pronounced in the traditionally disturbed central and Middle Volga provinces. Estate lands were seized and trees cut down. The violence intensified in June, and by July it seemed to be billowing out of control.

By the summer, then, workers, soldiers and peasants were deeply at odds with the moderate socialists who claimed to represent them. They were fed up with delay, with compromise, with turning the other cheek; they longed for action, and some were already taking it. True, the moderates had not yet finally exhausted their followers' patience. Yet it was hard to see how they could survive except by admitting the failure of the dual-power experiment and thus the bankruptcy of the entire strategy they had followed since February. It was not surprising that the Bolsheviks, after a bad start, were attracting more and more people with their anti-dual power slogan, 'All power to the soviets'. As the moderates floundered, the Bolsheviks could only benefit from the one fact most workers and soldiers knew about them: that they hated privileged Russia and were determined to smash it.

7

The Bolsheviks' wretched start to the revolution was due, as we saw, to the strong current in favour of unity and conciliation. Yet part of the reason why they seemed wrong-footed in these opening days was of their own, and in particular of Lenin's, making. Lenin had been utterly opposed to a bourgeois regime being installed after the revolution, but he had also insisted on the distinction between the bourgeois and socialist revolutions and rejected Trotsky's idea of merging the two. Had he taken Trotsky's line, then the Petrograd Bolsheviks would have had no doubt about what they ought to do: oppose the Provisional Government with might and main. As it was, however, they were left uncertain how to react once a bourgeois government had in fact installed itself. After some initial belligerence most of them swung to what in effect was the Menshevik position: this was the time for a bourgeois democratic republic. And caution remained the order of the day for them until Lenin came and scattered it to the winds in April.

The German government had provided the Bolshevik leader with a special train to bring him back from Switzerland in the hope that he would create trouble for the Provisional Government and so disrupt the war effort; and from the moment he arrived at the capital's Finland Station, on 3 April, to an ecstatic welcome from a throng of supporters, he started doing just that. Brushing aside a speech of welcome by Chkeidze, who urged the need for revolutionary unity, he insisted that 'The piratical imperialist war is the beginning of civil war throughout Europe . . . . The worldwide Socialist revolution has already dawned . . . Any day now the whole of European capitalism may crash. Long live the world-wide Socialist revolution!'[15] To any Menshevik these inflammatory words simply confirmed that Lenin was mad; but they were shocking too to many of his own supporters. And he shocked his supporters again the next day when he outlined what became known as his April Theses.

Rejecting a war of defence, Lenin urged soldiers to start fraternizing with the enemy; he also demanded the confiscation of landed estates and the nationalization of all land; and he called for the creation of a new kind of state – a republic of soviets rather than a parliamentary republic. He even suggested a new name for the party: 'instead of "Social-Democracy" . . . we must call ourselves the *"Communist Party"*'. Most important of all, he rethought his position on the bourgeois revolution, dropping his insistence on the strict separation of this from the socialist and in effect moved close to Trotsky's belief in telescoping the two. 'The peculiarity of the present situation in Russia', he argued, 'is that it represents a *transition* from the first stage of the revolution . . . to its second stage, which is to place power in the hands of the proletariat and the poorest strata of the peasantry.'[16] It was telltale that he no longer used the terms 'bourgeois revolution' and 'socialist revolution': instead he spoke of the 'first' and 'second' stages of a single revolution. And the first stage was already behind, the revolution was now in transition to its socialist stage. That being so, the only tolerable form of government was a revolutionary and soviet one. Such a government, he cautioned, would not set out to introduce socialism straightaway, but it would at once take control of the production and distribution of goods.

This was heady stuff – far too heady for most of Lenin's colleagues. *Pravda* dutifully printed the theses, only to disown them in an editorial by Kamenev. 'As for Lenin's general schema, it seems to us unacceptable in so far as it proceeds from the assumption that the bourgeois democratic revolution is finished and counts on the immediate conversion of this revolution into a Socialist revolution.'[17] When it came to a vote in the party's Petrograd committee, the theses were rejected by thirteen votes to two – a crushing defeat which underlined Lenin's position on the party's lunatic fringe. But Lenin fought his corner, as always. Time and time again he would argue, coerce and cajole his colleagues into adopting policies they had at first rejected as absurd, and never were his skills more evident than now. When the all-Russian party conference met in the last week of April, the theses won overwhelming approval. With this the Bolsheviks had the essence of the programme that would carry them to power in October (though they would, as we shall see, tack to the wind on the land question); and Kamenev and the others who formed what might be called the constitutionalist tendency within Bolshevism would from now on fight a losing battle against the combined might of the leader and an increasingly militant grass-roots following.

Why did Lenin win on this crucial issue? Partly of course because of his unique personal magnetism. Sukhanov, watching his arrival at the Finland Station, saw him as 'a bright, blinding, exotic beacon', obliterating everyone and everything else.[18] It was very hard to resist such a man. Moreover, with his slogans 'An end to the war', 'All land to the peasants', 'Peace, land and bread' and the most ringing of all, 'All power to the soviets', he had picked Bolshevism up from the floor and given it an immense popular appeal. And he had presented his followers with a clear choice of ways. Either they kept to the letter of Marxism, but lost him and never gained much of a popular following; or else they adopted his highly individual and very Russian interpretation of Marxism, and thus benefited from his leadership skills and had a real chance of conquering the masses. And his followers of course went for the second option.

While the Bolsheviks knew what they wanted, they were far from sure how to get it. Programme was one thing; tactics were another. 'All power to the soviets', were it ever implemented, would not give power to them: it would give it to their Menshevik and SR opponents. But even while they were a minority within the soviet movement, the slogan had its uses. It made clear their utter rejection of the dual-power idea. It underlined their commitment to the soviets as the only form of government compatible with socialism. (The Bolsheviks did, however, continue to pay lip service to the Constituent Assembly.) And it had the effect of taunting their rivals. 'Take power', it said, 'if you dare. Have the courage of your so-called socialist convictions.' That they themselves would take power, given the chance, they left no doubt. When, at the first All-Russian Congress of Soviets, Tsereteli declared that there was no party in Russia willing to assume power on its own, Lenin shouted back 'There is!' That was Lenin all over, and few outside his own following took his pretensions seriously.

The most obvious route to power was for the Bolsheviks to win a majority within the soviet movement. That would have seemed a remote prospect in February, but the party had grown rapidly since. There had been only 20,000 Bolsheviks at the time of the revolution; by May there were more than 80,000. True, they still had very little peasant following, and at the first All-Russian Peasant Congress in early May they were heavily outnumbered. However, they dominated a conference of Petrograd factory committees at the end of May and forced through a resolution demanding 'genuine workers' control', an end to the war and seizure of power by the soviets. Here and there soviets were doing just that, notably at Kronstadt, the naval base which guarded the capital. After these encouraging signs, the first All-Russian Congress of Soviets in early June came as an anti-climax: 105 Bolshevik delegates confronted 285 SRs and 248 Mensheviks, and the Central Executive Committee (CEC) was as a result swamped by their opponents. Yet if the Bolsheviks still lagged behind in the country as a whole, they were already poised to dominate Petrograd. The government's dilly-dallying over the Constituent Assembly played into their hands; so did the increasingly bitter struggle between workers and bosses and the Petrograd garrison's hostility to plans for a new offensive. Just how well the Bolsheviks were doing was shown on 18 June when a demonstration organized by the CEC was dominated not by its own slogans but by the Bolsheviks' – 'Down with the capitalist ministers', 'Bread, peace and freedom', 'All power to the soviets'. A popular head of steam was rapidly building up. The question was what the Bolsheviks would do with it and whether they could control it.

A crisis erupted in early July after the failure of Kerensky's offensive, which had led to a strong German counter-attack and the disintegration of the Russian army as soldiers abandoned their posts and fled. Had the offensive succeeded it would have stabilized the political situation, indeed tilted the power balance back towards the bourgeois, but its failure brought the passions of the Petrograd masses to fever pitch. On 3 July soldiers, sailors and workers converged in their thousands on the Tauride Palace, demanding that the CEC take power, and that there should be a purely soviet and socialist government. This was precisely what Bolshevik propaganda had been demanding since April. Yet events caught the Bolsheviks on the hop – they had not planned this bid for power and did not want it. The uprising was unwanted for two reasons: it was premature, and were it to succeed power would go not to the Bolsheviks but to the Mensheviks and SRs, who outnumbered them on the CEC by an overwhelming 203 to 35. Lenin rushed to Petrograd to try to limit the damage, but could do little. So indignant were the insurgents with the soviet leadership – this leadership which refused to take the power being offered it – that Chernov for one only narrowly missed being lynched. ('Take power, you son of a bitch, when they give it to you', someone shouted at him.) Then, however, the tide turned, helped by the release of documents which seemed to show Lenin as a German agent who was attempting to undermine the war effort on the enemy's behalf. Loyal guards regiments came to the rescue, the crowds dispersed, *Pravda* was closed down, and the Bolsheviks ran for cover.

The 'July Days' left several hundreds dead or wounded and were in other ways too a disaster for the Petrograd working class, whose members now suffered severe repression from a government which had recovered its nerve and was determined to end anarchy once and for all. The failed revolution was also a serious setback for the Bolsheviks. Kamenev was arrested; so too was Trotsky, who had returned to Russia in May, joined the Bolsheviks and was emerging as the party's most influential figure after Lenin; while Lenin himself, now widely reviled as a traitor, went into hiding and soon took refuge in Finland, where he would remain till October. The result of the crisis was a change in the power balance. The socialist ministers had been weakened, since they so obviously had no influence over the urban masses, and it was the Kadets who increasingly called the tune. The Kadets, moreover, were no longer a centrist party. Since March they had been inundated by people who would once have regarded them as dangerous radicals but now rallied to them as the last hope of stopping 'socialism'. The idea being increasingly floated in Kadet circles was that only a 'strong man' could restore order, and on 22 July General Lavr Kornilov, whom the Kadets saw as just such a man, was appointed commander-in-chief of the army. For the Kadets and their supporters, military dictatorship now seemed the only solution to the anarchy in the streets and at the front. The outcome of the July Days was therefore, in Bolshevik terms, a swing to counter-revolution, and a counter-revolution in which the moderate socialists were implicated by their continued membership of the government. Indeed, it was precisely in the aftermath of the crisis that Kerensky took over the premiership from Prince Lvov, who was not tough enough to deal with the disorder.

The July crisis sounded the death knell for dual power, though its burial was still three months away. The possessing classes had obviously given up any idea of dialogue and compromise – they would fight for their possessions; and any remaining loyalty to dual power among the workers drained away as a result of the repression which followed the crisis. Working-class support for the Mensheviks had been severely eroded even before July; now there were large-scale defections in addition from the SRs, who had hitherto won the support of most unskilled workers recently come from the countryside. Defectors inevitably turned to the Bolsheviks, whose membership had swollen by the end of July to over 200,000. As class hatred festered, the one party with an unblemished record of rejecting privileged Russia was bound to benefit. And newly recruited workers had every reason to feel at home among the Bolsheviks, for this was a proletarian party in reality as well as name. At the top, in the Central Committee, it was admittedly still a party of intellectuals. They, however, took pains to play the proletarian part – Lenin, for instance, had given up his bowler for a workman's peaked cap and spiced his talk with phrases like 'we, the workers'. Other than at the top, this was genuinely and overwhelmingly a party of the proletariat in culture and attitudes as well as in its policies. Moreover, it was increasingly a proletarian party, for as radical workers poured in, members of the intelligentsia moved away to the more congenial milieu of the moderate parties.

As right and left grew stronger and more uncompromising, the position of Kerensky and the moderate socialists became desperate: far from governing from an expanding centre, they found the middle position being rapidly eroded. 'I want to take a middle road', Kerensky lamented in July, 'but nobody will help me.'[19] The Kadets and the social forces arrayed behind them wanted a strong man to impose discipline on the army and the lower classes, while the supporters of the soviets were demanding a homogeneous socialist government with no middle-class participation. The government's position was weakened too by the lack of any representative body to uphold its authority: the Constituent Assembly remained a distant prospect and the Duma was discredited in the eyes of all but the propertied. Kerensky tried to make good the lack in mid-August by convening a so-called State Conference with representatives from all walks of public life; but the sharp divisions within it and the rapturous reception given by the right to General Kornilov merely underlined the gravity of the crisis. A fortnight later the right moved into action when Kornilov sent troops towards Petrograd with the aim of setting up a military dictatorship. The attempt at counter-revolution rapidly, however, degenerated into a fiasco. Kornilov's 'loyal' troops were half-hearted about their mission from the outset and were soon dissuaded from it by workers who rushed out from Petrograd to meet them. The working class as a whole and the various left-wing parties rallied in defence of the revolution; the coup fizzled out well before any troops got to Petrograd; and the would-be saviour of the nation then tamely gave himself up to arrest.

The Kornilov affair damaged Kerensky personally since he was widely suspected of being a party to it. It also destroyed any lingering shred of belief among the working class in dual power: for here was proof that the propertied were incorrigibly opposed to the revolution and determined to wrest back power from the people. Now, surely, the soviets' leaders would give up their alliance with the bourgeois; now, surely, they would insist on an all-socialist government. And for a time it seemed that they would. Yet when a Democratic Conference of socialist and working-class organizations met in mid-September, it failed to reach any clear-cut conclusion on whether Kadets should be included in the government. That left Kerensky with a free hand, and when a rejigged coalition was announced on 27 September it again contained half a dozen Kadets, including the deputy premier (A. I. Konovalov). Kerensky's idea was to hold on till the Constituent Assembly elections, now scheduled for 12 November, in the hope that against the odds they would legitimize his middle-of-the-road position. Meanwhile, he tried to boost his government by setting up a Council of the Republic, or pre-parliament, whose membership was dominated by moderate socialists. But support from the Council of the Republic could not disguise the fact that the dual-power arrangement had by now become little more than a ghostly pretence. A beleaguered and dwindling minority of intellectuals still clung to the idea; but it had lost all support among the working class and the soldiers of Petrograd, and support on the right was no more than lip service from people who for the time being could see no better alternative.

The setback to the right and the progressive collapse of the centre gave

the Bolsheviks their opening. For them the Kornilov affair had been a turning-point, ending whatever remained of the cloud which had hung over
them since the July Days. Now *their* patriotism could not be doubted: for
they had rallied to the defence of the endangered revolution and Bolshevik
party members, supporters and Red Guards had been the essence of the
resistance. Not only had Kornilov vindicated the Bolsheviks' hearts; he had
also vindicated their heads, showing how right they had been in distrusting
the traitorous and vengeful propertied classes. The ordinary people of
Russia had to make their own revolution and reconstruct society completely, eliminating the privileged from any position of influence within it –
few workers or soldiers in Petrograd now doubted that. The lesson was
rubbed in by worsening conditions of life. Real wages were now declining
relative to their spring levels. Food shortages were again becoming serious:
from now on there would be long queues for bread, milk and other essen-
tials. Factory bosses were staging their own version of the Kornilov offensive, closing factories or imposing lock-outs. Hunger and unemployment
inevitably increased the appeal of Bolshevik radicalism. On 31 August the
Bolsheviks reaped their reward when they gained a majority in the
Petrograd Soviet. On 5 September they did the same in Moscow. Urban
Russia, it seemed, was being swept irresistibly towards them. And a second
All-Russian Congress of Soviets, already postponed by a foot-dragging CEC
from September, was due to meet in October. When it met the Bolsheviks
would, if the present tendency continued, have a clear majority. This, admittedly, would be a congress of workers' and soldiers' deputies and hence representative of only a minority of Russians. The parallel peasant soviet
movement was still dominated by the SRs. But encouraging signs were
emerging for the Bolsheviks that the SR leadership was getting badly out of
line with its constituents. From July there had, as we have seen, been a
major upsurge in peasant seizures of land. And from September the peasant
mood turned uglier still: more and more violent attacks on noble properties
were being reported. The flames of burning manor houses in the autumn of
1917 gave the peasants' answer to the idea that there could be a peaceful
way forward by means of compromise and consensus. In the countryside, as
in the towns, whatever belief there had been in dual power had perished.

8

With the current running so strongly in the Bolsheviks' favour, it appeared
only a matter of time before they came to power. But how exactly would
they get power? And when? Both questions seemed to be answered by their
most famous slogan – 'All power to the soviets'. Once they had a majority
in the second Congress of Soviets they would come to power naturally,

almost constitutionally, and with any luck with a minimum of violence. That, however, was not at all the attitude of the most important Bolshevik. After the July Days Lenin had proposed that 'All power to the soviets' should be dropped. The government, he argued, had become a military dictatorship, peaceful development was impossible, and the only way forward was via an insurrection against the government and the soviet leadership. But to many of his colleagues this was perverse and even anti-Bolshevik thinking. 'All power to the soviets', the party's most famous and effective slogan, had seemed the very essence of Bolshevism. Now Lenin was proposing an uprising *against* the soviets, the outcome of which could hardly be a government of soviets. As usual, however, he won his opponents over, and the slogan was dropped. The soviets were not sacred; they were merely useful or not useful. And when the Bolsheviks got the upper hand in the Petrograd and Moscow Soviets and the soviets' usefulness was therefore no longer in doubt, the slogan was, to the general relief, reinstated.

From early September it looked as if the Bolsheviks could have the insurrection Lenin itched for and yet make a quasi-lawful take-over which would result in a government that was both soviet and Bolshevik-dominated. The rival claims of an armed uprising and a constitutional take-over continued nevertheless to divide the leadership. The obvious thing, many Bolsheviks argued, was to wait until the second Congress of Soviets. That, if it came up with the expected Bolshevik majority, would make the Bolshevik right to govern incontestable; and any violence they then had to use to make good their claim would be evidently justified. Lenin, however, fiercely opposed this 'constitutionalist' approach. In mid-September he fired off two letters from his Finnish refuge to his Central Committee colleagues, demanding that the party seize power straightaway rather than wait for the Congress. The majority of people, he insisted, were on the Bolsheviks' side; victory was assured; therefore, 'History will not forgive us if we do not assume power now'. Behind this argument for 'now' lurked a consideration that was not spelled out: if the Bolsheviks waited for the Congress and then took power in virtue of a popular vote, they would be accepting the electorate's absolute right to make and unmake governments. Lenin accepted no such right. 'We must not be deceived', he wrote on 12 September, 'by the election figures; elections prove nothing.'[20] The only way forward in fact was to seize power first and then, from a position of strength, create the conditions which ensured that they, not their rivals, won the approval of the people.

Lenin's colleagues were so alarmed by this demand for an immediate seizure of power that they ordered copies of the two letters to be burned. Yet again the extremist leader had been rebuffed by his more level-headed lieutenants. Lenin, however, kept hammering away. He fiercely attacked his colleagues for taking part in the Democratic Conference. He warned them against having anything to do with the Council of the Republic. He denounced Kamenev and Zinoviev, the leading 'constitutionalists'. And on 29 September he gave notice that if they insisted on waiting for the Congress he would resign from the Central Committee and campaign for an armed uprising among the party rank and file.

By now Bolshevik victory was certain, he believed, provided his colleagues did not frustrate it. The Bolsheviks could both win power and hold on to power. Not only did they have most Russians on their side; their victory would soon be consolidated by world-wide proletarian revolution. It was therefore necessary to think beyond the seizure of power to what the Bolsheviks should do once they had it. What kind of state would they set up? How different from any previous state? In what direction would it evolve? To answer these questions he wrote what proved to be his most famous work, *State and Revolution*.

Written in the peace of Finland, *State and Revolution* reverberated with the sound of crashing pillars and elemental rebellion in nearby Russia. In the first place, it was an onslaught on the state – not just on the tsarist state but on any state, on the very idea of the state. The state, Lenin insisted, was of its essence repressive. It transformed its officials into society's masters. It was incompatible with freedom of any kind. 'So long as the state exists there is no freedom. When there is freedom, there will be no state.'[21] He rejected the state as an administrative machine; equally vehemently he rejected any suggestion that it could reconcile the classes. The only thing to do with the state as it now stood was to smash it – and he used the verb 'smash' in its various forms repeatedly. But while the existing state had to be smashed, it was vital to replace it, as a temporary measure, by another, less objectionable form of state. This temporary state would have to be a dictatorship, because only a state which exercised the strictest control over people's activities would be able to prepare the ground for communism.

State and Revolution was thus the work of a passionate anti-statist who wanted in the near future to set up an extremely coercive state. Yet Lenin saw no contradiction here and he justified his statism as completely compatible with and indispensable to his anti-statist objective. First, he argued that the proletarian state would be different from any other state that had ever existed. It would be repressive only against the former exploiters, and since they were a defeated minority repressing them would be simple. For the majority there would be far more freedom than before and 'an immense expansion of democracy'. Indeed, this would not be a state in the proper sense of the word at all; it would merely be a 'transitional state', a 'semi-state', and even that would progressively wither away.

Second, the proletarian semi-state would not be imposed upon the majority. Those who believed that simply misunderstood what the Bolsheviks meant by 'democratic centralism'. Democratic centralism was voluntary centralism. What, he asked, 'if the proletariat and the poor peasants take state power into their own hands, organize themselves quite freely in communes, and *unite* the actions of all the communes in striking at capital, in crushing the resistance of the capitalists'?[22] The new state, in short, would be a people's state, a state created by rather than imposed upon the people, a state built from the bottom upwards.

Third, destruction of the bourgeois state machine and the creation of proletarian democracy would do away for ever with the scourge of bureaucracy. The old bureaucratic apparatus would be destroyed to its very roots and would never recover. There would of course have to be administration in the new society, but that would no longer be the preserve of a privileged and non-accountable group. Those who performed administrative functions would enjoy no special respect or privileges, would be paid no more than workers' wages, and would be elected and dismissable by the whole community. State officials would in fact be no more than modestly paid 'foremen and bookkeepers'. More radically still, he argued that capitalism had made administration so simple that almost everyone could take part in it. And his aim was 'an order under which the functions of control and accounting, becoming more and more simple, will be performed by each in turn, will then become a habit and will finally die out as the *special* function of a special section of the population'.[23]

The Bolsheviks would thus bring about a people's revolution which would create a people's state which would in time dissolve into a completely self-regulating society. This vision of Lenin's came up, however, against two uncomfortable facts. First, the Bolsheviks were not yet by a long chalk the party of the people. Not only were the propertied against them; they could count on very little, and diminishing, support among democratic intellectuals, while the peasant majority, however rebellious, had minimal rapport with them other than on the issue of land confiscation. Second, bureaucracy had deep roots in Russia and was hardly likely to respond to a wave of the Bolshevik wand. For centuries people had quailed before the power of non-accountable officials, who had run the country like little tsars at the autocrat's behest. And if Russia did somehow escape from the bureaucracy of primitivism, it faced another threat which Bolshevik ambitions made all the more menacing: the bureaucracy of modernity. Recent writing in the West (Max Weber, Robert Michels) had suggested that the very idea of a bureaucracy-free society was utopian. The complexity of modern society made administration increasingly, rather than decreasingly, difficult. Effective participation in the administration of a modern society by those without special training and know-how was impossible. Skilled administrators were indispensable, and they would inevitably wield immense power. The task was not to root bureaucracy out, but simply to find a way of stopping the administrative élite from becoming all-powerful.

These uncomfortable facts – lack of popular support and failure to achieve bureaucracy-free government – would catch up with Lenin in the final years of his life, creating not only a crisis for the fledgling Soviet state but a crisis of his own which would shake him to the core. His ability to reconcile the potentially warring elements within himself depended crucially upon two convictions: that what the Bolsheviks willed was what, in the end, the people of Russia willed; and that what they jointly willed would lead towards a self-governing and thus stateless society. Serious doubt about either or both would have destroyed the very bedrock of belief on which his revolutionary gamble rested.

But in Finland in the autumn of 1917, Lenin had no doubts. Bureaucracy after the revolution was simply not an issue for him. He had no time for bourgeois sociologists or for Mensheviks who harped on about Russia's 'Asiatic heritage', and he rejected with scorn their antidote to bureaucratism – a parliament, a system of checks and balances, and all the paraphernalia of constitutionalism. He did, however, meet head-on arguments that the Bolsheviks had only minority support and therefore had neither the right nor the ability to seize power. The claim was absolutely false. The Bolsheviks' programme – 'Power to the Soviets, Land to the Peasants, Peace to the Nations, Bread to the Starving' – would win them the support of 'nine tenths of the population of Russia, the working class and the overwhelming majority of the peasantry'.[24] Already the Bolsheviks had a majority behind them, but their potential support was much greater still. Once they actually held power they could draw massive support from what Engels had called 'latent socialism' – people who had been politically dormant and inert would be brought to life by realizing that power had passed to the oppressed. These people would be given what they had always wanted and would be drawn in their millions into running the new state. The argument was clearly intended to dispose of any Bolshevik constitutionalist who made heavy weather of unfavourable election results. The Bolsheviks might have the support of only a narrow majority just now, but soon they would be the party of the overwhelming majority, and the way to realize this potential support was to seize power and carry out Bolshevik policies. That was what people were crying out for. Even the battle within the party itself seemed to bear out his conviction that he and the masses were standing four-square against the privileged. For who were these Bolshevik constitutionalists? Bourgeois intellectuals! And which Bolsheviks responded unstintingly to his call for an uprising? Rank-and-file members, workers – and in particular the Petrograd committee of the party, which was solidly proletarian and militant, in contrast to the shilly-shallying Central Committee. In *What Is To Be Done?* he had envisaged the party leaders having to haul a reluctant working class along behind them. But now the scenario was the complete opposite: radical workers were helping him push his all too hesitant colleagues towards the inevitable insurrection.

By early October Lenin had been away from the theatre of action for a full three months; he could stay away no longer. *State and Revolution* would have to be left unfinished – as he drily remarked in the published version, 'it is more pleasant and useful to go through the "experience of revolution" than to write about it'.[25] At the end of the first week of October he returned in disguise to Petrograd, and at a Central Committee meeting on 10 October he put the case for having an armed uprising and having it soon.

Kamenev and Zinoviev opposed, arguing that the Bolsheviks still only had minority support and that the uprising would be defeated. By ten votes to two, however, the committee decided to make an armed uprising 'the order of the day'. Once the decision had been taken Lenin went back into hiding. He would not be centre stage again till late on the evening of 24 October, when the seizure of power was already under way, and it was his colleagues, led by the resourceful Trotsky, who would implement the Central Committee's decision.

9

How sound was Lenin's analysis? There was no doubt that the government and the political centre were in disarray. The dual-power experiment had failed utterly: in the capital at least the government was virtually without supporters and in the event of attack would be hard pressed to find any troops to defend it. But did hostility to the government translate into demand for a Bolshevik regime?

If Lenin's analysis applied anywhere it applied in Petrograd, and by early October the mood of Petrograd was bitter and disillusioned. Threatened by hunger and unemployment, people wanted a government that would act decisively on the workers' behalf – a socialist government. They wanted peace, they wanted bread, they wanted the peasants to have the land, and they wanted to take the control of industry out of the hands of capitalists who were using their control as a political weapon with which to crush them. Their wishes coincided completely with Bolshevik slogans, yet it was not a Bolshevik take-over as such that they were demanding. The Bolsheviks' most famous slogan had done its work all too well. 'All power to the soviets' was not, after all, a sectarian slogan: on the contrary, it united the masses with its suggestion of a government that in style and policies was distinctively their own. And while the people of Petrograd wanted a soviet government badly, they were not in an insurrectionary mood. October was not February, and the October Revolution would not be a spontaneous and euphoric popular outburst. The high hopes of February had been buried – bitter experience had destroyed any idea that the path to a better life would be easy. Since the July Days people had been wary and sceptical, unwilling to take risks, and fearful of falling into a still greater abyss of misery and impoverishment. They would fight if they had to, but reluctantly and only if the revolution seemed in danger.

Lenin was both right and wrong, then, in his view of the Petrograd masses. They wanted the peace, land and wellbeing the Bolsheviks offered, but it had not dawned on them that an exclusively Bolshevik regime would be the price-tag. They shared Lenin's hope for a self-governing society, but would have been astounded to hear what stages had to be traversed to get there; and until it was achieved they expected a government which represented and consulted all working people. Where Lenin got the mood wrong it was partly because his cast-iron convictions insulated him against inconvenient facts and partly because he was buried away in Finland. His colleagues on the spot, however, gauged the popular mood better. They understood people's nervousness and saw how incomprehensible Bolshevik sectarianism was to them. If the uprising were to succeed, both factors would have to be taken into account. The uprising would have to be mounted by the Soviet rather than the Bolsheviks; it would have to take the form of a defence of the revolution and workers' power against attack; and it would have to be legitimized by the Congress of Soviets.

The government's attempt to get rid of most members of the unruly Petrograd garrison by sending them to the front gave the Bolsheviks the chance to stage precisely such an uprising. The announcement swung any waverers in the garrison firmly on to the Bolsheviks' side, and it seemed to bear out what Lenin had been claiming for weeks – that Kerensky planned to give up Petrograd in order to crush the revolution. Since the government could no longer be trusted to defend the capital, the Petrograd Soviet would have to take on the role instead, and on 16 October it voted to create its own Military Revolutionary Committee (MRC) in order to fight off both the Germans and attempted counter-revolution. Though the MRC was a Soviet body it would in fact be dominated by the Bolsheviks, who now had the instrument with which to make a politically acceptable take-over. Tension was heightened on 21 October when the MRC anounced that *it* now commanded the garrison: no directives would be valid unless signed by it. Kerensky replied two days later by attempting to close down the main Bolshevik newspapers. This and accompanying rumours that he had ordered loyal troops to the capital created the 'revolution in danger' atmosphere which the Bolsheviks needed: now they could seize power under the guise of warding off counter-revolution and protecting the Congress of Soviets, which after further delay was due to assemble at last on 25 October.

The take-over began in earnest on 24 October, despite denials by the MRC and Trotsky of what was happening. No demonstrations occurred and the city remained uncannily normal; but though the workers stayed in their factories, mass meetings declared their support for the Petrograd Soviet. Kerensky and the government found themselves helpless. They had almost no armed defence, and they lost their last political prop in the evening when the hitherto loyal socialists of the Council of the Republic went over, in a death-bed conversion, to the idea of an all-socialist government which would begin peace negotiations and put through land reform. During the night of 24–25 October all major installations, including power stations, the telephone exchange and the railway stations, were occupied by the insurgents. In mid-morning on the 25th Kerensky left Petrograd for the northern front in a vain hope of meeting up with troops who would restore his government. Even before he left, Lenin had composed a manifesto announcing that the Provisional Government had been overthrown and that power was now in the hands of the MRC. That was somewhat premature since the other ministers remained in the Winter Palace, which did not fall until the early hours of the 26th. The Palace's capture, and with it the end of the attempt to create in Russia a dual-power and democratic government, was, however, inevitable and when it eventually occurred had little of the drama that Soviet propagandists would later endow it with. Defended by only a few officer cadets and threatened by the guns of the cruiser *Aurora*, the ministers simply gave up a hopeless struggle. They were taken away on foot to be imprisoned in tsarism's most notorious jail, the Peter-Paul Fortress, and despite threats of lynching they got there in one piece. The take-over had been remarkably easy and almost bloodless.

The Congress of Soviets had meanwhile begun its proceedings. Lenin had wanted to delay them until the seizure of power was complete, but the failure of the MRC to do its work more quickly, which frayed his nerves badly, in the end made little difference. The Congress opened with Menshevik and SR members of the old presidium looking out at a sea of unfamiliar and unwanted faces. These men had controlled the first Congress, which had underwritten the dual-power regime. They had desperately wanted to avert this Congress, but in the end the tide of opinion had overwhelmed them. They had good reason for being apprehensive. A few days before, John Reed, an American reporter with Bolshevik sympathies, had gone to the Smolny, the former school for privileged girls which was to house the Congress, and asked an official how the membership was shaping. '"These are very different people from the delegates to the first Siezd (Congress)", she remarked. "See how rough and ignorant they look"'![26] Nikolai Sukhanov thought much the same when the Congress assembled. 'Out of the trenches and obscure holes and corners had crept utterly crude and ignorant people whose devotion to the revolution was spite and despair.'[27] This was democracy all right; no one could deny that those who now occupied this elegant hall represented the hitherto excluded millions. But were these people with 'their morose, indifferent faces and grey greatcoats' the material for an experiment in socialism?

Of the 670 delegates, 300 were Bolsheviks; 193 were SRs, more than half of them Left SRs; and eighty-two were Mensheviks. The Bolsheviks had therefore won a moral victory somewhat similar to that won by the Kadets in the first Duma: they were the largest party, but could not form a majority without support from elsewhere (in this case, from the Left SRs). What was immediately clear, however, was that the moderates on the platform looked into the eyes of resounding defeat. They vacated their seats and were replaced by a new presidium of fourteen Bolsheviks and seven Left SRs. Martov, the distinguished left Menshevik and a founding father of Russian Marxism, then opened the debate by demanding a united democratic government – a coalition of all the socialist parties. The way to such a coalition seemed to have been smoothed by the last-minute policy change made by the mainstream Mensheviks and SRs. It was what the Left SRs, who were vital to the Bolshevik majority, wanted. It was what many of the Bolshevik rank and file took for granted. And it was the aim of a number of Bolshevik leaders, including Kamenev, who chaired the opening session of the Congress.

The rug was, however, pulled from beneath the feet of those who wanted a socialist coalition government by the Menshevik and SR spokesmen, who denounced the coup as a conspiracy arranged behind the back of the Congress and then marched with their followers out of the hall. When Martov again put the case for a coalition he had lost the sympathy of the audience and was jeered as a 'compromiser'. Then Trotsky, the most brilliant Bolshevik orator, moved in for the kill. He threw out any idea of concession or compromise. Why make concessions when no one in Russia was on the side of the compromisers any more? 'To those who have left . . . we must say: you are miserable bankrupts, your role is played out; go where you ought to be, into the dustbin of history.'[28] Few who heard this coruscating invective could have guessed that, like the departing Mensheviks and SRs, democratic politics would be consigned to the dustbin in Russia and would not be let out for more than seventy years.

Martov's group then decided by a narrow majority to walk out in sympathy with their fellow Mensheviks. With that the last hope of a general coalition of socialists disappeared. What remained on the cards was a Bolshevik–Left SR coalition, which would have suited Lenin and Trotsky well since the Bolsheviks would have easily dominated it. And in late November a number of Left SRs would in fact join the government. But for the time being the Left SRs drew back from such an idea, insisting on an all-socialist government or nothing; and the outcome was therefore a government drawn exclusively from the Bolsheviks, the most extreme of the socialist parties and until recently a party with a minority following even in the large cities.

On the face of it, this was a most surprising outcome. Most delegates had come to the Congress committed to the idea of a soviet government, and few were Bolshevik sectarians of the Leninist type. Part of the trouble, Sukhanov would lament, was that the Mensheviks and SRs by walking out had simply let Lenin do what he wanted: 'we gave the Bolsheviks with our own hands a monopoly of the Soviet, of the masses, and of the revolution'.[29] Yet it is hard to see how the moderates could have acted differently. How as democrats could they not protest against this armed take-over and all the trickery ('the art of insurrection', as Lenin called it) which lay behind it? How could the Marxists among them not regard the creation of a socialist government as premature and disastrously mistaken? By attacking the coup, however, they utterly lost the sympathy of the majority of delegates, to whom they came over as nothing other than spokesmen for the propertied. What the majority wanted was tough action against the hated Kerensky and the propertied plus a government that represented all working people. That combination, however, was simply not available. The moderates had to make their stand and then more or less had to walk out since they were left in no position whatever to bargain. After their walk-out it was easy for Trotsky to swing the majority, now burning with anger against them, behind the hard-line Bolshevik position.

Lenin had played no public part in this historic first session, which had seen the humiliation of his opponents and the triumph of his sectarian strategy. As we know, he had no great time for congresses: on the very eve of the take-over he had written a bitter rebuke to his dithering Central Committee: 'It would be a disaster . . . to wait for the wavering vote of October 25. The people have the right and are in duty bound to decide such questions not by a vote but by force.'[30] But while the Congress could not be allowed the decisive say, it was vital that it should endorse the Bolshevik programme; and Lenin spent the first hours of Bolshevik power away from the limelight composing the policy documents which would be put before the Congress. Towards the end of the first session his manifesto 'To All Workers, Soldiers and Peasants' was read out. The manifesto made a series of promises. The new government would propose a 'democratic peace' to all nations and an immediate armistice on all battle fronts. All land would be transferred without compensation to peasant committees. There would be complete democratization of the army. Workers' control would be established in industry. The Constituent Assembly would be convened on the late November date already set by the Provisional Government. All nationalities would be given the right of self-determination. There was something here, it seemed, for everybody. The people were at last being given what they wanted; and of those who remained in the hall, only two voted against the manifesto.

The next evening, 26 November, Lenin presented in person the decrees which made good the Bolsheviks' most important promises: on peace and land. The peace decree urged all warring nations to begin negotiations for a just and democratic peace, without annexations or indemnities. Meanwhile, an armistice should be declared immediately. The land decree abolished all private property in land without compensation and ordered that estates should pass to the control of peasant soviets and local agrarian committees. Land would be divided out among peasants on an egalitarian basis; there would be no more buying, selling or renting of land, and no one would be allowed to work his land with hired labour. Both decrees were met with thunderous applause and passed unanimously. To a downhearted Sukhanov, who had crept back into the hall, it seemed that the Bolshevik leaders had the delegates eating out of their hands. If these people represented Russia, then it was clear that the Russian people had been given what they wanted and could hardly believe their good luck.

The Bolsheviks had in fact done a volte-face on the land issue. Back in April they were still insisting that Russia's agrarian problems could only be solved by a large-scale, scientific and socialist agriculture. Land would be nationalized and peasants become the paid employees of collective farms. But the peasant revolution of the summer and autumn had made such thinking academic. The peasants had seized the land and turned Russia into a patchwork quilt of smallholdings. The Bolsheviks could do nothing but recognize the *fait accompli*, and when Lenin presented the decree he did his best to make a democratic virtue out of the necessity. Yes, he admitted, the Bolshevik decree did embody SR land policy – but so what? 'As a democratic government we cannot ignore the decision of the masses of the people, even though we may disagree with it.' The peasants had in the end to decide the land question themselves. 'Whether they do it in our spirit or in the spirit of the SR programme is not the point. The point is that . . . they themselves must decide all questions, and that they themselves must arrange their own lives.'[31]

Peasants and soldiers were thus given what they had been clamouring for within hours of the Bolshevik take-over. (Workers, however, would have to wait rather longer. Their problems were more complex. They were, in addition, more reliable and their loyalty could for the time being be taken for granted.) But while the peace and land decrees gave an impression of the Bolsheviks as reasonable-minded democrats, a less reasonable impression was given by the resolution, confirmed at the very end of the Congress, which established a workers' and peasants' government. The members of the government would not, incidentally, be ministers – to emphasize that this was a government entirely different from any other in history, they were, at Trotsky's suggestion, to be called 'commissars'. The Council of People's Commissars would be no more than a provisional government, since the Bolsheviks had reiterated their commitment to the Constituent Assembly. And Sovnarkom (the Russian abbreviation by which the government became known) would, as a soviet government, be accountable to the newly elected CEC of the All-Russian Congress of Soviets. The CEC was now, however, firmly in the Bolsheviks' pocket since its sixty-two Bolshevik members vastly outnumbered the twenty-nine Left SRs and six Mensheviks. And the fifteen commissars themselves, headed by Lenin as chairman and Trotsky with the foreign affairs portfolio, were exclusively Bolshevik.

The Bolshevik regime began in fact as a Janus, presenting two utterly different faces. The more obvious face was the democratic one. These commissars were not, after all, the members of an unrepresentative clique of adventurers who had seized power without regard to public opinion. The October Revolution may have been a carefully engineered coup, but the coup enjoyed enormous, if largely passive, support from the Petrograd masses. The Bolsheviks were, moreover, acutely aware of the need to win over opinion outside Petrograd. If they were not already the choice of most Russians, they wanted rapidly to become this. They had every reason to hurry because on 12 November voters would elect the Constituent Assembly, which would finally decide what government the country should have and which policies it should pursue. The Bolsheviks needed as a result to make converts very quickly, to stir the dormant masses with their revolutionary-utopian message and convert 'latent socialism' into active endorsement of Bolshevik policies. Their ambition was nothing less than to turn the people of Russia from the passive objects of government into the fully participant and fully developed members of a self-governing society. In his manifesto of 25 October Lenin had written that 'all power in the localities shall pass to the Soviets of Workers', Soldiers' and Peasants' Deputies'.[32] The transfer of all power to ordinary people, the creation of a people's state, was something no government in history had tried or even remotely considered before: it was a democratic ambition in the highest degree, breathtakingly and perhaps crazily so.

The other face of Bolshevism, however, jarred with the new regime's unprecedentedly democratic pretensions. Power had been seized against the advice of many Bolsheviks and most non-Bolshevik socialists when it could perfectly well have been acquired in a quasi-constitutional way. The Congress which legitimized the take-over had anyway scant claims to being representative since it contained very few peasant delegates. And the all-Bolshevik government which emerged from the Congress had not been anticipated even by many Bolshevik delegates. Had the moderates played their cards as Martov wanted and got the Congress to vote for an all-socialist coalition, Lenin would probably have persuaded his colleagues to defy it. Yet the Lenin who was so scornful of votes was also the inspiration behind the Bolshevik vision of a free and self-governing people. Bolshevism's two faces expressed this fundamental contradiction within its leader. If the dangerous gamble into which he had pushed the party was to succeed, the contradiction had somehow to be resolved – otherwise the outcome would either be a catastrophic defeat or a Bolshevik dictatorship. And what happened in the Smolny during the night of 25-26 October did suggest that a synthesis of the two faces might lie within the Bolsheviks' grasp. For the Congress had begun with the idea of soviet power and finished by enthroning the Bolsheviks; it had opened in an exhilarated, but tense and uncertain, mood and yet closed with thunderous applause for the Bolshevik leadership and the sense of a single will uniting these hundreds of individuals.

The scene in the Smolny when delegates rose to their feet in rapture and gave the Bolshevik leaders a prolonged and stormy ovation has an obvious relevance to the theme of this book. Tsarism's defenders had claimed that a common and recognized community of interests bound ruler and people, but the claim was clearly specious. Now, an observer might have thought, such a community had really come into existence: here in this hall rulers and people were locked in an embrace, united in mutual sympathy and understanding. Now at last a government of the general will was about to be created in Russia. The symbolism of these moving scenes in the Smolny was, however, deceptive. For the delegates did not, as we know, represent all or even most of the Russian people; and even those who were represented would before long become disenchanted with their new rulers.

Notes

1 Allan Wildman, *The End of the Russian Imperial Army* (2 vols, Princeton N.J., 1980 and 1987), vol. I: *The Old Army and the Soldiers' Revolt (March–April 1917)*, p. 92.
2 Michael T. Florinsky, *The End of the Russian Empire* (New Haven, 1931), p. 228.
3 Hans Rogger, *Russia in the Age of Modernization and Revolution 1881–1917* (London, 1983), p. 263.
4 Raymond Pearson, *The Russian Moderates and the Crisis of Tsarism 1914–1917* (London, 1977), p. 174.
5 George Katkov, *Russia 1917: The February Revolution* (London, 1967), p. 175.
6 *Ibid.*
7 V. I. Lenin, *Collected Works* (45 vols, Moscow 1960–70), vol. XXI, p. 216; vol. XXIII, p. 253.
8 Tsuyoshi Hasegawa, *The February Revolution: Petrograd 1917* (Seattle, 1981), p. 201.
9 Leon Trotsky, *The History of the Russian Revolution* (London, 1965), p. 125.
10 *Ibid.*, p. 171.
11 Katkov, *Russia 1917*, p. 410.
12 P. N. Milyukov, *Vospominaniya (1859–1917)* (2 vols, New York, 1955), vol. II, p. 310.
13 N. N. Sukhanov, *The Russian Revolution 1917: A Personal Record*, edited and translated by Joel Carmichael (Oxford, 1955), p. 46.
14 R. P. Browder and A. F. Kerensky, *The Russian Provisional Government, 1917* (3 vols, Stanford, Cal., 1961), vol. I, p. 158.
15 Sukhanov, *The Russian Revolution 1917*, p. 273.
16 Browder and Kerensky, *The Russian Provisional Government, 1917*, vol. III, pp. 1206–7.
17 Sukhanov, *The Russian Revolution 1917*, p. 289.
18 *Ibid.*, p. 273.
19 Alexander Rabinowitch, *The Bolsheviks Come to Power* (London, 1979), p. 115.
20 Lenin, *Collected Works*, vol. XXVI, p. 21; p. 19.
21 Lenin, *Collected Works*, vol. XXV, p. 468.
22 *Ibid.*, p. 429.
23 *Ibid.*, p. 426.
24 Lenin, *Collected Works*, vol. XXVI, p. 141; p. 67.
25 Lenin, *Collected Works*, vol. XXV, p. 492.
26 John Reed, *Ten Days that Shook the World* (Harmondsworth, 1966), p. 55.
27 Sukhanov, *The Russian Revolution 1917*, p. 635.
28 *Ibid.*, p. 640.
29 *Ibid.*, p. 646.
30 Lenin, *Collected Works*, vol. XXVI, p. 235.
31 *Ibid.*, pp. 260 and 261.
32 *Ibid.*, p. 247.

|6|

The power of the party, 1917–1928

1

Moderate revolution had failed, but the Bolsheviks' radical revolution would succeed, and it would propel Russia into a new era. Obvious parallels could be drawn with Peter the Great, founder of the previous era. Peter's challenge to tradition had been embodied in a new capital; the Bolsheviks too moved the capital, though instead of building a modernistic one they restored the government, in March 1918, to Moscow. Peter had changed the calendar; the Bolsheviks did the same, and on 1 February 1918 the country leapt 13 days to draw level in time with the West. Peter had wanted to slough off Russia's backwardness and import the technology and material civilization of the West; the Bolsheviks were no less determined to catch up. But there were also fundamental differences. Peter had created a westernized upper class; the Bolsheviks would destroy this class, close Peter's window on the West, identify themselves with those who, like the Smolny delegates, were almost wholly unwesternized, and soon retreat into an attitude of embattled hostility towards the West which had uncanny echoes of pre-Petrine Muscovy. Peter had been a hereditary ruler who carried out his revolution through existing institutions, and only a small number of Russians had had their lives transformed by it. The Bolsheviks, by contrast, were rank outsiders who wanted to smash the institutions, practices and attitudes of those they had dispossessed, and their revolution would launch a whirlwind of destruction and remaking which would touch every facet of the life of every citizen. Their long-term achievement would fall far short of their ambitions, but they would nevertheless transform Russia.

At the start, the odds had seemed to be stacked impossibly against them. Their defeated rivals consoled themselves that these adventurers could hardly hold on to power for very long, little guessing that

Communist rule would last a full three-quarters of a century. How then did the Bolsheviks entrench their power and soon make it impregnable? The explanation given by anti-Bolshevik historians in the West was that they succeeded by the use of coercion and terror, that behind high-sounding democratic and socialist ideals they resorted to every kind of skulduggery to create a totalitarian regime which held a helpless population in its grip. This view, which was fortified by the Cold War, has, however, been strongly challenged since the 1970s. The challengers have made two main points. First, the 'totalitarian' historians have concentrated too much on the top of the social pyramid, have been too concerned with high politics, and have as a result come up with a distorted picture of the ruling few victimizing an inert and helpless society. Had they studied the grass-roots, they would have seen that the relationship between the top and bottom of Soviet society was more complex, with movement between the two levels going in both directions, not simply one. Not all Soviet citizens were or felt themselves to be helpless victims. Millions *were* victimized, but millions more were the regime's beneficiaries and a minority became its enthusiastic collaborators or supporters. Second, the 'totalitarian' historians have been so obsessed with Bolshevism's unchangingly repressive and inhuman essence, as they see it, that they have more or less excluded accident and improvization from their picture. Soviet rulers were in fact often at the mercy of events rather than in control of them. Buffeted by unforeseen crises, they saved themselves by compromise and an unprogrammed pragmatism. Far from the party shaping events, it was events which tended to shape the party; and it emerged from the turmoil of the civil war very different from what it had been in February or even October 1917.

At times the revisionists have pushed their challenge to the totalitarian orthodoxy too far. The early Soviet government was indeed beset by crises, but the crises were very largely of its own making – the inevitable outcome of Bolshevik passions, beliefs and grandiose ambitions. The Russian Communist Party was never remotely a passive, amoeba-like body reacting to purely accidental disasters, and its improvizations were very far from random. As for the workers and Red Army veterans who crowded into it, they certainly had a profound influence but only in the sense that they made absolutely dominant the already strong tendency in the party to roughness, intolerance and authoritarianism. The revisionists have nevertheless given a more plausible explanation than their opponents of why the Soviet regime lasted so long and why it was so little challenged, and their great merit is that they have documented the two-way relationship between rulers and ruled. Russia would be Bolshevized with a brutality which the revisionists have sometimes underestimated; the survival of the regime would, however, be due to a steady process of cultural assimilation which made the new rulers heirs to traditions which in the bright dawn of October 1917 they had set out to liquidate.

2

The Bolsheviks' basic problem on taking power was that, whatever their claims, they were very much in a minority. They were the party of the workers, but in 1917 there were only four to five million of them out of a total population of more than 140 million; and even if some peasants and an appreciable number of soldiers are added, Bolshevik supporters still remained little more than a drop in the ocean. The support the Bolsheviks had, moreover, was only for a simple version of their programme – for their overthrow of Kerensky's government, their hatred of the privileged, their solidarity with the masses. Those who understood and sympathized with the more far-ranging Bolshevik ambitions were few indeed, but these ambitions were nevertheless vital. Removing the tsar and the nobs was to be no more than a beginning. In due course the bourgeois and any remnants of class differentiation would have to go as well; so too would the Church and organized religion in all its forms. The society the Bolsheviks aimed at would be collectivist and egalitarian, purged of all the self-seeking and acquisitiveness of the world they had destroyed; it would also be enlightened, rationalistic, scientific-minded and entirely free of the 'darkness' and superstition which had besmirched the old Russia. The Russia of Bolshevik dreams – classless, stateless and religionless – would in fact be utterly different from anything any Russian had ever known. The Bolsheviks would transform their poor, suffering and benighted country out of all recognition; and in the euphoric mood created by their unexpectedly easy seizure of power they had high hopes of realizing their vision fairly soon. Their isolation in the capitalist world would, they were convinced, be short-lived – revolution would triumph irresistibly in the advanced countries as well. Furthermore, their achievements in government and the effects of a vigorous programme of propaganda and re-education would soon vindicate their claims to be democrats and create spontaneous majority support for them at home. These two convictions – that their isolation would be short-lived and that they would soon have majority support – were essential. They would be forgotten or muffled once events had proved them utterly mistaken: but without them the Bolsheviks' gamble would have been unthinkable.

As commissar for foreign affairs, Trotsky assumed that after issuing a few revolutionary declarations he would be able to 'shut up shop' since there would be no more bourgeois regimes to deal with. That was of course naive in the extreme. Hopes of Germany in particular received a sharp setback: far from getting help from a revolutionary Germany, the fledgling regime was soon being pressed to the wall by an all too imperialist German state. The two countries had signed an armistice in December, but this was followed by harsh territorial demands from the Germans, which the Bolsheviks rejected. Trotsky tried to go over the imperialists' heads by appealing direct to the German people; the only outcome, however, of the stalled negotiations was a German advance deep into Ukraine and still harsher territorial demands. Those on the party's left responded defiantly – rather than capitulate, they would unleash a 'revolutionary war' against the predator. Lenin, however, insisted, and after a bitter struggle he got his way, that the German terms had to be accepted. The regime had no army worthy of the name; its hold on power was still precarious; what mattered was that the revolution should be preserved, even at the price of humiliation and major territorial sacrifice. And by the Treaty of Brest-Litovsk, signed on 3 March 1918, the Soviet state renounced its claims to Poland, Finland and the Baltic states, and – worst of all – agreed to recognize the independence of Ukraine. Thus by a stroke of the pen it lost two-fifths of the old Russia's industrial resources, three-quarters of its coal and iron mines, and much of its richest agricultural land.

Brest-Litovsk was a bitter blow, an 'obscene peace' in Lenin's words, but Bolshevik hopes of world-wide revolution revived strongly in November 1918 with the collapse of the German empire. Now there was a real whiff of revolution in the European air, so much so that *Pravda* announced that 'the world revolution has begun'; and when the Communist International (Comintern for short) was founded in Moscow in March 1919 by delegates from many countries, it was widely assumed that before long the organization would move its headquarters to Paris or Berlin. Again, however, hopes were raised only to be dashed. Soviet republics were set up in Hungary and Bavaria in 1919, but proved short-lived. Worse still, in 1920 the Red Army invaded Poland in the hope that Polish workers would join arms with their socialist brothers and overthrow their oppressors. The Poles did no such thing, however, and the Red Army, far from launching what more visionary Bolsheviks had seen as a revolutionary war for the whole of Europe, was soon driven out of Polish territory. Belief that the more advanced countries at least were 'pregnant with revolution' (Lenin's phrase) nevertheless continued to sustain the Bolsheviks. When H. G. Wells met Lenin in Moscow in October 1920, what Lenin wanted to find out from him was 'Why does not the social revolution begin in England?'[1] And why not in France? Why not, most important of all, in Germany? Had the Bolsheviks miscalculated?

International revolution would have mattered less if the Bolsheviks had been securely established at home: but they were not. There was a yawning gulf between their aspiration to be the party of the Russian people and the actual support they enjoyed, and the gulf was if anything widening. A moment of truth had come with the elections to the Constituent Assembly, which had taken place as planned, and in relatively free conditions, only three weeks after the Bolshevik take-over with rather more than half of the electorate participating. The Bolsheviks had been supported by some ten million voters (24 per cent of the total); they had swept Petrograd and Moscow and done well in the more industrialized central and western provinces and in the army. However, the SRs (who had fought as a single party, not as Right and Left) had done considerably better, winning over sixteen million votes – 37 per cent of the total. The Mensheviks by contrast had done badly and got less than one and a half million votes. What emerged nevertheless was that the electors had voted overwhelmingly in favour of socialism, four-fifths of them supporting a socialist party of some kind. They had voted decisively against the bourgeois parties: the Kadets, who had ridden high only eleven years previously, gathered no more than two million votes and made no impact at all outside the capitals. The question of what kind of socialist government people wanted could still not be answered with any certainty because of the failure to distinguish between the two kinds of SRs. What was clear enough, however, was that people had voted against an exclusively Bolshevik government. As the Bolsheviks had themselves admitted, their government was no more than provisional. Now that Russia's first ever democratic elections had taken place, they would surely have to share power with the victors.

A number of leading Bolsheviks, including Kamenev and Zinoviev, restated the argument in favour of a socialist coalition – the only alternative, they said, was a Bolshevik dictatorship maintained by terror. And in the aftermath of the elections seven Left SRs did join Sovnarkom, though they were to leave it the following March in protest against Brest-Litovsk. Most Bolsheviks, however, set their faces very firmly against co-operation with or concessions to any socialists other than the Left SRs. Their task, they agreed with Lenin, was to create a mandate for the policies they believed in. To have caved in to an electoral verdict passed after only three weeks of Bolshevik power would by their reasoning have been perverse. The logic of October committed them either to defying a hostile Constituent Assembly or to bending it to their will. When the Assembly convened in early January 1918, it was presented with a motion recognizing the authority of the Soviet government. By 237 to 138 votes the Assembly rejected the motion – thus dispelling any remaining doubts that the electors' verdict had been anti-Bolshevik. The Bolshevik and Left SR minority then withdrew. The remaining deputies passed a new land law replacing the Bolshevik one; but within hours Red Guards had made them disperse, and they were not allowed to assemble again.

Lenin had anticipated the dissolution with his 'Theses on the Constituent Assembly', published in *Pravda* a few days before. The Assembly, he argued, was a bourgeois institution which had been left behind by the tide of events. The election results reflected neither the wishes nor the interests of the people; the deputies should recognize Soviet power and agree to new elections, and if they did not, 'revolutionary measures' would be used against them. While Lenin did envisage the possibility of new elections leading to a more correct outcome, the thrust of his article suggested that the Assembly was an inevitable obstacle to socialist aspirations, for which only the soviets could serve as a proper vehicle. The dissolution decree went further and called the Assembly 'a screen for the struggle of the counter-revolutionaries to overthrow Soviet power'.[2]

The sweeping aside of Russia's only ever democratically elected parliament narrowed the bounds of political freedom very considerably, yet it did not amount to a rejection of democracy and pluralistic politics as such. The Constituent Assembly might be an outdated and invalid forum; a clear and open political struggle could, however, still be fought within the valid forum of the soviets. There democracy was still vigorously alive, and from the spring of 1918 soviet elections across the country gave clear signs that the Bolsheviks' rivals were recovering. The SRs did well in various places, surpassing the Bolsheviks in Kronstadt, for instance; even the Mensheviks seemed to be making a come-back. The Bolsheviks' declining popularity was hardly surprising: the voters were punishing them, as they had Kerensky, because of chaos and plummeting living standards. Unlike Kerensky, however, the Bolsheviks had contempt for constitutional democracy and their response to the upturn in support for their rivals was draconian. In January they had blackballed Constituent Assembly deputies for being elected under false pretences and to the wrong assembly; from that it was not a very large step to debarring their socialist opponents from political life altogether simply for being what they were. In June 1918 Mensheviks and Right SRs were excluded from the CEC of the soviets and also from the local soviets; in July the same fate befell the Left SRs after they had staged an unsuccessful uprising in Moscow. Mensheviks and SRs would not be completely removed from political life until 1921, but from the summer of 1918 the new state became to all intents and purposes a one-party one. From now on 'Soviet' meant 'Bolshevik', as Lenin had always meant that it should; and most Bolsheviks, faced with a challenge from resurgent SRs and Mensheviks, readily fell in with Lenin's sectarian attitude.

3

The Bolsheviks' left-wing rivals were disposed of easily enough, but it would be a very different story with their rivals to the right: the two million-odd people who had voted for the Kadets, the embittered and expropriated former privileged. The war between the Reds and the forces of the former privileged, the Whites, would last more than two years, devastate the country, shatter whatever remained of the inter-class harmony of 1917, and make the Bolsheviks' rejection of democracy irreversible.

The civil war was not, for the Bolsheviks, an unforeseen disaster. On the contrary, they expected nothing else – war was the inevitable outcome of what they had done since taking power. They had after all come to power by force; they had closed down bourgeois newspapers and channels of expression; they had dissolved the Constituent Assembly; they had begun an admittedly cautious nationalization of the economy and had endorsed 'workers' control' in industry; worst of all, they had underwritten the peasants' seizure of the land. In the eyes of the former ruling class they had acted in fact like barbarian usurpers, and it was only a matter of time before the representatives of the old order fought back.

The Bolsheviks had a great advantage from the outset – they controlled Russia's European heartland. They had won control of the heartland within a matter of weeks (relatively easily, except in the case of Moscow) and they would never relinquish it. The Whites, by contrast, were relegated to the fringe: to the south and south-east of European Russia, to the north, and to Siberia – areas that were non-Russian or marginally Russian or that lacked the strong working class which gave the Bolsheviks their core constituency. Controlling the heartland, the Bolsheviks controlled the railways, which radiated out from Moscow and Petrograd, and Trotsky's forays by armed train to crisis points became legendary. The Bolsheviks, moreover, were able to have a central command structure, whereas the Whites, scattered around the periphery, were unable to unite their armies or to develop a co-ordinated strategy. What should have helped the Whites was foreign intervention on their behalf: British in the far north, French on the Black Sea coast, American and Japanese in eastern Siberia, Poles in Ukraine, plus the assistance of Czech detachments making a long journey home via the Trans-Siberian railway. But the intervention rebounded if anything against the Whites. The foreign forces failed to make any major impact, and they helped the Bolsheviks win the war of minds by enabling them to play on traditional anti-westernism and to come over as Russian patriots. The Bolsheviks' greatest psychological weapon, however, was that they stood four-square for the agrarian revolution, whereas their opponents were associated indelibly with landlordism. Nor was it simply that the Whites were unable to live down their past. Where they took control they reinstated 'the ancient trinity of generals, high clergy, and landlords', and nothing did more to boost the appeal of the Bolsheviks.[3]

The Whites' advantage was that they could draw on a pool of officers and a military tradition. The Bolsheviks could do neither; indeed as a point of principle they did not believe in professional armies. Their principles, however, soon withered in the face of the military threat. Trotsky had left the Commissariat of Foreign Affairs for that of War, to which he was temperamentally far better suited, and he showed enormous flair in raising from scratch a new army, the Red Army, which for Bolshevik purists turned out to have disturbing echoes of the old one. This was not a people's militia, democratically run, in which the soldiers elected their own officers; on the contrary, an iron discipline was imposed on conscripted soldiers by officers appointed from above. Not only was the old command structure preserved, the officers were largely conscripts from the officer class of the imperial army (though their loyalty was assured by political commissars, who worked alongside them and had the right to execute them for treason). The Red Army flouted Bolshevik pre-revolutionary beliefs of what an army should be; it nevertheless grew into a formidable fighting force of more than five million men, and its traditionalism was vindicated by the eventual complete rout of the Whites, the last of whom had been evacuated from the Crimea by the late autumn of 1920.

The Red Army's work in defending the revolution was complemented by that of another new institution: the Cheka or security service. This too began as a temporary concession to expediency: police, together with bureaucracy and the standing army, made up in Lenin's eyes the three pillars of the bourgeois state, and he was committed to abolishing all of them. The Cheka had nevertheless been set up in December 1917, under the Pole Felix Dzerzhinsky, to fight counter-revolution, sabotage, and the general lawlessness, and it soon took on a security function similar to that of the tsarist Okhrana. Come the civil war, the Cheka became an organ of 'Red terror', making mass arrests of those regarded as class enemies of the regime in areas that inclined to the Whites or had been won back from them. 'Enemies of the people' – some of them not bourgeois at all but independent-minded workers or opposition socialists – were held in concentration camps, which were established from late 1918 at Lenin's prompting; and a considerable number of those arrested were shot. Terror, like the suspension of democracy, was from the Bolsheviks' point of view regrettable but absolutely vital: they could not defeat their enemies if their hands were tied by constitutional niceties. They had to be cruel; their terror had to be indiscriminate. But it should have been short-lived; and the replacement of the Cheka in 1922 by the GPU, which on paper had fewer extra-judicial powers, seemed to suggest that state lawlessness, having served its purpose, had now ended.

4

By 1921, then, the Bolsheviks had crushed their opponents to right and left. But though they ruled securely, the country they ruled over was in ruins. Some 800,000 people had died in the fighting since 1917. There had also been many deaths – perhaps 200,000 – from the Red and White terror. Disease had been an even greater killer: some two million had died of typhus and typhoid alone during 1919–20, while starvation too had taken an enormous toll. If the two to three million people who had fled abroad are added, the total population loss during the period of revolution and civil war rises to between seven and ten million. No other nation in modern times had suffered such a catastrophe.

In addition to the destruction of individual lives, there was the destruction of life as it had always been, the shattering of a civilization. 'Everything established, settled, everything to do with home and order and the common round, has crumbled into dust and been swept away in the general upheaval and reorganization of the whole of society', lamented Pasternak's Yurii Zhivago. 'The whole human way of life has been destroyed and ruined.'[4]

The ex-monarch and his family had been shot in July 1918 at the government's instigation – though it presented the execution as an initiative by the local soviet and tried to hide that the tsar's wife and family had been killed as well. Not for Nicholas the seemly judicial execution of a Charles I or a Louis XVI. The 'All-Russian Murderer', a newspaper rejoiced, had been shot as if he were a common brigand. 'Nicholas the Bloody is no more.'[5] Most aristocrats and major capitalists had also been eliminated by death or exile. Take any photograph of a high-society function in 1914: almost all of the people at the party would no longer be alive in Russia by the end of the decade. Landlords had entirely disappeared from the countryside, and their manor houses were often now crumbling or gutted ruins. A few artists and intellectuals fervently supported the Bolsheviks; most, however, were in opposition, many had gone into exile and many more would, like the writer Maxim Gorky, leave in the early 1920s. Many of the middle class, by contrast, stayed on, though they had now sunk to the position of a humiliated and exploited class. They had been evicted from their flats and houses or forced to share them with workers' families; they had lost their old jobs and many were now having with gritted teeth to serve the new regime instead. There had been an assault too on the spiritual prop of the old order: the Church had been disestablished in January 1918, lost ownership of its property, including its schools, and had its state subsidy taken away. Clergy were deprived of their vote; monasteries were sacked and closed down; here and there priests (among them the metropolitan of Kiev) were killed, and churches were plundered. Lenin was wary enough, however, of the Church's popular appeal to restrain the more hot-headed of the party's anti-clerics; churches on the whole remained open and systematic persecution would not begin until the late 1920s.

Such attacks, some brutal, others showing a certain subtlety, had destroyed 'the whole human way of life' as the former privileged understood it. But there had been no see-saw effect here: bourgeois misery had not been compensated by improved material conditions for the masses – instead, everyone had suffered. When H. G. Wells went to Petrograd in 1920, he found the city dead: trading had disappeared, there were no shops and no markets, and the streets were deserted. Money was so hard to come by that people were being paid in kind (e.g. with food rations), and many services, such as transport, were free. The disappearance of money made Communist visionaries rejoice at capitalism's imminent liquidation; ordinary Russians, however, had never in recent times faced so desperate a struggle for survival.

The economy had admittedly been severely disrupted when the Bolsheviks took power, but by 1920 it had reached a state of near total collapse. The more desperate the political situation, the more drastic economic policies had become. The Bolsheviks had begun cautiously enough, doing nothing more radical than to nationalize banking and credit; but with the eruption of full-scale civil war in the summer of 1918 they nationalized all large-scale industry, and they followed this two years later with the nationalization of small-scale enterprises as well. Not only did manufacturing become a state monopoly; private trading was banned, as H. G. Wells discovered, and all economic activity was placed under the nominal control of the Supreme Council of the National Economy. One concession to realism was that the government did its utmost, in the teeth of fierce left-wing criticism, to hold on to key industrial personnel – managers, engineers and technicians, who were now branded as 'bourgeois specialists'. But this was not enough to save industry, which was crippled by lack of supplies, by runaway inflation, by lack of investment, by the breakdown of transport, and by the organizational chaos caused by workers who interpreted Bolshevik power as a licence for them to manage their own industries. During the first ten months of Soviet rule, almost a third of large factories closed; by 1921 heavy-industrial production was only about 20 per cent of what it had been in 1913. No other nation had suffered so rapid and complete a collapse of its productive capacity. As for national income, that had fallen by 1921 to less than half – about 40 per cent – of what it had been in 1913.

The economic policies which produced these ravages became known as War Communism. Left-wing theorists, Nikolai Bukharin for instance, believed that the sooner Russia got rid of money, markets and the whole paraphernalia of capitalism, the nearer socialism would be. One of War Communism's consequences, however, horrified even its passionate defenders: the very class that provided the Soviet regime with its base, its justification and its spearhead, was fast disintegrating. The Bolsheviks had counted on a steady expansion of the proletariat; far from that, it seemed to be disappearing before their very eyes. In 1917 the two capitals had four million inhabitants; in 1920 they had little more than one and a half million between them. The population loss was particularly severe in Petrograd, and the rate of the loss was at its highest among the industrial working class. As factory after factory closed and hunger menaced, there was little or nothing to hold the workers. The lucky ones got jobs in the expanding administration, many were conscripted into the Red Army, where they formed the core units, and about one million fled the large towns altogether for the countryside in a desperate hope of finding food and a livelihood there. Of the three million industrial workers in 1917, little more than one million remained in 1920. Soviet Russia was becoming de-industrialized and de-proletarianized, many of its workers were turning back into peasants, and at the end of the civil war the Communist Party had an even smaller social base in the country than the slender one it had had in October 1917.

5

Economic recovery, if it ever came, would of course ease the situation. But beyond the problem of the dwindling proletariat loomed the still more daunting problem of how the Bolsheviks were to win over, or at least manage to co-exist with, two much larger segments of the population: the non-Russians and the peasantry.

In the case of the non-Russians, Lenin had, as we know, taken a stand on the right of national self-determination, while clearly hoping that in practice it would not be exercised. How to persuade the minority peoples that their best interests would be served by staying within the Soviet state therefore lay at the heart of the Bolsheviks' nationalities problem. Who in any case constituted 'the people'? If working-class Ukrainians or Balts wanted to join the Soviet state but the middle class and peasants did not, would the Bolsheviks feel bound by the majority verdict? The answer to that had been suggested by what happened to the Constituent Assembly. In the Assembly elections the Bolsheviks had in fact done well in what became Estonia and Latvia; they had also found areas of solid support in Ukraine, Belorussia and the Caucasus. Knowing that they had considerable minority support fuelled their intolerance towards 'bourgeois separatists', and their conviction that the international society of socialism was anyway just around the corner made concessions to separatism seem a step in entirely the wrong direction.

Once Imperial Germany had collapsed, the way seemed open to regaining the territories lost at Brest-Litovsk. The attempt to impose Soviet regimes in Poland, Finland and the Baltic states in the event failed and by the end of 1920 the Soviet government had had to recognize the independence of all three areas. Soviet regimes were, however, established in Belorussia in 1919 and in Ukraine after prolonged fighting in 1921. In addition, the lost Caucasian areas were reconquered – Azerbaijan and Armenia in 1920 and Georgia, after a period of Menshevik rule, in 1921; and by 1921 Central Asia too had been brought back within the fold.

The reconquest of the empire's lost lands raised a host of technical and moral problems. How were these very different areas to be formally bonded together? What had conquering small peoples got to do with socialism? Could coercion possibly be reconciled with Bolshevik principles? The task of finding a way through this moral and practical maze and devising an acceptable nationalities' policy fell in particular upon the Georgian Iosif Dzugashvili, known since 1912 as Stalin, who had been chosen as commissar for nationalities precisely because as a non-Russian he seemed unlikely to act like a Russian chauvinist. Stalin and the party's left insisted that self-determination was a right not of the bourgeoisie but only of the working masses of a nation. The slogan had to be 'self-determination for the workers'. Not only was self-determination of limited application; it was valid only if it clearly served the overriding principle of socialism. Another amendment made to the Bolshevik nationalities policy was the concept of federalism. Lenin had earlier rejected this as an unsatisfactory half-way house – nations had to choose between outright independence and full participation in the Soviet state. By 1918, however, giving the non-Russian areas a separate status which fell well short of independence had acquired an obvious appeal. Under its constitution of that year, the country became the Russian Socialist Federated Soviet Republic (RSFSR), though the rights of the federal units *vis-à-vis* the centre were very largely, and deliberately, left unspecified. Ukraine, Belorussia and the reconquered Caucasian areas for the time being remained nominally independent republics allied to the RSFSR by military and other treaties; the federal idea nevertheless pointed towards the way by which they too might be integrated with Russia while enjoying some recognition of their non-Russianness.

Whatever the exact formalities, Bolshevik intentions were clear: to bring the minority peoples wherever possible into the Soviet state, though ideally with their agreement. The spread of socialism and the increasingly evident economic advantages of the union would in time, it was confidently assumed, make the minorities happy enough to waive their constitutionally guaranteed right of secession. But in the meanwhile their reluctant acquiescence would have to be won by giving them broad cultural freedom, in particular the right to use their own languages; by letting fellow nationals administer them; by allowing them their own forms of statehood, however empty; and by sparing them any overt russification. All of this made the Soviet nationalities policy very different from the tsars'. Yet the fact remained that the minority peoples had been bludgeoned; the autonomy of the non-Russians within the RSFSR and the independence of the Ukrainians, Belorussians and Caucasians were a mere formality. More scrupulous Bolsheviks were troubled by the feeling that behind a radical smokescreen the regime was pursuing a nationalities policy little different from the tsarist one, and the suspicion would trigger a crisis in the leadership in the early 1920s.

Even more agonizing, however, than the nationalities question was the question of the peasantry. With the loss of Poland, Finland and the Baltics the non-Russians had, after all, become a minority grouping; the peasants, by contrast, were more than 80 per cent of the population. When you thought of Russia, you thought of peasants. The peasants *were* Russia, and by seizing power in so overwhelmingly peasant a country the Bolsheviks – townsmen of the pith and marrow – had stored up enormous problems for themselves. So far the peasants had, notionally at least, been the proletariat's allies in the struggle. October had, however, brought a parting of the ways. Now that the bourgeois revolution was behind and the task of building socialism lay ahead, the peasants became a major obstacle to Bolshevik ambitions, and anti-peasant prejudice, which had been damped down somewhat during the decade of tactical alliance, was rapidly rekindled.

Bolshevik attitudes to the peasantry were in fact through and through ambivalent. Gut reaction tended to be that the peasants were stupid, backward, brainwashed by religion, and inordinately greedy – in a word, petty-bourgeois. Yet Bolsheviks could not write the peasant majority off entirely without damning their own chances of creating a socialist Russia, and so they persuaded themselves that the peasants nevertheless had a proletarian potential. The average peasant was torn between petty-bourgeois instincts (acquisitiveness, etc.) and a natural sense of identity with the workers, and the poorer he was the more likely, or so the view went, were his pro-worker instincts and sympathies to come out on top. In the long run the problems of rural Russia could be solved only by a massive assimilation of rural ways and values to urban ones, of the peasant petty bourgeoisie to the proletariat. Agriculture would have to become large-scale, scientific and collectivized, with farms being turned into efficient food-producing factories worked by wage labourers. The problem, however, was that this would be a take-over of the overwhelming majority by a small (and currently a dwindling) minority, of a way of life with deep national roots by one which hardly existed so far outside the minds of a few theorists. That was why collectivization was not on the agenda for the time being, even though Lenin made much in his talk with H. G. Wells of the handful of collective farms which had been set up. It could only be achieved with the peasants' willing co-operation, of which there was no sign whatever at a time when other issues were making the town–country relationship fraught in the extreme.

The heart of the problem was that too little grain was getting to the towns; workers were therefore going short of bread; and to suspicious minds this looked like a peasant attempt at sabotaging the revolution. In reality the matter was more complicated. The disruption of transport had reduced the grain supply; so had the collapse of industry, since the peasant found that he could buy little or nothing if he did market his produce. But the underlying cause of the slump in the grain supply was the transformation of the rural economy brought about by the revolution. The supply of grain for the market had come overwhelmingly from the large estates and from the richest peasants. Now the large estates were no more, the peasants who had broken away under the Stolypin reform had had their land reincorporated into the communes, and there had been a general equalizing of landholdings. Russia had become a country of small peasant farmers, nearly all of them very poor but more or less equal in their poverty, who cultivated their strips in the time-honoured way under the umbrella of the village commune. Peasant traditionalism had triumphed at the expense of the recent modernizing impulses, and the outcome was a small-scale, subsistence farming and farmers who had neither the surplus nor the incentive to sell.

The Bolsheviks, however, were inclined to read the situation very differently. At the very time when the old ruling class was trying to defeat them by armed force, the peasants, they decided, were trying to achieve the same end by starving them into submission. Not that the peasants as a whole were counter-revolutionaries – that would have been an utterly demoralizing admission. The villains of the piece clearly enough were the rich peasants, the kulaks. These were natural anti-Bolsheviks, and they were defending their class interest as the rural bourgeoisie by holding back grain. This insight decided how the regime would respond to the grain crisis: it would declare class war in the villages and set the poor peasants against the rich.

In the early summer of 1918, committees of 'poor peasants' were set up throughout rural Russia and ordered to seize surplus supplies from their supposedly grain-hoarding richer neighbours. On paper the task looked easy: Lenin calculated that there were ten million poor peasant households as against only two million kulak households. The poor peasants would, moreover, be helped and spurred on by armed detachments of workers sent out from the towns. Under this two-pronged attack, kulaks would be forced to disgorge their grain at prices fixed by the state; those who tried to resist would be declared 'enemies of the people', handed over to revolutionary tribunals, and given at least ten years in prison.

The Bolsheviks had, however, deluded themselves. Very few peasants were now landless (less than 5 per cent) and very few were appreciably better off than the rest. The idea that a sizeable minority of kulaks was oppressing a majority of landless peasants was a Bolshevik fantasy – the reality was that the overwhelming majority were middle peasants who lived off the cultivation of their own strips. There were no class divisions for the Bolsheviks to exploit, and the villages simply closed ranks against these urban invaders. The government soon accepted that setting peasant against peasant was not going to work and by the end of the year the poor peasant committees had been abolished; but it continued denouncing the kulaks and sending armed detachments from the cities to forage. Not only that; from 1919 the requisitioning became harsher. Previously limited to grain, it now included all the peasants' produce. And where before the brigades had worked with local estimates of the peasants' surpluses, they now had quotas which had been calculated in the light of the state's needs rather than the size of local surpluses. This was nothing other in fact than indiscriminate confiscation. Thuggish methods had to be used to carry it out, and whenever they could the peasants replied to violence with violence.

So it came to outright warfare between town and country; Lenin's prerevolutionary alliance had utterly split asunder. The peasants had welcomed the October Revolution and seen the Bolsheviks as their liberators, but within a year harmony between the two had been replaced by bitter enmity. The oppression the peasants suffered now seemed in many ways worse than the old oppression and in some ways undoubtedly was worse. Above all, it was more intrusive. They had begun running their own affairs through the village communes; now soviets controlled by outsiders were ordering them about. There was talk of taking the land from them and turning them into labourers on huge collective farms run by townsmen. There was talk too – sometimes more than talk – of closing the churches and driving out the priests. They were being conscripted into the new army just as they had been conscripted into the tsar's army. The worst intrusion, however, was the violent theft of their grain and other produce by town hooligans and the terrible punishments inflicted on anyone suspected of hoarding. Even in the days of serfdom, the masters had not pillaged their produce. A curious peasant slogan of the time – 'We are for the Bolsheviks, but against the Communists' – expressed something of the peasants' confusion and anger at the regime's turnabout.[6] The 'Bolsheviks' had given them land, but now 'Communists' had come along who bullied and cheated them and even threatened to take the land back. (The confusion may have stemmed from the party's change of name: in March 1918 it became 'The Russian Communist Party'.) The revolution had come, Yurii Zhivago reflected, like the fulfilment of the peasant's 'ancient dream of living anarchically on his own land by the work of his own hands, in complete independence and without owing anything to anyone. Instead of that, he found he had only exchanged the old oppression of the tsarist state for the new, much harsher yoke of the revolutionary super-state.'[7]

One thing only held the peasants' urge to retaliate in check – the fear that things could get even worse. The Communists might be awful, but if the Whites won the landlords would come back, and then for sure the peasant would lose his land. By the summer of 1920, however, it was clear that the Whites were beaten, and now across the country the peasants broke into open revolt. In effect they called a plague upon both Reds and Whites, upon new bosses and old ones, and made a desperate bid to be allowed their own way of life. 'Green' rebels roamed the countryside. In some places they were no more than bands of guerrillas; in others – Ukraine, western Siberia and the province of Tambov – sizeable peasant armies took to the field against their oppressors.

The only consolation in this for the Bolsheviks was that peasant hostility was predictable. The peasants had been on the receiving end of War Communism and could not have been expected to like it. Moreover, the peasants' revolts were localized and thanks to the neutering of the SRs had no organizing nucleus; they would be put down in the end. A severer blow for the Bolsheviks, however, was the discovery that they had strained to breaking-point the patience of their own natural supporters, the urban workers. It was bad enough that this class with which all their hopes were associated was fast dwindling; worse still, they now had evidence that their much-diminished core of supporters questioned Soviet rule and even in some cases rejected it entirely.The warning signs had begun with waves of strikes and demonstrations in Moscow and Petrograd early in 1921. The real shock, however – the 'lightning flash', as Lenin called it – came when the sailors and workers of the fortress island of Kronstadt broke into revolt at the end of February 1921. For these were not ordinary Bolshevik supporters – they had been the heart and soul of the 'July Days', had delivered the final blow to the Provisional Government by training the *Aurora*'s guns on the Winter Palace, and had acquired a place in Bolshevik mythology similar to that of the Bastille's captors in the mythology of the French Revolution. But now the Kronstadt sailors and workers had risen against their party, demanding new and truly free elections to soviets, freedom of speech and assembly, freedom for socialist political prisoners, a multi-party political system, and a fully democratic worker and peasant state.

The lightning struck as the tenth Party Congress was about to gather in Moscow. A number of delegates left at once for Petrograd and went with Red Army units across the ice to fight this 'counter-revolutionary conspiracy', as the government had chosen to call it. After a week the uprising was crushed with massive losses on both sides; a bloody repression then followed. But while the Bolsheviks' hold on power remained for the moment secure, the reality Kronstadt had illumined for them could hardly have been more depressing. They had not gained the majority support they had counted on; quite the contrary – they had lost even the cast-iron working-class constituency they had once had. On Zinoviev's perhaps overpessimistic estimate, they now had no more than 1 per cent support from a working class which had itself shrunk to a tiny fraction of the population. Equally depressing, defeat of a Communist uprising in Berlin, almost simultaneous with Kronstadt, seemed to sound the death-knell for their hopes of help from a victorious Western proletariat. The bitter truth was that they were confronted by hostile and apparently impregnable capitalist powers, while in Russia itself they were hated and rejected by the overwhelming majority of the people. The regime found itself suspended in the air with no apparent social underpinning. Both of the assumptions upon which the October gamble had been premised had turned out to be mistaken. Their Menshevik and other opponents had been vindicated, and it was surely only a matter of time before the regime collapsed and the Bolsheviks' experiment was terminated.

Nothing of the kind happened, however. Intensely unpopular though it was, the regime had put its enemies to flight and would continue doing so. The leaders would, as we shall see, make concessions, but for the time being they could manage without majority support or even large-minority support. What they had instead of support was absolute power, and the instrument of their power was the relative handful of people who made up the Communist Party.

6

Things should have worked out very differently, of course. The party should not have been a ruling force in its own right, simply the vanguard of a ruling proletariat which rapidly won the allegiance of most of the population. Once the revolution was accomplished, the party's role should have been fairly minor: October was meant to have ushered in not the rule of the party but the rule of the soviets.

As for the soviets, they were intended as the Bolsheviks' improvement on the pseudo-democracy of the despised bourgeois parliament. Their worker, peasant and soldier deputies would not develop into a class of professional politicians cut off from the lives and opinions of ordinary people: real democracy would be ensured by the deputies keeping their everyday jobs and being subject at any time to recall by their constituents. The Bolsheviks' addiction to this new form of representative government was shown in the name they gave to their state; in Lenin's *State and Revolution*, where the soviets got frequent mention and the party none at all; and above all in the RSFSR's 1918 constitution. The first article of the constitution declared: 'Russia is proclaimed a Republic of Soviets of Workers', Soldiers' and Peasants' Deputies. All power at the centre and in the localities shall be vested in these soviets.'[8] Supreme power, according to the constitution, belonged to the All-Russian Congress of Soviets, an unwieldy body which would meet only once or twice a year, and when it was not in session to its Central Executive Committee. The CEC appointed Sovnarkom – the government – and Sovnarkom was answerable to it and ultimately to the Congress. As for the Communist Party, that was the ghost at the feast. There was not a single reference to it in the 1918 constitution or the 1924 one, and it would receive only a passing mention in the 1936 constitution. Anyone taking these early constitutional documents as a guide to political life in the new state would have assumed that but for two, admittedly serious, shortcomings – the disfranchizing of the former 'exploiting classes' and the weighting of the voting system in favour of town dwellers – what had been established was a model democracy.

The reality, however, would prove utterly different, and Soviet democracy would turn out to be a travesty of the intended soviet democracy. At the root of the problem was the Bolsheviks' grossly misplaced optimism that once they had power there would be a rapid convergence between what they wanted and what the masses wanted. This belief that proletarian support would broaden out into general support had been an absolutely necessary piece of wishful thinking for them. They wanted power very badly; they considered themselves democratic socialists and embodiments of the highest ideals of humanity; therefore there *had* to be potential majority support for them which would quickly, once they had power, be converted into actual and enthusiastic support. But they were deluding themselves, and how completely would be shown by the civil war. Their gut response to the peasants as more or less incorrigible petty-bourgeois individualists had proved much closer to the mark than their view of the rural masses as a semi- or potential proletariat. As long as the peasants remained more petty-bourgeois than proletarian, Bolshevik power and soviet democracy would be incompatible; and faced with a choice, the Bolsheviks naturally enough put their power before their principles.

They had made another mistake in seeing the Russian working class, raw and not long out of the villages, as a proletariat. Had the workers lived up to Lenin's expectations of them, the regime might at least have practised some neutered form of democracy, discriminating against peasants perhaps as liberal regimes in Western Europe had once discriminated against those with little or no property. But once in power the Bolshevik leaders very quickly became disillusioned with this working class which had nominally empowered them. It showed no signs whatever of a proper proletarian consciousness, as the upsurge of Menshevik and SR sympathies among its members revealed all too clearly. Far from peasants being proletarianized, the reverse process seemed to be happening before the eyes of a disbelieving Bolshevik leadership: the workers were behaving more and more like greedy, stupid and short-sighted peasants.

The problem had begun in the factories, where the workers' interpretation of 'workers' control' as a licence to manage the factories themselves had led to anarchy and a rapid collapse of the industrial sector. The workers were simply too uncultured, Lenin judged, to be capable of industrial self-management. They had a right, certainly, to be consulted and to supervise, but management had to be left to managers, who for the time being would be drawn inevitably from the bourgeois intelligentsia. What was at issue was not merely knowledge but *authority* – there had to be 'unquestioning subordination to a single will' and even, Lenin argued, a form of individual dictatorship within the factory.⁹ Democracy, it followed, stopped strictly short at the factory gates, and once the worker crossed that threshold the order of the day was obedience to authority. Factory committees were placed under the control of the trade unions, whose task was to protect not their members' rights but their members' interests by increasing discipline and productivity within the factories. Just as they had lost the right of self-management, so the workers lost the right to do what they wanted with their own labour. They were made to work where the authorities decreed; they were conscripted into the Red Army; and when the war was over many would be drafted into 'labour armies', which carried out civilian tasks under military discipline. Even outside the factory or the army they did not have the rights of citizens, let alone the rights of a ruling class. If the workers were considered too anarchic and too stupid to be allowed to run the factories, they could hardly be allowed any say in the running of the state. There was no proletariat, only an immature working class which fell far short of its proletarian vocation. Therefore there could be no dictatorship of the proletariat other than in name. What replaced it was a dictatorship of the party.

The dictatorship had been accomplished, first, by the party's take-over at all levels of the soviets. It had of course from the outset controlled the top level of the soviet movement – the All-Russian Congress, the CEC and Sovnarkom. But these were simply the apex of a vast pyramid, the lowest level of which was formed by small town, district and village soviets, and these had remained relatively independent in the opening months of Bolshevik rule. By 1918, however, the opposition parties had, as we have seen, been removed from them. Not only that: the soviet assemblies had lost power to their executive committees, the committees had become dominated by their secretaries, and the secretaries were acting as agents of the government in Moscow. When Lenin commented in 1919 that the soviets, which ought to have been organs of government *by* the workers, were in fact only organs of government *for* the workers, he was more or less admitting that soviet democracy as he had envisaged it until October 1917 had been shelved.

But the party had done more than take over the soviets lock, stock and barrel: it was increasingly encroaching upon functions which had been designated as soviet rather than party ones. Party and soviets had parallel organizational structures, each a chain of many links which went from the top of society to the very bottom, from congress in Moscow to village soviet or party cell in a factory. The dominant partner should have been the soviets, but in the critical conditions created by the civil war the party proved a more versatile instrument and its officials far more effective as troubleshooters. Beginning at the lowest levels, the encroachment soon spread to the most important decision-making body in the state, Sovnarkom itself. Though its members were all Bolsheviks (apart from the brief period of coalition with the Left SRs), Sovnarkom nevertheless came firmly on the soviet side of the divide and was answerable, as we have seen, to the CEC. In 1919, however, reorganization at the top of the party led to the creation of a rival to it: the Political Bureau or Politburo, which had the task of taking decisions that could not wait until the next meeting of the party's Central Committee. The Politburo consisted of a mere five full members; they happened to be the most important people in the party and the state (Lenin, Trotsky, Stalin, Kamenev and Zinoviev), and the meetings of this handful more and more became the chief decision-making forum.

Since the soviets were by now so thoroughly Bolshevized, the steady erosion of the line distinguishing soviet from party responsibilities might not have seemed to matter that much. What did matter, however, since this had in effect become a one-party state, was that the party with monopoly control should remain a democratic one at least in the sense of being accountable to its own members. Yet the conditions which had helped eliminate the party's rivals worked against free speech, accountability and toleration of differences within the party itself. What had happened in the soviets happened at the lower levels of the party as well: general assemblies became a formality, officials took their instructions from above with no regard to opinion from below, and soon elections disappeared altogether and appointment of officials became the normal practice. Just as the regime ducked any accountability to the general electorate, so the party took care not to be accountable to its particular electorate. And the erosion of accountability was all the easier within the party since it was subject to the rules not of democracy but of democratic centralism. Authority was imposed from above, and the flow of energy and initiative from below, which in Lenin's original idea of democratic centralism should have had a balancing effect, rapidly dried up. The ruling party itself was therefore no less divided between rulers and ruled than society as a whole. At the summit a tiny number of what Lenin called 'the party's old guard' took all the decisions that mattered; beneath them a burgeoning cohort of full-time party officials spread across the country saw to it that the oligarchs' decisions were carried out; and beneath them the party's rank and file, who continued at the factory bench or in other ordinary employment, acted as intermediary between this two-tier élite and the politically excluded masses.

This concentration of power at the top and the authoritarian way in which in conditions of civil war the power came to be used created obvious dangers of abuse, and in 1920 the party tried to safeguard against these by setting up so-called 'control commissions' which would receive and investigate complaints against officials. The commissions, however, were soon perverted from their purpose of protecting the party rank and file against their bosses, and before long were being used instead by the bosses to silence their critics. Even had the commissions been effective, they would not have gone far enough for those who resented the stifling of democracy in the party and believed that democracy alone offered a real safeguard against abuse. As the civil war drew to an end, determined efforts were made to restore the party's democratic character. The Democratic Centralists set out to reverse the tendency towards appointing party officials, demanding proper elections and free and open debate on issues of importance. A more formidable challenge to the leadership came, however, from the Workers' Opposition, which voiced the frustration of workers who had seen the hopes and ideals of 1917 come to nothing. A chasm had opened up, the group's spokesmen warned, between the workers and those who ruled in their name, and this had to be closed as a matter of urgency. The party's bureaucrats had to be held in check; its democratic principles had to be put into practice; industry should be run by the trade unions rather than by government managers; and there should be a general increase in the workers' influence at the expense of that of intellectuals and bourgeois specialists. The party, in a nutshell, had to become more democratic and more genuinely proletarian; and by the winter of 1920–21 the Workers' Opposition was making these twin demands very loudly.

The background to this debate was provided by the changes to the party since February 1917. From 20,000 members it had expanded massively to 732,000 members in March 1921. At the leadership level intellectuals still dominated, though less strikingly than in 1917. Virtually 70 per cent of the 1921 membership, however, originated from the manual labouring classes (41 per cent workers, 28 per cent peasants, most of whom had been radicalized in the Red Army). These newcomers who had swamped the Old Bolsheviks were mainly poorly educated young men who had fought in and been moulded by the civil war. If they were talented and energetic, they moved easily into important positions in the soviets, the army, the Cheka and the party itself. These 'cadres' (the military term by which key person-nel became known) are often portrayed as revolver-touting thugs; they were certainly tough and prepared to be brutal; and from them a proletarian rul-ing class was beginning to take shape. Promotion to important party or soviet posts inevitably took such people away from the factory floor. An analysis of party members has shown, for instance, that in October 1919 only 11 per cent still worked in factories. The new ruling class was in dan-ger, therefore, of losing what proletarian roots it had; moreover, it was only a ruling class in a very conditional sense. Certainly it had nothing in com-mon with the Marxist ideal of a working class which governed collectively with a minimum of coercion or centralization. The members of the new rul-ing class were professional executives who ruled over their working-class comrades and everyone else. They had a striking functional resemblance in fact to the old discredited and destroyed ruling class, even if they originated from the opposite end of the social spectrum. Like the members of the old ruling class, they had enormous powers and a wide scope for arbitrary action; like them, they were handsomely rewarded; and like them they were bound in absolute obedience to the real rulers, on whose behalf they ran the country with an iron hand.

Behind the demand for a more democratic and more proletarian party lay the assumption that proletarianization would make for greater democracy. Events would, however, disprove it, and the mass recruitment of workers in the 1920s would simply play into the hands of the most authoritarian of the party's leaders. The undemocratic nature of the party was anyway some-thing which the leadership as a whole was not willing to sacrifice. Originally a defence of the party against the might of the tsarist state, it was just as nec-essary now when by a baffling reversal the party itself had become a besieged power-holder facing mass hostility. The rulers in the Kremlin after all had next to no support and no democratic legitimacy whatever. That was why they needed the tough new ruling class of cadres. That was why they fell back so unreluctantly upon the autocratic tradition, which throughout had exercised a strong subliminal fascination on the party. The brute fact was that the party's powers were all that stood between it and political oblivion, and this was why they were absolutely non-negotiable.

7

Concessions were nevertheless vital. In the long run three-quarters of a mil-lion party loyalists could not hold down 140 million deeply disaffected peo-ple; but what made the need for change urgent was that the economy was grinding to a halt. Almost no goods were being produced or exchanged any more. People could be bludgeoned into obedience, but bludgeoning did not make them produce. It was a situation reminiscent of the 1918 one, when Lenin had had to insist against fierce opposition on an unfavourable peace with the enemy. The enemy in this case were the peasants, and a hurtful peace had to be made with them. War Communism had failed, Lenin reluctantly concluded. There were simply too few Communists as against too many peasants. Given that ratio, changing the peasants over a short timescale was impossible. The immediate need was to conciliate them by giving them what they wanted – otherwise they would send the party to the devil. And in March 1921 Lenin initiated a dramatic volte-face by announcing the New Economic Policy (NEP).

NEP had two elements. First, the hated requisitioning of produce was abolished. Instead, peasants were to pay a food tax, a fixed proportion of their produce, which was set at a much lower level than the requisitioning targets. The government would as a result take only a part of the peasant's produce rather than everything it could lay hands on; the more the peasant produced, the more would be left for his own benefit. The aim of giving the peasant an incentive to grow as much as possible would, however, be thwarted unless he could market the surplus and buy goods with what they earned him. And this need led to the second element in NEP. Restrictions on trading were gradually relaxed; small-scale private enterprises were again allowed in order to provide the goods which would persuade the peasants to disgorge their produce; and before long private entrepreneurs, 'Nepmen' as they became known, had set trade flowing once more between town and country.

Gentleness and gradualism – a reformist approach rather than a revolutionary one, Lenin called it – replaced intolerance and impatience in other spheres of life as well. Non-party intellectuals now breathed more easily, and the NEP period developed into an oasis of cultural freedom. Even now there were of course limits to the permissible. Someone who went too far was Yevgenii Zamyatin, whose novel *We* satirized Bolshevik ambitions by depicting a society in which people were no longer known by names, simply by numbers, and enjoyed the happiness of absolute non-freedom. The time when they got up and went to bed, their work and their leisure, their thought processes, their meals, their sexual activities, even when they drew the blinds – everything was decided for them by the Benefactor and the Guardians. This commentary on Bolshevik collectivism (hence the 'we' of the title) and anti-individualism went far too close to the bone; not surprisingly, *We* was suppressed, and it never achieved Soviet publication. NEP nevertheless stands out as an easy-going interlude between the periods of draconian control which preceded and followed it; and with the resumption of trading and greater freedom in general (even for prostitutes), life in the cities regained something of its pre-revolutionary character. The 'peasant Brest-Litovsk' had not of course changed the Bolsheviks' objectives. NEP was no more than 'a necessary retreat', a case of one step back in order to take two forwards, though subsequent progress, Lenin warned, would take place 'infinitely more slowly than we expected'.[10]

Not only was the retreat temporary; it was by no means on all fronts. The party had conceded an NEP but not a NPP – there would be no political relaxation. The peasant rebels had been bought off, but the Kronstadt mutineers were not offered the freedoms and the multi-party system they had fought for. It was precisely at this juncture in fact that the Menshevik and SR parties, which might so easily and justifiably have capitalized on the Bolsheviks' difficulties, were struck out of existence. Some 2,000 Mensheviks, including the whole Central Committee, were arrested just before the new policy was announced; leading SRs were put on trial for crimes against the state; and numerous liberals and socialists were deported not long afterwards. Lenin justified this harshness by arguing that 'When an army is in retreat a hundred times more discipline is required than when it is advancing'.[11] He threatened anyone who publicly opposed the government with the death penalty, and in correspondence marked 'strictly secret' he recommended making an example of reactionary clerics and bourgeois by shooting them. 'It is precisely now that we must teach these people a lesson, so that for several decades they will not even dare to think of any resistance.'[12]

Not content with crushing opposition outside the party, the leadership turned equally relentlessly against its own internal critics. The tenth Party Congress condemned the Workers' Opposition as a 'syndicalist and anarchist deviation', and passed a resolution on party unity which dissolved all such groups and imposed a ban upon so-called factions, upon pain of expulsion from the party, which would last until the party's downfall. This congress which endorsed the economic liberalism of NEP thus set the seal upon the party's rejection of democratism. Until the tenth Congress, those who opposed official policies had been allowed to organize and to argue their case in party forums. That, however, was a luxury the party could no longer afford. From now on it would have to be unchallengeable, and in order to be that it would have to look monolithically united.

NEP was therefore a very mixed bag indeed. It offered considerable concessions to peasants and petty entrepreneurs, yet the state still kept control of 'the commanding heights of the economy', i.e. all major industry and large-scale economic activity. Intellectuals were held on a much looser leash, yet there was a distinct tightening in the party's control over the state and the élite's control over the party. Thus at one and the same time the party bowed to what people wanted and increased its capacity to make them do what it wanted.

By general agreement, NEP was much too contradictory to last long. The concessions made to peasants and intellectuals had been bitterly resented by many party zealots, whose dream of communism around the corner had been dashed. They had also been badly received by urban workers, who feared that the peasants' gains would be their losses – so much so that 'New Exploitation of the Proletariat' went the rounds as a sardonic translation of NEP. The new policy was no more in fact than a holding operation which had defused current problems at the price of storing up future ones. It gave no clear-cut answer to the party's fundamental dilemma – how to create socialism in a country utterly unprepared for it. Instead, it pointed towards solutions that were very different and indeed incompatible. Letting the country go towards socialism at its own pace, which meant slowly and with detours in the direction of capitalism; or else using the party's now unlimited powers to impose whatever seemed necessary in the interests of socialism.

In the final years of his life, however, Lenin clung to the hope that a middle way could somehow be found between these extremes. The Bolsheviks, he admitted, had done things in the opposite order from the one envisaged by Marx: they had had their political revolution before the social, economic and cultural revolutions which should have prepared it. The October Revolution had not for all that been a mistake; but having had to take power prematurely, the Bolsheviks themselves now had to do the economic and cultural spadework which others should have done for them. And at the end of his life Lenin clutched at the idea of cultural revolution as the way by which the Soviet regime could escape from the anomalous position in which it found itself. Cultural revolutionaries, whose method would be persuasion rather than coercion, would teach literacy, science and a Marxist understanding of the world, thus reshaping the mentality of the masses and opening their eyes to the benefits of socialism. The village schoolteacher had a vital role here, but formal education would have to be supplemented by propaganda. Reading rooms, or at least 'Red Corners' in public buildings, would be set up in every village; the new art form of the cinema would be exploited to the utmost; and celebration of the great revolutionary anniversaries (9 January, 1 May, 7 November, etc.) would help create a secular popular culture which would oust Christianity – thus May Day would take over as a spring holiday from Easter.

The idea of cultural revolution brightened the end of Lenin's life because it seemed to offer an escape from a hard choice between postponing socialism into the infinite future and turning once more to violence. But whatever the promise of the future, there were ominous signs that here and now the party was losing its way, and the unresolved question of the nationalities provided particularly disturbing evidence of this. In 1922 Stalin proposed that Ukraine and the other soviet republics should be incorporated into the RSFSR with the status of autonomous republics. Lenin, however, objected, insisting on the need for a federation of republics enjoying equal rights. Each republic should keep its own government, and above the republican level there should be a Moscow-based Union government for the whole state. Stalin gave way and as a result the Union of Soviet Socialist Republics (USSR) was created; its constitution, modelled on that of the RSFSR, was drawn up in 1923 and finally ratified in January 1924. But while Lenin had achieved a state structure which gave the nationalities formal equality with the Russians, the reality, he soon realized, was very different. When evidence emerged that Stalin and his henchman Ordzhonikidze had beaten and bullied the Georgians into the Union (literally so, since Ordzhonikidze had struck a leading Georgian Communist), he became infuriated. Just as the party had leant over backwards to the peasants, so it was vital, Lenin now believed, to treat the nationalities with utmost consideration. Russian chauvinism – exemplified here, ironically enough, by the Georgians Stalin and Ordzhonikidze – was utterly intolerable. It might actually be necessary to discriminate within the Union *against* the Russians; and at the end of his working life he was even contemplating limiting the responsibility of the Union government to foreign affairs and defence and passing everything else to the republics.

High-handed treatment of the nationalities, moreover, reflected a wider malaise which he agonized over during his final working months. The party and state machine – the bureaucracy – had expanded monstrously, seemed to be getting out of control, and was coming to have a sickening resemblance to the old bureaucracy, which the revolution had been meant to extirpate once and for all. There were far too many officials; and too many of them were inefficient and incompetent, if not downright dishonest, oppressive and corrupt. The trouble was that Lenin's desire for a self-governing, bureaucrat-free society had proved incompatible with his equally fervent desire for the party to take control of all aspects of life, including the economic. That desire, which was essential to the Bolsheviks' ambition of transforming Russia, had made a huge army of apparatchiks unavoidable. Sovnarkom, for instance, had to his horror spawned no less than 120 commissions. What could be done? The obvious solution of curbing the activities of this proliferating officialdom by making the officials' political masters publicly accountable was ruled out by the very fact that it was unconstrained executive action which kept the party in power. The hateful reality was that Lenin and his colleagues depended upon this bureaucratic machine, arbitrary, incompetent and corrupt though it often was. The most that could be done was to tighten and redefine accountability at the top, and with this in mind Lenin proposed that an enlarged Central Committee of the party should claw back authority it had lost to the Politburo and that an élite corps of inspectors should be given a free hand to monitor all party and state activities.

What terrified him was the prospect of cadres behaving in an abominable and utterly un-Bolshevik way – in fact like the tsarist satraps of old. The danger had of course been shown graphically and at the highest level by Stalin's bullying of the Georgians. The problem would have seemed less pressing if Lenin, who was only in his early fifties, had been in good health. He, after all, could curb his headstrong colleagues. But he had suffered a stroke in May 1922 and had been poorly ever since; and the prospect that he might not be around much longer raised as a matter of urgency the question of who should succeed him. Though no dictator, he had in effect been responsible for all the major strategic decisions. He had also acted very much as the party's conscience and court of appeal. It was almost certain, however, that someone else would have to guide the party out of the ambiguities of NEP and ensure that it went by the right road and at the right pace towards socialism.

The obvious successor was Trotsky. Lenin admittedly had reservations about him, which stemmed from the past conflicts between them. Yet Trotsky stood head and shoulders above his rivals in terms of ability, charisma and popularity; he had masterminded the October Revolution and he had had a brilliant record of achievement during the civil war. Furthermore, Lenin and he were at one on the need to fight bureaucracy. Since that issue had become enormously important, it was perfectly clear that the one person Lenin could not allow to succeed him was the party's arch bureaucrat, and incidentally Trotsky's *bête noire*, Stalin.

In December 1922 Lenin dictated a series of notes on his senior colleagues in which he warned that Stalin might not use his 'unlimited authority' as General Secretary of the party 'with sufficient caution'. That was fairly mild, and what reduced its sting was that he passed strictures on the others as well. However, in January 1923 he added a much sharper appendix: 'Stalin is too rude, and this defect, though quite tolerable in our midst and in dealings among us Communists, becomes intolerable in a secretary-general'. For that reason Stalin should be removed from his post and replaced by someone 'more tolerant, more loyal, more polite and more considerate to the comrades, less capricious, etc.'.[13] Two months later Lenin suffered a further stroke, which incapacitated him entirely, and on 24 January 1924 he died. The aftermath, however, would have dismayed him. For it was not Trotsky but Stalin who emerged as the Soviet Union's new leader, and under Stalin the evils which had distressed him would be magnified a hundredfold.

8

On the face of it, Trotsky should have strolled to an easy victory. Stalin was no more than a competent mediocrity: neither a brilliant intellect nor a brilliant orator nor a brilliant organizer. He was of course no fool – he was well read in Marxism and had quite enough grasp of theory to keep his end up in political infighting. By comparison, however, with his rival, the Georgian cobbler's son seemed uninspired, ordinary, a man on Moscow's Clapham omnibus. Yet Trotsky's outstanding abilities were not wholly to his advantage. His very superiority, worn all too evidently on his sleeve, alienated colleagues and led Kamenev and Zinoviev to gang up with Stalin against him.

It was not just envy which drove the three of them into an anti-Trotsky alliance. The Bolsheviks, finding themselves in uncharted revolutionary waters, grasped at any guidance history might seem to give them. The obvious precedent was the French Revolution, which warned of the dangers of a military dictator taking over; and the person who threatened to be Russia's Bonaparte was of course the charismatic and haughty founder of the Red Army.

It did not help Trotsky that, for all his popularity, he had failed to create a solid power-base for himself in the party. Probably he saw no need for one. Stalin, however, had by no means made the same mistake. In 1922 he had acquired the new position of General Secretary of the party, which made him head of its 600-strong secretariat. In a democratic party this might have been no more than an important backroom job, and that is how the other party leaders seem to have seen it: suitable employment for a plodder who would never shine in public. But in the Russian Communist Party the secretariat and the General Secretary in particular had enormous scope to direct and control the members. He allocated party personnel, supervised local party organizations, and, crucially, appointed the secretaries who ran the local organizations. What became known as a 'circular flow of power' was thus created: the General Secretary appointed, and could of course dismiss, the secretaries who dominated the localities; they in turn repaid him and ensured his continuing good will by sending delegates to party conferences and congresses who would loyally support him against opponents. By his control of party patronage the General Secretary was therefore able to build up a clientele of dedicated followers who could determine the make-up of the top party bodies and thus indirectly of the Central Committee and the Politburo. Trotsky had no equivalent weapon; and his fierce attacks on bureaucracy in the party during 1923 clearly reflected a fear that the weapon would be used against him.

The reality was that, despite appearances, it was Trotsky who was the underdog. He had no power-base and, despite his brilliance, no ability at political infighting; and Stalin had both of the things he lacked. At the thirteenth Party Conference, held in January 1924, Trotsky suffered a severe defeat; from then on his following in the party, which had been considerable among intellectuals, white-collar workers and soldiers, went into a rapid decline. The success of the anti-Trotskyites owed much to Stalin's cultivation of Kamenev and in particular Zinoviev, who had the prestige of being widely regarded as Lenin's heir. And these two did Stalin another vital service by using their influence to have Lenin's criticisms of him suppressed. Had the criticisms been published, as Lenin seems to have intended, Stalin's career would almost certainly have been finished.

It was not only in dealing with his colleagues that Stalin proved an adroit politician; he had a sharp eye too for what appealed to the rank and file. His 'man of the people' image – quite different from Trotsky's aloof and supercilious intellectuality – was not wholly bogus: he understood popular instincts and how to manipulate them, and showed this clearly enough after Lenin's death. The death had made little practical difference since Lenin had been out of action for a long while; its impact was nevertheless enormous and potentially devastating. For Lenin had been an unpopular regime's trump card; he had become genuinely respected and something of a father figure. The problem of how to give him a fitting send-off was, therefore, linked to a vital broader one – how could his popularity be kept alive for the party's benefit?

On the first issue, Stalin's position was clear-cut. Even before the Leader's death he had opposed the idea of cremating him (which Lenin himself seems to have wanted), arguing that cremation was un-Russian and would cause offence. He had also, though rather tentatively, floated the idea that Lenin should be embalmed rather than buried. The idea of preserving Lenin's body had, however, met strong opposition from Trotsky, Bukharin, Kamenev and other leading Bolsheviks, and also from Lenin's wife and family. For Trotsky, preserving Lenin smacked of the Church making a holy relic out of the bones of a saint. 'Apparently we, the party of revolutionary Marxism, are advised to behave in the same way – to preserve the body of Lenin. Earlier there were the relics of Sergius of Radonezh and Serafim of Sarov; now they want to replace these with the relics of Vladimir Ilich.'[14] That putting Lenin's body on show to be venerated was un-Bolshevik hardly needed to be laboured: the Bolsheviks had, after all, set out as rationalists and enlighteners who wanted to replace superstition and religiosity by a man-centred, secular socialism.

Yet the preservers, led by Stalin, got their way. Instead of being buried, Lenin's body would be embalmed and put on display in a wooden mausoleum in Red Square, to be replaced in 1930 by a grandiose porphyry and granite construction; and during seven decades millions of Soviet people would come here 'on pilgrimage' (Stalin's phrase) to gaze at the founder. To intellectuals like Trotsky and Bukharin this was an obscene exploitation of primitivism; it was also a warning that the party might easily get deflected from its enlightenment mission and be contaminated by the petty-bourgeois culture which lapped about it. To the former seminarist Stalin, however, and no doubt to many other party bosses with a feel for the grass-roots, such fastidiousness was absurd: Lenin's death had unleashed enormous popular grief and affection, which the party had to make the utmost of. There was nothing wrong in harnessing popular credulity to socialist purposes. If the ancient Russian belief that saintly rulers continued after death to protect and watch over their people could be used for the party's benefit, why not?

Bolshevik purists might object to the religious overtones, but they could hardly deny that the party needed to make special claims for Lenin. During his lifetime there had been none: his own modesty had forbidden it, and special treatment would anyway have been un-Bolshevik. The country had only just got rid of one tsar, and to have instituted another under any guise whatever would have been out of the question. The Bolsheviks believed in collective leadership; Lenin was seen as first among equals, nothing more. But if he had not been the Leader in life he became so to general party acclaim in death, and once he was dead the leadership, with Stalin in the van, set about vigorously creating a cult of him. The former capital was renamed Leningrad; a Lenin Institute was established; despite protests from his wife, Nadezhda Krupskaya, statues and memorials in his honour rapidly proliferated; and soon even remote villages had 'Lenin Corners' which, with their busts, photos and paintings of the Leader, recalled the icon corners of old Russia.

'Lenin lives!' was the message on the billboards. The cult of Lenin as Leader nevertheless implied that someone else had to take on the role which he had partially at least now vacated. As General Secretary Stalin was well placed for the succession, but control of the party machine was not in itself enough to ensure his success. He had to prove himself the heir, and soon he was posing as the Leader's champion against anyone – Trotsky being the chief alleged offender – who tried to belittle him or to stray from his 'commandments'. Guarding the heritage of course included the vital task of defining it. What was Leninism? What it was not, Stalin made clear, was Trotskyism.

All Bolsheviks had, as we have seen, taken it for granted that the success of socialism in backward Russia was dependent upon its success in the West. Though generally accepted, the belief had been stated most clearly by Trotsky in his theory of 'Permanent Revolution'. By the early 1920s, however, the belief had become an embarrassment and an anomaly. For there had been no world-wide revolution, nor did revolution look imminent in any developed country. Did that mean that Soviet communism was doomed to wither and die on its exposed limb? That was certainly not what most party members assumed, yet their commitment to achieving socialism irrespective of what happened elsewhere was not yet reflected in theory, and this discrepancy gave Stalin his chance. In adjusting theory to the reality – that the Soviet Union was building socialism on its own – he would also strike a blow against the outstanding proponent of the view that socialism in Russia had to depend upon revolution in the West. The opportunity was too good to miss, and Stalin took it in December 1924 with an article, clearly targeted at Trotsky, in which he argued that socialism could be achieved by one country on its own, even a backward one. He was careful to add the rider that the final victory of socialism would still depend on international proletarian revolution; but even with this qualification Socialism in One Country, as the doctrine became known, was a masterstroke which struck a blow at Trotsky and drew national feeling on to Stalin's side.

One of the Bolsheviks' weaknesses was that their internationalism risked wounding Russian feelings; and how un-Russian they were had been shown by the name they had just given their state – Union of Soviet Socialist

Republics, which made no reference to Russia at all. In the international socialist community the Bolsheviks envisaged there would, as we have seen, be little place for anything distinctively Russian. Socialism in One Country, however, brought the party firmly back into line with national feeling. Russia, Stalin was saying, needed no favours from the West. Backward it might be, but it could lead other countries in the building of socialism. Whereas Trotsky's approach – in effect the Menshevik one, he suggested – left the Russian revolution having 'either to rot away or to degenerate into a bourgeois state'. In fact, 'Lack of faith in the strength and capacities of our revolution, lack of faith in the strength and capacity of the Russian proletariat – that is what lies at the root of the theory of "permanent revolution".'[15]

As a Jew and a highly westernized intellectual, Trotsky was all too vulnerable to such insinuations of anti-Russianness. Stalin was playing the national card against him, knowing that among the party masses he could count on a response to anti-semitic and anti-intellectual innuendo. He was appealing, moreover, not only to prejudice but to realism: the party was going it alone, and the only alternative to that was an unthinkable surrender. With popular feeling and Stalin's cohorts behind it, Socialism in One Country became official doctrine at the fourteenth Party Conference in 1925. 'Under the dictatorship of the proletariat', Stalin wrote after the conference, 'we possess, it appears, all that is needed to build a complete socialist society, overcoming all internal difficulties.'[16] Russia might be Bolshevized, but Bolshevism was at the same time being russified, and the architect of its russification was, curiously enough, someone who spoke Russian with a Georgian accent.

9

Rather late in the day, Kamenev and Zinoviev woke up to the danger from their fellow 'triumvir'. Stalin had accumulated far too much power; he was also, they decided, pursuing wrongheaded policies. Trotsky had for some time been questioning NEP and arguing the case for tough economic planning and forced industrial growth, even if it meant forcing the peasants to pay for it through higher prices and higher taxes. Kamenev and Zinoviev now swung to the side of their old enemy on a platform of rejecting NEP and demanding more rapid industrialization; in addition, they came out firmly in opposition to Socialism in One Country. Stalin's control of the party machine was by now, however, almost complete, and when Kamenev and Zinoviev challenged him at the fourteenth Party Congress in December 1925 they went down to a humiliating defeat by 553 votes to 65. From then on the 'Left Opposition', as they and Trotsky became known, faced an uphill struggle. At the fifteenth Party Conference in October 1926 they were not allowed to speak, and when they tried to address fringe meetings party militants intervened and broke the meetings up. The next year they went back to pre-revolutionary tactics and used a secret printing press to produce leaflets to circulate among delegates at the fifteenth Party Congress; but the GPU discovered their press, and for this breach of party rules all three were dismissed from the Central Committee and Trotsky and Zinoviev were excluded from the party altogether. For Kamenev and Zinoviev, that for the moment was enough: they agreed to recant their errors and to denounce 'Trotskyism'. It was weak-kneed behaviour, though their surrender to Stalin did at least have the justification that he seemed to be coming round to their viewpoint on NEP. Trotsky, however, was made of different stuff and refused to abase himself. For his recalcitrance he and his leading supporters were deported in 1928 to Alma-Ata in Central Asia, and in 1929 he was expelled from the Soviet Union altogether, never to return there.

Thus the most distinguished living Bolshevik was shut out altogether from the task of building socialism in Russia. Not only would he be vilified; he would be turned in time into an 'unperson', blotted out from the historical record even to the extent of being removed from photographs. This spectacular downfall was in some ways a special case. Stalin hated Trotsky with a venomous hatred he felt for no other rival and pursued him with unremitting virulence. Moreover, Trotsky suffered from a fateful combination of dazzling abilities and political ineptitude not possessed in the same degree by anyone else. His downfall nevertheless set the pattern for many later ones. He tied his hands firmly behind his own back by persuading himself that the party could do no wrong and that to fight it would be a betrayal of all he had worked for. And like many later victims he came from that élite group of cosmopolitan, free-thinking intellectuals, many of them Jewish, which the populist, ultra-patriotic and not very intellectual General Secretary all too clearly felt threatened by.

During the struggle with the Left Opposition, Stalin's closest ally had none the less been a classic representative of cultured Old Bolshevism, Nikolai Bukharin. A fierce leftist during War Communism, Bukharin had undergone a conversion in 1921 and from then on he was the outstanding advocate of the NEP approach. The outline of NEP had of course been etched by Lenin. Yet it was Bukharin, very much Lenin's disciple and favourite in this final period, who put flesh on the bones, and after the Leader's death he presented NEP as the true Leninism: no mere temporary retreat but a qualitatively different approach which provided the only true path to socialism in the Soviet Union. NEP, as Bukharin conceived it, was a gentle and evolutionary creed which excluded coercion of any kind and aimed to persuade the peasants that socialism would be best for them. To the Left's advocacy of rapid industrialization, Bukharin replied that forcing the pace would be ruinous – it would destroy the worker–peasant alliance Lenin had regarded as fundamental. Industrialization was of course essential, but it should be achieved by natural development. The peasants should be allowed to prosper, and as they did their taxes, savings and increased buying power would fuel industrial growth. Leaving them in peace was not, however, tantamount to giving over the countryside to kulak-dominated capitalism. In a mixed economy with state and private enterprise existing side by side, the state sector would gradually prevail as peasants came to see that state credit was cheaper than private credit and co-operative trading more effective than private trading. Competitive conditions would in fact prove the superiority of the socialist economic system, and the market would as a result die a natural death. 'As it turns out, we will arrive at socialism through market relations themselves. One can say that these market relations will be destroyed as a result of their own development.'[17] Giving people economic freedom was not, however, an argument for freedom in politics. The dictatorship of the proletariat had to remain and opposition to the Communist Party would not be allowed. Yet even here Bukharin's gentle touch was apparent: he condemned arbitrariness, encouraged the growth of grass-roots activism as an antidote to it, worried that the party might be turning into the instrument of a new ruling class, and wanted broad freedom of thought and expression under the umbrella of a tolerant one-party state.

Stalin put up with all of this, but it was Bukharin he valued rather than Bukharinism. The alliance was simply a marriage of convenience to him: Bukharin was useful for his powerful opposition to Trotsky and his Leninist credentials. Once the Left Opposition had been defeated, however, he had served his purpose. Stalin now swung from his pro-NEP stance to a more leftist one, and soon he was taking a pro-industrialization and anti-peasant line which differed little from the programme for which Trotsky, Kamenev and Zinoviev had gone down to defeat except that it was, if anything, more intransigent than theirs.

There were good reasons why Stalin should reject NEP for an approach which harked back to War Communism. NEP had, as we have seen, been contentious from the outset. Lenin had come to see virtue in the necessity, but few of the party rank and file had done the same. For most, NEP had been and remained a pact with the devil, and the longer it lasted the more the chances of breaking decisively with Russia's backwardness and advancing to socialism were endangered. Bukharin's idea of 'riding into socialism on a peasant nag' was in the eyes of such irreconcilables pure illusion; where the peasant nag would take the country was, on the contrary, into the arms of capitalism. What rankled, too, was that NEP had seemed to discriminate against the party's own supporters. While peasants were encouraged to get rich, workers lost their free rations and services, were given money wages which bought very little, and suffered worsening unemployment. The pampering of the peasants might be justified by their numbers, yet in the party it was of course the workers who dominated. As the 1920s went on, moreover, the Communist Party became more and more a workers' bastion. The

Workers' Opposition had been defeated, but its plea for the party of the proletariat to become more fully proletarian had been accepted. Lenin's insistence that the party needed quality rather than quantity had acted as something of a brake; once he was dead, however, an intensive recruitment campaign, aimed above all at workers, got under way. By 1929 the party had 1,091,000 members (and a full million and a half if candidate members – those undergoing probation – are included as well). These people who flooded into the party were young, poorly educated and overwhelmingly from the towns – in 1927 there were 319 members for every 10,000 urban residents as against a mere 25 for the same number of rural residents. The urban predominance inevitably swung the party against NEP; and so too did the strong representation of Red Army veterans, who bristled at NEP's softly-softly 'civilian' approach.

Party pressures might have been resisted had NEP seemed to be doing what Bukharin had hoped. The signs, however, suggested the opposite: far from advancing towards socialism, the country was if anything slithering towards capitalism. Class differentiation was growing apace in the country-side: more peasants were doing well enough to hire labour, but the other side of the coin was that more were being forced to hire themselves out. The growth of a kulak class was suggested, too, by the problem of grain supply, which remained unreliable and well below pre-war levels. From 1926 demands to cancel the concessions to the peasants became louder, and they were increasingly linked to pressure for collectivization. If the peasants, or significant elements of them, were incorrigible enemies of socialism rather than the potential socialists of Bukharin's imagining, then the kid-glove treatment of the peasantry had to stop. Collectivized agriculture would do away with the threat to Soviet power posed by nests of capitalism in the countryside. It would be a lot more productive, since collective farms would be much larger and have the benefit of mechanization. Moreover, since the farms would be state-controlled, a reliable supply of cheap grain to the towns could be guaranteed. That was vital. Without a reliable grain supply it would be hard to industrialize. Without industrialization there could be no socialism.

The case for preserving NEP and a conciliatory approach towards the peasant masses crumbled in 1927–28, and it was no coincidence that it crumbled at the very time when the Left Opposition was being liquidated. Despite a good harvest in 1927, the grain collection was less than half what it had been the previous year. The result was more abuse of the kulaks and a speech by Stalin to the fifteenth Party Congress in favour of collectivization. Partial collectivization would not be enough: Soviet power, he now argued, had to rest upon a wholly socialist economic base. Pressures for an end to the slowness and sloppiness of NEP were intensified by a war scare, triggered by the breaking off of diplomatic relations with Britain in May 1927. If the capitalist powers, led by Britain, were indeed intent upon war against the Soviet Union, as Stalin made out, then achieving industrial self-

sufficiency and building the heavy-industrial base essential to modern warfare became a matter of urgency. Not only were there enemies abroad: the
country's attempts to achieve socialism were being subverted, or so Stalin
claimed, by enemies at home. In May 1928, fifty-three engineers at Shakhty
in Ukraine were put on trial for industrial sabotage, and eleven of them were
sentenced to death. It was the start of a campaign against the bourgeois specialists, whom Lenin had protected and made use of to the indignation of
proletarian militants. The Shakhty sabotage was very far, Stalin warned,
from isolated: 'wrecking by the bourgeois intelligentsia' had in fact become
one of the most dangerous forms of opposition to developing socialism.

As the case against NEP gathered strength, Bukharin gave ground: he
admitted the need for greater investment in industry and for an offensive
against the kulaks. Any hopes he may have had that Stalin still had an open
mind and was prepared to read the evidence objectively were, however, misplaced – Stalin had made his mind up and was fixing the evidence accordingly. There were problems with grain procurement, but the supply crisis of
1927–28, and the still greater crisis of 1928–29, were caused by the government *choosing* to set grain prices too low. There were indeed tensions with
Britain in 1927, but talk of imminent military intervention by the West was
a politically useful piece of fantasy on Stalin's part. As for sabotage by the
bourgeois intelligensia, that was almost certainly a figment of the imagination. Yet these claims, too, served a political purpose – they added to the
impression of a regime surrounded by enemies which, as in 1918–20, could
only save itself and build the new world it had promised by turning to heroic
and ruthless self-assertion.

Systematic harassment of the peasants began in 1928 with barn searches,
seizures of grain, prosecutions, and road blocks to prevent private trading.
It was like War Communism all over again. These measures to boost the
grain supply would be accompanied, Stalin declared, by collectivization.
The collectivization was supposed to be voluntary, though given the party's
commitment to it and the peasants' fierce attachment to their plots, strong-
armed methods looked more or less inevitable. The mechanization of agriculture was considered equally vital, and plans were announced for a huge
tractor factory in the Volga town once called Tsaritsyn, now Stalingrad.

A minority in the Politburo – Bukharin, Alexei Rykov, chairman of
Sovnarkom, and Mikhail Tomsky, head of the trade unions – resisted the
new policy. The Right Opposition, as they became known, wanted to
retain the broad NEP approach, avoiding coercion of the peasant, holding industrial growth rates at a modest level, and keeping friendly and
trustful relations with the intelligentsia. Stalin's battle with the Left
Opposition had been more a conflict of personalities than of policies; this
time, by contrast, real policy-issues were at stake and the outcome would
have a profound bearing on the direction taken by the Soviet state. The
Right found themselves outnumbered and outmanoeuvred; and when in
the summer Bukharin made a secret overture to Kamenev (which Stalin

– 'Genghis Khan' as Bukharin now called him – soon knew about), he only worsened the Right's position. In September Bukharin made a last stand with an article in *Pravda* in which he attacked the 'mad pressures' to industrialize and the planned destruction of the balance between agriculture and industry. In November the Central Committee committed the party to forced industrialization with Bukharin's reluctant assent, and shortly afterwards he resigned as editor of *Pravda*. The way forward, it was thus decided, would be by rapid industrial growth, with targets set by an overall economic plan. A desperate attempt would be made to drag the Soviet Union out of backwardness and bring it abreast of the West; and unless the country achieved parity quickly, Stalin warned, the West would destroy it. This was not of course the first time Russian rulers had decided on a headlong rush to catch up the West. It would be Peter the Great and Witte all over again, and Stalin even cited Peter's example. This time, however, the tempo would be still faster, the methods more ruthless, the scope of the change more all-encompassing.

Stalin's triumph over the Right Opposition in 1928 was a decisive turning-point. NEP was not formally repudiated; Lenin's and Bukharin's attempt at resolving its contradictions was nevertheless rejected and with it the whole ambiguous NEP legacy. There would be no peaceful and evolutionary path to socialism – such a path, it was now made clear, did not exist. Threatened, Stalin suggested, by enemies both at home and abroad, the regime either stormed its way to socialism by mobilizing the population as if for war or else it capitulated before the capitalist world, the petty bourgeoisie, and the country's backwardness. Those being the options, the party had very little choice. The course adopted – the return to revolution, to coercion, and the fomenting of an upheaval even greater than that of 1917–20 – was not of course what most Soviet citizens, given the opportunity, would have chosen. The regime had long since, however, come to terms with the fact that it could not expect majority support, just as it had learned to live with and even exploit the hostility from abroad; and its spokesmen no longer talked about any imminent withering away of the state. For the foreseeable future the state had vital functions to perform, and among the most immediate was to hold the peasants and other malcontents in a tight grip.

And if the revolution on which the leadership was about to launch the country was not wanted and would be bitterly resisted by the masses of the people, the leadership could at least count on the wholehearted support of nearly all the million-plus militants and careerists who made up the party. During the NEP years they had had absolute power and the privileges which went with it, yet they had been left deeply insecure by policies which threatened to erode their recently-won position as a ruling class and the very basis of Soviet power itself. The new policy spoke to both their insecurities and their ambitions. An all-out onslaught on the regime's opponents would entrench their position, while a crash industrialization programme would make the Soviet Union invulnerable against its external enemies and create in this backward country the world's first socialist society.

The Stalin revolution called the party to superhuman effort and offered it enormous rewards. It gave an outlet to the new rulers' energies and it assuaged their insecurities. And if it suited the men, and the very few women, who had stepped into the shoes of the old ruling class, it also suited the man who had become and was determined to remain the Leader. The Bukharinites had paid lip service to the one-party state and the proletarian dictatorship, but the pluralist and libertarian implications of what they wanted had been clear enough between the lines. Just as Bukharinism had implied a steady reduction in centralized control, so the Stalin revolution implied the opposite. Violent onslaught on the peasant masses, together with a campaign against intellectuals and a forced industrialization programme, would necessitate an immense increase in the regime's directive powers and a still greater concentration of authority at the apex. The party would impose its iron rule on the country; the party élite would rule the party; and the General Secretary would rule the party élite in what was beginning to look like a fulfilment of that prophecy made long ago by the now vanquished and vilified Trotsky.

Notes

1 H. G. Wells, *Russia in the Shadows* (London, 1921), p. 131.
2 V. I. Lenin, *Collected Works*, vol. XXVI, p. 436.
3 Victor Serge, *Memoirs of a Revolutionary, 1901–1941* (Oxford, 1963), p. 95.
4 Boris Pasternak, *Doctor Zhivago* (London, 1958), p. 362.
5 Edvard Radzinsky, *The Last Tsar: The Life and Death of Nicholas II* (London, 1992), p. 326.
6 Orlando Figes, *Peasant Russia, Civil War: The Volga Countryside in Revolution (1917–1921)* (Oxford, 1989), p. 209.
7 Boris Pasternak, *Doctor Zhivago*, p. 202.
8 Aryeh L. Unger, *Constitutional Developments in the USSR: A Guide to the Soviet Constitutions* (London, 1986), p. 25.
9 V. I. Lenin, *Collected Works*, vol. XXVI, p. 269.
10 V. I. Lenin, *Collected Works*, vol. XXXIII, p. 271.
11 *Ibid.*, p. 282.
12 E. A. Rees, ed., *The Soviet Communist Party in Disarray* (London, 1992), p. 126.
13 Robert C. Tucker, ed., *The Lenin Anthology* (New York, 1975), p. 728.
14 Nina Tumarkin, *Lenin Lives! The Lenin Cult in Soviet Russia* (Cambridge, Mass., 1983), pp. 174–5.
15 J. V. Stalin, *Works* (13 vols, Moscow, 1952–5), vol. VI, p. 394.
16 J. V. Stalin, *Works*, vol. VII, pp. 117–18.
17 N. I. Bukharin, *Izbrannye proizvedeniya: Put k sotsializmu* (Novosibirsk, 1990), p. 60.

|7|

Stalinism, 1929–1953

1

Stalinism had two essential features. First, there was the absolute and despotic rule of one man, who pushed through a revolution as sweeping as the October one with the declared aim of creating socialism but with the undoubted ulterior motive of making his own absolutism unassailable. Second, there was a massive and unprecedented expansion in the scope of state power. The few remaining no-go areas for the state vanished. Now it could intrude in the name of its lofty aims into any aspect of life, destroy or assimilate any non-state groupings and associations, and cut across any loyalties (those based on family, friendship or religion, for instance) that might get in the way of the supreme loyalty – to itself.

At the heart of Stalinism lay the cult of Joseph Stalin, a plain and in many ways mediocre man who was turned into someone all-wise, infallible, and god-like in his perfection. The cult can be dated to 1929 – to be exact to 21 December 1929, the Leader's fiftieth birthday, when *Pravda* came out with a full-page picture of him and devoted six and a half of its eight pages to his praise. The cult had in fact begun in advance of full-blooded Stalinism and would help pave the way for it. It was of course blatantly at odds with the party's democratic ideals and its oligarchic practices, and Stalin's colleagues probably intended, or at least hoped, that it would be no more than a ceremonial façade. Until the Great Purge of the late 1930s, the leadership did remain to some degree collegial. The Purge, however, completed the process of converting Stalin's supremacy into personal power exercised independently of the party's decision-making bodies, though with due genuflections to the party and the sovereign people, whose servant Stalin pretended to be. The extraordinary circumstances of the Second World War forced him to share power to some extent with his top civilian and military advisers. But this group presented little real threat to him since the organ through which its members might have challenged him, the party, remained in practice suspended, and once victory had been achieved, and his stature as a result further enhanced, his personal despotism returned in full force.

During the Stalin years the state, society, the economy, culture and attitudes would be transformed. Russia had suffered many 'revolutions from above', but never had it been exposed to change so concentrated, brutal and far-reaching as this. Most familiar things which had survived the storms of 1917–20 would be razed as by a hurricane. On this waste ground would be built a Russia which at first sight looked entirely new: industrialized, urbanized, highly educated and provided with welfare services – in short, a socialist society, or so the claim went. The socialist society would also, however, emerge as one of the world's two superpowers; it would be master not only of the territory of the old empire but of half of Europe and potentially the patron of much of the underdeveloped world as well. But while immense social and economic development and modernization were one side of the coin, the other side was unprecedented destruction, the wreaking of havoc and misery, and behaviour so barbarous that accounts of what happened can still, half a century later, make the blood run cold.

Stalinism presents many problems for historians, but two in particular have preoccupied them. First, to what extent should what happened be put down to Stalin himself? Was Stalin of the essence of Stalinism? How important were his wishes and his personality to the outcome? It was not, after all, Stalin who built the steelworks or notched up productivity records or beat and bullied prisoners in forced-labour camps: but to what extent were the hands and arms which did these things set in motion by the Leader? Historians of the 'totalitarian school' have agreed in effect with Soviet propaganda as to Stalin's ultimate responsibility. Stalinism is inseparable on this view from Stalin, who as devil – or demi-god – was the moving force behind everything. Revisionists, with J. Arch Getty in the vanguard, have, however, been sharply critical of this approach. We simply, they say, do not know enough to justify it. Take, for instance, the murder in December 1934 of Sergei Kirov, the Leningrad party boss, which is widely regarded as having triggered the terror. There is no convincing proof that Stalin organized the murder; and if, as is more than likely, he did not, then one of the principal props of the view that he masterminded the terror falls away. Furthermore, what we do know suggests that he was a fallible, blundering politician, often undecided and unsure of himself, who far from enacting a long-term strategy held the ring among contending colleagues and pressure-groups.

We should be careful, however, not to turn Stalin into a Clement Attlee. If he was not an all-knowing devil or demi-god, it is hard not to see him as a devil of a more fallible sort and an extremely adroit one at that. For he approved and he far more than anybody else was the driving-force behind policies which led to the ruining and destroying of millions of lives. He pushed ahead relentlessly with an exercise in social engineering which was unparalleled in its ambition and its inhumanity. We cannot pinpoint his exact responsibility in particular cases or the exact amount of suffering his policies inflicted (historians' disagreements as to the number of victims run in the millions rather than the hundreds of thousands), but there is no doubt whatever about his general responsibility for one of the great calamities in history. The problem of Stalinism is bigger, needless to say, than the problem of Stalin; but Stalinism without Stalin is nevertheless inconceivable.

The second problem, and a still more crucial one, is how all this could have come about. How did the great leap forward manage at the same time to become a great leap *backwards*? Why did economic advance and a rapid closing of the gap with the West go together with a grotesque political retrogression? Soviet propaganda would focus exclusively on the advance, but the most striking feature of Stalinism for nearly everyone else has been its regressiveness. What happened between 1929 and 1953 came as a complete surprise to all but a handful of the highly prophetic and overturned the expectations of nearly all enlightened Russians, Bolshevik and liberal alike. Bolsheviks had after all assumed that once in power they would guide Russia in a more or less straight line towards a self-governing, uncoerced, egalitarian and stateless society. Liberals had taken it for granted that the revolution which overthrew tsarism would open the way towards a more humane, law-abiding, democratic and pluralistic society. Each conviction rested upon the accumulated wisdom – or wishful thinking – of several generations of enlightened Russians. Whatever remained of each would be destroyed upon the great pyre of Stalinism.

The reversion to personal absolutism was in itself perhaps not so surprising. A few years of unacknowledged oligarchy as tsarism tottered towards its fall had been followed by a few years of more or less acknowledged Soviet oligarchy. Democracy, however, remained a far cry, and it was clearly on the cards that a precarious oligarchy – the rule of the few, as Aristotle long ago pointed out, is a most unstable form of government – would give way to some revamped version of autocracy. Nevertheless, it would be wrong to see Stalinism as a return to tsarism without the crown. The cult of Stalin was far more effusive and inescapable than that of any tsar. His effective powers were much greater. And these powers would precipitate an upheaval incomparably more far-reaching than anything achieved by a tsar. The parallel, if there is one, is not with any recent Russian ruler but with Peter the Great and even Ivan the Terrible. Stalin himself was drawn to these two and seems in particular to have fancied himself as a modern Ivan destroying the boyars of his time. Not that there is anything very remarkable about this fantasy of his. Someone with Stalin's neurotically insecure, vengeful and vicious personality would naturally enough have taken Ivan as his hero and role-model. But what is remarkable is that he managed to play out his fantasy upon the stage of twentieth-century Russia, and that the Soviet Union under his leadership regressed to a form of government which in certain ways recalled not recent Russian

absolutism but its distant and primitive ancestor, whose brutalities and sim-
plicities had long since, it had seemed, been outlived. History, for whatever
reason, played a peculiarly cruel trick upon the Russians in allowing an Ivan
to come back in a buttoned-up communist tunic.

There were two constraints upon change which had inhibited all rulers
since Peter – and both, as it happened, were absolutely inapplicable to
Stalin. The first was an underlying awareness that fundamental change was
dangerous. Even Peter had aimed his changes largely at the upper class and
had not wanted, or felt able, to transform the lives of the peasantry. And
when Alexander II tackled the peasant problem he had, as we know, moved
extremely gingerly: the emancipation was a policy for containment. Safety
lay in keeping the peasants where they were and maintaining a separate,
self-contained peasant world; and once this approach was dropped, disaster
quickly followed. But not only did the tsars hold almost until the end to the
belief that fundamental change was dangerous. They and their ruling class
had since Peter's day been increasingly exposed to cultural westernization. They might shy away from a constitution, yet ideas of humanity, justice, the rule of law, and the rights and dignity of man meant something at
least to higher level officials. They flouted them if they had to, but with a
certain embarrassment; and one of the results of this reluctant and partial
acceptance of Western values was that the tsarist police state was, by later
standards, remarkably unrigorous and incompetent. Perception of what the
state's own interest required plus a half-hearted recognition of others' interests had resulted in a policy of not stirring things up and of less than ruthless repression of anyone who did create trouble.

Neither constraint applied to Stalin. Having climbed to absolute power
from nothing, he had every reason to feel insecure. But insecurity did not
make him, like the tsars, fear change – quite the contrary; nor was he ham-
strung by any of the old regime's scruples. The Bolsheviks after all believed
in change, had been carried to power by change, were the apostles of
change. Salvation by massive, all-encompassing change was their creed.
They set out to create not only a new material order but a new moral order,
to change life ceaselessly and universally until nothing needed to be changed
any more; and the old order and everything that pertained to it, including its
moral standards, were for them absolutely invalid. (This did not mean that
Bolsheviks as a breed lacked ordinary humanity, but it conveniently legitimized the activities of any who did.) The Provisional Government's fum-
blings had shown how futile were ideas of a peaceful coalescence of old and
new. The obstacles to socialism had to be ruthlessly removed, and in 1918
the Bolsheviks launched an onslaught on the most entrenched of them: the
peasantry. The resulting convulsion was a forerunner of the still greater one
of 1929–31. Never had the plough of government cut so deep into the social
soil, reaching down to the enclosed, archaic, primitive peasant world and
churning it up. Whatever security the peasants had known was lost, everything familiar to them was put in peril, and their world seemed on the brink

of that final destruction which had always haunted their imagination. In 1921, however, the Bolsheviks admitted temporary defeat, and their agents – most of them not long removed from the village, products of the same social subsoil as their victims – were left for the time being to lick their wounds. But the militants would be unleashed again in 1929, and the second time round they would not accept defeat.

This world of savagery and turmoil was not of course of Stalin's making, but it proved to be his natural element. During the NEP years he had perforce put on a moderate face, always taking the middle position against extremists, but now the time for moderation was past. By 1929 he had eliminated all his major rivals and become the acknowledged Leader. His supremacy was, however, still precarious. It was thoroughly un-Bolshevik, to start with; and the party's machinery and its doctrines could yet be used, should he make a false move, to topple him and establish what his enemies would then claim was proper Bolshevism. Only a return to revolution and turmoil could convert this prize which skilful politicking had won him into a supremacy that was absolute and unassailable. He was by no means a natural radical, but his ambition made radicalism the only tactic open to him. And luckily his radicalism coincided, as we have seen, with that of the semi-peasant workers and proletarianized peasants who made up the backbone of the party, though did not yet dominate its upper levels. These were men who had climbed out of the peasant world but still kept its darkest, most violent features; and they identified naturally enough with Stalin, since he was the supreme example of their own type.

2

No one now openly disputed that collectivization of agriculture had to go ahead; that without this, socialism and the party's own long-term survival would be in jeopardy. It was still assumed, however, that the collectivization would be voluntary. Bolsheviks had never assumed anything else. Voluntary agreement seemed the only possible way of proceeding; it also seemed the only correct way. A party claiming to be democratic could hardly make a majority of the population go collective against its will. A voluntary collectivization would inevitably be a gradual one, lasting perhaps for decades. It would also in the early stages be a partial one within each community, with some households joining the collective and others, particularly kulak ones, staying outside.

These assumptions were, however, overturned during the winter of 1929–30 in the wake of the Right's defeat. Forcible methods had worked well in getting the peasants to give up their grain; now they were used to 'persuade' them to enter kolkhozes – collective farms. With the Right intimidated into silence, no one in the party was going to protest that the peasants were simply being coerced. All the pressure from the party was in the opposite direction – to get the matter over and done with, to end rural capitalism and ensure a decent bread supply for the workers. No one was brazen enough to admit that the voluntary principle had become no more than a figleaf. Quite the contrary – at its November 1929 Plenum, the Central Committee declared that the poor and middle peasants were 'spontaneously' moving towards collectivization. This in fact was the assumption on which the whole upheaval would rest. The party was helping the people to do what they wanted (which happened to be what *it* had always wanted); and hypocrisy reached its height in March 1930 when Stalin, as we shall see, turned on local officials and castigated them for flouting the voluntary principle.

The claim that the peasants wanted collectivization and were spontaneously moving towards it gave the go-ahead for an immediate and wholesale transformation of agriculture. This, however, highlighted that perennial problem group, the kulaks, who were least likely to want to be collectivized and might well prove disruptive if they were. The problem of the kulaks split the party. Moderates – probably a majority – wanted them to be assimilated to the collective system. In December 1929, however, Stalin came out decisively against this approach. The old policy of merely containing the kulaks would have to be dropped, he said. Instead, they would be liquidated as a class. The month in which the cult of Stalin began thus produced the first flourish of mature Stalinism. The justification for this savage action was that the people demanded it: what was driving poor and middle peasants towards the kolkhozes, or so the ruler claimed, was their desire to escape kulak exploitation.

The decision to collectivize the countryside and purge it of kulaks ('dekulakization' in official jargon) was bound to cause an immense upheaval, but the upheaval by no means took the form the leadership had suggested. 'Spontaneity' had implied that a willing populace would move eagerly into the new structures and way of life. In reality, collectivization would be imposed upon extremely unwilling people. Party militants from factories in Moscow, Leningrad and elsewhere spearheaded 'collectivization brigades', which were helped out not only by local party and state officials but by Red Army and GPU units. In all, one-quarter of a million agents of the state fanned out throughout the countryside to collectivize some twenty-five million peasant households. Stalin's slogan 'There are no fortresses the Bolsheviks cannot storm' set the tone of the exercise. This was a military offensive against rural petty-bourgeois capitalism; military images pervaded it and civil war memories deeply influenced it. The zealots had come, moreover, not only to set up the collective farms but to stay and manage them. What was at issue in the end was not a form of agriculture but a philosophy and way of life – the collectivization brigades were building socialism and extirpating its enemies. That was why the village church had to be closed, its bells taken down and its interior stripped, since religion gave succour and support to the rural capitalists.

The peasants were helpless; and the fearful question 'Are you against Soviet power?' was in most cases enough to stifle any inclination to resist. By March 1930, fifteen million peasant households – well over half – had enrolled in kolkhozes. They had lost more than their land; for socialism's sake they had lost ownership of their houses, the plots surrounding them, their cows and other livestock, even their poultry and rabbits. But then, alarmed by signs of welling discontent, the party suddenly pulled back. In an article entitled 'Dizzy with Success', Stalin berated local officials for violating the principle of voluntary agreement and mocked zealots who went in for revolutionary overkill – 'Just imagine, removing the church bells – how r-r-revolutionary!'[1] Houses and surrounding plots, small livestock, poultry and some cattle should be restored, he insisted, to private ownership. It was tough on the cadres, who had simply been zealously doing what the leadership had seemed to want. But the peasants were of course overjoyed – for some, Stalin's statement seemed as momentous as Alexander II's emancipation of seventy years before. Joining a collective was, they inferred, genuinely a matter of personal choice; many as a result withdrew from the kolkhozes they had been bullied into, and between March and June 1930 the proportion of collectivized peasants fell from over half to under one-quarter.

There was no mercy, however, for the kulaks. The very notion of kulak was of course vague and elastic: having two horses and a clutch of cows got you branded one, but so too did putting up any resistance to collectivization or even being suspected of it. (You could also get labelled a 'kulak's lackey' – *podkulachnik*.) The richest and most actively hostile were condemned to deportation; even the innocuous were to be evicted to inferior land outside the village. Some poor peasants were eager enough to take advantage of the kulaks' misfortune. The real threat to them, however, came not from hostile fellow villagers – most showed solidarity with them – but from the invading cadres, who were driven not only by ideological militancy but by the fear that any softness would be interpreted as 'rotten liberalism'. The kulaks put up a spectacular resistance: rather than let this hated state have their belongings, many slaughtered their animals and some even burned down their houses. But they were helpless against the might of the GPU, backed if necessary by Red Army units, and their fate proved to be a terrible one. By the end of 1930 one and a half million people had been deported as kulaks, most of whom had been uprooted during the frenzied period of February to April. Families were broken up and children left uncared for; people were transported like cattle in unheated railway wagons with little food or water across the vastnesses of Russia; and many died before reaching the remote settlements or labour camps intended for them.

For those who remained in the villages, the respite inaugurated by Stalin's article proved short-lived. In the autumn of 1930 the collectivization drive began again, though the methods used now were somewhat more subtle. Peasants could if they wished stay outside the kolkhoz, but if they did they had to pay more in taxes and grain delivery obligations and were relegated to inferior land. As a result of these various pressures the number of collectivized households rose again during 1931 to over half; and by 1937, 93 per cent of peasants had joined kolkhozes. By unleashing his urban militants and then following up their initial onslaught with a softly-softly approach, Stalin had won his war with the peasantry.

The outcome was not quite as terrible as some peasants had feared. There was no pooling of women, nor did all the villagers have to sleep together under a common blanket in a single hut. A way of life and a world had nevertheless come to an end – the world of immemorial peasant Russia. The collectivization had caused far more upheaval than those two other landmarks (for good and ill) in the peasant memory: the emancipation and the post-revolutionary onslaught. Through them the agricultural system had remained unchanged, and the two great institutions of the *mir* and the Church had continued as staples of peasant life. But now everything familiar had been swept away, and the *mir* for one was officially abolished in June 1930. The peasant now became a cog in a large enterprise, labouring in a brigade and doing what he was told by urban militants-turned-kolkhoz bosses, and he was more interfered with and pushed around even than in the days of serfdom. Nor was there any compensation for his loss of independence: he did not enter the promised era of prosperity and did not even get a guaranteed wage. Workers on the small number of sovkhozes (state farms) got this; but the kolkhoz worker was simply left the residue of grain and cash when the enterprise had paid all its obligations. Since an unspoken purpose of the collectivization had been to transfer as much produce as possible to the state for as cheap a price as possible, what was left over was, as we shall see, all too little. Up to 40 per cent of the produce – a far higher percentage than had been marketed before – went to the state; in addition, further payments in money and kind had to be made to the Machine Tractor Stations (MTSs), set up to provide the kolkhozes with tractors and combines but also as political fortresses to exercise tutelage over a hostile countryside. This pitifully rewarded work did not even end the peasant's obligations – he also had to perform other kinds of labour-service, such as road-building and timber-hauling. It was no wonder that peasants felt that a second serfdom had been imposed upon them.

Conditions spiralled downwards into a crisis in 1932–3. A law of April 1932 made pilfering of kolkhoz property a criminal offence punishable by shooting or at least ten years of detention. Produce came within the definition of kolkhoz property, and by now peasants had every reason to pilfer it. For the 1931 harvest had been bad, and the government's procurement demands combined with the demoralized state of the workforce and the general disorganization of agriculture rapidly turned a crisis into a disaster. The old peasant saying 'a bad harvest comes from God but famine comes from the tsar' could hardly have been more applicable. During the famine of 1921, the government had at least done its utmost to alleviate the problem. This time, by contrast, a stony face was turned towards the starving. No relief measures were taken and no word of the disaster was allowed into the papers. Famines were of course a recurrent evil of Russian life, but this was the most terrible of all the Russian famines. People ate the bark of trees, cats and dogs, even other human beings. Across Ukraine, the north Caucasus and the region of the lower Volga perhaps seven million people died from the famine of 1932–3. Meanwhile grain was still sent to the towns and the army, and throughout the crisis a steady flow of grain exports helped finance the drive to industrialize.

The countryside had thus been turned into a place of desolation. The government had won its war, but the price of victory was an apathetic and dispirited workforce which lacked any incentive to effort and hence an agriculture which even in better times would be woefully underproductive. And while most stayed and suffered this unexpected second enserfment, the more spirited or more desperate left the countryside altogether. Between 1930 and 1932, for every three peasants who joined a kolkhoz, one left to work elsewhere. During the period 1926–35, eighteen million people would migrate and join the urban labour force. This was exactly of course what the party wanted. Only massive migration could end the anomaly of a Marxist government ruling a society of peasants. But while the party needed an urban majority, it did not want a huge uncontrolled movement of starving peasants, and to stop this it went back to the old tsarist practice of issuing internal passports. The passports were given automatically to townspeople, but to peasants only in special circumstances, and for those who did not have them migration was illegal. Another obstacle to movement was that residence in a town now had to be registered with the police. Anyone with a guarantee of employment could still move, but the peasant who simply wanted to escape misery and look for a better life now found his way barred. Throughout the ages the tsarist state had pinned its peasants like moths to a board, and the Soviet state acted in a similar spirit in the 1930s. The 'military-feudal exploitation of the peasantry', which Bukharin had warned against in the late 1920s, was now in full swing, though nobody dared say so.

Yet even with the Red Army and the GPU at its back the government could not get everything it wanted, and it made an important concession to the peasants in allowing them to keep private plots and some domestic animals. Without this, there could be no peace between party and peasantry; with it, there was the making of a *modus vivendi*, which would last through the Soviet period. The concession was confirmed by the Kolkhoz Statute of 1935, which allowed each household to have a maximum area of about one acre, one cow and calves, one sow, four sheep, goats, and unlimited poultry. This was a lifeline. Not only did the private plots feed their owners; surplus produce was allowed to be sold in special kolkhoz markets, and the private sector soon developed into the main supplier of meat, milk, eggs and many other commodities. In 1935 the average household earned twice as much from the sale of its own produce as from work for the kolkhoz. Could the plots and the herds have been larger, how much more peasants and urban consumers would have benefited. The party, however, had granted even this miserly concession with reluctance and would later pare it down. The trouble was that the more the private plots flourished, the more they set a question mark against the underlying thesis of the collectivization: that the peasant was a potential socialist and soon, once his life had been reconstructed, would become a full-blown one.

3

Collectivization was accompanied by a desperate industrialization drive, directed by the first Five-Year Plan. Planning was crucial and from now on the party would be obsessed by it. Socialists had always of course believed in planning, i.e. in making a rational, balanced and just distribution of resources. By now, however, the purpose of the plan was not to distribute resources rationally but rather to push the economy forward at a furious pace, whatever the resulting distortions and sacrifices. The first Five-Year Plan was commissioned in December 1927 and became operative in October 1928, but its production targets were finalized in April 1929 at levels which at the outset would have seemed fantastic; even so, they were twice more hoisted during the life of the plan. The coal target went up from an initial 68 million tons – itself almost twice the actual production at the beginning of the plan – to a proposed band of 95–105 tons; oil and iron-ore targets were raised similarly. Planners vied with one another to set sky-high targets, fearful that if they did not they would be dubbed 'right-deviationists' and dumped in prison. In the ideological climate of the late 1920s, setting a realistic growth target was as out of the question as defending the kulaks. Even the unrealistic targets set were not maxima: the plan, it was constantly emphasized, had to be not only fulfilled but overfulfilled. And in the event it was declared completed in December 1932 after a mere four years and two months.

Stalin drove the workforce relentlessly, and the swelling working class at least responded eagerly to him: after the shilly-shallying of NEP this socialist offensive, this storming of fortresses, was what the party's core supporters had yearned for. Only rapid growth, he insisted, would do, and he punched the message home by appealing to Russian as much as to Soviet patriotism. Any slackening of the pace, he told an audience in February 1931, would lead to defeat. Russia had been repeatedly defeated in the past – by Mongols, Turks, Swedes, Poles, Britons, French, Japanese. 'All beat her

– because of her backwardness, because of her military backwardness, cultural backwardness, political backwardness, industrial backwardness, agricultural backwardness.' Only hard work would save her now from the foreign predator. 'We are fifty or a hundred years behind the advanced countries. We must make good this distance in ten years. Either we do it or we shall go under.'[2] It was Witte's message, though still starker and more urgent; and unlike Witte, Stalin had complete control of the machine of state and zealous followers whose commitment to industrialization verged on the fanatical.

Consumer industries had the lowest priority of course and would only double their output. Coal, oil and electricity rated higher, and electric output was scheduled to increase by a full 600 per cent. The greatest emphasis, however, was given to iron and steel. This in fact was an age of steel, the metal of modernity, and Stalin for one was obsessed by it. How far-sighted (or simply lucky!) that way back before the war he had chosen to rename himself 'Stalin'. For 'Stalin' meant something – unlike 'Lenin', which conjured up nothing other than a Siberian river. *Stal* was Russian for steel, and 'the man of steel' would preside over the most rapid expansion in a country's metal-making and -processing capacity in history. Regional party bosses fought one another for the prize of a steel or engineering or machine-tool or tractor plant, and Bolsheviks everywhere rejoiced that these plants, which were the emblem of socialism and seemed to close for ever the book of Russian backwardness, were not only the biggest but the best in the world.

A high price was, however, paid for the transformation. Peasants poured in vast numbers, as we have seen, into the expanding old towns and the new ones being created amidst the forest and on the steppe. In 1928, there had been fewer than seven million workers; by 1940, there were twenty million. Services inevitably failed to keep up with the expansion – housing was in dreadfully short supply and families were lucky if they could get a single room to themselves. Real wages slumped; shortages of food and other basic items became endemic, and queues an inescapable aspect of the Soviet townscape. In Moscow certain days were declared meatless; in Leningrad consumption of meat, milk and fruit fell by two-thirds during the first five-year plan. Alec Nove commented that 1933 saw 'the culmination of the most precipitous decline in living standards known in recorded history'.[3] Standards then stabilized for a while, even rose a little, only to fall once more in the late 1930s, when resources were once more switched to heavy industry; and the level of 1928 would not be achieved again until the late 1950s.

Attempting the impossible, the Bolsheviks were bound to fail, and none of the major targets of the first Five-Year Plan was fulfilled. The achievement was nevertheless spectacular. During the period of the plan, electricity output all but trebled, output of iron ore more than doubled, that of coal, oil and pig iron almost doubled, while steel production increased by a more modest half. Perhaps most important of all, a mighty engineering industry was in the making and would be in full production well before it was needed for the war effort. By 1940, industrial production would be about three times what it had been at the start of the first Five-Year Plan. That showed what could be done when ruthless government went together with an explosion of working-class energy in pursuit of an earthly heaven. The peasantry had been conquered; nature too had been tamed in the service of socialism; and the rise of great industrial complexes amidst the forest and steppe triumphantly proclaimed that there were indeed no fortresses which party and working class together could not take.

But it was not only agriculture and industry which were transformed by this state-directed assault of the zealots. Thought, education, culture and know-how were equally affected; and here too coercion from above went together with a largely spontaneous impetus from below. The turn to radicalism in 1928–9 had of course implied a wholly different atmosphere from that of NEP. The coercion needed to force through collectivization and a painfully rapid industrialization left no room for dissent and bred a climate in which even the neutral looked suspect. Life became more difficult for non-party intellectuals, as it did for those within the party who had backed the wrong side.The bourgeois intellectual would no longer be safe provided he kept his head down and got on quietly with his job. He who was not clearly for the party would be suspected of being against it. On Stalin's fiftieth birthday, Bukharin, Kamenev and other leading heretics ate humble pie and praised the Leader to the skies. 'It is now already completely clear', wrote Yurii Pyatakov, another former oppositionist, 'that it is wrong to be for the party and against the existing Central Committee, to be for the Central Committee and against Stalin.'[4] Opposing Stalin from now on implied opposing the Central Committee and Soviet power itself: Leader, party and state had, for the ordinary citizen at least, become one and indivisible.

What had happened at the top was mirrored in the rise of a legion of little Stalins who drove the revolution forward in the localities. The little Stalins in turn depended upon the zeal and energy of party militants, and since they needed ever more of them, still more workers were recruited to the party. By 1932, 65 per cent of a total membership of more than three million were workers by origin (whereas only 8 per cent were white-collar by origin), and as many as 44 per cent were workers by actual occupation. The party had never been before, and would never be again, such a bastion of the working class. The worker-militants' agenda was very largely at this stage what the leadership wanted: to build socialism, make the revolution irreversible, and destroy whatever remained of the old order. The collectivization brigades might have overdone things, but their urge to get rid of the rural menace was basically sound. The same went for the activities of the League of Militant Atheists: maybe it was not necessary to close quite so many churches or outrage quite so many worshippers, but sooner or later religion would have to be uprooted. Militant passions flowed above all, however, into a sustained attack on the bourgeois and the institutions and way of life associated with them, and here too leadership and workers were largely of one mind.

It had not always been so. The bourgeois had not only been tolerated, they had been pampered and taken into key positions throughout Soviet life. But the party's compromise with them, always an uneasy one, was now over. The Shakhty trial and the dismissal and arrest of thousands of bourgeois engineers after it had made that clear enough. The bourgeois were now fair game and a ferocious campaign, driven by age-old hatreds, welled up against them. Plays of bourgeois life were jeered and booed off the stage. Bourgeois types – professors, teachers, bureaucrats, technical specialists, Academy of Sciences scholars – were thrown out of their institutions and sometimes beaten up as well. To survive in the new climate, you had to be 'proletarian', and the proof of that was provided by your hands – 'Show us your calluses!' If your hands were soft and white, you did not have a chance. Students who failed the proletarian test were excluded from colleges and universities. Conversely, there was a massive influx into higher education of workers, who were given crash courses and then enrolled in some branch of practical study. In 1928, there had been only 40,000 students of worker origin; by 1932, the number had shot up to 120,000. Within a short time, the whole direction of education changed: it became more vocational and more heavily politicized. Schools were handed over to collective farms and factories, and traditional subjects were abandoned or downgraded. Ten out of twenty-one universities were closed, but this deletion of institutions that contributed little to socialist construction was more than compensated for by a huge proliferation of technical colleges. The workers and peasants who flocked to college in these years were mainly party members, and from their ranks would come the political leaders of the post-Stalin era – Khrushchev, Brezhnev and Kosygin among them. The excesses of the cultural revolution would shortly be halted; but by educating the cadres who from the late 1930s would form an almost exclusively worker and peasant ruling class, it would leave an indelible mark upon the rest of the Soviet era.

4

The effect of this whirlwind of change was 'a profound revolution ... equivalent in its consequences to the Revolution of October 1917'.[5] Stalin's claim was obviously self-glorifying, but it was by no means an empty boast. The question mark which during NEP had hung over the future of socialism in Russia had been swept away. The country now had a heavy-industrial base, a socialized agriculture, and the makings of a technically educated worker and peasant ruling class. Whether socialism had, in the main, been achieved, as the party claimed from the mid-1930s, was very much open to dispute. But what could not be denied was that something tremendous had been achieved, as a result of which the country had become irrevocably different from what it had been in 1917. Socialism was not of course the end of the matter. What now lay ahead was the still greater leap forward into communism, and that leap too, it appeared, would have to be made without help from abroad, indeed, in the teeth of capitalist hostility.

The Great Leap Forward of 1929–31 was, however, followed by the Great Retreat – or so claimed Nikolai Timasheff, an *émigré* Russian sociologist, in a famous book of the 1940s.[6] The party would not of course have admitted any such thing. But it was clear from the early 1930s that the phase of heroic, frenzied and euphoric advance – the 'storming fortresses' phase – was over. Now the emphasis was on steady growth, consolidation, and brains rather than brawn. There were two reasons for the change. First, the previous pace was simply unsustainable – society, like the individual militant, was in danger of exhaustion. Second, the forces unleashed by this revolutionary heroism presented dangers, to which discipline and level-headedness were the obvious antidote. This had not, after all, been a tightly controlled 'revolution from above' in which change was imposed tsarist-fashion on a passive and immobile population. Millions of people had left the villages for a shatteringly different way of life in industry. This unregulated movement had created what the historian Moshe Lewin was to call a 'quicksand society', and it threatened chaos. The migrants brought with them what Bolsheviks saw as the fecklessness of the village – they drank too much, worked erratically, and in general showed little of the self-discipline and sober devotion to duty which Bolsheviks insisted upon. And in the unfamiliar surroundings of the industrial town, these traits became more pronounced: there was more fighting, more drunkenness, more shoddy workmanship and absenteeism. Unless order was imposed on this teeming mass of unruly ex-peasants, there was a danger that the party and its experiment would go under.

The response was still more interference, still more repression. The state's powers had been increased to bring the great transformation about; now that the very success of the operation had led to undesirable results, the case for tightening the ratchet of state control still further was irresistible. In factories, managers acted like replica Stalins and demanded absolute obedience. Campaigns were launched against 'flitters', 'idlers', 'disorganizers'. Workers who broke the labour code risked losing not only their jobs but their accommodation and food rations as well. Disciplinary powers would be stiffened as the decade went on, till in 1940 absenteeism became a criminal offence punishable by up to six months of detention. The party, too, came in for harsh treatment. The massive expansion of the past years stopped, and instead there was a purge. This reduced total membership from three and a half million in 1933 to just under two million in 1937, and its aim was 'to ensure iron proletarian discipline' and cleanse 'the party's ranks of all unreliable, unstable and hanger-on elements'.[7]

Being a poor workman or an unreliable party member was not the same as being a class enemy. Yet as the decade went on, the distinction between politically innocent shortcomings and opposition to socialism became increasingly blurred by claims that the country was suffering from an epidemic of 'double-dealing'. 'Double-dealers' were class-enemies who, having been defeated, carried on their struggle by masquerading as loyal communists and trying to subvert the party from within. The revelation in the mid-1930s that such famous Bolsheviks as Kamenev, Zinoviev, Bukharin and Rykov were double-dealers and enemies of the people – men who had, moreover, only recently sung Stalin's praises – created universal distrust. If *they* had been double-dealers, then the most lily white might be. Your boss and even your own family were potential suspects; you had to be on your watch all the time and report anything untoward. The most notorious case of putting duty to the state before personal loyalties came in 1932, when the child Pavlik Morozov denounced his father as a kulak, was killed by indignant relatives, and was then turned by the press into a socialist martyr.

But increasing repression was not easy to reconcile with basic Bolshevism. It was lucky that most Soviet citizens had short memories and that idealistic tracts like Bukharin and Preobrazhensky's *ABC of Communism* (1919), which had envisaged a rapid withering away of the state, had been largely forgotten. But repression hardly fitted, too, with the regime's current claim that socialism had in the main been achieved and the exploiting classes eliminated. Surely, in these conditions the coercive role of the state ought to have been diminished? Not so, Stalin declared. The exploiters had been eliminated as a class, but remnants of the class lived on; and it was precisely now, when they had been made desperate by defeat and isolation, that they were most dangerous. Since the class struggle was intensifying as it entered its death throes, there could be no question of state power being reduced. On the contrary, before the state withered away there would actually, Stalin announced in January 1934, be an increase in its powers. From then on, anyone who tried to argue for the withering away of the state was a potential wrecker and guilty of a criminal offence.

With so many criminals, the secret police, known from 1934 as the NKVD, expanded and worked overtime. More and more of the arrested were sent to forced-labour camps. It was not simply that the existing prisons (often former monasteries) could not cope; the leadership had woken up to the advantages of forced labour. So-called corrective labour would help redeem the criminal, but it also had tremendous economic potential for the state. Detainees could be sent to remote areas of northern Russia and Siberia where no free citizen would go. They could be made to work more than twelve hours a day in appalling conditions for meagre rations and no pay. If they died, as very many did, no questions were asked and there were anyway many more to replace them. The camps' administration, the so-called

Gulag, burgeoned during the early 1930s into a great industrial empire, whose slave labourers felled and hauled timber and worked in mines and on construction sites in the most inhospitable areas of the country. The Gulag's most trumpeted achievement was the building of a canal between the Baltic and the White Sea in 1931–3, which was proclaimed a triumph of socialist construction. In order to build the canal, however, hundreds of thousands had laboured with tools more reminiscent of Peter the Great's Russia than of contemporary Europe – picks to break the frozen soil, wooden cranes, horse-drawn drays; and many thousands had died in the making of something that proved to be of very little use.

The emergence of a police state which recreated, and often far exceeded, the worst horrors of tsarism, confirmed what had been fairly obvious anyway: that the party had lost all contact with Marxism's libertarian side. The commitment to equality had, however, been more serious, and its abandonment was the most striking aspect of the 'retreat'. The emphasis now was on realism and efficiency. The second Five-Year Plan (1933–7) actually had its initial targets scaled down, and the campaign against bourgeois specialists was called off. After 1931, all that mattered was that you were capable and loyal. The dismissed specialists were welcomed back into industry, and college doors were once more opened to their offspring. Not only did industry need the best irrespective of class origins; so too did the party. When recruitment began again after the purge, the party's criteria had changed considerably. In 1929, workers had made up 81 per cent of recruits; during 1936–9, they were only 41 per cent, while intelligentsia and white-collar recruits, previously negligible in number, went up to 44 per cent.

The leadership wanted 'the best', and in order to get them it was prepared to pay well and treat them well. 'Wage-levelling', Stalin announced in 1931, was a petty-bourgeois prejudice: which was hard on the many workers who took Marxist egalitarianism seriously. The conditions that would prevail under communism were very different, it was emphasized, from those appropriate to socialism. 'From each according to his ability, to each according to his needs' was the formula for communism. Socialism's basic principle, however, was 'from each according to his ability, to each according to his work'; and the reference to the individual's work was used to justify a considerable widening of wage differentials during the 1930s. Lenin had laid it down that no party member should be paid more than a skilled worker. This 'party maximum' was, however, abolished in 1932. Qualified engineers were soon earning eight times the pay of unqualified workers. By the late 1930s, the differences between top and bottom pay were even greater than in the United States. Workers who overfulfilled their norms benefited as well. From 1935, a cult developed of the Ukrainian miner Alexei Stakhanov, who with two assistants in one shift cut fourteen times the expected amount of anthracite. Soon all branches of industry had their 'Stakhanovites'; the party glorified them, and their workmates, under constant pressure to do as well, often loathed them.

Since there was an endemic shortage of goods and services, it was not only money that mattered: so too did privileged access to whatever was scarce. In large factories, canteens were often allocated according to rank – those for the higher ranks served meat, the others did not. Bosses and the highly qualified usually had chauffeur-driven cars and got first-class railway tickets. Many kinds of preferential treatment were not, however, openly acknowledged. The privileged were given access to special stores in which they could buy goods never seen on the open market. They would have larger and better flats, dachas in the countryside, the right to use special clinics, and access to sanitoria by the sea or in the mountains that were really hotels in disguise. Such a lifestyle assured the loyalty of a swelling class of bosses, specialists and top administrators, some proletarian or peasant by origin, others bourgeois by origin, but all bonded by common membership of the party and an increasing sense of themselves as rulers.

The retreat from ideological radicalism and the settling of the ruling class into a comfortable groove was reflected in a turn towards conservatism in morality, education and culture. The early revolutionary years had been a time of moral permissiveness. Bolshevik enthusiasts had often denounced the family as a bourgeois institution and extolled free love and cohabitation without marriage. Lenin, who had been something of a prude in such matters, had reluctantly tolerated this permissiveness, but in 1934 Stalin brought it to a halt. Far from being a bourgeois relic, the family was now declared to be the basic unit of socialist society. If society was to be stable, stable families had to underpin it; and the subtext of the message was that Soviet society itself was an extended family, presided over by a patriarch of patriarchs, who laboured tirelessly on his children's behalf. Weddings came back into fashion – brides in white went through a secular equivalent of the traditional ceremony and even received gold rings. Divorce became difficult; abortion was forbidden in 1936 save in exceptional cases; and the great Bolshevik apostle of free love, Alexandra Kollontai, spent years in effective exile as Soviet ambassador to (appropriately enough) Sweden.

The pattern was similar in education and culture. After the educational revolution of 1929–31, with its emphasis on practicality and spontaneity, there was a marked swing back to traditionalism. Children went back to classrooms, learned their 'three Rs' by conventional methods, and normal academic subjects once they had mastered them, and were made to do exams and wear uniforms. The Soviet classroom of the 1930s had much in common in fact with its tsarist predecessor, though with the vital difference that all children now went to school and that Marxism–Leninism, not Orthodox Christianity, was the staple of the curriculum. It was much the same in culture. The iconoclasm and experimentalism of the early revolutionary years had fallen into disfavour, and not a trace of artistic freedom remained. The classics, much mocked by the Bolshevik avant-garde (though not by Lenin), had been restored, and a visitor to Moscow's Metro, built as a showpiece of socialism during the 1930s, would see people hunched over thick volumes of Dickens, Balzac, Tolstoy, etc. In the 1920s there had been no 'official line' on art: now there was. The artist had to follow the principles of 'socialist realism', which meant that he had to be ideologically committed, party-minded, and make his own contribution to socialism, just as the miner and steel worker did. Art had to be accessible, optimistic and positive – and when an artist broke these rules, as Shostakovich did with his opera *Lady Macbeth of Mtsensk* (1935), he was punished. (In Shostakovich's case, by Stalin storming out of the performance. He was not arrested, but *Pravda* denounced him and the opera was not seen again until the 1960s.) The paintings which adorned ruling-class apartments included of course the obligatory portrait – and often portraits – of Stalin. Otherwise they showed happy, healthy men and women working on collective farms or building sites; and the same vitality, earthiness, and message of 'we, with the Communist Party at our head, are building a better life' pervaded the novels on the shelves.

The country was indeed forging ahead. During the period of the second Five-Year Plan coal production doubled, that of steel and machine-tools trebled, while even agricultural production went up by half. People, it seemed, were accepting the new order and making the best of it. Peasants, however reluctantly, were adjusting to the kolkhozes; the new working class was responding to the government's stick and carrot techniques and learning some discipline; while the ruling class was, in the eyes of its own members at least, amply earning the comfortable living standard it had achieved.

The sense of settling was reflected in a new constitution – the 'Stalin constitution' of 1936. So much had changed during the preceding decade that the previous constitution badly needed updating. The fundamental premise of the new one was that socialism had been achieved. Society was no longer divided between exploiters and exploited. Now it consisted instead of two 'friendly' classes, the working class and the peasantry, plus a 'stratum' – the white-collar workers, somewhat misleadingly labelled the 'intelligentsia'. The victory of socialism meant more democracy. Since there were no longer any exploiters, the suffrage now became universal (from the age of eighteen). The ballot would be secret – another democratic gain. A new legislature, the Supreme Soviet, was introduced, and this was to be elected directly rather than indirectly and without the previous bias in favour of urban voters. Yet another sign of the democratizing spirit was that this constitution, unlike its predecessors, had a sizeable section devoted to 'fundamental rights'. Among the rights guaranteed were freedom of assembly, freedom of the press, and freedom to demonstrate. The citizen's person, home and correspondence were, in addition, declared inviolate. What mattered, too, was that the strident tone of the previous constitutions was missing. Admittedly, the notion of dictatorship was not disavowed; true, too, the democracy at issue was defined as 'socialist' rather than 'bourgeois'. What was set out nevertheless provided a framework within which, if words meant what they seemed to, people would be able to choose their government and the government would be accountable to them. It was, Stalin commented, 'the only thoroughly democratic Constitution in the world'.[8]

The reality was of course very far from democratic. All power belonged to the party, which got no more than a passing reference, and most of it to the Leader. The Supreme Soviet would be powerless (despite some fanciful provisions for what should happen if its two chambers fell out with one another); those who elected it would have no choice of candidate, still less of party; and the citizens' so-called freedoms were pure make-believe. The constitution might, despite all this, have expressed a democratizing aspiration. Nikolai Bukharin had as it happened been its main draftsman, and the party would shortly launch a democratizing campaign and even allow the idea of multi-candidate elections to be floated. The calm and benevolence of this admittedly deceptive document did, moreover, suggest a society edging its way back towards normality. Someone who knew the history of the French Revolution might well have decided that the Russian one had at last reached its Thermidorean stage – the stage when people get sickened by violence, upheaval and fanaticism, and common sense, tolerance and the desire for a quiet life reassert themselves. But if so, he would have been mistaken. It was not peace and quiet which lay around the corner, and this constitution with its democratic pretensions was the harbinger not of democracy but of unmitigated despotism.

5

The Great Retreat had been a natural enough reaction to the convulsions of 1929–31. It was followed, however, by one of the most baffling episodes in Russian history: the Great Purge, which went counter to any aims of stability and growth, was utterly destabilizing and in every possible way destructive. The Great Purge was a holocaust which destroyed not only high-profile opposition figures but the Bolshevik party itself as it had been until then. The majority of the party's leading members were purged – executed, that is, or sent to labour camp. The cream of the nation's talent as a whole was purged. Not only the political leadership but the military leadership, the industrial, scientific and technological leadership, the artistic and intellectual leadership. The knock-on effects of the Great Purge involved people at all social levels, but in essence it was a blow against talent and leadership. The loss to the national life is incalculable; historians have not even agreed on the number of victims, but many thousands were executed; and in 1939 more than one million people (on Robert Conquest's estimate, as many as nine million) were being held in the Gulag's labour camps.

The Great Purge erupted in 1937, but its origins can be traced back to 1934. In January that year the party's seventeenth Congress had met in a mood of complacency tempered by a certain unease. There was much for this 'Congress of Victors' to be complacent about: the great upheaval was, after all, behind and the party's aims had been triumphantly achieved. Was it not time, then, to settle down and seek peace with the opposition? Delegates who felt this way looked in particular to Sergei Kirov, the popular Leningrad party chief, whose reception at the congress was almost as enthusiastic as Stalin's. Doubts as to whether Stalin was the best leader for a time of peace and consolidation seem to have been reflected in voting for the new Central Committee. There are suggestions that Kirov actually got more votes than Stalin and that 300 delegates had the nerve to cross Stalin's name off. The results were promptly falsified of course, but rumours of the true outcome even prompted some Old Bolshevik delegates to ask Kirov to take over as General Secretary. Another blow to Stalin's pride was congress's decision to change his title to 'secretary', which put him nominally on a par with Kirov and two others. Stalin would, however, before long have his own back on this treacherous congress, and only a minority of its almost 2,000 delegates would survive in freedom until the next congress.

The first victim was Kirov himself, who was assassinated in Leningrad on 1 December 1934 by a young communist dissident. Whether Stalin was responsible for the death remains an unsolved mystery. He was almost certainly needled by Kirov's popularity and he may well have regarded him as a dangerous rival; in any event, he put the murder to use. The next day the NKVD was given wide-ranging powers of trial and summary execution. Three months later, a so-called Leningrad Centre with links to Zinoviev, Kirov's predecessor as Leningrad party chief, was declared to be behind the murder. In January 1935 Kamenev and Zinoviev were put on trial, accused of 'moral and political responsibility' for Kirov's death. They denied any direct involvement but admitted general political responsibility, and they were sentenced to five and ten years' imprisonment respectively. By the end of the year, anyone else who had been remotely associated with the Left Opposition had been arrested, together with many others unlucky enough to have been the oppositionists' acquaintances.

In April 1936, Kamenev and Zinoviev went on trial again. This was to be the first of three great show trials in which eminent Bolsheviks were paraded as enemies of the people. In each, fantastic allegations of evil-doing were made; in most cases the accused, broken in body and mind by torture, confessed to planning murder and mayhem; and for most of the accused the outcome was execution by shooting. By now the distinction between Left and Right Opposition had been obliterated: the country was in danger from 'a united Trotsky–Bukharin gang of fascist hirelings',' the alleged leader of which, Nikolai Bukharin, was the chief defendant in the third trial (March 1938). Bukharin admitted leading the opposition bloc and accepted general responsibility for its alleged actions, but made a detailed rebuttal of personal involvement in any of the crimes imputed to him, the most fantastic of which was that he had plotted to kill Lenin and seize power in 1918. A brilliant defence could not, however, save him, and after his execution he would be obliterated from the official memory for half a century – only to return to prominence in the late 1980s as a prophet of perestroika. In his closing speech, Andrei Vyshinsky, the public prosecutor, had gloated over the downfall of this morally and intellectually most impressive of the Bolsheviks still in Russia. He and his accomplices were filthy dogs and accursed reptiles. The country demanded that they be wiped out. Weeds and thistles would grow over their graves. Meanwhile, Vyshinsky assured the court, 'Guided by our beloved Leader, Great Stalin, we will go forward to Communism along a path that has been cleansed of the sordid remnants of the past.'[10]

Without the climate of terror created by Stalin's vendetta against his former colleagues, the Great Purge would have been impossible. The Purge and the campaign against these unfortunates were nevertheless different. The victims of the show trials were household names, men who knew far too much for Stalin's comfort and had been at least as close to the ultimate authority, Lenin, as he had. If anyone could shout 'The Emperor has no clothes!', these Old Bolsheviks could; and it was understandable that he saw them, even in defeat, as a potential threat. By contrast, those eliminated by the Purge were, with a few exceptions, altogether lesser figures, and they were disposed of without any publicity. The show-trial victims had long since been branded as oppositionists; there was therefore nothing very surprising about their final downfall. The Purge victims, however, were struck down out of the blue. Far from being already stigmatized as oppositionists, they were people with unblemished records. And that is what is so breathtaking about the Great Purge: its main target was not past or, by any rational criterion, likely future trouble-makers but the very heart of the party, its loyal middle-ranking leadership.

This unexpected attack on the party's regional and local leaders did, however, have a precedent – in Stalin's volte-face during the collectivization campaign. His 'Dizzy with Success' article had castigated local party officials for doing what in effect he had told them to and had clearly been intended to deflect popular grievance on to the local leadership. The idea was being implanted that the party – i.e. the central leadership, Stalin himself – could do no wrong: any mistakes committed and any injuries suffered as a result were the fault of local leaders who had failed to understand or wilfully misunderstood what the leadership wanted. The idea that an infallible leadership was being let down by all too fallible local bosses hardly stood up, yet it reflected an attitude towards power which had deep roots. Central power had traditionally been seen as benevolent and infallible – only local power-holders were capable of acting unjustly. What was new, however, was for the central power to exploit this attitude at its satraps' expense. The price paid in 1931 by local officials for this offloading of blame on to them had been no more than to lose their jobs. In 1937, the attack on local officials would be more devastating and their punishment execution or years in a labour camp.

This time, Stalin not only attacked local leaders; he tried to stir up the party's rank and file against them and placed himself squarely on the side of 'the little person' against 'the heartless, soulless bureaucrats' who made his life a misery. There had, he insisted, to be democracy in the party, including the secret election of leaders. The many who had been wrongfully expelled from the party had to be allowed back. 'Simple people', he remarked in February 1937, 'sometimes prove to be far nearer the truth than some highly placed institutions.'[11] The grass-roots had to be given their say, and bosses had both to criticize themselves and to let others criticize them. This was all very disorientating for the bosses. Stalin was blaming the party at the local level for being the intolerant and autocratic body that he had made it and was posing as the champion of ordinary people against the consequences of Stalinism. The arch Stalinist was about to strike down the petty Stalins in order to make his personal absolutism even more secure; but, in a brazen piece of populism, he would smite them as the people's friend and the apostle of democracy.

When the campaign for greater democracy began, there was no suggestion that the bosses would suffer any worse punishment than rebuke or dismissal. They might be inadequate; they were not enemies of the people. This distinction was, however, wiped out after the sensational arrest in May 1937 of Marshall Tukhachevsky, the deputy commissar for defence, and a clutch of other military leaders. They were charged with Trotskyism, espionage, treason, and plotting to overthrow the Soviet government, and by mid-June they were dead. In the wake of this purge of the military, the mass arrest of party leaders began. The thin line between inadequate performance and treachery now vanished: all who incurred the leadership's criticism had to be eliminated. It was Stalin and the people against the enemy.

Stalin nevertheless tried to stand aloof from the actual purge process. The chief investigator was the NKVD chief, Nikolai Yezhov, who was so identified in the public mind with the bloodletting that the period of the Purge became known as the *Yezhovshchina*. Anyone with any political nous ought to have realized that Stalin had not only approved but instigated what was happening. He and Molotov, the head of Sovnarkom, would regularly sit down and sign the list of death sentences prepared for them by Yezhov; and his pose of aloofness was once breached by a sharp-eyed Fitzroy Maclean, who spotted him watching Bukharin's trial from behind black glass high above the court. Yet there was a general assumption that Stalin was oblivious of the details. 'If only someone would tell Stalin about it', Boris Pasternak said to his fellow writer Ilya Ehrenburg. 'It's those hell-hounds, the investigators – they make up all those lies', another convict told Evgenia Ginzburg. 'And He trusted Yezhov, who let Him down.'[12] Some even died with the cry 'Long live Stalin!' on their lips.

The peak of the arrests came in the summer and early autumn of 1937.

Most arrests occurred at night, and so widespread and arbitrary were they that no member of the élite could go to bed without fear. Many slept with a packed bag, and Maxim Litvinov, the foreign commissar, may well not have been alone in sleeping with a revolver by his bed. The arrested were not told why they had been arrested – it was up to them to confess to crimes appropriate to the sentence decided for them. Each arrest led to a large number of others. The arrested person's family, friends and colleagues would be pulled in, and with the help of torture – whose use was legitimized in 1937 – he would be made to implicate others. The arrests continued at a somewhat lower level throughout 1938. Yezhov was, however, removed as head of the NKVD in December 1938, and he would be shot in 1940. Under his successor, the Georgian Lavrentii Beria, the Purge was in effect wound up since it had served its purpose of wiping out the élite.

Of the 139 persons elected to the Central Committee at the seventeenth Party Congress, 110 had been arrested before the next congress met in 1939; and of the 1,966 delegates to the seventeenth Congress, 1,108 had been arrested and only 59 made it as delegates to the eighteenth Congress. By that congress, the party was no longer a ruling party except in name. It might not have been democratic, but it had been a reasonably broad-based oligarchy: now it merely anointed Stalin's personal dictatorship. The military leadership suffered equally: marshals, admirals, all deputy defence commissars, and most divisional and regional commanders had been purged. It was a similar story with industrial managers, scientists, diplomats and writers: they too had been scythed down. A new ruling class would of course replace the old – for every boss struck down there was a young worker not long out of college eager to take his place. And unlike their predecessors, the new rulers would be relatively safe; many would even grow old in high positions, becoming eventually the gerontocrats of the 1980s. There was, after all, little for Stalin to fear in this post-Purge ruling class. It had not risen to power alongside him but was very much his own creation; it had no links to Lenin and the Old Bolsheviks; and its members were untainted by the independent-mindedness and café-society mentality of the old intelligentsia. The country had now at last, Stalin told the eighteenth Party Congress, got the intelligentsia it needed. That was a moot point, but what was beyond doubt was that he had got the loyal, technically educated, plebeian ruling class that he wanted.

Stalin's success owed much to the residual dislike of the bosses, of 'them', which he exploited with great skill and turned into a political weapon. Ordinary people seem to have been at best indifferent to the Purge's victims, at worst hostile and even savagely hostile to them. The accusations were widely believed, and the fact that the culprits confessed their crimes made belief easier. There was public rejoicing at the overthrow of the 'arch fiends'. Mass meetings which demanded 'the extermination of the fascist vermin' were stage-managed, but nevertheless provided an outlet for real passions. People did hate the fascists, even if, as some later writers would argue, it was mass hypnosis which made them do so. In January 1937, some 200,000 people gathered in sub-zero temperatures in Red Square to demand immediate execution for those convicted in the second show trial. In a world which had been turned upside down, 'they' had become more menacing than ever before, and there was a desperate need to believe in Stalin and the moral certainties he stood for.

How Stalin exploited these age-old resentments was seen in the treatment of political prisoners – those sentenced under the catch-all Article 58 of the criminal code. In tsarist times, the 'politicals' had been treated with some leniency: by and large they belonged, after all, to the same class as those who sentenced them, whereas common criminals were riff-raff. Under Stalin, however, the evaluation was reversed: thieves and murderers were seen as a 'socially friendly' element, whereas the politicals were 'socially hostile'. 'Even though you're a bandit and a murderer,' the reasoning went, 'you are not a traitor to the Motherland, *you are one of our own people.*'[13] But it was not just that common criminals were spared the barbarous treatment meted out to the educated men and women sentenced under Article 58. There was a policy of encouraging the common criminals to plunder and persecute the politicals. As far back as 1901, Solzhenitsyn records, Stalin was accused by party colleagues of using common criminals against his enemies.[14] By the 1930s, no one could stop him. Evgenia Ginzburg, incarcerated with other women politicals in a ship's hold, was attacked by 'murderers' and 'sadists', a 'half-naked, tattooed, ape-like horde' of women criminals who invaded the hold and 'set about terrorizing and bullying the "ladies"'.[15] Not that politicals were real 'ladies' and 'gentlemen', but they had been educated and civilized, which was enough to put them into the world of 'them'. And these dregs of the underworld, spurred on by the authorities, were acting out in an extreme form the still unassuaged desire of many Russians to settle scores with 'them'.

This climate of opinion in the 1930s had nothing to do with Bolshevik enlightenment and everything to do with the mentality of the Russian village. Through the centuries the Russians had lived under the rule of God and the tsar. They had also had to put up with a legion of real or imagined enemies – landlords, bandits, demons, evil spirits – against whom they looked to God and the tsar for protection. But God and the tsar had been distant and all too imperfect protectors, and by 1917 both were a fading force in the life of the peasantry. That year both were toppled from their plinths, and it had not of course been the Bolsheviks' intention to replace them. But here Stalin was out of step with his colleagues. The novelist Anatolii Rybakov has given a plausible portrait of him as someone who prided himself on *understanding* the Russians and was privately critical of Lenin because 'he did not know Russia well enough'.[16] This 'understanding' seems to have come down to the belief that the Russians were natural collectivists and that they needed a charismatic ruler who would protect them, maintain group solidarity, hold the bosses on a tight leash, and keep everyone equally prostrate before him. By turning Lenin into the Leader, he gave them someone to worship – God and the tsar had come back, but now they were fused in a single figure, at once human *and* divine, who promised happiness in this life rather than the next. The dead Leader needed a living complement, however; and Stalin, as the propaganda tirelessly repeated, was 'the Lenin of our days' and 'the Great Successor'.

By the Purge, the cult of Stalin had reached dizzying heights. People claimed to have fainted or gone into ecstasy on seeing or hearing him. Victims of the Purge died, as we know, praising Stalin; some may even have believed that they deserved to die for their personal disloyalty to him. An eight-sided gramophone recording of his speeches consisted of seven sides of speeches and one with nothing but applause. 'When the woman I love presents me with a child,' an enthusiast exclaimed, 'the first word it shall utter will be Stalin.'[17] Soon men would go in to battle shouting 'For Stalin! For our country!' – in that order. He was 'the great leader, teacher and friend' of the peoples; he was a genius; but he was more than a supremely able mortal. He had brought men to birth, or so the ecstatic claimed; he had fructified the earth, he had made the spring bloom; and the individual could have a personal relationship with him, much as with God. As a post-war biography put it: 'we talk to Stalin as to Lenin. He knows all our innermost thoughts; all his life he has cared for us'.[18]

Stalin, then, was a perfect being who was privy to every thought and word of his children. But in the dualistic world of the Russian peasantry, there could be no god without devils, no light without darkness. The people had always been tormented by enemies, and in the 1930s enemies threatened again. The most popular book of the decade, the *Short Course* of Communist Party history, which people read as if it were the Bible, teemed with references to them. They were 'double-dealers', 'lickspittlers of the defeated classes', 'fascist hirelings', 'assassins, spies and wreckers', 'Judases', 'despicable tools and agents of the fascists', 'dregs of humanity', 'Trotsky–Bukharin fiends', 'Whiteguard pygmies' and of course 'enemies of the people'. The names were not traditional, but they aroused traditional enough emotions. In one important respect, however, this struggle of good against evil was different from all the previous struggles. For Stalin's enemies were the people's, and the people's enemies were Stalin's. Ruler and subjects stood shoulder to shoulder in an unbreakable unity against them. That was why the enemies were being defeated, had all but been defeated already, and now faced the prospect of complete and eternal extinction.

'The Soviet people approved the annihilation of the Bukharin-Trotsky gang and passed on to the next business' – with such contemptuous briskness the *Short Course* disposed of the enemy.[19] The 'next business' was the elections of December 1937 to the country's new legislature, the Supreme Soviet. The proposal for multi-candidate elections had been dropped: by the autumn of 1937, the democracy campaign had served its purpose – which was not of course to introduce democracy. Despite the lack of

choice, people went in droves to the polls. Of the ninety-four million electors, 97 per cent voted, and 99 per cent of the voters opted for the official
candidate (i.e. did not do what a brave 632,000 did – cross him or her
off). The result was, as the *Short Course* put it, 'a brilliant confirmation of
the moral and political unity of the Soviet people'.[20] The claim would have
been rejected as fraudulent by Western electoral observers – had any been
allowed in. Yet it did reflect a partial truth. People voted as they had to,
but probably only few acted under duress: if we exclude Gulag victims and
some intellectuals, people had been bonded by the bright light and the
darkness of Stalinism.

The eighteenth Party Congress, which met in March 1939, was utterly
subservient to the Leader. So many 'victors' of the 1934 Congress had
become victims that no one dared risk being suspected of dissent by even so
much as clapping for too short a time. Socialism having been achieved, the
task ahead was to go on and build communism unaided. The idea of 'communism in one country' was in fact wholly un-Leninist, though no one
dared say so. In one respect, however, Stalin's communism would have
much in common with what had gone before. If capitalist hostility continued, then the state, he insisted, would have to be preserved. There would
therefore be that unheard-of thing – a communist state. This was not the
first time that Stalin had used the 'capitalist threat' to justify repression. This
time, however, the danger was all too real.

6

Initial Soviet contempt for the Nazis had turned to apprehension once Hitler
entrenched himself in power. In 1934, the Soviet Union joined the League of
Nations and began pressing for collective action against fascism. The following year, the Comintern instructed communist parties to form popular
fronts with other parties, even the hated social democrats, in order to stop
the fascist advance. But still the advance continued; and far from resisting
Hitler, the West turned to appeasement, which to suspicious Soviet minds
looked like a capitalist ruse to turn Hitler eastwards. However, two could
play at the game of diverting Hitler, and in August 1939 the Soviet Union
and Germany signed a non-aggression pact – the so-called Molotov–
Ribbentrop pact. If Hitler attacked the West, the Soviet Union would sit out
the conflict. In fact it stood to benefit from any general war, since under a
secret protocol the two powers would carve up the territory which lay
betwen them. Germany would get western Poland and Lithuania, while the
Soviet Union would acquire eastern Poland, the remaining Baltic states,
Finland and Bessarabia.

The deal with Hitler was a surprising volte-face reminiscent of Alexander

I's unpopular pact with Napoleon: once again Russia's ruler was willing, it seemed, to sup with the Devil, and fulsome messages passed between Hitler and Stalin on the occasion of the latter's sixtieth birthday. Once again the Devil would prove utterly untrustworthy, but while the pact lasted the Soviet government took advantage of its secret provisions to get back tsarism's lost lands. During September 1939 the two powers invaded Poland, and they then divided up the country as agreed. The areas of eastern Poland which were now added to Ukraine even included territories that were not lost lands at all but had formerly been Habsburg rather than Russian. In all cases, an effort was made to avoid the appearance of annexation: people's assemblies or governments elected by overwhelming popular vote requested, and were duly granted, admission to the USSR. In June 1940, Estonia, Latvia, and (after a revision of the protocol) Lithuania were acquired in a similar way, and these became constituent republics of the Union. The same year, Bessarabia and northern Bukovina were taken from Romania, some of the territory passing to Ukraine and the rest forming a new Union republic, Moldavia. Of the areas allocated to the Soviet Union by the secret provisions, only Finland put up significant opposition. The Finns inflicted major losses on the Red Army during the Winter War of 1939–40 and Stalin had to make do in the end with a fairly small gain of territory, which was formed into the Karelo-Finnish Republic (later downgraded to an autonomous republic within the RSFSR).

These spoils gave Stalin good reason to be happy about the deal he had struck. He even seems to have imagined Hitler and himself ruling the world between them after the war. His complacency blinded him, however, to increasing signs, especially after the fall of France, that Hitler was preparing an attack. Intelligence reports which suggested this got dismissed as a provocation. As a result the country was entirely unprepared for the German invasion, 'Operation Barbarossa', which began on 22 June 1941. The Germans, by contrast, had prepared meticulously for what they intended as a knock-out blow; and this time, unlike in the First World War, they were able to throw their whole force against the Russians without any distraction on the western front.

At first, there was no resistance – indeed, Stalin himself was so pole-axed by the news that he seems for several days to have been in a state of collapse. Within twenty-four hours, 1,200 planes sitting uncamouflaged on airstrips had been destroyed. Within three weeks, a million Soviet troops had been killed or wounded and a million more captured, while twenty million inhabitants had fallen under German rule. By the end of August, Leningrad had been besieged and Kiev was on the brink of capture. By October, German tanks had reached as far as the edge of Moscow. The country's fate hung by a thread; government offices were evacuated and Lenin's body was removed, while Stalin himself left the capital for a time. In December, a supreme effort, directed by Grigorii Zhukov, who was to prove the greatest of the Soviet wartime commanders, in fact threw the Germans back. In

1942, however, they renewed the pressure, this time thrusting deep into Ukraine. They pushed the Red Army further and further eastwards until a stand was finally made at Stalingrad on the Volga. The battle for Stalingrad lasted four months, led to the death of some two million soldiers, and finished with a Soviet victory. It proved to be the turning-point. From then on, the Red Army, with morale enormously boosted and ever-improving supplies, was on the offensive. During 1943, much of Ukraine, including Kiev, was recovered. In January 1944, the siege of Leningrad was lifted. In late April 1945, Red Army units under Marshal Zhukov entered Berlin, and on 8 May 1945 Germany surrendered.

Such an outline can convey little of the horror. The Second World War – the Great Fatherland War, as the Russians came to call it – was a far worse experience for the Soviet Union than for any of its allies. The material destruction was enormous. The Germans completely or partly destroyed 1,700 towns and 70,000 villages. They made about twenty-five million people homeless. They destroyed 32,000 industrial enterprises, 65,000 kilometres of railway line, 40,000 hospitals, and 84,000 schools and colleges. They killed millions of cattle, horses, pigs and other livestock. But the worst slaughter was of human beings. Western historians have generally estimated the Soviet population loss as a result of the war at between twenty-five and thirty millions. Some recent Russian estimates have put the loss as high as forty to fifty million. Even the lower figures represent a devastating proportion of a total population which in 1939 stood at just under 200 million.

Most of the deaths were civilian ones, and the greatest single concentration of civilian misery was in Leningrad. The siege of the city lasted for the two and a half years – from August 1941 to January 1944. The besieged had no heating or lighting (this in a city as far north as the sixtieth parallel), no public transport, no water supply, and so little food that they ate dogs, cats, birds, even human beings. People sat in their homes and slowly starved or froze to death. During the winter of 1941–2, when the blockade was at its worst, 800,000 died: the toll during these few months in this one Soviet city exceeded the entire British and American war losses. Nowhere else were conditions quite so bad over a sustained period as in Leningrad, though in other parts they were often not much better. The war inflicted unimaginable suffering on a nation which in the previous four decades had already had far too much of it. The trauma would take a long time to exorcise, and its short-term effect was to strengthen national characteristics we have already noted: a desperate patriotism, intense distrust of the supposedly civilized West, vigilance against anyone who might threaten national unity, and a readiness to accept draconian centralized government and minimal personal freedom in order to provide a shield against the apparently limitless hatred of Russia's enemies. If Russians since 1945 have at times seemed prickly or even paranoid towards the outside world, their suffering during the war does much to explain it.

But why after such a bad start did the country emerge victorious at all?

Admittedly, it is hard to imagine a country of Russia's size losing its independence for long. But if some sort of Russian regime was likely to survive the assault, it was far from obvious that the Soviet regime would: that might easily have collapsed under the ordeal, as its tsarist predecessor had. And the Soviet regime was, as we have seen, very much to blame for the poor initial resistance: the officer corps had been half wiped out, the remaining commanders terrified into utter passivity, and the armed forces left completely unprepared for attack. Yet while the regime's pre-war madness had damaged the country's ability to resist, when the actual crisis struck, the very ruthlessness and hyper-centralization which had been so damaging before now turned into an advantage. Once Stalin had regained his grip, a highly effective war government was created with power vested in a tiny State Defence Committee, chaired by Stalin, with initially no more than five and never more than eight members. Constitutional formalities were set aside; the State Defence Committee had supreme authority in everything. Stalin of course dominated, but there was genuine debate and a real sharing of responsibility among the members; and under the Defence Committee's leadership the regime responded far more effectively to the crisis than its tsarist predecessor had. One of its achievements was a massive evacuation of people to the country's eastern areas; another was the rapid creation of military–industrial plants in the Urals, Siberia and Central Asia, well beyond the Germans' reach, and thanks to these the Red Army would come to be better equipped, in many respects, than its opponent.

But the war was won in the end because most Soviet people saw their government as a proper embodiment of the national will. They trusted the government, fervently carried out its instructions, and were willing, as the Leningrad siege showed, to undergo the most terrible hardships rather than surrender. The Germans made Stalin's work much easier of course by treating the Slavs as subhuman. However, much of the credit was due to Stalin himself, who quickly nullified whatever appeal the invaders might have had by making it clear that this was a war not to save the party or communism but to save everything that was sacred to the Soviet, and especially the Russian, people.

When on 3 July 1941 he made his first wartime speech to the nation, he addressed his listeners as 'brothers and sisters' and 'my friends', and he appealed to them in the name not of the Communist Party but of 'the motherland' (*rodina*) – a term which had returned in the mid-1930s after having been banished at the revolution. And when on 7 November 1941 he spoke at the annual revolutionary parade with the Germans almost at the walls, he invoked the great military commanders of Russia's past: Alexander Nevsky, who had defeated earlier German invaders, the Teutonic Knights; Dimitrii Donskoy, vanquisher of the Mongols; and Mikhail Kutuzov, architect of Russia's victory against Napoleon. Reconciliation with the Russian past was impossible, however, without an overture to the Orthodox Church, and this came with permission for a new patriarch to be elected after a gap of almost twenty years and with the reopening of seminaries and very many churches. The resurgence of Russian nationalism had already been prepared by the cultural changes of the 1930s and the retreat from Bolshevik internationalism. During the 1930s, Stalin had manipulated traditional attitudes in order to create an impregnable position for himself. But now that a genuine 'enemy of the people' had appeared at the gates, implicit and unstated Russianness turned into a direct annexation of Russia's great-power and cultural traditions. Stalin's role as party leader now dropped out of sight. Instead, he was the latest in a line of heroic ruler defenders of Russia, tireless, indomitable, and ready to fight to the last, as everyone else was exhorted to, for the sake of the motherland.

The regime's atttempt to assure Russian support by donning the mantle of Russianness could only, however, complicate its relations with the non-Russians. These had already deteriorated markedly during the 1930s as the Georgian leader, more Russian than the Russians, cracked down on 'national deviationism'. The 1920s' policy of encouraging local languages and cultures (vigorously applied in Ukraine in particular) had been overturned: Russian was again promoted at the expense of local languages, and the local political leaderships had been savagely purged. Not surprisingly, many non-Russians, not only ethnic Germans but Ukrainians, Belorussians, Balts and Caucasians, were ready to welcome the Nazis as liberators from a Soviet state which had come to look like the imperial Russian state in camouflage. But the very possibility that a minority people might 'collaborate' damned it utterly in Stalin's eyes, and terrible collective punishments were meted out to those suspected of disloyalty. The deportation of peoples had begun even before the war, when more than one million Ukrainians and Belorussians from eastern Poland and several hundred thousand Balts had been transported into the Soviet interior. During the war years, entire peoples accused of collaborating were rounded up and deported: the Crimean Tatars, the Volga Germans, the Kalmyks, and the Balkars, Chechens, Ingushes, Karachais and Meskhetians from the Caucasus. In all, more than three million people were uprooted and resettled during and immediately after the war.

In those areas of western Ukraine that had never been Russian, a guerrilla war against the Soviet occupiers continued for several years after the war. In the core areas of the state, however, the effect of the struggle – of unspeakable shared suffering and the eventual euphoria of victory – was to bond people more tightly to the regime than before and to set Stalin on a still higher pinnacle. This had been a victory for socialism and Stalin, who now took the title of 'Generalissimo' (not, however, a victory for Marshal Zhukov, who was quickly removed from the limelight). But it had been a victory achieved by the Soviet and above all the Russian people, in whose mythology its episodes of endurance and heroism would from now on play a crucial part. The Russians did indeed have every reason to hold their heads high. They more than any other people had defeated the Germans, and their country had emerged from the war as a great player on the world stage. Not even at the end of the Napoleonic Wars had a Russian state cut so large a figure. The Soviet Union was one of the three 'superpowers', and with Britain's superpower status largely honorary it was one of the two states which would from now on dominate world affairs.

7

Victory had in fact brought the country a new geopolitical situation. The territory lost to the Germans had of course been regained, and at the end of the war two areas which had never been Russian before had been added. The East Prussian city of Königsberg, together with its surrounding area, was taken from Germany, renamed Kaliningrad, and made into a detached part of the RSFSR (from which it was cut off by the now Soviet republic of Lithuania), while further to the south Sub-Carpathian Ruthenia was ceded by Czechoslovakia and added to Ukraine. But not only had the booty of war given the Soviet Union more westerly frontiers than any previous Russian state. Beyond its new frontiers there now began an 'outer empire' of satellite states which reached into the very heart of Europe.

In 1944–5 the Red Army had swept over Poland, eastern Germany, Czechoslovakia, Hungary, Romania and Bulgaria. Britain and the US had conceded the Soviet Union a dominant role in these areas and, in most, 'people's democracies' were rapidly established, the 'exploiting classes' were expropriated, and a political system closely modelled on the Soviet and backed by a Soviet-type secret police was set in operation. Separating what became the GDR from the other Allied sectors of Germany of course took some time. There were, moreover, special problems in Czechoslovakia, which had a Communist Party with genuine popular support but also a stronger democratic tradition than the other countries. That too, however, was in the bag by February 1948. The only country to escape was Yugoslavia: here Tito's communist regime had been set up without Soviet aid, and as a result Tito was able to win his confrontation with Stalin when the latter tried in 1948 to turn Yugoslavia into a satellite. Despite this one setback, the creation of the 'socialist camp' gave the Soviet Union a solid buffer of subservient allies against the West. And on its other flank, the triumph in 1949 of Mao Tse-tung's Communists after a twenty-year struggle and the creation of the Chinese People's Republic was further proof of what Soviet citizens had long been told and most had probably come to believe: that the cause of socialism was irresistible and its world-wide triumph sooner or later inevitable.

Triumph in war and the apparent security provided by the 'outer empire' did not, however, bring the 'enlightenment and liberation' (Pasternak's words) which many had hoped for. The British got a new government and a new deal, but the Russians got neither. Stalin alone of the Allied leaders remained in power, and he went on as if he had learned nothing and forgotten nothing. The wartime relaxation had been no more, it seemed, than an unavoidable concession: no longer vulnerable, the regime returned to its pre-war policies and emphases.

Peasants were among the victims. During the war private agriculture had been allowed to expand, and there had been signs that the kolkhoz system might be, if not abolished, at least humanized and made more efficient. One sign had been increasing use of the 'link' system, under which a dozen or so peasants, often an extended family, were given complete responsibility for a tract of land. The drift towards a more peasant-friendly agriculture was now, however, firmly reversed. All land acquired from kolkhozes was ordered to be returned; the kolkhozes were amalgamated into still bigger units; and peasants were made to work again in large brigades rather than the more intimate and productive 'links'. Nor were the areas recently acquired allowed to miss out on collectivization: so thoroughly was the pre-war drama replayed that 100,000 Balts were deported as 'kulaks' to Siberia and Kazakhstan. All of this had a disastrous effect on agricultural productivity, which was no higher at the end of Stalin's rule than in 1913. If the country was saved from starving, it was mainly because of the meat, milk, potatoes and other produce from the peasants' diminished and derided private plots.

If the peasants suffered, so too did intellectuals. For them, Stalin's final years had much in common with the final period of Nicholas I's reign. During both phases Russia was at the mercy of an aged and ailing despot whose paranoia had been exacerbated by a recent cataclysm; during both intellectuals reacted with cynicism, apathy and despair to a cultural wasteland ruled over by talentless sycophants; and during both what lay at the root of the repression was a carefully manipulated surge of anti-Western xenophobia.

Stalin had always done well out of 'enemies', and it was not surprising that in the post-war years the theme returned with the West in the leading role. The perception of a hostile West was far from new, of course. The West had been there in the background pulling the strings behind the 'Trotsky–Bukharin gang' in the 1930s, and its predatory designs went back to the Middle Ages. But what made the West particularly dangerous now was that the regime's ideological defences had of necessity been lowered during the war. Millions of Soviet citizens had gone to the West or at least been exposed to its influence as never before. It was the experience of Alexander I's reign all over again, and the danger was that the returnees might turn into a new breed of Decembrists. The most dangerous were the prisoners of war, many of whom had spent years in German camps; and in order to nip the danger in the bud these were rapidly sent off to the Gulag's camps, if not shot as traitors. By the time Winston Churchill spoke at

Fulton, Missouri, in March 1946, of a 'Red Threat' and an 'iron curtain dividing the continent', the Cold War was under way in earnest and Stalin had all the pretext he needed to wage a relentless campaign against the ideologically contaminated.

Though it was an Englishman who signalled the onset of hostilities, the real enemy was of course America. Not an exhausted imperial power, a senile, class-ridden monarchy easily traduced by Soviet propagandists, but a youthful and vigorous republic unencumbered with old-world liabilities whose power, now enhanced by the atomic bomb, presented an obvious threat and whose wealth and democratic spirit had an all-too evident appeal to the impoverished and the downtrodden. What Tocqueville had predicted back in the 1830s had come to pass: the fortunes of the world now lay in the hands of America and Russia. However, there was no chance of the peaceful condominium betwen them that Stalin had once hoped for between himself and Hitler. Tocqueville's claim that the one country represented freedom and the other 'concentrates the whole power of society in one man' was as valid now as it had been then, and the different heritages and political systems of the two made the rift between them inevitable.[21]

The Truman Doctrine, the Marshall Plan, NATO, the dispute over Berlin, culminating in an unsuccessful Soviet blockade of the city in 1948–9 – all were cited as proof of the capitalist powers', and especially America's, unlimited hostility to the Soviet Union and everything it stood for. In response to this apparent threat, nationalist fervour rose to a crescendo. Everything Soviet and Russian was held up as superior to its foreign equivalent; every device and every thought worth having had, as it turned out, been created by the genius of the Russians; and the worst thing that could be said about anyone was that he or she was kowtowing to the West and wanted to copy it. These were the accusations hurled by Andrei Zhdanov, the party's ideological chief, at two Leningrad periodicals in 1946, and they set off a campaign to purge Soviet intellectual life of foreign taint and restore its purity and party-mindedness after the easy-going (in this respect) wartime years. The campaign became known as the *Zhdanovshchina*, just as the pre-war repression had been known as the *Yezhovshchina* – in both cases, Stalin distanced himself from what his henchmen were doing (and not until long after his death would there be talk of a *Stalinshchina*). Poets, novelists, composers, painters, and social scientists were at great risk; so, too, were those who worked in the natural sciences. Nuclear physicists were highly prized because of the regime's anxiety to acquire nuclear parity with America, and many who had fallen foul of the Great Purge served their sentences in special scientific institutes – Solzhenitsyn would portray one of these in *The First Circle* (1968). Biologists, by contrast, were pitifully vulnerable and interference by party hacks had devastating effects on them, particularly on geneticists. A rather different victim of this late-Stalinist xenophobia was the Uniate Church in western Ukraine, which used the Orthodox liturgy but, impermissibly, recognized the authority of the

Roman pontiff. This was abolished in 1946 and its property handed over to the Orthodox, an act of persecution which more than anything else fired the partisan resistance in western Ukraine.

In this anti-Western climate, Jews were especially in jeopardy. The Bolshevik Party had of course prided itself on not being anti-Semitic; it had numerous Jewish members, and Stalin's own anti-Semitism had until the post-war period been relatively repressed. The two and a half million Soviet Jews who died during the war were victims of the Nazis rather than the Soviet regime. After the war, however, a campaign against 'alien influences' and 'cosmopolitanism' was clearly targeted at Jews. It did not help that the leading figures in intellectual and cultural life – the intelligentsia in the traditional meaning of the term – were disproportionately Jewish; and internal passports, in which they were registered as 'Jewish' rather than 'Russian', made it hard for even the most loyal and assimilated Jews to hide their origins. Another suspect community were the people of Leningrad. Their troubles began with the mysterious death, in August 1948, of Andrei Zhdanov, who had been the city's party boss from 1934 to 1944. There then followed a purge of his former colleagues in the Leningrad apparatus, men who had led the city's defence during the siege, and a large number of leading figures were executed. The most likely explanation of this bizarre butchery is that Stalin in some way felt threatened by this most westernized Russian city, stamping ground of the intelligentsia, one-time power-base of Zinoviev and Kirov, a city which he had always resented and which had emerged from the ordeal of the war with a new lustre. In the aftermath, every effort was made to wipe out Leningrad's war record: the museum dedicated to the defence of the city was closed, its director was arrested, and books, newspapers and archives on the subject of the war were withdrawn from access.

Anti-westernism, anti-intellectualism, and anti-Semitism had sturdy native roots, but their vigorous encouragement now, as in the past, was a sure sign that the ruler wanted to destroy any vestiges of pluralism and to make his personal power unassailable. The State Defence Committee was abolished, and the military were put firmly in their place. After four years on the sidelines, the party was restored to a nominal central position, but party rule simply meant Stalin's rule. Even the formalities went by the board. A party congress had last met in 1939; there would not be another until October 1952. There were no party conferences at all. The Central Committee, too, was brushed aside, though it should have been convened every four months, and it did not meet between February 1947 and August 1952. Even the Politburo ceased to meet regularly from early 1949, after one of its members, Nikolai Vosnesensky, had been arrested (he would later be shot); from then on, Stalin assigned Politburo members to committees to deal with particular problems. These henchmen of his vied with one another for his favour, but he did not trust even them and played them off against one another in the classic manner of dictators. The chief rivalry in the early post-war years was between Zhdanov on the one hand and Malenkov and

Beria, the security chief, on the other. Zhdanov's death and the destruction of many of his followers in the 'Leningrad Affair' then cleared the way for Malenkov and Beria's ascendancy among the courtiers. Towards the end of Stalin's life, his most senior colleagues, Molotov and Mikoyan, fell into deep disfavour, and signs appeared that a purge of his closest associates might be looming. One sign was that the nineteenth Party Congress, in October 1952, abolished the Politburo and replaced it by a much larger Presidium, in which the long-serving henchmen would be swamped. The congress made one other change, too, which showed how much the party had become the ruler's plaything: its name was changed from 'All-Union Communist Party (Bolsheviks)' to 'The Communist Party of the Soviet Union', and the historic title of 'Bolshevik', which had such irksome associations for Stalin, was dropped.

Three months after the congress, storm signals flashed when *Pravda* announced that nine doctors who worked in the Kremlin's medical centre had been arrested on various heinous charges: among them, that they had murdered Zhdanov, had links with an American Jewish organization and with British intelligence, and that they planned to kill others of their Kremlin patients. The most obvious target were Jews, since seven of the nine 'white-coated assassins' were Jewish: but there were suggestions, too, that the security police, who had been lax enough to let the 'assassins' infiltrate the Kremlin, were intended victims as well, and hence that Beria, Stalin's right-hand man and fellow Georgian, was now at risk. The country may even have been on the verge of another show-trial and more high-level bloodletting, as in the late 1930s. Certainly, no member of the leadership could feel secure. All were at the mercy of the sickly and capricious seventy-three-year-old: however abjectly they fawned upon him, they could never win immunity from his suspicions, and the fact that the wives of two members of the inner circle – Molotov and Poskrebyshev, Stalin's secretary – had been thrown into labour camps underlined how precarious their situation was.

The constitution and the rules of the party could do nothing to protect them, but mortality now intervened to save them. On the night of 1–2 March 1953, Stalin was paralysed by a stroke, and on 5 March he died. The death was announced the next day as if it were an event of earth-shaking importance: which in a sense it was. 'The heart of Joseph Vissarionovich Stalin – Lenin's Comrade-in-Arms and the Genius-Endowed Continuer of his Work, Wise Leader and Teacher of the Communist Party and of the Soviet People – has ceased to beat.'[22] Exiles, prisoners and some intellectuals may have rejoiced at the news, as Herzen had rejoiced at the death of Nicholas. Yet the reaction of most people seems to have been grief, a sense of personal bereavement, and alarm at the prospect of a Stalinless future. How, one person wondered, could life possibly go on without him? – 'hadn't God died, without whom nothing was supposed to take place'? 'All Russia wept', the poet Yevtushenko would recall. 'So did I. We wept sincerely with grief and perhaps also with fear for the future.'[23] There were even reports of convicts weeping in the Gulag camps. People who would later fight against everything Stalin had stood for were engulfed by the general grief. Andrei Sakharov, the distinguished future dissident, was overcome by 'the great man's death' and only years later would he understand 'the degree to which deceit, exploitation and outright fraud were inherent in the whole Stalinist system'.[24] Dmitri Volkogonov, son of a Purge victim, who in the late 1980s would publish a damning biography of the Leader, believed on hearing of his death that 'the sky had fallen in', and not until much later would he see the link between his family's tragedy and Stalin.[25] If men as intelligent as these had fallen under Stalin's spell, it was hardly surprising that more ordinary subjects had succumbed to him. The loss of father, friend and Leader must have been almost unbearable. Enormous crowds streamed towards Moscow's Hall of Columns, where the Leader lay in state before being placed with Lenin in the mausoleum, and so great was the crush that large numbers of mourners were trampled to death as they tried to get to the Hall. Even dead, Stalin had managed to inflict suffering and destruction upon his subjects.

Notes

1 J. V. Stalin, *Works*, vol. XII, p. 204.
2 *Ibid.*, vol. XIII, pp. 40–1.
3 Alec Nove, *An Economic History of the USSR 1917–1991* (Harmondsworth, 1992), p. 210.
4 R. W. Davies, *The Industrialization of Soviet Russia* (3 vols, London, 1980–9), vol. I, *The Socialist Offensive, 1929–30*, p. 175.
5 *History of the Communist Party of the Soviet Union (Bolsheviks): Short Course* (Moscow, 1939), p. 305.
6 Nikolai Timasheff, *The Great Retreat: The Growth and Decline of Communism in Russia* (New York, 1946).
7 Central Committee resolution of 12 January 1933. See T. H. Rigby, *Communist Party Membership in the USSR, 1917–1967* (Princeton, N.J., 1968), p. 201.
8 J. V. Stalin, *Problems of Leninism* (Peking, 1976), p. 820.
9 *Short Course*, p. 326.
10 Fitzroy Maclean, *Eastern Approaches* (Harmondsworth, 1991), p. 109.
11 J. Arch Getty, *Origins of the Great Purges: The Soviet Communist Party Reconsidered, 1933–1938* (Cambridge, 1985), p. 147.
12 Robert Conquest, *Stalin: Breaker of Nations* (London, 1991), p. 207; Evgenia S. Ginzburg, *Into the Whirlwind* (Harmondsworth, 1968), p. 225.
13 Alexander Solzhenitsyn, *The Gulag Archipelago 1918–1956* (3 vols, London, 1974–8), vol. I, p. 505.
14 *Ibid.*, p. 506.
15 Ginzburg, *Into the Whirlwind*, p. 281.
16 Anatoli Rybakov, *Children of the Arbat* (London, 1988), pp. 205–7.
17 T. H. Rigby, ed., *Stalin* (Englewood Cliffs, N.J., 1966), p. 111.

18 *Joseph Stalin: A Short Biography*, prepared by the Marx-Engels-Lenin Institute (London, 1950), p. 96.
19 *Short Course*, p. 348.
20 *Ibid.*, p. 352.
21 Alexis de Tocqueville, *Democracy in America*, ed. J. P. Mayer and Max Lerner (2 vols, London, 1968), vol. I, p. 511.
22 Ronald Hingley, *Joseph Stalin: Man and Legend* (London, 1974), p. 423.
23 Vladimir Bukovsky, *To Build a Castle: My Life as a Dissident* (London, 1978), p. 83; Yevgeny Yevtushenko, *A Precocious Autobiography* (London, 1963), p. 89.
24 Robert Conquest, *The Great Terror: A Reassessment* (London, 1990), p. 314.
25 Dmitri Volkogonov, *Stalin: Triumph and Tragedy* (London, 1991), p. 564.

|8|

Khrushchev and communism, 1953–1964

1

Stalin's death meant the end of Stalinism. At least, it did unless another such person slipped quickly into the dead man's shoes, and most members of the ruling circle were determined not to allow that. There would be no second Stalin and there would be no more terror. The secret police would of course remain, but from now on they would be subject to strict control. All this, however, raised a daunting problem. How could the regime survive without either a charismatic leader or terror? Collective leadership was not in itself new, but in the early Soviet period there had at least been a charismatic number one. Now there was no one to believe in. 'People said openly: "Who is there to die for now? Malenkov? No, the people won't die for Malenkov!"'[1] Nor would they die for Beria, Molotov, Khrushchev or any other of Stalin's heirs. And these men who were not worth dying for were so unsure of themselves that their first act was to appeal to the population not to panic. If there was panic anywhere, however, it was in the Kremlin itself. The heirs had somehow to command obedience; more than that, they needed to win people's willing and eager co-operation. But how?

The only way, it seemed, was to revive a spirit of revolutionary idealism and enthusiasm. They had to show themselves as Lenin's heirs, wrap themselves in his mantle, and so bring the revolution's original vision back into focus. Though high-flown talk would not be enough in itself, and it would have to be accompanied by real changes. There would have to be more personal freedom and a marked improvement in the miserably low standard of living. Nothing, after all, was more likely to ensure their subjects' loyalty than better living conditions. Stalin had ruled by fear and hypnosis; his successors would have to earn people's gratitude.

An outside observer might have gone further and said that the regime needed to make a radical change of direction. During the Stalin years, it had

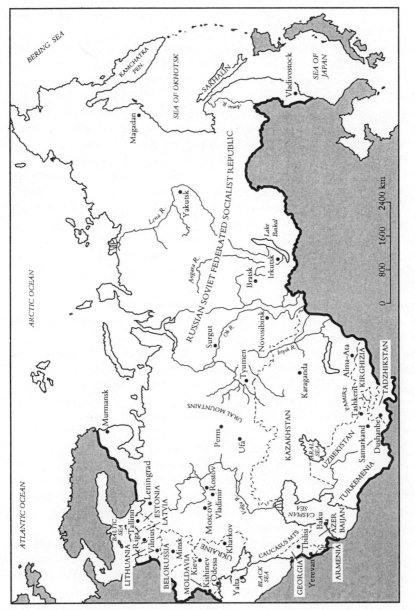

The USSR, 1945–1991

lost touch with the revolution's original purposes almost entirely. The modernizing achievements of the regime had been enormous, but these very achievements had made it an anomaly and underlined how badly it had gone astray. The party's dictatorship had been intended for a backward country with a tiny working class; it had also been justified by internal and external enemies. But Russia was no longer the country of peasants in 1953 that it had been in 1917, nor was the regime under any threat. The proportion of the population which worked on the land had fallen to under half: in 1917 it had been four-fifths. And now there were ninety million townspeople as against only twenty-six million then. As for the argument about 'enemies', that had become utterly implausible: kulaks, Nepmen and members of the old ruling class had long since been disposed of, while in international affairs the Soviet Union was no longer a vulnerable outcast but had become one of the world's two superpowers. Real enemies were, in other words, either non-existent or harmless, and there was very little appetite to pursue fictive ones. The dictatorship had as a result lost the justification it had once had. It was surely time, high time, to get back to the revolution's original aims and to wrestle with the problem of how to achieve them. The aims, remember, were freedom and material abundance: there were few signs of either in the Russia of 1953. The key problem of means, which had caused Lenin such torment in his final years, was how to make the party a genuine instrument of the people's will. How did it win voluntary and enthusiastic support for its cause? How could it be democratic, yet keep true to socialism? How could it relax controls without risking chaos and move towards a largely self-regulating and self-motivating society?

Such questions would be asked by leading figures in the party three decades later. They were not asked in the early 1950s, though in his final years of power Khrushchev would seem to be edging towards them. 'Back to Lenin' would be a motto of the post-Stalin leaders, but they were incapable of putting Stalinism behind them. That was by no means surprising – they were, after all, its products. They had lived in fear of the dictator but they had also been the beneficiaries of his regime, and each had played his part in its achievements and its crimes. Extricating themselves from the assumptions of Stalinism would be hard: these men, too, no less than ordinary subjects, had been mesmerized by Stalin. (His mesmeric power and the difficulty of escaping it come out very clearly in Khrushchev's memoirs.) There were also tactical constraints. Any sharp break with the past – and with a ruler who had been seen as almost sacred – might have undermined them. They needed to preserve all the power of Stalin's regime intact, even if this power would from now on be wielded by a collective leadership and with more sensitivity to the subjects' needs and opinions.

The broad outlines of what should be done were agreed among the leading figures. The terror would be wound down and the secret police demoted to a state committee under party control. Life would become orderly and predictable; the government would act in accordance with clearly understood, if not written, rules. Something would be done about the camps, if only because an ugly spirit of mutiny was spreading in them. There would be a determined drive to raise living standards, to tackle the housing short-age in the towns and the wretched poverty and neglect of the peasants. Yet despite such broad agreement, collective government turned out to be diffi-cult. There was of course little tradition of it. In addition, there were no external constraints, such as a parliament or a free press, to help prevent one leader rising above the others, nor were there the necessary institutional structures to preserve a rough equality among them. Sooner or later one of them would usurp the others, and the policy issue on which the inevitable struggle for supremacy turned was the reforms. How far should they go? How fast should they go? The leader who came out on top, Nikita Khrushchev, was the most radical, and he would take a first step towards the more thoroughgoing reforms of Mikhail Gorbachev. Khrushchev was, however, ousted by his colleagues in October 1964, and his fall would be followed by two decades of extremely cautious rule – by what became known as 'the period of stagnation'.

Toppling a Soviet leader was unprecedented, but there were two reasons why by 1964 his colleagues wanted very badly to get rid of Khrushchev. First, there was his attack on Stalin. This had initially been kept within the party, but in the early 1960s he had taken it into the public forum. The attack had, admittedly, been on Stalin rather than on Stalinism: on terror and arbitrariness rather than on the fundamental structures and assump-tions of the Stalinist state, on the way Stalin had used his power rather than dictatorial power in itself. Any such attack was, however, dangerous. Once the party had been shown to be guilty, directly or indirectly, of wrongdoing, even in a limited area, then its claim to infallibility, its mystique, and the jus-tification for its monopoly of power were in jeopardy. Stalin had of course made serious mistakes, and their consequences had wherever possible to be rectified. But harping on what had happened might all too easily make people suspect an underlying flaw in the system.

Second, there was Khrushchev's Bolshevism – his 'back to Lenin' em-phasis. As a piece of public relations, 'back to Lenin' was fine. But Khrushchev had done more than use Lenin in order to bolster the party and give it a touch of the old man's magic. Despite those long years of Stalin, he had turned out to be a Bolshevik idealist with something of the naiveté and impetuosity of the 1920s. Communism for him was not merely a distant goal which gave the party legitimacy and a purpose but something to be achieved in the very near future. To be exact, it would be achieved during the 1980s, by which time the Soviet Union would have overtaken the USA in its living standards. Now, there were obvious advantages to such an approach. The prospect of living better than the Americans would galvanize people and ensure their loyalty, all the more so since it was backed up by a marked improvement in current living standards. Khrushchev's promises were nevertheless extremely hazardous for the party. The timetable was unrealistic, indeed positively reckless. Communism would not be achieved in the 1980s, and there would be mud on the party's face when it was not. (When the 1980s were reached the party would, as it happened, be facing not imminent communism but a dead-end, from which the only escape was to renounce its utopian ambitions altogether.) The trouble was that the great economic advance of the 1950s was showing distinct signs of faltering by the early 1960s. Boasts about communism and overtaking the Americans had begun to look foolish.

There was another problem as well. Communism needed a highly developed industry and material abundance: these would provide the base. But what would be built on the base was a life in which there would be no coercion and thus no state – a life with the greatest possible degree of freedom. If communism was as close as Khrushchev claimed, then the transition to statelessness and the wind-down of the state's repressive machinery would have to begin at once. He was already taking the first steps in this direction and laying much emphasis on the role of voluntary, non-state organizations and of grass-roots initiative. But this encroachment on the state's monopoly was most unwelcome to his fellow oligarchs and to the perhaps one million members of the ruling class – party and state apparatchiks, managers of enterprises, military and KGB leaders – who ran the country on the oligarchs' behalf. An allied grievance was his restlessness and frequent administrative reorganizations, which made office-holders feel deeply insecure. That alone was reason enough for ousting him.

Undeniably, Khrushchev had been undignified and impulsive – 'a real peasant'; and he had made the mistake of going for changes that were well ahead of their time. No wonder the sober men who succeeded him would accuse him of 'hare-brained schemes' and 'voluntarism'. Yet he had focused once more on the revolution's central themes, which Stalin had utterly disregarded. The revolution had been made so that people should live decently and in freedom. Communism was a faith, a vision of life transformed which drew on age-old currents in the Russian peasant experience. It was a faith which would be judged in the end by its results, by loaves of bread and degrees of wellbeing; and so would the party, whose claim to rule depended vitally upon the faith being valid and hence effective. What made Khrushchev an original among Soviet leaders of the time, and even something of a tragic figure, was that he believed what he preached.

2

Of those around Stalin, Khrushchev had in fact seemed the least likely to emerge as the new leader. The more obvious contenders were Beria, Molotov and Malenkov, though each as it turned out had a flaw. Beria's drawback was that he looked likely to be the new Stalin. Not only was he a Georgian and the dictator's former crony; as minister of the interior and thus head of the secret police he was quite capable of getting rid of his colleagues. But in June 1953, a conspiracy masterminded by Khrushchev succeeded in having him arrested. He was then accused of being a traitor, a fascist hireling, and of plotting to seize power, and on these implausible grounds he was executed. The man whom his colleagues had feared as the new Stalin was thus disposed of brutally and under false pretences in the classic Stalinist manner.

The 'new Stalin' had, as it happened, given signs of becoming a reformer. With Molotov, the elements of the problem were the other way round. No one could have been drabber, less awesome and less charismatic than this prim man who had served Stalin as both prime minister and foreign minister. He was too old and too grey to be a threat. Yet he was also too committed to the old ways – in that sense a genuine Stalinist – to be a serious candidate for supremacy in a period that cried out for change; and his main function would be to guard the heritage and try to curb more reform-minded colleagues.

The most prominent of the reformers was Georgii Malenkov, and Stalin himself seems to have seen him as his heir. At Stalin's funeral, it was Malenkov who gave the main speech, and he at once took over the two key positions of prime minister and head of the party. He was plump, charming, and gave the impression of being soft in character as well as body – 'a man with a womanish face', was how the poet Yevtushenko described him.[2] He was also a sophisticated intellectual and he had a strong commitment to change, in particular to improving things for the consumer. Here, it seemed, was the new image of the Soviet Union in this leader who was youngish (fifty-one), had a popular touch, and knew what to say and do at a cocktail party. The new image turned out, however, to be premature. Within a fortnight Malenkov had given up the party leadership, and from then on he was fighting a slowly losing battle with Khrushchev, who had made the party his power-base. In February 1955 he resigned from the premiership in favour of Nikolai Bulganin, an amiable nonentity who looked likely to do Khrushchev's bidding; and in June 1957 he, together with Molotov and Kaganovich, was expelled from the leadership altogether after mounting an unsuccessful challenge to Khrushchev. Part of the trouble was that his struggle with Khrushchev became a struggle between the government and the central economic bureaucracy on the one hand and the party apparatus on the other, and the party proved the stronger. But the main reason for his fall was that as a politician he could not hold a candle to his tougher and wilier opponent. His weakness was captured in a fable in a literary magazine. 'A sparrow was appointed Eagle. Then the other birds wondered: Is he really right for the job?'[3] The true Eagle was Nikita Khrushchev.

Khrushchev had been born into a peasant family in southern Russia in 1894. When he was only a boy, however, his family moved to the mining and industrial area of the Donbass in Ukraine. That made him a member of the peasant proletariat which has figured so much in this book: as a child he had tended cows, as an adolescent he worked in a factory and a mine. The young Khrushchev became fiercely radical and naturally enough joined the Bolsheviks after the revolution. As he rose through the party's ranks, he was very much a second-generation member. He had none of the sophistication or knowledge of the outside world of the Old Bolsheviks, and what little education he had was largely picked up in party institutions during the 1920s. All this made him a natural follower and devotee of Stalin. His support for Stalin no doubt reflected the peasant instinct to side with the majority and throw out splitters. Most probably, however, an element in it was his visceral rejection of party leaders who, like Bukharin, still kept the stamp of their bourgeois origins.

By 1935, Khrushchev was head of the Moscow party organization, and he remained in high office throughout the Stalin years. How he survived is not easy to say. It may have helped that he was away from Moscow for much of the time as Stalin's viceroy in Ukraine. It may have helped, too, that he was bold enough to look Stalin in the eye and tell him what he thought. But part of the reason seems to have been that Stalin saw him as a simple peasant, to the extent that he sometimes made him perform Ukrainian peasant dances. With his pair of warts, his enormous bald head, his upturned nose and his protruding ears, Khrushchev certainly looked the *muzhik*. And while he could play the part to perfection when it suited him, he did have undoubted peasant characteristics: he was warm, ebullient, given to explosive outbursts, and never happier than when hobnobbing.

This 'peasantness' made Khrushchev very different as a ruler from Stalin, who was austere, buttoned-up, and except on great ceremonial occasions never showed himself. Whereas Stalin was aloof and cultivated a godlike image, Khrushchev was all too available and human. Ordinary Russians might respect him, but the very fact that they could identify with him made reverence out of the question. Both leaders have been called 'populists', yet Stalin's populism was quite different from Khrushchev's. Stalin understood popular instincts and had the knack of exploiting them – the need to revere the leader, for instance. Khrushchev by contrast constantly rubbed shoulders with ordinary people and without any particular effort passed himself off as one of them. Not only was he a peasant, he was seen as such – the one and only thoroughly peasant ruler in modern Russian history.

Like his peasant ancestors, Khrushchev was a true believer, though his faith, unlike theirs, was in communism. He took the faith more seriously than any other Soviet leader apart from Lenin, and he tried to prepare for communism by making society more egalitarian and more uniform. Wage differences, which had become glaring under Stalin, began to be narrowed. He tackled the gulf between town and country by launching a grandiose scheme to break up villages, settle peasants in 'agro-towns' (*agrogoroda*), and turn agriculture into a form of industry. He tried to erode the difference between mental and physical labour by making all school-leavers spend at least two years in ordinary jobs before they went on to higher education. And he spurred people on by giving a clear picture of the life that lay around the corner. Under communism, Soviet citizens would live in 'communal palaces' of 2,000 or more inhabitants. They would even eat all together in huge cafeterias and so the unproductive chore of household cooking and washing up would disappear. The working week would be cut to between twenty and twenty-five hours. Work, moreover, would become a pleasure which people performed from love of the public good; and having freely given, they would freely receive the food, clothing and everything else they needed. These visions were inspired of course by Marx and Lenin, but it is not hard to see that they also had roots in the communal traditions of the Russian peasantry.

If communism was to be achieved, however, two major changes were essential. First, there would have to be a moral change – people would have to cast off all the undesirable character traits and patterns of behaviour inherited from the old society. There could be no more dishonesty or self-ishness, no drunkenness, abuse of women, or anti-social behaviour in general. 'Comradely mutual assistance' would replace the bourgeois principle of 'each for himself or herself'. And since the old evils had all too obviously not been eliminated, an enormous propaganda effort had to be brought to bear on them. One of the victims of this was the Church: during the later Khrushchev years, thousands of churches were closed and more than half the parishes were disbanded.

Secondly, the 'material-technical base' of communism had to be created. That meant developing a modern highly technological industry and bringing about conditions of material abundance. The society that would achieve communism had not only to be more just and on a higher moral plane than its American rival; it had to run more efficiently and its people had to live better than the Americans. Khrushchev's communism was not a matter of mere pious moralizing and lofty abstractions; it was very much about bread and sausage, and beating the Americans was a recurring theme. 'We shall overtake and outstrip the USA in per capita production of meat, milk and butter' was a boast of his which shouted from the billboards – and would later embarrass him.

This transformation could certainly not be brought about by orders from above, by bullying and terrifying people in Stalinist fashion. It could only be achieved by a highly motivated society, by people who were no longer repressed and eagerly put their shoulders to the wheel. Khrushchev talked a great deal about participation and about democracy. He wanted soviets, trade unions and other local bodies to assert themselves, and he denounced as conservatives and bureaucrats those who tried to restrain them. 'The dic-tatorship of the working class' hardly tallied with this approach and was replaced by the more tolerant and inclusive notion of 'the state of the whole people'. The masses, declared one of the basic propaganda texts of the time, 'must not be submissive performers of someone else's orders, but conscious architects of the new forms of their social life'.[4] Such talk did not of course mean that Khrushchev had become a liberal: far from it. 'Socialist democracy', the same text declared, 'is not a democracy without direction, but a directed democracy – directed by the Party and the state in the interests of the further development of socialism.'[5] The party would not only remain as infallible and authoritative as ever – in the run-up to communism, its role would actually increase. When Khrushchev talked of 'democracy' he was in fact straining after the same will-o'-the-wisp as Lenin: a society in which people willingly worked towards the goals laid down for them by the party and accepted without question its claim to embody their collective will and intellect. But what mattered was that he had turned decisively against Stalinism.

Stalin's methods, he saw, would lead neither to material abundance nor to freedom; they pointed in entirely the wrong direction. The party had to provide strong leadership, but at the same time it had to trust people rather than treat them as children or, worse still, as potential enemies. This trusting attitude had to be applied, moreover, to the outside world as well. And it was in foreign relations that the new attitude was first put conspicuously on display. Khrushchev visited Belgrade to make peace with the former heretic and outcast, Tito, established diplomatic relations with West Germany, withdrew Soviet troops from Austria, and gave up the naval base maintained since the war in Finland. But the real foreign break-through came in February 1956 at the twentieth Party Congress, the first congress since Stalin's death. This threw out one of Stalin's basic beliefs – that war with the capitalist powers was inevitable – and replaced it with the idea of peaceful co-existence between states with different social systems. There would of course be vigorous competition between the two systems, but the competition would be economic and ideological rather than military. The new thesis told people at home that they would be held on a looser leash; it also justified shifting resources from military to peaceful purposes, which was vital if Khrushchev's ambitions were to be realized.

The burning issue, however, was Stalin's domestic policy and the terror and repression with which he had implemented it. On this, the leadership had, admittedly, to some extent already voted with its feet. The release of several thousand people from the camps, the reopening of the Kremlin after many years to the public, the general relaxation which had become known as 'the thaw' – all this made an anti-Stalinist statement. Molotov, moreover, had been forced to recant his view that the Soviet Union had done no more than lay the foundations of socialism – a view which had seemed to imply that communism still lay well beyond the horizon. That was the standard Stalinist line, and when he recanted it the ghost of Stalin ate humble pie as well. There had, however, been no explicit criticism of Stalin or his policies. On the contrary, he was still revered as one of the two giants of Soviet history; and the Beria affair had in its way continued a tradition of deflecting criticism away from him on to his lieutenants.

The leadership's nervousness was understandable. Stalin was, after all, inseparable from the system. Soviet society had been made very largely to his design – how could you criticize him without criticizing all its structures, institutions and attitudes? How could you criticize Stalin without suggesting that the party had got it wrong and thus cutting the ground from beneath the feet of the current leadership? There were also more personal considerations. Molotov and Kaganovich had been Stalin's long-standing colleagues, and even the younger leaders had been closely associated with him. To some degree, they all had blood on their hands. How, then, could they attack Stalin without inviting awkward questions about themselves? 'We'll be taken to task!' was the frightened response of two Presidium members when Khrushchev tried to insist that the Stalin question could not be ducked at the twentieth Party Congress.[6] But Khrushchev got his way in the end, and he seems to have won over his reluctant colleagues by an argument not dissimilar from the one Alexander II had put to opponents of emancipation. The issue could not be postponed much longer because people were already coming back from the camps and many more would come soon. Much better for the leaders to raise the issue themselves than to wait until people took matters into their own hands.

3

That was true enough no doubt, yet it does not fully explain the fervour of Khrushchev's anti-Stalinist crusade. He, too, had been a faithful Stalinist; he, too, had wept at the dictator's funeral, and he had continued to believe in him well after his death. But then the spell had been broken, partly it seems by evidence of Stalin's brutalities unearthed by a secret party commission. Once converted, Khrushchev no longer saw Stalin as a leader of genius but rather as someone who had butchered friends and colleagues of his and had inflicted untold suffering upon the peasantry. This undoubted moral outrage in Khrushchev's anti-Stalinism was blended, however, with political calculation. Opponents such as Molotov and Kaganovich were far more implicated in Stalin's crimes than he and would therefore be harmed more by their exposure. And strategy as well as tactics made the Stalin issue one that he had to take up. For Stalin was emerging as the key symbol in the looming battle about how far and how fast the regime should reform. Conservatives were grouping themselves around the totem of Stalin; those who wanted a very different relationship between state and citizen and rapid progress towards communism simply had to take an anti-Stalinist position. And in the wake of Khrushchev's speech to the twentieth Party Congress, 'Stalinist' and 'anti-Stalinist' would become synonyms for 'conservative' and 'reformer'.

The circumstances of the speech were dramatic. The congress had already finished its work when, shortly before midnight on 24 February 1956, the 1,500 delegates were summoned back to the Kremlin, and they then heard Khrushchev speak for four hours 'On the Cult of Personality and its Consequences'. So sensitive was the subject that this was a closed session, to which only those with special passes were admitted. Not even all of them had strong enough stomachs for what they heard. Some delegates are said to have fainted, while some later suicides could be indirectly put down to the speech.

Khrushchev in fact launched a fierce assault on Stalin for having committed 'a whole series of exceedingly serious and grave perversions of party principles, of party democracy, of revolutionary legality'.[7] And he added weight to the attack by reading out Lenin's previously suppressed 'Testament', including the damning postscript on Stalin. These negative characteristics noted by Lenin had in time, Khrushchev commented, led to a grave abuse of power by Stalin. He had become intolerant, capricious and despotic in character, and he had acted brutally towards anyone he suspected of opposing him. The attack was sharpened by statistics which caused ripples of indignation in the hall: of the 139 Central Committee members elected at the seventeenth Party Congress, ninety-eight (70 per cent) had been arrested and shot, while 1,108 of the delegates – the predecessors of these very listeners – had been arrested on anti-revolutionary charges. Such figures are familiar enough now, but to the flower of the political nation hearing them in the early hours of 25 February 1956, they must have come like a douche of icy water.

Despotism – or 'the cult of the individual', as Khrushchev more diplomatically called it – had not only led to countless personal tragedies: it had resulted in thoroughly bad government. Stalin had not been the military leader of genius the legend made out; his management of the war effort had in fact been highly incompetent. And in society, the result had been over-caution, a crushing of initiative, and excessive formalism and bureaucracy. But how could all of this have happened? How could the cult have reached such monstrous dimensions?

Chiefly, Khrushchev replied, 'because Stalin himself, using all conceivable methods, supported the glorification of his own person'.[8] But that was not so much an answer as an evasion. Why had his Politburo colleagues not been able to stop him? Khrushchev's reply was that for many years Stalin had been a faithful Leninist who had 'actively fought for Lenin and against the enemies of Leninist theory and against those who deviated'.[9] Everything he had done until 1934, including collectivization, forced industrialization and the routing of the opposition, had been correct and had therefore fully deserved his colleagues' support. From 1934, however, Stalin's character had degenerated, and this had led to the tragedies of the time. The safeguard against such evils was collective leadership; but as to how that could have been maintained in the circumstances of the 1930s, Khrushchev said not a word. To have suggested that the Stalinist tragedy revealed a fundamental flaw in Soviet democracy would have been out of the question. He had been bold enough in tackling the symptoms of Stalinism; to have plunged into an analysis of its causes would have been madness. What he did do, however, was to point an emphatic moral. The party had to abolish the cult of the individual and return to Marxism–Leninism, whose most important teachings he summarized as follows: the people were the creators of history; the party had to have a decisive role in transforming society; and the victory of communism was inevitable.

The attack on Stalin thus turned into an endorsement of the Khrushchevite line with its emphasis on party-directed participation and the imminence of communism. The mistakes of the past were now safely behind; guided once more by Marxism–Leninism, the party was on the high road to communism. It was doubtful, however, whether the Stalin decades could be shrugged off quite so lightly. Many in the audience resented Khrushchev's assault on someone they still revered; others were frightened of the consequences of the assault and did not share Khrushchev's confidence that the party could admit Stalin's mistakes and still keep people's confidence. Fedor Burlatsky, a young party intellectual, met his boss straight after the speech and found him 'as white as snow – or more grey than white' and incapable at first of saying anything. When he had at last collected his wits, the man described what he had heard as a time-bomb. 'We don't know when it will explode, and what will remain of our ideology when it does.'[10]

There were two possible kinds of explosion to fear. The more immediate threat was of an enraged pro-Stalin outburst from people who still regarded him as a god and would therefore see any aspersions on him as sacrilege; and in the event there would be rioting in the Georgian capital, Tbilisi, where the cult was most entrenched. The alternative danger was that anti-Stalinism would unleash a movement against the party and the revolution itself. That the speech was indeed dynamite was soon shown by reactions in Eastern Europe, where reports of it caused a sensation. At home, marked copies were sent to local party secretaries, who read it to closed meetings of party members and then promptly returned the copy to the Central Committee. But what, if anything, was to be said to the non-party masses?

Letting them read the speech was out of the question – the tradition of treating ordinary Russians as children not capable of responding sensibly to the unadorned truth was too deeply ingrained. Nevertheless, a gradual process of desacralizing Stalin had to be begun. The existence of the 'secret' speech was acknowledged, and the congress resolution which followed it was published: 'to put an end to the cult of personality which is alien to Marxism–Leninism, to liquidate its consequences in all spheres of Party and state activity and of ideological work, and to ensure the strict maintenance of the standards of Party life worked out by the great Lenin and of the principles of collective Party leadership'.[11] Thus the content of the speech was hinted at but all the details were withheld. Khrushchev had denounced

Stalin's 'crimes'; when *Pravda* editorialized on the cult of personality, it spoke only of 'serious mistakes'. The message that Stalin had fallen from favour was borne out, however, by more than *Pravda*'s circumspect remarks. In March, the big paintings of Stalin disappeared from the Tretyakov Gallery. Large numbers of his victims began to come home from exile and the camps. In May, Lenin's 'Testament' was at long last published. The changes were nevertheless cautious and the caution resulted in glaring inconsistencies. Stalin might have gone from the Tretyakov, but there were still monuments to him in every Soviet town, and Stalingrad remained Stalingrad. Comments in which Lenin had damned Stalin and said positive things about Trotsky, Zinoviev and Bukharin had been released, yet the opposition leaders remained heretics and outcasts, while everything Stalin had done up to 1934 was endorsed.

By means of this fudging, Khrushchev got away relatively unscathed at home; but he had not guessed the effect his words would have in Eastern Europe, where Stalin was seen of course as a foreign tyrant. Georgians and Russians might demonstrate on Stalin's behalf; in the satellites, by contrast, Khrushchev's speech triggered anti-Stalinist and anti-Soviet outbursts. And what from the Soviet point of view made the anger in Eastern Europe more alarming was that it engulfed not only intellectuals but workers. Trouble erupted at Poznan in Poland in June 1956 with anti-Soviet riots which quickly led to a change of government, sweeping into power Wladyslaw Gomulka, a Stalinist victim who was determined that Poland should take its own distinctive road to socialism. That was bad enough; but while the Soviet leadership was trying to come to terms with Gomulka, still worse was happening in Hungary.

On 23 October, anti-Soviet riots erupted there too, and there too another victim, Imre Nagy, rode to power. The difference was that in Poland the party had kept control of events, even if it had struck out on a somewhat independent line. In Hungary, by contrast, party power collapsed altogether. Faced with a general strike against which he felt helpless, Nagy gave the rebels what they wanted. Hungary withdrew from the Warsaw Pact and announced its neutrality, and thus looked as if it would leave the Soviet sphere of influence altogether.

But this was more than Khrushchev could tolerate. Hungarian defiance was not only a threat to the entire 'outer empire'; it posed a mortal threat to his own, still precarious, ascendancy within the Presidium. If he lost Hungary, he would be doomed – the Stalinists, with Molotov at their head, would oust him. Only armed intervention could save him; and on 4 November 1956, under the pretext of putting down 'counter-revolution', Soviet troops invaded Hungary, deposed Nagy, and set up a loyal government under Janos Kadar. It was 107 years since the last time Russia invaded Hungary and crushed an independence movement. Then a conservative ruler had wanted to save conservatism by propping up someone else's empire; now a reformist ruler was propping up his own empire in a desperate attempt to save an imperilled reform programme.

4

In the spring and summer of 1956, Khrushchev had been on the offensive. Now, however, the Stalinists counter-attacked, buoyed up by incontrovertible evidence that criticizing Stalin had jeopardized the whole system. And Khrushchev seems at this point to have come close to panic. 'We were scared – really scared', he recalled in retirement. 'We were afraid that the thaw might unleash a flood, which we wouldn't be able to control and which would drown us.'[12] Nothing dramatic in fact happened, though in Russia too there had been disturbing ripples among students and writers. In his alarm, Khrushchev clamped down hard. In December 1956, a lot of students were expelled from Moscow University, while erring writers were whipped back into line with stern reminders that what was required of them was 'party-mindedness'. In May 1957, Khrushchev went as far as to threaten to shoot writers at the first sign of Hungarian-type troubles. That was a measure of how little 'liberalization' under him had in common with real liberalism: intellectuals were allowed to speak their minds only if, and in so far as, it suited the leadership.

The limits of freedom were shown by the fate of two great writers, Boris Pasternak and Vasilii Grossman. Pasternak was everything Khrushchev could be expected to dislike: a refined, westernized Jewish intellectual steeped in the traditions of 'bourgeois' pre-revolutionary culture who had come to see the revolution as a disaster, had lived through the intervening years as an 'internal *émigré*', and now took advantage of the thaw to try to publish a novel which passionately rejected the revolution's – and Khrushchev's – assumption that life could be reshaped for the better. 'Reshaping life! People who can say that have never understood a thing about life – they have never felt its breath, its heart.'[13] *Doctor Zhivago* was not the 'vicious lampoon' on the revolution nor the 'act of treason against the Soviet people' that some of its enemies claimed. Pasternak's work was nevertheless of its essence anti-Soviet, a rejection of the revolution's philosophy, an indictment of its brutality, and a lament for its victims. What made the offence worse was that, having been rebuffed at home, he allowed *Doctor Zhivago* to be published in the West, where it caused a sensation and in 1958 won him the Nobel Prize for Literature (which he accepted but in the ensuing furore had to turn down). Pasternak suffered no formal punishment other than expulsion from the Writers' Union – he was simply denied the right to be read and he was harassed intolerably, in effect to his death. There was similar treatment of Vasilii Grossman, whose novel about the battle of Stalingrad, *Life and Fate*, came close to heresy by implying that the Soviet and Nazi systems and the concentration camps in the two countries had a great deal in common. The manuscript was confiscated, Grossman was told by the party's chief ideologist (Mikhail Suslov) that his work would not see the light for at least 200 years, and shortly he, too, was harried to his grave.

Yet while Khrushchev defined the limits of freedom in a way which appeased the Stalinists, he refused to give ground on the economy and early in 1957 he returned to the attack with a radical economic reform that abolished most of the central economic ministries and devolved economic decision-making to some hundred regional councils (*Sovnarkhozy*). This decentralization was wholly in line with his general strategy; it also had the advantage that it delighted the party's regional bosses and redoubled their loyalty to him. On the other hand, it infuriated a huge army of Moscow bureaucrats, who either lost their jobs or had to transfer to the provinces, and it confirmed the feeling among many influential people that Khrushchev was fundamentally unsound and a potential wrecker.

The conflict within the élite came to a head in June 1957, when Stalinists and those who wanted reform to proceed more slowly ganged up against him. A Presidium resolution demanding his resignation as First Secretary was passed by seven votes to two, with one abstention. Khrushchev refused, however, to accept this as a definitive verdict, claiming that since the Central Committee had appointed him, only it (to which the Presidium was in theory accountable) could dismiss him. With great reluctance, his opponents, who had not expected to be thwarted by this constitutional nicety, gave way. They had little alternative in fact since Central Committee members, having heard what was afoot, were already gathering in Moscow and demanding a meeting. The meeting lasted a full week, and during the course of it Khrushchev turned the tables on the Presidium majority completely. The regional party bosses who had gained so much from his economic reorganization rallied fervently to him; so did the military, led by Marshal Zhukov. By the end of the meeting, the tradition of unanimity had so strongly reasserted itself that a motion condemning the opposition to Khrushchev was passed by 308 votes to none, with only Molotov having enough courage of his convictions to abstain. He, Malenkov and Kaganovich, together with Foreign Minister Shepilov, who had joined them late in the day, were then branded as an 'anti-party group' and expelled from the Presidium and Central Committee. (Other opponents were for the time being left in peace so as not to advertise the embarrassing fact that a *majority* of the Presidium had turned against Khrushchev.) They were formally condemned for having violated the party's ban on factionalism; for having opposed economic reform and attempts to relieve international tensions; and, most resonantly, for their stubborn opposition to 'those measures which the Central Committee and our entire party carried out to eliminate the consequences of the cult of the individual leader'.[14] This victory of the 'entire party' over a handful of malefactors was in effect a victory of the oligarchy's outer circle over its core. It therefore reflected a very slight broadening of the power-base; but the people of Russia had, needless to say, as always been left on the sidelines.

In victory Khrushchev was, by the standards of Soviet politics, remarkably generous. His opponents were not cast into outer darkness, still less liquidated as 'enemies of the people'. Instead, they were given minor posts and allowed to keep most of the perks which went with membership of the ruling class. He had, after all, fought them on the issue of Stalinism, and it would have been incongruous had he acted like Stalin once he had routed them. The light punishments reflected the new temper of the times; they even in a sense went beyond it, suggesting late-1920s thinking rather than the early-1930s thinking on which Khrushchevism was officially based. To their credit, his opponents had in the end yielded to his constitutionalist point: that, too, may have weighed with him and persuaded him not to eject them from the élite altogether. And it may also have occurred to him that new and more humane rules of the political game promised a soft landing for himself, should he ever come out the loser from any future confrontation.

A sequel to the affair came in March 1958, when Nikolai Bulganin was forced to step down as prime minister. From then on Khrushchev held both of the top jobs in Soviet politics. His domination of the political scene dated, however, from June 1957. Lip service continued to be paid to collective leadership, but since the expulsion of the 'anti-party group' the Soviet Union had had an unchallenged leader who was determined to push it hard towards its communist destiny.

5

In 1957, people in the West were astounded to hear that Soviet scientists had launched the world's first artificial earth satellite, the Sputnik; and there was still more astonishment in 1959 when they landed a rocket on the moon. Opponents of the regime made much of the absurdity of sending rockets to the moon when it still could not properly feed, clothe and house its people. Yet these triumphs of space technology (there would be another in 1961 when Yurii Gagarin made the first manned space flight) did seem to say something about the success of the Soviet system. Some observers in the West – Harold Macmillan, for one – began to fear that the Soviet economy would indeed overhaul the advanced capitalist ones. Directed by the reforming Khrushchev, the Soviet system seemed to be at the point when it was about to make good the regime's promise of wellbeing for its people.

Admittedly, Soviet industrial production in 1959 was only half that of the USA. But optimistic Soviet predictions, and gloomy Western ones, were based on rates of growth. The Soviet economy had for some years been growing at an annual rate of around 9 per cent, whereas the USA could manage only a growth rate of some 2 per cent. If these rates were kept up, the Soviet triumph would be inevitable. At the party's twenty-first Congress, which met in 1959 in a mood of euphoria, Khrushchev predicted that real income per head would increase by 40 per cent during the next seven years, while the Soviet Union would overtake the USA in output per head in 1970.

The twenty-first Congress was billed as 'the Congress of the Builders of Communism'. The transition to communism had been occurring, it was claimed, ever since 1936, and the final phase of the transition was now under way. The twenty-second Congress, which met in October 1961, then fleshed out the prospects in a new Party Programme, which replaced one adopted as long ago as 1919. The national income, the programme predicted, would increase 150 per cent in the next ten years and 400 per cent in the next twenty. By 1980, real income per head would have gone up by more than 250 per cent. Low-paid jobs would disappear. Within a decade, the Soviet Union would have the shortest working-day in the world; the Soviet working-day would also be more productive and better paid than anywhere else. By 1970, the housing shortage would be solved, and by 1980 every family would have its own comfortable accommodation. Moreover, standards of consumption would rise rapidly, giving the Soviet Union a higher living standard than any capitalist country. Everyone, the programme said, 'will live in easy circumstances'; all farms would become 'highly productive and profitable enterprises'; and 'hard physical work will disappear'. During the decade 1971–80, the work of building the material and technical base for communism would be completed; and by 1980, the programme promised, 'a communist society will in the main be built in the USSR'.[15]

It was an exhilarating prospect. But Khrushchev had taken an enormous risk in doing what no previous Soviet leader had done – putting a date (an early one at that!) on the achievement of communism. And not only did he go out on a limb in that respect, he took another risk at the congress by re-opening the Stalin question. This had seemed to be settled by a tacit agreement that Stalin should be subjected to no more than low-level public criticism for the personal mistakes of his later years, and the Presidium had decided against raising the question at the congress. But then Khrushchev made a last-minute change to his speech, and to his colleagues' surprise and almost certainly to their dismay he launched into a fierce attack on the Stalin cult and the 'anti-party group' as supporters of it. The criticisms may have been no harsher than in 1956. However, it was a crucial difference that those criticisms had been made to a closed meeting of the élite; these were for all the world to hear.

Further drama was provoked by an elderly woman delegate who announced that Lenin had come to her in a dream and told her that he felt uncomfortable lying beside Stalin. That very night, Stalin's body was removed from the mausoleum and buried under a granite slab near to the Kremlin wall. The implications of moving the dead Leader were of course immense. With this one gesture – a gesture prepared of course by six years of cautious sniping – the demi-god was desacralized, turned into someone human and fallible. And since he was no longer the object of a cult, all symbols of the cult had to be removed. Stalingrad became Volgograd, while busts, portraits, statues and all other remaining pieces of memorabilia rapidly disappeared throughout the country.

That was not the end of Stalin, of course. The Stalinists would fight back hard and they could draw on a deep reservoir of popular support. Khrushchev had for the moment given radicals what they wanted, but they were all too few and their patron was all too mercurial. So precarious was the victory that the poet Yevgenii Yevtushenko appealed in a poem to the government 'to double and treble the sentries guarding this slab, and to stop Stalin from ever rising again and, with Stalin, the past'.[16] Khrushchev's personal approval had been needed to get Yevtushenko's poem into print; its chilling implication was that a legion of unreconstructed Stalinists was poised to seize power again. The most remarkable anti-Stalinist statement in the wake of the twenty-second Congress came, however, from a completely unknown writer, Alexander Solzhenitsyn, who did not directly raise the Stalin question at all.

Drawing on his eight years as a Gulag victim, Solzhenitsyn had written a fictional account of a day in the life of a prisoner, beginning with reveille long before the winter dawn and finishing with the prisoner falling into an exhausted sleep after a final tussle with the guards. *One Day in the Life of Ivan Denisovich* looked at camp life through the person of a simple, apolitical peasant who had been arrested on trumped-up charges, was all too obviously not an 'enemy of the people' and equally clearly not a radical or an intellectual or anyone else on the margins of the Russian experience but rather the quintessence of decent, everyday suffering Russianness. The novella was stark, concentrated, devoid of comment or authorial consciousness, and made the more powerful by its tight-lipped understatement. The impact was similar to that of Tolstoy's writings about the Crimean War. Tolstoy had brought an entirely new character before the reading public – the peasant in uniform, the common soldier suffering and dying in the hell of Sevastopol. Solzhenitsyn introduced the *zek* (detainee) in the hell of the camps. 'That was how it was', his work said; and the injustice of how it was cried out between the lines. He sent the work to the most progressive literary periodical of the day, *Novyi mir* (New World), whose editor, Alexander Tvardovsky, had become expert at pushing free expression to the limits of the possible. Tvardovsky reacted much as literary St Petersburg had reacted to Tolstoy's first manuscripts – here out of the blue had come the work of a master. Here was someone who shone a powerful light on the Russian darkness. Here at last was reality. But after the fabrications of socialist realism, such unadorned truth was unpublishable. He dared not publish it – yet he had to.

Tvardovsky did the only thing possible: he went to Khrushchev. 'Comrade Khrushchev, I think this work is very good', he said. 'From this work I can see that its author is going to become a great writer.'[17] Khrushchev then read the manuscript and approved it for publication. Not that great art concerned him; what mattered was that this provincial schoolmaster had written a powerful exposé of the camps. Moreover, the writer gave the impression of a down-to-earth Soviet citizen: there was nothing here of the over-refined bourgeois intellectual with his visceral anti-Sovietism. *One Day in the Life of Ivan Denisovich* was published in the November 1962 number of *Novyi mir*, and the 120,000 copies sold out at once. The schoolmaster became a celebrity overnight. Little can Khrushchev have guessed that this writer he had let loose would soon, like some calf butting an oak, begin a one-man literary struggle against the might of the Soviet state.

The campaign against Stalin was now out in the open because Khrushchev, an old man in a hurry, needed to clear away the obstacles to his promises, and prominent among them were the conservatives and more cautious reformers whom he regarded, rightly or wrongly, as Stalinists. The new anti-Stalinism did not, however, seem to go any deeper than the old. 1934 was still maintained as a firm watershed: before that, all had been well. There was no question, therefore, of rehabilitating the opposition. As for Stalin's mistakes, they were personal and did not reflect on the system. Not only did Khrushchev rule out fundamental objections to Stalinism. At the very time when he was attacking the cult and its supporters most vigorously, something of a cult of himself was beginning to take shape.

The Khrushchev cult was not of course in the same league as the Stalin one. Yet official pronouncements no longer stressed the collective nature of the leadership; instead, they used formulas such as 'the Central Committee with N. S. Khrushchev at its head'. At meetings, speakers showered fulsome praise on Khrushchev, and a film glorifying him went the rounds. It was partly that the old and hard to eradicate Russian tradition of one-man leadership was reasserting itself. There were, as we have seen, no effective mechanisms for maintaining equality of power among the oligarchs, and probably few people apart from the oligarchs themselves would have wanted such restraints. But there was more to it than that. Khrushchev had risen to the top thanks to the party apparatus. It was party loyalists who had saved him in 1957. Now, however, support for him within both the narrow circle of the oligarchy and the broader circle of the ruling class was haemorrhaging away. There were two obvious responses to this loss of support. One was to turn himself into someone special and so beyond the reach of envious rivals. The other was to win such popularity outside the élite that no one would dare to challenge him.

6

But why had he lost support among those who mattered? Why was he having to trawl for it among the masses? Part of the problem was the serious setback his agricultural ambitions had suffered. He had come to power with a strong commitment to improving the wretched condition of the peasantry and to providing more meat, butter and other foodstuffs for everyone. His headstrong ways and his doctrinaire Bolshevism, however, seriously obstructed the ambition. He believed in irresistible, military-style campaigns and in simple, all-encompassing solutions, but his campaigns and his solutions tended to go wrong. Early in his period of power he had aired a grandiose scheme to plough up the 'virgin lands' of Kazakhstan and south-eastern European Russia and grow grain on them. Expert objections that these arid steppe-lands were unsuitable for large-scale grain production were brushed aside. The 'virgin lands' project was launched with great fanfares, and hundreds of thousands of young people were in due course sent, or volunteered, to harvest the crop. For a time all went well and high yields resulted; but then, as the experts had predicted, serious problems of soil erosion appeared, and by the beginning of the 1960s the virgin lands campaign had come to look like a costly mistake. It was much the same with the maize campaign. A trip to the USA in 1959 had given Khrushchev the idea that maize was an ideal crop for the Soviet Union, and he then insisted that it be grown across the country irrespective of soil and climate conditions. The campaign won him the derisive name of 'maize-nut', and poor results once more did nothing for his prestige. The combination of bad judgement and bad luck in the form of poor harvests in fact made the agricultural record of Khrushchev's final years a dismal one. Output hardly increased. A hike in food prices in 1962 led to serious riots. And in order to avoid a repetition of the trouble, he had to resort to the humiliating measure of importing grain from abroad. Whereas tsarist Russia had *exported* grain, the communist regime appeared to have bungled things so badly that it had become a net importer. Such a comparison was, however, not wholly fair to Khrushchev. The tsars, after all, had exported grain while people went hungry; so had Stalin. It was a sign of the changing times that Khrushchev spent precious hard currency in order to keep people happy; and Brezhnev after him would do the same.

The story of industry was rather similar. During the 1950s, the industrial economy had performed very well and had given solid ground for Khrushchev's predictions. But around the end of the decade a decline in growth rates set in, and by the early 1960s the overall growth rate had fallen to some 5 per cent per year. Part of the problem was a decline in the rate of growth of labour productivity, which was extremely worrying given the general belief that labour productivity would be a vital – perhaps *the* vital – factor in the victory of the Soviet system. Lenin was frequently quoted to this effect, and the 1961 Programme had re-emphasized the point. If Soviet labour productivity continued to decline relative to that of the West, then a communist society would for the foreseeable future be unachievable. The labour productivity problem raised questions about management of the economy, levels of technology and the attitudes of the workforce, which reform-minded economists began to grapple with. Finding solutions consistent with party orthodoxy was not easy, however, and it was clear that any that breached it would get short shrift from Khrushchev. But by the early 1960s, one thing at least was certain. The downturn in the once dynamic Soviet economy had made his predictions of abundance and communism by 1980 look laughable.

Foreign affairs, too, had given Khrushchev's swelling army of opponents ample reason to want to get rid of him. His peaceful co-existence thesis had led to an attempt at *détente* with America, which had the advantage that it checked the growth of military expenditure but the disadvantage, for Khrushchev, that it angered the military. Another unfortunate effect was a worsening of relations with China, which strongly resisted the peaceful co-existence approach. By the early 1960s, the bad blood between the two, and between Khrushchev and Mao Tse-tung in particular, had resulted in an open split in the world communist movement and fierce polemics in which Soviet spokesmen called the Chinese 'dogmatists' and were damned as 'revisionists' and 'social imperialists' in return.

The split in the communist movement would have mattered less if the policy of *détente* with America had gone smoothly, but it had not. An unexpected stumbling block proved to be Cuba. The overthrow in 1959 of the Batista regime in Cuba by the young Fidel Castro, who once in power soon became a communist fellow traveller, had seemed a marvellous piece of luck for Khrushchev. Here was further evidence, in a quite new theatre, of the irresistibility of communism; and it opened up the possibility that much of the rest of Latin America would go the same way, leaving the USA as the beleaguered bastion of a doomed capitalism. The Americans, however, reacted badly to having a pro-communist and Soviet client state so close to their shores; and when in October 1962 they discovered that the Soviet Union had installed short-range nuclear missiles there, disquiet turned to fury. The ensuing stand-off reached crisis point when an American reconnaissance aircraft was shot down over Cuba. The two superpowers appeared to be on the brink of a nuclear war. The peace was then saved by Khrushchev backing down and removing the missiles; but the price of peace was a considerable loss of face for him.

Mismanagement of the economy and clumsy posturing in foreign affairs were bad enough. But Khrushchev was more than an incompetent: to many members of the political nation (i.e. his fellow oligarchs plus the million-odd members of the ruling class), he had become an enemy because of the threat he presented to their security and their privileges. One hateful change, introduced at the twenty-second Party Congress, was to set fixed limits to the length of time a top position could be held – thus, members of the Central Committee were limited to sixteen years and party officials at the provincial (*oblast*) level to a mere six. He followed this up in 1962 with a major restructuring of the party, which split it down the middle. From then on, the party had quite separate industrial and agricultural sections which did not converge until the Central Committee apparatus was reached. The reform created enormous confusion; it also resulted in inconvenience and dislocation for a large number of officials, who had to change the place or the nature of their work and sometimes both. Yet worse even than this tampering with the machine of state were the suggestions that he was in principle against it, that he saw the country being strangled by the machine and wanted the masses to assert themselves against it. His administrative reforms were a nuisance; his anti-Stalinism in its more radical form and the populist, anti-bureaucratic rhetoric which went with it were, however, positively dangerous since they threatened to destroy the controls on popular spontaneity which were a necessary defence against anarchy.

Khrushchev had in fact edged away from the traditional view that the élite's role was to give orders and the masses' role was to obey them uncritically. At first, he had aimed to do no more than ginger ordinary people into being more creative and showing more initiative at work; now he wanted to use them against those in the political nation who were trying to obstruct him. Not only had a lot of raw recruits been brought into the party at the bottom. He was also trying to stir things up at the top – non-party specialists, for instance, were being invited to take part in Central Committee plenums. Further pressure was applied to the party by his insistence that plenum proceedings should be published. True, he claimed to want a larger rather than a smaller role for the party in the run-up to communism. Yet he was also trying to expand the rights of other organizations which the party had long since neutered – soviets and trade unions in particular. And he had the idea that state (as opposed to party) organizations should begin shedding some of their functions to voluntary local organizations – for instance to 'comrades' courts', which would try minor offences in place of normal courts. Perhaps most galling of all, he was encouraging ordinary people to answer back and to 'wrangle' with officials, whom he all too readily labelled as 'bureaucrats'. Lenin had admittedly had similarly crazy ideas. But nothing could have been more alien to the Stalinist society which Khrushchev's Russia in many respects still was than grass-roots activism and answering back. The apparatchiks would have been alarmed also, had they known about it, by a group of young Turks who, with some official encouragement, were drafting new constitutional proposals which would have provided for free and multi-candidate elections, a proper working parliament, separation of powers, an independent legal system, and a president directly elected by the people.[18]

Yet whether Khrushchev would have implemented such ideas is extremely doubtful. Frightening apparatchiks with the threat of popular retribution was one thing; establishing constitutional democracy would have been quite another. He wanted to trust people and give them their heads, but not to the extent of letting them make serious mistakes. Imposing real constraints on the party would have gone against the principles and attitudes of his whole adult life. He wanted a freer and more spontaneous relationship between party and people with a two-way flow of energy and ideas; he would not, however, have wanted genuine pluralism or anything that might have jeopardized the party's ultimate control. His ideal was not a party reduced in power and authority but, rather, one purged of drones and capable of infecting the masses with its vision and its dynamism.

This neo-Leninist ideal was shared by a group of young radicals, who as chastened veterans would provide the shock troops for perestroika. There was, however, only 'a very thin layer' of such people, as Khrushchev's son Sergei would later point out.[19] Among the political nation as a whole, and perhaps even among the nation as a whole, de-Stalinization had made Khrushchev more enemies than friends. And even the loyalty of the young Khrushchevites could not, by the end, be counted upon. During the Brezhnev years, they would look back nostalgically at the freedom and opportunities offered by Khrushchev, but while he had power he was at best a mixed blessing for them. Khrushchev, one would comment, 'walked on two legs – one boldly striding out into the new era, the other hopelessly stuck in the mire of the past'.[20] Many later radicals, among them Mikhail Gorbachev, shed no tears about Khrushchev's political demise and hoped for less erratic progress under successors who were more disciplined and less torn by conflicting impulses than he was.

Khrushchev's problem was that he had alienated the political nation without winning much of a following among the disfranchised. In many ways, he deserved to be popular. Living standards had improved considerably during his period of power. Peasants had benefited especially, but he had also helped townspeople by a crash attack on the housing problem – the modern Russian city with its forest of high-rise apartment blocks owes much to him. Yet he got little thanks. Peasants remembered him mainly for his hostility to their private plots and his campaign against the Church; townspeople complained about the awful quality of their flats and the lack of amenities around them. He was too Bolshevik to appeal to the peasants, but also too peasant to fit anyone's idea of what a Soviet leader ought to be. Russians had never before had a leader who showed himself to be all too like themselves, and on the whole they did not appreciate it. Leaders were expected to be dignified and to keep their distance: this clowning, garrulous, back-slapping peasant, moody and all too uncultured, was quite wrong for the part. An incident at the United Nations when he interrupted a speech of Harold Macmillan's by taking off his shoe and banging it seems to have caused particular offence. Khrushchev had done much to humanize the image of the leader; but in the early 1960s people still wanted, if not a god, then someone who hid his character and foibles behind a mask of impersonal authority.

Even had Khrushchev won an enthusiastic popular following, he would have been hard put to translate it into effective support against his opponents. The mechanisms simply did not exist; not until the late 1980s would a Soviet leader find a way of admitting the masses to the political nation.

Anyway, he had no such support. Not only had he alienated and scared the élite, the masses looked at him with indifference if not distaste. When the blow fell, he was as a result helpless. On 13 October 1964, he was brought back from holiday in the Crimea to face the denunciation of his Presidium colleagues. The next day, Mikhail Suslov, whose support had helped save him in 1957, delivered a comprehensive indictment of him before a full meeting of the Central Committee. He was condemned on many counts, but the essence of the case against him was that he had concentrated all power in his own hands, slighted and ignored members of the Presidium, and encouraged a cult of himself which outdid even the cult of Stalin. There was no replay of 1957 – none of the provincial bosses rallied to him. The session ended with the Central Committee formally approving Khrushchev's 'request' to be relieved of his duties 'in connection with his advanced age and worsening condition of health'.[21] The real reasons for removing him were of course covered up. As usual, ordinary people were given no say in the matter of how and by whom they should be ruled – though in this case most of them were, as it happened, probably not too unhappy about the change.

The fallen ruler was given a flat in Moscow and a dacha, a car and a pension, and he would live on in obscurity as an 'unperson' until his death in 1971. When the crisis came, he had decided not to fight. 'Could anyone', he told his accusers, 'have dreamt of telling Stalin that he didn't suit us anymore, and suggesting that he retire? Not even a wet spot would have remained where we had been standing. Now everything is different. The fear's gone and we can talk as equals. That's my contribution.'[22] It was a fitting epitaph. Khrushchev had left the country freer, happier and more prosperous. Many who supported him only half-heartedly at the end would come to miss him and to idealize the Khrushchev era. Two decades later, they would begin a more thoroughgoing reform than his. By then the time would be ripe for change, but in a sense it would be overripe. They would no longer be able to believe in the great myth of the revolution – the myth of communism.

Notes

1 Vladimir Bukovsky, *To Build a Castle: My Life as a Dissenter* (London, 1978), p. 83.
2 Yevgeny Yevtushenko, *A Precocious Autobiography* (London, 1963), p. 95.
3 Alec Nove, *Stalinism and After: The Road to Gorbachev* (Boston, 1989), p. 127.
4 O. Kuusinen, ed., *Fundamentals of Marxism-Leninism* (London, 1961), p. 833.
5 *Ibid.*, p. 633.
6 *Khrushchev Remembers*, edited and translated by Strode Talbott (2 vols, Harmondsworth, 1977), vol. I, p. 374.

7 *The Anti-Stalin Campaign and International Communism* (New York, 1956), p. 3.

8 *Ibid.*, p. 89.

9 *Ibid.*, p. 81.

10 Fedor Burlatsky, *Khrushchev and the First Russian Spring* (London, 1991), pp. 63–4.

11 Wolfgang Leonhard, *The Kremlin since Stalin* (Oxford, 1962), p. 187.

12 *Khrushchev Remembers*, vol. II, p. 113.

13 Boris Pasternak, *Doctor Zhivago* (London, 1958), p. 305.

14 Robert V. Daniels, *A Documentary History of Communism* (2 vols, London, 1987), vol. I, p. 335.

15 See 'Programme of the Communist Party of the Soviet Union', in Leonard Schapiro, ed., *The USSR and the Future: An Analysis of the New Program of the CPSU* (New York, 1963), esp. pp. 284 and 293–6.

16 Stephen F. Cohen, Alexander Rabinowitch, Robert Sharlet, eds, *The Soviet Union since Stalin* (London, 1980), p. 43.

17 *Khrushchev Remembers*, vol. II, p. 196.

18 See Fedor Burlatsky, *Khrushchev and the First Russian Spring*, p. 200.

19 Sergei Khrushchev, *Khrushchev on Khrushchev* (Boston, 1990), p. 14.

20 Fedor Burlatsky, *Khrushchev and the First Russian Spring*, p. 274.

21 Robert V. Daniels, *A Documentary History of Communism*, vol. I, p. 355.

22 Sergei Khrushchev, *Khrushchev on Khrushchev*, p. 154.

|9|

Conservatism, 1964–1985

1

Anti-Stalinism was not in fact part of the case against Khrushchev: on the contrary, the suggestion was that he had become something of a Stalin himself. His fall nevertheless ushered in a more cautious period, and caution hardened in time into positive conservatism. The great gain of the post-Stalin years was, however, preserved. Leadership was collective, and even when Brezhnev became fawned upon he was really no more than first among equals. Life was secure, predictable and governed by tacitly understood rules. Brezhnev's watchwords were 'stability of cadres', and accordingly he allowed high officials to grow old in their posts. Many had entered the élite remarkably young as a result of the Great Purge of the 1930s; now, as men in their sixties, seventies and even eighties, they clung on and resisted the normal generational turn-over.

The great beneficiaries of the Brezhnev era were in fact the members of the political nation, for whom this was to be a golden age of wellbeing. Now they enjoyed the best of all possible worlds. Under Stalin the price of power and privilege had been to live in constant fear of the ruler; even under Khrushchev, top people had to fear for their jobs if not their lives. But now they kept their firm control of the disfranchised, while getting rid of the fear and insecurity which had previously gone with it. Accountability of a kind had been established within the political nation, and as a result its members were shielded against threats from both above and below.

While political reform had disappeared from the agenda, economic reform stayed on it because of the very fact that the economy was doing so badly. If the relative decline of the Soviet economy continued, people were bound to start questioning the effectiveness of the socialist economic system. In addition, military parity with the USA would be quite impossible to maintain. Fears that the regime would sooner or later become vulnerable both to its own subjects and to the capitalist powers drove the leadership in the mid-1960s into an attempt at economic reform. Put through by premier Kosygin, the reform sprang from the assumption that overcentralization was damaging the economy. This was still the 'command economy' created by Stalin in the late 1920s and early 1930s: everything was done in accordance with the plan and all significant decisions were made in Moscow. During the 1930s, these methods had worked wonders, but by the 1960s they had become much less effective. Draconian centralization had laid the foundations of a modern economy: the more complex the economy became, however, the less it responded to old-style directives. The Kosygin reform aimed to decentralize, creating more freedom for managers and more scope for incentives for workers.

The reform ran into serious resistance, however, from the ruling class and in the end came more or less to nothing. The trouble was that any economic reform which went beyond tinkering had political implications. The Stalinist system had been all of a piece: the command economy was but one aspect, though a vital one, of the regime's total control of society. Giving some freedom in the economic sphere could well prompt demands for other freedoms – a lessening of censorship, say, or allowing lawyers to observe the letter of the law. But it would also in itself dilute that supreme concentration of power which was Stalinism's special hallmark.

If there were any doubts about the close connection between the economic and the political, they were dispelled by what happened in Czechoslovakia in 1968. The Czech Communist Party had put economic liberalization to the fore of its reform programme; but by August 1968 it was giving way to clamour for free and multi-party elections and an end to the communist monopoly. That economic competition and market mechanisms were inevitably linked with political competition and a political market could not have been more graphically illustrated. The lesson was not lost. The Soviet invasion of August 1968 did more than crush the Czech reform movement; it put paid to any hope of economic or political reform at home.

The leadership had in effect made its choice. The long-term dangers of not reforming and the consequent loss of economic dynamism would have to be lived with. Something might anyway turn up: technology and in particular computerization might yet make the command economy efficient. The dangers were in any event less alarming than the almost certain threat to the party's monopoly and even its ruling position which would flow from reforms that allowed individual initiative and a market element in the economy.

During the late 1960s and 1970s, dissidents, many of them scientists or writers, protested against the regime's conservative and repressive course. But they were few and divided among themselves, and they won little active support from the educated and next to none from workers and peasants. Getting rid of Soviet power by force was out of the question. The dissidents

were as isolated and as outnumbered as tsarism's critics at the very beginning of the nineteenth century, and by the end of the 1970s their movement
– though it hardly amounted to that – had been crushed. Within a decade
the regime would collapse, but those living in the late-Brezhnev era had very
little inkling that its demise was so close.

Then, as in the early nineteenth century, a formidable machine of repression seemed to rule out any real challenge. Then, as in the early nineteenth
century, the regime could count upon the passive, if not the active, support
of the most numerous group in society. Then, as in the early nineteenth century, critics were an unrepresentative handful who were quite unable to
establish any rapport with the masses. And the Soviet state for its part could
expect more than mere acquiescence from its rank and file. The revolution
had, after all, been made on the workers' behalf. The current rulers were
themselves very largely working class in origin. And workers had good reason to feel grateful: there had been a vast improvement in material conditions, especially since Stalin, even if the regime's ultimate promise of
communism remained unfulfilled. Real benefits had been supplemented,
moreover, by skilful use of propaganda. Ordinary people had come to
believe that conditions for workers in the West were terrible, and until very
recently few had doubted that their own socialist system was intrinsically
superior. The increasing problems the regime faced had created what the
Sovietologist Seweryn Bialer called 'a crisis of effectiveness', yet they hardly
suggested that it was on the eve of its downfall.[1]

Foreshadowings of the coming trouble had, however, already appeared.
They could be seen in the non-Russian republics, where Sovietization was
resented as simply russification under another name. They could be seen
among the burgeoning middle class, whose members were irked by policies
that seemed to benefit workers and peasants at their expense. But perhaps
most ominous for the regime were signs that it was losing touch with the
workers themselves. Not that it had come to open opposition. Occasionally
there were riots, but these were provoked by specific issues, usually food
shortages or price rises, and the regime always moved quickly to defuse the
issue. Russian governments had, after all, been used to spontaneous outbursts throughout the ages – 'anarchy' could be coped with. What was happening now, however, was both less dramatic and more serious: the regime
was losing its power to motivate and manipulate. Back in the 1950s,
Khrushchev had tried with some success to make the party once more a
dynamic force, but its power to inspire and to reshape society had now
fallen almost to zero. The most glaring symptoms of the trouble could be
found at the work place. There was more absenteeism, more shirking on the
job, more shoddy workmanship, more pilfering and corruption, more
drinking and hence more illness and more violence. The dominant attitudes
of the workforce as it entered the decade which should have been the decade
of communism were apathy and cynicism. The party had once excited people and given them hope and belief. But now morale was in steep decline,

and society, which the party had held together by the power of inspiration as well as repression, was beginning to unravel.

The problem began at the top. This was a regime of old men, and inevitably it had run out of vitality. Rulers as elderly and as set in their ways as those who lined the Lenin Mausoleum for the great parades could hardly communicate excitement or infect people with ideals. They were complacent, lacklustre and often corrupt, and complacency, lack of lustre and corruption went all the way down the chain of command. They used the traditional rhetoric, but few people believed it any more. Words and reality had grown dangerously far apart. They talked of communism, but a communist future was simply not credible. They talked of the increasing homogeneity of Soviet society, but people sensed that it was actually becoming more divided and differentiated. They talked of the high morality, selflessness and social consciousness of the new Soviet man: but everyone knew that they themselves were greedy and selfish 'old men' (in both respects) who lived lives of inordinate privilege. There were no 'new men', nor would there be; and the trouble with the Soviet system was that it was incapable of getting the best out of an obstinately imperfectible workforce.

It was not only the minority who listened to Radio Liberty or the BBC who knew that the communist experiment was faltering and was almost certainly doomed. This was widely sensed, and the result was a feeling of being morally adrift. What was there to believe in? Your grandparents had probably believed in God and the tsar, and their beliefs had done something to explain the suffering and mess around them. Your parents had believed in Lenin, Stalin and the communist future. Until recently, you had at least believed that every year would bring a modest improvement in living standards. Now even that was in doubt.

It had not yet got to a visible crisis: there was order in the streets and the normal pattern of life carried on. But more perceptive members of the political nation knew that a crisis was looming and that its immediate cause was economic. The various methods of stimulating the economy that the ideology sanctioned – disciplining workers, exhorting them, offering them minor incentives – had proved useless. Fundamental change might open a Pandora's box of troubles, but nothing else offered any hope. What had to be done in fact was to begin again where Nikita Khrushchev had left off.

2

In October 1964, however, the leaders had been determined to prevent any repetition of the Khrushchev episode, and the Central Committee plenum had decided that from now on the two top jobs should not be held by the same person. The premiership went to Alexei Kosygin, a melancholy technocrat who was particularly associated with the consumer industries, while the more important position of party First Secretary went to Leonid Brezhnev. Compared to previous party leaders, Brezhnev did not stand out: he lacked the brilliance of Lenin and the masterful presence of Stalin, and he did not even have the energy and ebullience of Khrushchev. What could be said, however, for the new man was that he was dignified and charming, and he seemed in addition to have decent instincts and to be at least modestly competent. Some of the main players in the October 1964 coup, such as the former KGB boss, Alexander Shelepin, may well have seen him as no more than a useful interim front man. Yet against the apparent odds, this undistinguished man survived in the top job right through until his death in November 1982. He had, as it turned out, more political acumen than most people credited him with, and in due course he removed those like Shelepin who might have threatened him; and the very fact that he was not especially clever or wilful, and was therefore inclined to be guided by consensus rather than to impose, proved to be a positive merit in the eyes of most of his colleagues.

Not only did Brezhnev last, gradually he rose above his fellow oligarchs. At the twenty-third Party Congress in 1966 he took for himself the more glorious title of 'General Secretary' (and at the same time the Presidium went back to its old name of Politburo). After the twenty-fifth Party Congress in 1976, a cult of him began to develop, and in 1977 he added the post of President to that of General Secretary. During his final years he was something of an emperor, inordinately vain, and demanding not only flattery but tribute: on his visits to Azerbaijan, for instance, he was twice presented with a diamond ring by the local first secretary. The Khrushchev saga was, however, most unlikely to be repeated. For one thing, Brezhnev, now in his seventies, was too old and infirm to be dangerous. And the very factor which explained his longevity in office – that he left people to grow old in their jobs – denied him the political leverage which would have been available to a leader who reshuffled office-holders and so built up a clientele beholden to him. There was no 'circular flow of power'. Brezhnev played the part which Stalin's colleagues may well have hoped initially that he would play: he was a fatherly and reassuring presence, performed his duties with dignity, and acted as arbiter between contending factions.

Brezhnev would go down as a conservative, but that was by no means how he appeared in 1964. The case against Khrushchev had, after all, been that he was a budding Stalin. His 'hare-brained schemes' were soon disposed of: the party apparatus was reintegrated, the regional economic councils were replaced by centralized ministries, while the limitations on term of office were quietly discarded. The rejection of Khrushchev's reforms did not, however, imply a rejection of economic reformism. This remained very much on the agenda, and in 1965 reform-minded economists achieved a major break-through when Kosygin, who as premier had direct responsibility for the economy, introduced proposals which incorporated much that they had been asking for. More freedom of decision-making was to be given to enterprises; prices would be more directly related to costs; and managers would be allowed to draw on the profits they had made so as to offer additional incentives to workers. Here was the beginning, it seemed, of a movement away from hyper-centralization towards an industrial structure more in keeping with economic and human realities. The hopes aroused by the 1965 reform were, however, to be dashed. No gradual dismantling of the command economy took place; and by the end of the decade the reforming impetus, with its emphasis on market mechanisms, profit, incentives and quality of production, had very largely petered out. The reform failed because it threatened too many highly placed functionaries and too many vested interests. Brezhnev himself seems to have been lukewarm towards it because of the implicit rivalry between himself and the reform's initiator, Kosygin. But what brought about the final ruin of the reform movement was the crisis in Czechoslovakia.

East Germany and other satellites had put through economic reforms considerably more radical than anything in the Soviet Union, and that in itself had not alarmed their Soviet overlords. What was worrying about Czechoslovakia was the close connection between the economic and the political. Under the leadership of a new First Secretary, Alexander Dubček, the Czech regime set out not only to decentralize the economy but to democratize it as well. Rather as in Russia in 1917, there would be elected workers' councils with considerable powers over the management of enterprises. Moreover, this development reflected a wider democratizing tendency. There would be democratization within the Czech Communist Party itself, with elections by secret ballot and the right to express minority views, and while the party would in principle keep its 'leading role', other groups would be allowed to organize and to stand against it. To Soviet politicians who had been reared on the assumptions of Stalinism, all this was of course rank heresy. Admittedly, the Czechs did not make the Hungarians' mistake of trying to leave the Warsaw Pact. What they were proposing to do, and were indeed rapidly doing, was, however, provocative enough. On 21 August 1968, Soviet troops invaded under the pretext, as in 1956, of resisting counter-revolution and defending socialism. What then followed was a 'normalization' of Czech life, at first under a cowed and defeated Dubček but from April 1969 under the hardline Gustav Husak. The whole episode was subsequently justified by what became known as the 'Brezhnev Doctrine', which gave the Soviet Union the right to intervene and offer 'fraternal assistance' to the workers of any satellite country in which it considered socialism to be in danger.

The crisis had in fact divided the Politburo. Kosygin had opposed armed intervention and urged a political solution, some other Politburo members, including the ex-ambassador to Hungary, Yurii Andropov, had argued for force, while Brezhnev himself had wavered. What seems to have swung him to the hardline stance was fear that, were the Czech 'revisionists' to win, his position as General Secretary would be in jeopardy – 'You see, I would have lost Czechoslovakia'.[2] The decision to declare the Czech reformers heretics and to use armed force against them proved a turning-point in Soviet domestic development. During the early Brezhnev years, there had been a rough equilibrium within the oligarchy between conservatives and the reform-minded. But now that the dangers of reform and the close link between economic and political liberalization had been exposed, the conservatives could with some justification say 'We told you so'. From then on, they were very much in the ascendant. Brezhnev, who had been somewhere in the middle, aligned himself easily enough with them, and Kosygin fell increasingly into his shadow.

Criticism of Stalin was now regarded as bad taste. The Leader was not formally rehabilitated, but a bust placed over his grave indicated the much more positive official attitude towards him. Ideas associated with Khrushchev, by contrast, went into eclipse. The 'state of the whole people' rarely got a mention, while the promise of communism by 1980 was not mentioned at all. For the Communist Party to abandon communism was of course unthinkable, but it was now postponed until the safely indefinite future. Far from being on the eve of communism, the Soviet Union was declared to be in the period of 'developed socialism', and this would continue for a long time – perhaps as much, Brezhnev implied, as half a century. Khrushchev's timetable of development was in fact unceremoniously scrapped. Communism was by no means imminent; even the transition to it had not yet begun. The country found itself instead at a stage ('developed socialism') which Marx and Lenin had never made any mention of. One of the advantages of spinning out socialism was that it removed any need for the state to start shedding its functions. Under developed socialism, the party now taught, the state would have to be 'perfected' rather than weakened – its control of society, in other words, would have to be made more effective.

The conservative swing stopped well short, however, of a return to Stalinism. Terror was after all a two-edged weapon: once used against the subjects, it could all too easily be turned against the rulers as well. Opponents of the regime were as a result repressed rather than terrorized. And despite repression, the second half of the 1960s saw a steady increase in their numbers and a broadening of their activities. The turn to moderate conservatism had given rise in fact to the dissident movement.

3

Under Stalin, dissenting activity had of course been impossible. Most potential dissidents were in detention; any who remained free were terrified into silence. A quarter of a century of indiscriminate terror and mass coercion had extinguished the very idea of defying the regime. Without Khrushchev's thaw, the lessening of fear and the new emphasis on socialist legality, dissident activity could never have begun. But if Khrushchev put the preconditions in place, it took the threat of re-Stalinization during the early Brezhnev years to make organizing resistance a matter of urgency.

Intellectuals began meeting in small groups to discuss the threat, and these groups became linked by something equally unheard-of: copies of manuscripts expressing dissenting viewpoints which circulated among them. 'Samizdat' – do-it-yourself anti-regime publishing – began in the late 1950s and from the mid-1960s developed into a flourishing cottage industry. There were even samizdat periodicals. Roy Medvedev's *Political Diary* circulated from 1964 among a small number of party intellectuals, challenging communist orthodoxy in the name of a genuine Leninist socialism, while *The Chronicle of Current Events*, founded in 1968, documented violations of human rights, giving details of arrests and trials, and percolated widely enough to create something of a nationwide information agency.

The arrest in September 1965 of two writers, Andrei Sinyavsky and Yulii Daniel, proved a turning-point. The two were charged with 'anti-Soviet propaganda' for stories they had published in the West, and their cases flashed a clear warning that the regime would tolerate no defiance. Yet far from quashing opposition, the arrests provoked it. On 5 December 1965, 200 or so demonstrators, some with protest banners, gathered in Moscow's Pushkin Square in the first mass public defiance of the authorities since the 1920s. And the sentences eventually passed on Sinyavsky and Daniel – seven and five years in labour camp respectively – prompted a wave of protests against the regime's apparent violation of its own laws.

Dissidents came overwhelmingly from the highly educated. An analysis of 738 who protested against a dissidents' trial in 1968 showed that 45 per cent were academics and 22 per cent were engaged in the arts, while a mere 6 per cent were workers. Even among the educated, the dissidents were a drop in the ocean. No more than seven people demonstrated in Red Square in August 1968 against the Brezhnev regime's most outrageous action – its invasion of Czechoslovakia. By the early 1970s, those taking an active part in human rights campaigning were, on one estimate, down to between 1,000 and 2,000. The dissidents did, admittedly, have a vast circle of sympathizers among the educated. But people had good reasons for not showing any open solidarity with them. Every institution was riddled with informers – they amounted, one dissident guessed, to 15 to 20 per cent of his colleagues. The slightest suggestion of support for a known dissident would result in a phone call from a local party official. Anyone who persisted beyond this would lose any chance of promotion and perhaps risk his job and even his freedom. Not surprisingly, most passive sympathizers saw no point in sacrificing themselves in so hopeless a cause. Could they not anyway be more useful, many persuaded themselves, by continuing as ostensibly loyal party members and doing their best to change things from within?

Among the masses, there was not even a glimmering of a potential following. The regime was artful at playing on ordinary people's feelings – their patriotism, their fear of subversion and foreign attack – in order to stir up resentment against these dissident intellectuals. When dissidents went on trial, the prosecution always put a stridently patriotic case, suggesting that the accused were traitors who had been working for Western governments or anti-Soviet *émigré* organizations. Dissidents, *Pravda* wrote in 1977, were 'unconcealed enemies of socialism' who 'exist only because they are supported, paid and praised by the West'. Andrei Sakharov, *Izvestiya* commented in 1980, was guilty of 'direct betrayal of the interests of our motherland and the Soviet people'.[3] The accusation of being fifth columnists led on naturally to claims that the movement was inspired and dominated by Jews. The KGB agents who charged the Red Square demonstrators in 1968 shouted 'They're all Jews! Beat up the anti-Soviets!'[4] The authorities resorted to other underhand methods as well. When the Red Square demonstrators went on trial, people in the vicinity were told that it was currency speculators – always hated – who were being tried; and free vodka was distributed to stir passions further and encourage local stalwarts to beat up anyone who came to show solidarity with the accused.

Dissidents were helpless against this all too exploitable popular dislike, which was rooted in age-old anti-westernism and anti-intellectualism. There simply was no common ground, many felt, between themselves and the masses. 'To the majority of the people the very word "freedom" is synonymous with "disorder"', wrote the dissenting Andrei Amalrik. 'As for respecting the rights of an individual as such, the idea simply arouses bewilderment.'[5] Only two ideas, as he saw it, meant anything to the people. One was force , which made them all too responsive to the state's cult of its own internal and external strength. The other was justice, which in practice meant that 'nobody should live better than I do'.[6] Both ideas went completely counter, Amalrik believed, to democracy. The Politburo, another dissident commented, hunted witches and burned heretics because 'the Russian people are still ready to believe in witches and heretics'. The masses were of course the regime's prime victims, but they were so thoroughly brainwashed that Populist-type ideas of intellectuals forming a common front with them seemed utterly futile. 'I'm not yet demented enough', a dissident doctor wrote, 'to risk my head trying to "help" them. Do you understand that they feel *I'm* the enemy – not the brutes who enslave them?'[7]

Isolated and outnumbered, the dissidents could have no great ambitions. Unlike nineteenth-century revolutionaries, they did not draw up grand blueprints for social and political change. Willy-nilly, they accepted the Soviet state and the leading role of the Communist Party. Overthrowing the regime was unthinkable; the most they could hope was to be allowed a more tolerable life beneath its umbrella. Since getting new laws was no more than a dream, their main aim was to have the existing laws observed. Thus the Committee for Human Rights, founded in Moscow in 1970, had the modest ambition of wanting to be allowed 'to cooperate in a consultative way with the organs of state power in developing and applying guarantees of human rights'.[8] Human rights were the heart of the matter – without them, proper political opposition and the development of a civil society were impossible. Dissidents asked that the rights of free speech, assembly, etc. granted by the constitution should be implemented. They asked that the regime's basic promise of democracy should be honoured. They asked to be allowed to act in ways which the law did not specifically forbid, such as to talk to foreigners, circulate manuscripts, and read non-Marxist books. And they asked the authorities at least to listen to what they had to say, to treat them as citizens rather than as potentially rebellious children. 'All my conscious life', one of the Red Square demonstrators commented, 'I have wanted to be a citizen – that is, a person who proudly and calmly speaks his mind. For ten minutes I was a citizen.'[9]

The emphasis on socialist legality gave them an opportunity: they called their rulers' bluff, and sometimes successfully. When Alexander Yesenin-Volpin approached a court-room in which dissidents were about to be tried and flourished a copy of the criminal code, the guards felt obliged to let him in. The code after all stipulated the right to public trial. Defendants, too, took heart. They tended not to admit any guilt, and as in tsarist times some made impassioned speeches on behalf of their cause. They still got sentenced, and many dissidents were still dealt with by 'administrative methods'. Yet the slogan 'Respect the Constitution!' managed at least to wrongfoot a regime which was anxious to prove to the world that lawlessness had been put behind it.

The dissidents were united in defending basic human rights, but beyond this fundamental issue they divided. Some – most notably the historian Roy Medvedev – had high hopes that spontaneous developments within the party would bring about the changes they wanted and therefore did their utmost to encourage the reformists within it. The party's natural tendency, Medvedev believed, was towards democracy. Since the party was the sole power in the land, there were obvious reasons for making the best of whatever democratic potential it had. But Medvedev's party orientation was more than a matter of tactical convenience. He was a fervent believer in Leninist socialism, saw Stalinism as a tragic accident, and hoped that the party would now shed the remaining tinges of that aberration and lead the country towards a genuinely democratic socialism. These hopes were, however, dealt a crushing blow by the Czech invasion; and in the aftermath Medvedev was expelled from the party for having circulated in samizdat his *Let History Judge*, a fiercely anti-Stalinist study of Stalinism which would be published to acclaim in the West in 1971. Yet even outside the party, as an overt critic and hence a dissident, Medvedev still clung to the hope that reform-minded members would manage to turn the party in a democratic direction.

The two towering figures among the dissidents, Andrei Sakharov and Alexander Solzhenitsyn, did not, however, share Medvedev's faith that the party could still be an instrument of progress. Sakharov was a brilliant physicist, widely regarded as the 'father' of the Soviet hydrogen bomb, who had first become involved in public affairs because of the regime's apparent indifference to the hazards presented by nuclear weapons. From the mid-1960s, his great influence as the country's most eminent scientist was used in defence of human rights. In 1970 he, together with two others, addressed an open letter to the leadership in which he argued for democratization. So far he had not yet rejected socialism; he wrote as someone who aimed at 'maintenance and strengthening of the Soviet socialist system, of the socialist economic structure ... and socialist ideology'.[10] But soon afterwards, disillusioned by the leadership's bone-headedness, its repression of dissidents, and accumulating evidence that the socialist economic system was incapable of competing with capitalism, he broke with the party and its socialist aims, and he would spend the rest of his life as the embattled proponent of a liberal and essentially Western path for Russia.

Solzhenitsyn, like Sakharov, was a Nobel Prize winner (though the prize in his case was for Literature, not Peace). Like him, he was an unflinching opponent of the regime who seemed to be hewn from granite; and like him he had come to reject not only the CPSU but socialism. Unlike Sakharov, however, Solzhenitsyn had not exchanged socialism for Western ideals of liberty and democracy. If Khrushchev had sensed that the author of *One Day* was an honest Soviet citizen uncorrupted by bourgeois and westernizing tendencies, he had at least partly got him right. Solzhenitsyn had become a Russian nationalist and his case against the Soviets was that they were violators of all that was quintessentially Russian. For him, the only way out of the current cul-de-sac was to rediscover traditions and resources the Soviets had ignored, if not desecrated: the Church; rural Russia and especially the expanses of the north-east; the peasantry; and respect for the individual within a tradition of communal solidarity. Despite his commitment to human rights, Solzhenitsyn did not set a premium on democracy, at least in the near future. For 1,000 years, he wrote, 'Russia lived with an authoritarian order – and at the beginning of the twentieth century both the physical and spiritual health of her people were still intact.'[11] The country was likely in his view to remain authoritarian for the foreseeable future, but its rulers should at least respect the people, allow freedom of expression and belief, and give up their utopianism and intolerance.

Despite his acceptance of authoritarian rule, Solzhenitsyn was a worrying opponent for the regime since his nationalism and his coolness towards Western constitutional forms gave him what the liberals manifestly lacked – a potential popular following. Moreover, he had dealt a devastating blow to the regime's pretensions with *The Gulag Archipelago*, published in Paris in 1973, whose three volumes were a passionate and massively documented exposé of the maltreatment of the Soviet state's opponents in prisons and labour camps. His world-wide fame and his utter fearlessness protected him, however, against normal anti-dissident measures, and in 1974 the authorities put an end to the dilemma he presented them with by simply having him bundled on to a plane and expelled to the West – the first Soviet citizen to suffer such an expulsion since Trotsky.

Sakharov was similarly protected by fame and fearlessness, and he was given some additional protection by his status as an Academician. However, in June 1980 he was taken into custody by the KGB and sent, without trial, into internal exile in the closed city of Gorky, where he could have no contact with foreigners. By the time he was removed from Moscow, the dissident movement had in effect been broken. Its members were abroad, or in prison or labour camp, or scattered in remote places of internal exile, or suffering the peculiarly totalitarian punishment of being confined in a psychiatric hospital (opposition to such a state raising by definition, in more blinkered traditionalist minds, a suspicion of mental derangement); and many had by then been browbeaten into silence or simply given up because of the apparent hopelessness of their cause.

The suicide of Alexander Radishchev, with which this book began, must have rung with special poignancy in the ears of defeated dissidents of the 1970s. By an irony of history, it must have seemed to them, their situation bore an uncanny resemblance to that of this man who had lived in the backward, illiterate Russia of 1800. So much for progress! A handful of highly developed individuals faced an insuperable leviathan of a state. They dangled in a limbo between this state they abhorred and a population which had no understanding of their aims and saw them as aliens if not as enemies. Their chances of getting what they wanted in defiance of the state were nil. They could only achieve change through the state, yet it was hard to have much hope of it as an agent of reform. Russia could not, it seemed, be saved *from* the CPSU. Was there really any chance of Russia being saved *by* the CPSU?

Of the various categories of dissent, one of the most important was religious, with Baptists, rebel Orthodox believers and Lithuanian Catholics having the leading role. Religious dissidents were repressed as savagely as secular ones. The desolation of the dissidents was, however, relieved by one success story – that of the Jews. As dissidents, Jews were a special case. Other dissidents wanted to change the Soviet Union; most Jewish critics simply wanted to leave it. Soviet citizens had no right of departure, and therefore Jews could not use the socialist legality argument. They had, however, a still more powerful weapon: pressure from the United States, whose good will the regime needed in order to pursue *détente*. Thanks in large part to American pressure, some 200,000 Jews left the country during the 1970s. The authorities probably consoled themselves that they were getting rid of trouble-makers; the reality was that they had driven out many talented scientists, artists and intellectuals whose loss could only impoverish the country.

A number of Germans and Armenians were allowed to go as well, but otherwise the situation of the minorities was bleak. Brezhnev's regime was more sensitive to the small nations than Stalin had been; the centralizing and unifying thrust of Soviet nationalities policy nevertheless remained unchanged. Ideology still laid down that the different nations would 'draw together' and eventually 'fuse'. Brezhnev had enough tact not to emphasize this eventual 'fusion', but the concept of a 'Soviet people', which was promoted vigorously from the early 1970s, was from the small nations' point of view just as bad. Sovietization could mean nothing other than russification. It was not simply that the Communist Party was dominated disproportionately by Russians. By 1982, there were twenty-four million Russians living in non-Russian republics, and in Ukraine, Kazakhstan, Estonia and Latvia they formed a worryingly large segment of the population. Resistance to these Russians, almost none of whom learned the local language, was channelled through vigorous cultural movements, especially in Ukraine and the Baltics. In Ukraine the movement had the luck to be protected by the first secretary, Pyotr Shelest, who tried to conciliate intellectuals and sympathized with at least a limited show of national assertiveness. Shelest was, however, removed in 1972 and replaced by the hardline V. V. Shcherbitsky, who immediately cracked down on dissidents. There was similar repression in the Baltic states, especially in Lithuania, where Catholicism gave a powerful boost to national feelings. Lenin had hoped that socialism would in time erode national self-consciousness, but the resentments among intellectuals from the smaller nations and their resistance during the Brezhnev era to russification showed how unrealistic that hope had been. The authorities crushed these minorities' dissidents as easily as they had crushed the Russian ones. Repression was, after all, what they were good at. But what was quite beyond them was to create that union of minds which Lenin had seen as essential to the building of socialism.

Repression went together, as so often, with window-dressing. By taking their stand on socialist legality and the constitution, the dissidents had touched the regime on a tender spot. The 1936 constitution had long since become obsolete; and it had of course been wildly at odds with reality from the start. A post-Stalin constitution was badly needed, and one was at last produced in 1977. Dissidents had wanted the gap between reality and the constitution to be closed and in one important respect it now was – though they would naturally have preferred reality to be adjusted to the constitution rather than the constitution to reality. In previous constitutions, the party's role in Soviet life had been more or less passed over. This one openly acknowledged it. 'The Communist Party of the Soviet Union', ran article 6, 'shall be the guiding and directing force of Soviet society, the core of its political system and of all state and social organizations.'[12] In other respects, however, Brezhnev's constitution belonged even more to the world of make-believe than Stalin's had. Whereas Stalin's document had guaranteed the 'rights' of the citizen, Brezhnev's guaranteed the citizen both 'rights' and 'freedoms', committed itself to the expansion of these rights and freedoms, and delineated them in rather more detail than before. The new constitution laid much emphasis, in addition, on democracy. This was a 'society of genuine democracy', the preamble declared, though it also, seeming to contradict itself, spoke of 'striving towards the further development of socialist democracy'.[13] This commitment to rights, freedoms, and a democracy which scarcely existed was in keeping with the regime's previous propaganda, yet in the circumstances it gave something of a hostage to fortune. Within a decade of the constitution's appearance, its hypocrisies would have been turned against the upholders of Soviet traditionalism.

4

The Soviet Paradox: External Expansion, Internal Decline was the title a leading Sovietologist gave to a study of the Soviet Union written during the early 1980s.[14] Judged by the country's military power, its international standing, and the awe with which most foreigners regarded it, the regime had every ground for complacency. It had five million men under arms, and by spending far more on defence than the Americans (between 15 and 25 per cent of the national product) it had equalled or even overtaken the military capacity of its rival. Control of the inner and outer empires seemed unassailable. In 1979, the regime had even taken on a new defence commitment by sending 100,000 troops to prop up what proved to be a highly unpopular Marxist government in Afghanistan. The steady increase in defence expenditure – of some 4 per cent per year for most of the Brezhnev period – had the added advantage that it kept the generals happy and ensured their undeviating loyalty.

Yet behind this impressive façade, things were going badly wrong; and one cause of the trouble was that the country was spending far more on defence than it could afford. It had achieved superpower status despite having no more than half the GNP of the United States. As a result, there was a serious mismatch between the commitments this status brought with it and the country's resources. Moreover, the commitments were increasing at a time when the Soviet economy was falling back relative to the American one. Sooner or later, something was going to have to give. By the late 1970s even Brezhnev was getting worried, and in November 1978 in a moment of unusual candour he admitted that the economic problems were bad enough to present a threat to political stability.

The continuing decline in growth rates was the chief source of worry. An annual growth rate of 5 per cent through the 1960s had fallen to 2.5 per cent in the late 1970s. The Soviet Union had been overtaken as an industrial producer by Japan; even China had begun to replace the Soviet economic model by one that incorporated market mechanisms and incentives. Rapid growth in the past had been made possible by ample supplies of labour and of raw materials. But falling birth-rates (except in the Muslim republics of Central Asia) meant that there was no longer a large surplus population to draw into industry. Nor were there inexhaustible supplies of raw materials; and revenue from the most profitable, oil and gas, fell away markedly during the later Brezhnev years. Further growth would depend on intensive rather than extensive development – on making more efficient use, in other words, of the existing human and natural resources. But that would require a spirit of innovation and enterprise, qualities which the command economy had more or less killed off; it also required a far higher level of technology than the country could currently muster.

A warning of what might happen came in 1980 from Poland, where a strike of shipyard workers broadened out into a national movement against the government and led to the creation of an independent trade union, Solidarity, which the authorities at first seemed helpless to deal with. What made the Polish movement so hard to counter was that the driving-force came not from intellectuals but from workers: its leader, Lech Walesa, was a shipyard electrician. Yet though the Polish events were disturbing, they also underlined how secure the Kremlin's hold over its own subjects was. Russia was not Poland: the Russian masses were quiescent, and there were good reasons over and above traditional passivity to explain why they were. 'You've never had it so good', that electoral slogan of Harold Macmillan's, could equally well have come from the lips of Leonid Brezhnev. For by the Soviet people's admittedly miserable levels of expectation, conditions of life had become remarkably good, and peasants and workers in particular had strong reasons to feel grateful to the government.

The Brezhnev regime had continued Khrushchev's emphasis on agriculture. High prices were paid to the peasants for their produce but were not passed on to the consumer, with the result that agriculture received a massive net subsidy. Kolkhoz workers now got a regular wage rather than simply the residue of the collective's earnings, and the restrictions Khrushchev had placed on their other source of income, the private plots, had been lifted. By the end of the Brezhnev era, the gap between rural and urban wages had narrowed considerably. But not only were peasants better off. By granting them internal passports and the full range of welfare benefits, the regime had at last put them on an equal footing with other citizens.

Most people lived better. Meat, milk and butter were more plentiful, even if shortages remained. There had been improvements across the whole range of consumer goods, especially in the field of consumer durables. By the early 1980s, the great majority of homes had television sets and refrigerators, and over half had washing-machines. Welfare benefits had increased as much as fivefold since the Stalin era, with notable increases in pensions and family allowances. Housing was still a problem in the towns and it was very hard for the newly married to find a place of their own, but here too the improvement since Stalin had been immense. Moreover, workers and peasants had every reason to be grateful to the regime for continuing the egalitarian wages policy begun by Khrushchev. During the decade 1965–76, the average wage of industrial workers had risen by 65 per cent and that of collective farm workers by a staggering 86 per cent, while that of white-collar workers had gone up by no more than 25 per cent. This policy of narrowing wage differentials flew in the face of what reform-minded economists advised: but it was clear proof that the regime's commitment to the traditional dispossessed of society was more than mere talk.

All this suggests that anti-communist Westerners who explained the regime's survival by its powers of repression alone were taking too simple a view. The powers of repression were of course immense, as any handful of dissidents who unfurled a banner in the street soon discovered; but they were little needed and much KGB activity was frankly superfluous. The regime survived because it gave most people much of what they wanted and in particular because it gave them more and more of what they wanted. Nearer the mark were those historians who floated the idea of a tacit agreement, an unwritten 'social contract', between rulers and ruled.[15] The regime gave people security, cradle-to-grave welfare benefits and steadily improving conditions of living; it also gratified their patriotism by making the country cut an impressive figure in the world. The 'contract' was seen most clearly in the relationship between state and workers. What the state expected of the industrial workforce was very little compared with what capitalist employers demanded. Workers could arrive late, leave early, do very little in between, even get drunk on the job, and despite all it was very hard for managers to sack anyone. In return for this kid-glove treatment, however, workers had to do what they were told, were forbidden to strike, and received poor wages. 'You pretend to pay us and we pretend to work' was a famously cynical view of the relationship: but in its way, the trade-off was a fair one.

This understanding between rulers and ruled underlined how much the two sides had in common. The members of the Soviet élite did of course lead highly privileged lives. Some people even argued that they had come to form a distinct class – the 'new class', as Milovan Djilas called it in a well-known book.[16] That they did not strictly speaking own the means of production, the argument went, was a mere formality: they had effective control of the means of production, and this was quite enough to enable them to live as if they were capitalists. Yet for all this, they were not set apart from ordinary people to the extent that tsarism's ruling class had been, and they were not generally seen as exploiters and parasites. Given the regime's egalitarian pretensions, they did of course have to hide their privileges or at the very least take care not to flaunt them. But what stopped any strong sense of 'them' and 'us' was that most bosses themselves had only recently climbed out of the working class and the peasantry. They simply had not had time to acquire the special ambience of a privileged caste. They spoke the same language as the people, and they had very much the same culture, attitudes and tastes. Rulers and ruled were bonded in fact by a common demotic Russianness which had been very little affected by westernization. Another stabilizing and consolidating factor was social mobility. Those who had made it to the top had been careful not to kick down the ladder of opportunity up which they themselves had climbed, and it was still relatively easy for a working-class boy of talent and ambition to rise into the élite.

All this said, however, the 'social contract' between rulers and ruled was not a perfect guarantee of stability. One problem, as we shall see, was that a significant section of the ruled felt excluded from it. But even more serious was that the rapport between regime and workers was beginning to break down. The problem was seen most obviously at work. Absenteeism was more common than ever; the quality of production and services was deteriorating; corruption was becoming rampant; and the endemic scourge of alcoholism was on the increase. All these were in their different ways symptoms of an underlying problem of morale. People were becoming dissatisfied, frustrated, and cynical. The regime bombarded them with propaganda and did its utmost to shut out alternative voices, yet despite its monopoly of the media it was failing to stop the rot. At risk were certain cardinal beliefs or myths which had once had an inspiring and bonding effect, and upon these the special relationship between party and people in the end rested. That Marxism–Leninism was an exact and infallible science. That, guided by it, the Communist Party could do no wrong. That the party represented the will and intellect of the whole people. That the Soviet Union was the most democratic country in the world, whereas workers in the capitalist countries were exploited and oppressed pawns. That Soviet society was becoming ever more united and free of divisions and frictions. That living conditions would continue their steady upward curve of improvement; and that the communist era of abundance for all was close at hand, even if an exact date could not yet be put upon it.

By the early 1980s, these myths were either losing credibility or had already lost it entirely. The gulf between words and reality had become too broad for even the most systematic propaganda machine in the world to cover over. Where they could be most easily assessed, the claims made were simply not sustainable. The divisions and hence the tensions within society were becoming more, not less, noticeable. The rate of growth of labour productivity was falling rather than rising. In its overall economic performance, the country was slipping further behind, rather than overhauling, the West.

People might put up with false claims and fairy stories, but were the regime to default on its basic promise of material betterment they would be bound to react badly. And by now it was hard to hide that the period of steady improvement in living standards had ended. The government was devoting huge resources to agriculture, yet food shortages were getting worse and the situation was kept bearable only by imports. There was increasing difficulty in finding goods to spend your money on. More and more money was going into bank accounts, and this steep rise in savings was a sure sign of consumer frustration. An inevitable side-effect of this failure of goods and services to keep pace with incomes was a spreading miasma of bribery and corruption and a flourishing black market. If you had the money and the know-how you could get what you wanted, and the authorities usually turned a blind eye. The growth of this semi-tolerated black market eased many hardships, and yet it pushed a still broader wedge between the idealized world of the regime's official pronouncements and the sordid realities of life as the ordinary citizen experienced them.

Disaffection had not yet turned into revolt. Unless the economic tendency were reversed, however, crisis was inevitable. The regime would stand or fall in the end on its ability to deliver communism, which above all implied abundance, and all the signs by the early 1980s were that it would fall. Economic failure would do in fact what continued oppression and arbitrariness were most unlikely to do: it would shake ordinary people out of their passivity. Lack of freedom could be put up with; lack of meat, which by 1982 had disappeared from shops in wide areas of the country, was a far more serious matter. To make things worse for the authorities, the decline in labour discipline was both a consequence and a cause of the country's economic plight. People were finding it hard to believe in the regime's pretensions, and the resultant apathy and cynicism simply worsened the conditions which had produced the original disillusionment. Whatever could be done to break this vicious downward spiral?

Punishing people Stalinist-fashion was hardly likely to do much good. They were not likely to respond to traditional communist exhortation either. Increased material incentives might, by contrast, have an effect. Unfortunately, the very doctrines which justified the party's rule placed a limit on how far it could go in this direction: it claimed, after all, to be creating a society in which greed would have no place. And a fair number of intellectuals and high-level party functionaries had by now come to see that nothing less than fundamental change could stop the drift to disaster. The reforms of the Khrushchev period would have to be resumed, but this time there would have to be a real return to Lenin.

5

One of the finest historians of Soviet Russia, Moshe Lewin, has described Soviet history as 'a two-act play replayed several times with different sets and casts'.[17] The two acts represent, he argued, quite different Soviet experiences, the one autocratic and intolerant, the other pluralistic, idealistic and relatively tolerant. The autocratic 'act' had of course hogged the stage for most of the time: only during the first few months of the revolution and during NEP had the other Soviet experience got a look-in. But though the autocratic experience had dominated, the very fact that the early period of Soviet history had shown glimmerings of a gentler and more genuinely democratic socialism gave intellectuals who were yearning for reform something to clutch at. The pluralistic and tolerant act, they persuaded themselves, was the real one.

The Alternative Tradition, as I shall call this outlook, saw the pre-Stalin years as a golden age before the Fall. The promises of October had not been delusory and the experiment on which Lenin had launched Russia had not been a mistake. Stalinism and the administrative command system had been a terrible perversion of Lenin's intentions, but if only the party would now turn to Lenin again it could still save itself and lead the country to socialism. The Alternative Tradition thus did what Khrushchev had been unable to: it rejected Stalinism in its entirety and drew the firmest possible line between it and Leninist socialism. Beliefs like these appealed to people who saw the utter futility of dissent because they did not in the least challenge the fundamentals of the Soviet state or of Marxism–Leninism. On the contrary, they promised proper socialism and an end to the Stalinist counterfeit; and as the post-Stalinist regime tottered towards its crisis, their time, it seemed, had all but come.

Roy Medvedev, the philosopher of the Alternative Tradition, had great hopes of those in the party whom he called the 'party democrats'. So far there were not many of them, but he believed that their numbers would increase and thanks to them socialism and democracy would sooner or later be fused. Two things were, however, essential, one in the economic sphere and the other in the political. Central planning and market mechanisms would have to be reconciled in a 'socialist market'; and the party would have to grant freedom of expression and even allow those who thought otherwise to organize themselves. Granting freedom would not, he insisted, harm the party. On the contrary, 'The point about open dialogue with dissidents is that it will strengthen communism and the CP.'[18] Socialism, Medvedev was convinced, would always be the creed of the overwhelming majority, and only the party's monopoly and its intolerance and obscurantism presented any threat to socialism's dominance. Were real socialist democracy to be established, then all non-Marxist parties would rapidly lose any mass following. Western-style institutions and practices would in fact ensure the triumph of a renovated party and a redefined, yet strictly Leninist, socialism. The 'alternative' approach thus came up with myths of its own: planning and the market could be reconciled, and so could party-implemented socialism and democracy.

These two fundamental beliefs went hand in hand. The market required freedom, and freedom in turn could not survive without the market. It helped, however, that the economic and political arguments could be advanced separately and that their interdependence did not have to be stated. Medvedev had put himself out of court by challenging the party's monopoly; the hope for anyone who wanted to change things from within, through the party, was to work on the economic thesis. That the country needed economic reform was, after all, undeniable. And by the early 1980s some pioneering economists, with Abel Aganbegyan, Tatyana Zaslavskaya, A. P. Butenko and B. M. Kurashvili to the fore, were mapping out new approaches to the problems of the Soviet economy. Members of what Medvedev called the 'loyal opposition', they accepted the basic principles of Soviet life and were careful not to topple over, as he had, into dissidence; they were nevertheless pushing at the very frontiers of the permissible.

The command economy, such economists argued, had been appropriate to the 1930s: now it had outlived its day and should be replaced by a system that stimulated people rather than coerced them. The claim that Soviet society was becoming more homogeneous and that no antagonistic divisions were to be found in it was, they suggested, rubbish. This belief was in fact vitally important since it underpinned the party's claim to a monopoly: if there was no more than a single interest in society, then it was right and proper for a single party to represent it. But to the economic reformers this was an untenable dogma – the evidence simply contradicted it. Those with high positions in the hierarchy inevitably pursued their own interests and expanded their own privileges, which in turn made for antagonistic divisions and increased the potential for social conflict. What the reformers wanted was not to eliminate the role of self-interest but, rather, to devise an economic system that recognized and made proper use of it and was as a result more efficient as well as more just and more realistic. The system as it stood was quite unable to make full use of the worker's potential. People, Zaslavskaya argued, ought to be treated as human beings, not cogs in a machine. At present, she said, 'they do not act but are "utilized", do not perform actions but "function", do not change their place of work but are "distributed" and "redistributed"'; and so long as they were treated like this, they would be incapable of showing any creative initiative.[19]

All this had implications that went far beyond the economic. No wonder that the leaking of Zaslavskaya's views to the West caused outrage! An inefficient economic system which allowed the ruling few to prosper but kept the majority in poverty and which was sustained by coercion and ideological make-believe could not be transformed without a relaxation of centralized control. Economic reform in fact implied democratization. Without democracy, there could be no economic progress. Without it, there could also be no long-term social stability and there would be a real risk of Polish-type eruptions. Exactly what changes were necessary the reformers were careful not to specify, though Kurashvili went so far as to reject 'quasi-reform', arguing instead for a reform that changed the relationship between apparatus and society and would have to be carried through 'despite the resistance of conservative and inert elements in the state apparatus'.[20]

That was a vital lesson learned from the 1965 failure: economic reform without political reform – without change in power relationships – would get nowhere. But though the oppositionists were committed to political change, they had to appear loyal and not to repeat Medvedev's mistake of challenging the party. Luckily, they could hide behind the hypocrisy which had given 'democratization' an honoured place in official thinking. But was there any chance that their ideas would ever be implemented? That the 'party democrats' would come to power? That the pluralistic 'act' would again take the stage and that the players in the other act would be sent packing?

One factor strongly favoured such an outcome. Throughout the so-called 'stagnation period' Soviet society had continued to develop very rapidly, and the result was that by 1980 the party ruled over a society very different from the one in which it had originally taken power. That had been overwhelmingly rural, peasant and uneducated. Paradoxically, this very backwardness had, as we have seen, helped the Bolsheviks to impose themselves. By now, however, most traces of that age-old backwardness had disappeared, and a striking discrepancy had emerged between the all-powerful state, which continued to treat its subjects with traditional contempt, and a sophisticated, multi-faceted society which cried out for fine-tuning rather than crude manipulation and coercion. The Bolsheviks had come to power as modernizers, yet they had been shaped by backwardness and had benefited from backwardness, and the effect of their sustained attack upon it had inevitably been to remove some at least of the conditions that had made it possible for them to flourish.

Modernization had brought about one change of enormous importance: the average Soviet citizen was now a town-dweller. During the early 1960s, the urban population had overtaken the rural, and by 1979 62 per cent of the inhabitants (70 per cent in the case of Russia itself) were classified as urban. A considerable proportion of the urban population, moreover, lived in large cities: by 1979, sixty-five cities had between one-quarter and one-half million inhabitants and twenty-three had more than one million. Moscow and Leningrad left all other cities far behind. Moscow had some eight million inhabitants and Leningrad four and a half million, and as always they had an influence disproportionate to their size. Urbanization had been accompanied by a striking change in the pattern of employment. By 1979, some 45 per cent of the employed worked in industry, construction and transportation and almost 35 per cent were in white-collar occupations, while no more than 20 per cent were engaged in the traditional mainstay of agriculture. But not only was Brezhnev's Soviet Union more urban and industrial than rural; it had put illiteracy and ignorance well behind it. In 1939, only 1 per cent of the population had a higher educational qualification and only 11 per cent had completed secondary education; in 1979, the respective figures were 10 per cent and 70 per cent. Educational advance had, however, outpaced the growth of the economy, and by doing so it had created problems. Before the war, there had been a desperate shortage of the highly skilled; now, if anything there were too many of the well qualified chasing too few jobs appropriate to their skills.

As a result of these changes, the country now had many people who might be called 'middle class' – were well educated, that is, did skilled and usually non-manual jobs, and had some at least of the tastes and aspirations of a Western bourgeoisie. In Soviet terminology, these as we have seen constituted the 'intelligentsia', the third officially recognized element in the social mix alongside the workers and the peasants. Engineers and technical specialists made up the biggest group among them, but perhaps one-quarter – out of a total of some thirty-five million – were intelligentsia in the traditional sense of having the educational and cultural background likely to breed independent thinking and a detached, if not critical, attitude towards authority.

The middle class had good reason for dissatisfaction since it was the one sector of society left out of the 'social contract'. Wage differentials had, as we know, narrowed very considerably during the Khrushchev and Brezhnev years. In Brezhnev's Soviet Union, doctors, teachers, engineers and office workers were in fact generally paid less than skilled manual workers, and they in turn were being caught up by unskilled workers. But not only had the relative material position of the middle class worsened; it had suffered far more than other social groups from the loss of the precarious and partial freedoms granted by Khrushchev. As a consequence, middle-class disaffection presented the regime with a problem. Worker discontent could still be contained fairly easily: not only did the regime flatter the workers by regarding them as society's 'leading class', but it took care to molly-coddle them as much as declining economic performance would allow. It could cope, too, with the grievances of a much diminished peasantry – collective-farm workers, after all, now earned more than doctors. But by the end of the Brezhnev era, relations with the middle class and with the intelligentsia proper in particular had become strained, and for the first time in half a century the regime found itself facing a public opinion which was something other than the echo of its own dictates.

Talented middle-class people were often deeply frustrated by the state's nannying, and they were the natural supporters of any movement to curb state power and give more scope to individual initiative. People like this, the first shoots of an emerging civil society, were asking in effect for three things. First, they wanted to be allowed areas of personal privacy from the state – and how un-Russian a demand this was can be seen from the fact that the Russian language did not even have a direct equivalent of the word 'privacy'. The implication of their demand, again un-Russian and especially un-Soviet, was that much in the individual's life concerned him or her alone and the state had no business to interfere in it. Second, they wanted the right to join together in unofficial groups or associations with like-minded people in order to pursue interests and engage in activities – artistic or business, for instance – that were, properly speaking, outside politics. Third, and most contentiously, some at least of them wanted wide areas of public life to be reclaimed from the exclusive control of the tiny handful who ran the state and made over to genuine public control.

But despite these tensions between party and middle class, their relationship had not yet reached the point of breakdown. One reason for this was that the party was to a considerable extent a middle-class body. Its formal commitment to the workers remained, yet for all that the party was far from being the working-class bastion it had been in the early 1930s. By the early 1980s, the intelligentsia (in the official sense) made up one-half of the membership; and within the party élite it was still more heavily over-represented. As society had become more educated, so too had the party. In 1927 only 1 per cent of members had completed higher education; by 1977 one quarter had. And by now the party had become a magnet for the highly qualified: one half of Candidates of Science – the equivalent of PhDs – and rather more than half of the still more lofty Doctors of Science were enrolled in it.

The CPSU had in fact become very different from what it had been originally intended to be – an élite drawn from or representing the proletariat, whose task was to restructure society from top to bottom. The average party member now was an ambitious and well-qualified product of the middle class who had joined for reasons of career advancement rather than ideological commitment, and if he or she had broader aims it was to bring party and state more into line with society rather than to adapt society to the party's demands. The party was of course still tightly controlled at the top: 'democratic centralism' was as undemocratic as ever. Yet it was no longer capable of performing the vanguard role Lenin and even Khrushchev had wanted it to. The party was not in fact an instrument that was isolated from society and could therefore be used against society. On the contrary, it was coming under increasing pressure from within its own ranks to do what society, middle-class society in particular, wanted. For the time being, conservatives held it in a firm grip. Yet Roy Medvedev's hope of well-educated 'party democrats' who saw the need for greater freedom coming out on top was not implausible. Looking from across the Atlantic, Moshe Lewin saw a very similar possibility: scholars, administrators and politicians might one day join forces and put through a really radical reform, which would then 'bring the political system into accord with the growing complexity and modernity of society'.[21]

6

By the beginning of the 1980s, such a coalition was in fact taking shape. Its members could do little while supreme power remained in the hands of an ailing and now deeply conservative Brezhnev. But in November 1982 Brezhnev died and was succeeded as General Secretary by Yurii Andropov, who had recently completed a fifteen-year stint as head of the KGB. That was hardly a good augury from the reformers' point of view since Andropov had been at the KGB when it had expelled Solzhenitsyn, sent Sakharov into exile, and more or less crushed the dissident movement. Another illiberal credential of his was that he had been Soviet ambassador in Hungary in October 1956. Yet there was more to Andropov than the record suggested, and would-be reformers had good reason to welcome his appointment. In mind, character and tastes the new General Secretary was very different from Brezhnev: he was undoubtedly intelligent, well-read and something of a sophisticate, even if suggestions that he enjoyed jazz and collected icons were a KGB concoction. And he seems to have been entirely untouched by the corruption and extravagance which had become a hallmark of the Brezhnevian élite. The new leader was personally incorruptible and austere almost to the point of asceticism; he lived in a one-bedroomed flat, made his children live modestly, and was so far removed from the sordid wheelings and dealings of the Brezhnev clan that in his KGB capacity he had launched an investigation into a diamond scandal involving Brezhnev's daughter, Galina.

Puritanism did not by any means imply liberalism. Yet if Andropov was not a liberal, he was certainly more open to new ideas than most other of the oligarchs. As head of the KGB, he had hardly had a chance to develop this side of his political personality. However, in his previous position in the Central Committee apparatus he had gathered around him a kitchen cabinet of many of the brightest and most progressive minds in the party. Men who would become leading proponents of perestroika – among them, Arbatov, Bogomolov, Bovin and Shakhnazarov – were the protégés of Yurii Andropov and came to respect, even revere, him as a man with a fine mind and decent instincts who was caught in a quagmire. But it was not only leading intellectuals who moved in his orbit. His eye had been caught by a politician who was making a mark in his own home province of Stavropol in southern Russia. Mikhail Gorbachev, too, was an Andropov protégé.

Andropov's short term of office – November 1982 to February 1984 – turned out, however, to be a disappointment for those who had hoped for great things from him. He made a large number of personnel changes – 'stability of cadres' had outlived its day and was jettisoned. He cracked down hard on absenteeism, drunkenness and low production standards at work, and even sent police into shops, bars and public baths to hunt for absconding workers. He launched an anti-corruption drive which was targeted at both high and low – at ministers who abused their positions but also at ordinary workers who went in for 'moonlighting'. Thousands of arrests were made, and some of the more flagrant offenders were even executed. These measures fell short, however, of an adequate response to the looming system crisis: for all his toughness, Andropov was doing little more than tinkering. Of course he understood the country's dire economic situation and its implications for stability, yet he failed to come up with any solution which broke through the meshes of orthodoxy. How tightly he was hemmed in by the old thinking came out in an article of his in which he discussed the basic problems of socialism. Here was an intelligent man who seemed at least partly to recognize the utopianism of the communist experiment and the unreality of the party's ideology, yet was too old and set in his ways, or simply too much a victim of his circumstances, to rethink either. There was a suggestion of defeat and even of despair in his admission that individual psychology had proved far more resistant to change than had been expected. Changes in property relations were not enough, he conceded, to remove 'all the negative features of human relationships that have accumulated over the centuries'.[22] Experience showed that 'the turning of what is "my own" and privately owned into what is "ours" and common to all is no simple matter'. Because of these unanticipated problems, the country was now at no more than 'the beginning of this long historical stage' called developed socialism.[23]

How the party had changed its tune in twenty years! Communism had dropped beyond the horizon, even the final phase of developed socialism now seemed scarcely in sight. How Andropov would have squirmed to have been reminded that, according to the party's pronouncements of twenty years earlier, communism should already have arrived and with it abundance for all. In the face of mounting problems and glaring misjudgements, he clung to what must have seemed to him the only possible source of short-term safety – the pillars of ideological orthodoxy. Anyone inclined to 'anarcho-syndicalism, to splitting society into independent corporations competing with each other, to democracy without discipline, to the notion of rights without duties', was sternly reminded that none of these pointed the way towards communism. In the Soviet Union there was no discrepancy, he insisted, between the interests of the state and those of the citizen. Those who pretended otherwise were simply putting their selfish interests before those of society, and such people needed to be re-educated (there was a distinct echo here of the psychiatric hospital, to which Andropov's KGB had sent many a dissident). The constitution of course gave Soviet citizens broad rights and freedoms, but at the same time 'it underlines the priority of public interests, service to which is indeed the supreme manifestation of civic duty'.[24]

An ideology which had once been inspired by a vision of transforming life had thus been reduced to clichés of deadening pomposity whose only function was to justify the monopoly, power and privileges of those for whom power had become an end in itself. These were in fact the clichés of an ideology and a ruling élite at their last gasp, and before the end of the decade they would have been consigned to the dustbin by Andropov's Stavropol protégé.

Andropov was already sixty-eight when he became General Secretary, and soon he was being afflicted by the kidney disease which in February 1984 would kill him. Had he enjoyed good health and had longer in office, he might perhaps have responded more adequately to the country's problems: though in all probability, even his admirers admit, he would not have. His rule, as it turned out, marked an ending rather than a beginning; but the nadir of the *ancien régime* would come not with him but with his successor, Konstantin Chernenko.

Chernenko had been Brezhnev's crony and favourite for the succession, but in November 1982 he had been defeated by an obviously abler man. In February 1984 there was also a much abler man in the running. From his sickbed, Andropov had proposed that Mikhail Gorbachev should stand in for him, clearly implying that he should be his heir, but the proposal had been brushed aside. Chernenko, the Politburo kingmakers decided, would be more amenable. He was certainly unlikely to upset anyone by wielding a new broom. Whereas Brezhnev and Andropov had become seriously ill while in office, Chernenko was already in poor health when appointed General Secretary: he suffered from emphysema and heart trouble, walked with difficulty, and would sometimes find it an ordeal to read out the speeches set before him. This frail man of seventy-two was in fact gerontocracy embodied, and the months of his nominal leadership were to be 'the agony' of the old order, as one Soviet memoirist put it.[25] The running of the country was, however, already very largely in the hands of his defeated rival, a mere stripling (by Soviet standards) in his early fifties who represented a new generation of leaders and would bring great energy and rare political skills to the task of saving the regime and Soviet civilization from shipwreck.

Notes

1 Seweryn Bialer, *The Soviet Paradox: External Expansion, Internal Decline* (London, 1986), p. 75.
2 G. A. Arbatov, *Zatyanuvsheesya vyzdorovlenie (1953–1985gg). Svidetelstvo sovremennika* (Moscow, 1991), p. 147.
3 Joshua Rubenstein, *Soviet Dissidents: Their Struggle for Human Rights* (London, 1981), pp. 269 and 272.
4 *Ibid.*, p. 88.
5 Andrei Amalrik, *Will the Soviet Union Survive Until 1984?* (Harmondsworth, 1980), p. 37.
6 *Ibid.*
7 Rudolf L. Tökes, ed., *Dissent in the USSR: Politics, Ideology and People* (Baltimore, 1975), pp. 423-4.
8 George Saunders, ed., *Samizdat: Voices of the Soviet Opposition* (New York, 1974), p. 414.
9 Marshall S. Shatz, *Soviet Dissent in Historical Perspective* (Cambridge, 1980), p. 127.

10 Andrei D. Sakharov, *Sakharov Speaks*, ed. Harrison E. Salisbury (London, 1974), p. 117.
11 Aleksandr Solzhenitsyn, *Letter to Soviet Leaders* (London, 1974), p. 52.
12 Aryeh L. Unger, *Constitutional Developments in the USSR: A Guide to the Soviet Constitutions* (London, 1986), p. 234.
13 *Ibid.*, p. 233.
14 Seweryn Bialer, *The Soviet Paradox: External Expansion, Internal Decline* (London, 1986).
15 See, for instance, Stephen F. Cohen, *Rethinking the Soviet Experience: Politics and History since 1917* (New York, 1985), p. 151.
16 Milovan Djilas, *The New Class: An Analysis of the Communist System* (London, 1957).
17 Moshe Lewin, *Political Undercurrents in Soviet Economic Debates: From Bukharin to the Modern Reformers* (London, 1975), p. 124.
18 Roy Medvedev, *On Socialist Democracy*, tr. and ed. by Ellen de Kadt (London, 1975), p. 103.
19 Tatyana Zaslavskaya, 'The Novosibirsk Report', *Survey*, 28, no. 1 (1984), pp. 88–108, at pp. 89–90.
20 Cited from John Gooding, 'Perestroika and the Russian Revolution of 1991', *The Slavonic and East European Review*, 71, no. 2 (1993), pp. 234–56, at p. 243.
21 Moshe Lewin, *Political Undercurrents in Soviet Economic Debates*, p. 353.
22 Y. V. Andropov, *The Teaching of Karl Marx and Some Questions of Building Socialism in the USSR* (Moscow, 1983), p. 16.
23 *Ibid.*, p. 10.
24 *Ibid.*, p. 27.
25 G. A. Arbatov, *Zatyanuvsheesya vyzdorovlenie*, p. 334.

|10|

The success and failure of perestroika, 1985–1990

1

Why ever did Mikhail Gorbachev begin the 'perestroika' (reconstruction) of Soviet society and the Soviet system? He surely ought to have realized from the start that real reform would damage the Communist Party. And so it turned out: a process of change that had been intended to reform the Soviet system finished by destroying it. By the end of 1991, the party had been abolished, socialism was discredited, and the Soviet state itself had disintegrated, while Gorbachev himself had been unceremoniously removed from office and had become so unpopular that a man unlucky enough to resemble him would be regularly assaulted in the street.

Gorbachev was of course no kamikaze politician and he did not in the least intend such an outcome. But even if we put the finale on one side, there is still a paradox at the heart of perestroika. When Gorbachev became General Secretary, the Communist Party was all-powerful and he was in a position to exercise immense personal power; but as a result of his policies, the party's power and his own would be whittled away and the controls with which the state held society in check would be steadily dismantled. Given the outcome, some have argued that Gorbachev entered office with no intention of making fundamental reforms. What he aimed at, rather, was modest, within-system change which would have gingered the economy and so safeguarded the regime against internal and external threats; but his changes developed a momentum of their own which forced him to yield position after position until, like some sorcerer's apprentice, he had entirely lost control of the process he had instigated. There are important elements of truth in this interpretation. Like all politicians, Gorbachev improvised and learned on the job. Certainly, he had no exact blueprint in March 1985 of what would become the perestroika programme. Reform would be very much a two-way movement: he and his allies would shape the changes, but they themselves would in turn be shaped by the reform process and the problems it threw up. Like all politicians, he gave way to pressure when it became irresistible; and from 1990 he did increasingly have the air of reacting to events rather than guiding them. Yet for all this, Mikhail Gorbachev was not an apparatchik of limited vision who muddled along with *ad hoc* feints and thrusts. His problem was not that he lacked a strategy but that the strategy he developed turned out to be seriously flawed. The flaw, and the key to the paradox of perestroika, lay in his belief that democratization was not merely compatible with the party's dominant role but vital to its preservation. The party and the Soviet system would be saved by democratic socialism.

This belief in moving towards democracy did not come to Gorbachev from books and was not the result of any deep-rooted libertarian principles. It hardly needs to be said that this masterly politician and arch-opportunist was no dissident, and the Alternative Tradition meant little to him except as an arsenal of useful ideas. There has been much discussion of whether his democratism was genuine or merely 'instrumental'; but whatever his personal preferences, there were powerful considerations pushing him towards democracy. First, those whose support would be vital to him demanded a fair measure of it. Second, like Witte he realized that society could not be dynamic unless it were free, and that economic vitality could not be achieved without giving far more scope to individual initiative. Third, and most immediately important, anything less than real democratization would be useless since resistance to reform came not merely from the middle level of the power pyramid but from its very apex. Shopwindow change would be beside the point; so too would any real but limited democratization that broadened freedom at the bottom but left the supreme political organs untouched. The only way of arresting the country's decline was to prise absolute power from the hands of an incorrigibly conservative ruling class. Faced with an apparent choice between democracy and disaster, Mikhail Gorbachev not surprisingly chose democracy.

The new General Secretary had the sharpest and best-stocked mind of any Soviet leader since Lenin, and among his intellectual gifts was a sense of history. On his reading, the regime was now nearing a dead end: the original revolutionary impetus had petered out and only a second round of revolution would restore vigour and a sense of direction. Just as the English and French Revolutions had needed follow-ups (1685 and 1832, he suggested, in England; 1830, 1848 and 1871 in France), so did the Russian.[1] Yet the last thing he or anyone else wanted was more upheaval; on the contrary, what he aimed at was change that would prevent upheaval. That did not, however, mean that he believed in another instalment of 'revolution from above'. The changes would inevitably have to be initiated and directed 'from above', but what would make them different from the ruler-imposed changes of Russia's past was that they would be 'simultaneously a revolution "from above" and "from below"'.[2] The initial revolution from above would in fact unleash and merge with a movement at the grass-roots, and the outcome would be change that was fundamental yet not in the normal sense revolutionary at all: an unviolent and undisruptive transformation.

Gorbachev was not the first Russian to aim at what I have called a 're-volution from within', but he was far better placed to achieve one than his predecessors, Speransky and Stolypin. They had been no more than advisers to the leader; he was the leader, even if by no means an autocratic one. Speransky had dreamt of a middle class that would underpin the liberal institutions he believed in, while Stolypin had 'wagered' on a property-owning and contented peasantry that was as yet no more than a gleam in his eye. Gorbachev, by contrast, had no need to dream or wager since he had a large potential following among the middle class and the intelligentsia in particular. Frustrated professionals would be his battering-ram against the implacable diehards of the ruling class – the successors to those conservatives who in the 1960s, as he knew all too well, had broken Khrushchev. What was in the making in fact was an alliance unique in Russian history in which the leadership and a wide swathe of the intelligentsia would unite against the conservatives of the ruling class.

Democratization had to stop well short of full democracy, of course. Since it was being sold to the ruling class as something that would safeguard the party's interests, there could be no question of lifting the ban on rival political parties. The party's draconian control of society was, nevertheless, very greatly relaxed. People were allowed to speak more freely; a question-ing and innovating spirit was encouraged, while passivity, dependency and unthinking conformism were deplored; the worth and dignity of the indi-vidual began to be emphasized; there were attempts to give people a sense of involvement in policy-making; and the outcome, Gorbachev hoped, of this unprecedented interaction between party and people would be a broad con-sensus as to aims and a willing readiness to implement them. Thus the merg-ing of socialism and democracy would at long last take place: people would act in a socialist spirit without having to be coerced or repressed. Non-socialist tendencies would still be opposed, but in a democratic manner, for 'there is no present-day socialism, nor can there be, without democracy'.[3] That left it rather unclear how far the limits of freedom would go. In prac-tice, however, they were steadily extended: by 1989, there was more or less complete freedom of speech, and from March 1990 there was even freedom of political activity and organization.

Gorbachev's success was striking and unexpected. In 1989 he inaug-urated what till shortly before would have seemed quite unbelievable – a more or less genuine Soviet parliament. In February 1990 he still more breathtakingly persuaded the party to renounce its monopoly. Using con-summate political skills, he in fact almost single-handedly cajoled, coerced and duped the élite into making a voluntary renunciation of the absolute power the party had wielded since 1917. From the spring of 1990, the Communist Party was no more than one, if much the most influential, of the country's various political organizations. The party would of course continue and even, Gorbachev assumed, flourish; but the communist system, of which its privileged position had been the cornerstone, had been quietly dismantled. All of this amounted to a magnificent achievement, and the miscalculations and the disasters which lay ahead should not detract from the credit Gorbachev deserves for doing what no other politician of the day would have been capable of. His triumph had, moreover, aroused remarkably little overt opposition within the party. He had come to be widely seen by the party élite as a Machiavel and a destroyer, yet the tradition of obedience to the leadership still inhibited open opposition. Among the broad public, he had fervent support from many intellectuals (which waned, however, from the summer of 1989), while workers, though less enthusiastic, had tended at least to give him the benefit of the doubt.

With the abolition of the party's monopoly, what one might call the first stage of perestroika had been completed. The authoritarian structures which curbed vitality and initiative and stunted economic growth had been largely got rid of, while freedom of the individual had been recognized as the chief value in life. What now lay ahead was a second and more positive stage in which the priorities were to transform the economy and to attract broad support for the renovated party and its new-look, democratic socialism. During the first stage, Gorbachev had triumphed against the apparent odds; the second would, however, be even more challenging, since with every success the difficulties and dangers of his position increased. Till the summer of 1989, he had at least kept control of the reform process in the sense that he could regulate its pace and scope and suspend or even rescind the reforms. But now that a lively parliament and public opinion existed, the critical threshold, the point of no return, when change becomes irreversible was looming very close.

In Speransky's ideal scenario, the ruler would at this point accept defeat and cede formal power to the apparently harmless institutions which he had been duped into allowing to grow up. In this case, however, it was the ruler himself who had made all the running: far from being the victim of cunning advisers, *he* had done the cajoling and the arm-twisting. The fact that he had pushed through reforms widely seen as having harmed the party meant that as the threshold approached he faced opposition on two sides rather than just one – from radicals who demanded more rapid and fundamental change but also from diehards who were desperate to claw back what had been lost. Pressured from opposing sides, Gorbachev willy-nilly became a man of the centre. Between the extremists to either side he would stand for a middle way that was democratic to the extent that people were able to cope with, and economically reformist without breaking too violently with accepted traditions and current welfare levels. His hope had to be that a moderate, sensible democratic-socialist approach would win general and enthusiastic support and enable him to marginalize his rivals.

Back in 1987, still firmly in control, he had written in a somewhat abstract way that the revolution from above would unleash and converge with a revolution from below, without which the reform programme could not possibly succeed. What had then been little more than an aspiration had by 1990 become a reality. Soviet society was in motion; it was being stirred and shaken by more spontaneous activity at the grass-roots than at any time since 1917. Gorbachev and his fellow leaders were no longer absolute rulers; from now on, they would rule with the consent of those they had freed. Mass support, if they won it, would vindicate their perestroika; but without it, they faced the threat of being unseated by the very changes they had set in motion.

2

Democracy would come later, but the creed Gorbachev had grown up with was socialism. His father had been a party member and his maternal grand-father had been a Bolshevik zealot who had headed the collective farm on which Gorbachev himself worked as a youngster. This inherited socialism was to be the basic principle of Gorbachev's life. Rejecting it, he would tell a 1990 gathering of his Moscow University classmates, would be as unthinkable as rejecting his own father and grandfather.[4] The socialism of General Secretary Gorbachev was, however, very different from his prede-cessors' in the Soviet leadership. It was not visionary or emphatically egali-tarian like Khrushchev's, nor was it the frozen, dogmatic and intolerant creed of Khrushchev's successors. The socialism Gorbachev preached was down to earth, allowed wide freedom beneath the umbrella of party rule, and encouraged individual initiative and the instinct for material self-better-ment. Furthermore, it had in effect broken loose from communism and become an end in itself. The word 'communism' rarely passed Gorbachev's lips when he was leader, and after the nineteenth Party Conference in the summer of 1988 he stopped referring to it altogether.

This special brand of socialism – pragmatic, tolerant and with a streak of individualism – can be explained in part by his background. Gorbachev had been born far from the Russian heartland in the province of Stavropol in the rich lands immediately north of the Caucasus. This area had never known serfdom; indeed peasants had fled to it in order to avoid being serfs, and as a result the mentality here was somewhat different from that of the heart-land. People had not been bred to submission; they were less fatalistic and less inclined to accept oppression without a struggle. Their long tradition of independence had in fact only ended in the 1930s, when they were firmly yoked to the Soviet state by the collectivization drive. Gorbachev's maternal grandfather had sided with the collectivization, though like many party activists he had then fallen victim to the terror and been imprisoned. His non-party paternal grandfather suffered still more harshly and was sent for some years to Siberia. Gorbachev thus lost both grandfathers for a time to the purges and grew up in a family that was politically tainted. It was perhaps not surprising that when he and his friends got together to talk seriously in the Moscow of the early 1950s, they chose to turn Stalin's portrait to the wall.

Gorbachev was also very much a child of his time. The men who ran the Soviet state before him had kept a living link with the tsarist past and with the revolution. Their education, apart from some technical and vocational training, had largely been in the 'school of life', and their political personalities had been shaped by profound insecurity. The priority for them had been survival – on a regime and a personal level. Hence the immense importance they attached to unity, to centralization, to absolute obedience to superiors, to unswerving formal adhesion to party doctrine. But Gorbachev, born in 1931, belonged to a generation that had been shaped by very different experiences. Tsarism and the revolutionary struggles he knew only by hearsay, he had been too young to take part in the war, and Stalin died while he was still a student. He knew about raw reality from the farm, but from his distant village he had managed to get to the country's premier educational institution, Moscow University. When he began his career, Khrushchev's de-Stalinization was already under way, and he would climb the rungs of the apparatus during the calm and stable Brezhnev years. Thus, unlike his predecessors, he rose within the secure élite of a regime that seemed unassailable. They would never lose the rigidity and intolerance born of their early experiences; but there had been little to cast him in the same mould, and when problems loomed he would respond to them imaginatively and be willing to rethink fundamentals.

That said, the future leader was no more of a rebel than Stolypin had been. He accepted the basic Soviet structures and values and his aim was to protect and strengthen them in the cause of socialism. He would always be scornful of people who were not realists, who were too impulsive or muddle-headed to distinguish what was achievable from what was not, and he had shed no tears at the overthrow of Khrushchev. Such a person could only make his career in the party. He had joined while a student, taken up full-time party work in his native Stavropol straightaway after graduating, and in 1970 had become the local party boss. Brezhnev's inertia must have disappointed him, but he kept his opinions to himself and managed to win the good will of both Andropov and the conservative grey eminence, Mikhail Suslov. (It helped that both patrons had Stavropol connections.) In 1971 he joined the Central Committee and thus the oligarchy proper. In 1978 he moved to Moscow as Central Committee secretary responsible for agriculture; in 1979 he entered the oligarchy's inner circle by becoming a member of the Politburo; and a year later, aged only forty-nine, he was raised to full Politburo membership.

The story of the boy from the factory or farm making it to the top was a

Soviet commonplace. But what was special about this particular boy from the farm was that by the time he got to the top he had become a sophisticate who had left his peasant background (though not his southern accent) far behind. Whereas Khrushchev was very much a peasant leader, Gorbachev had turned himself into an educated professional and representative of the burgeoning middle class. He had not, of course, contrary to what some of his enemies would suggest, so far abandoned his background as to become a fifth columnist. Gorbachev's historical affinity was not with Speransky, a genuine saboteur, but with the true-believing Stolypin, who wanted desperately to save tsarism but came to see that only by being transformed could it be saved. We know from Gorbachev's Czech friend, Zdenek Mlynar, that even as a student he was inclined to question fossilized truths and outdated practices.[5] Yet his criticisms were all contained within a frame, whose limits were provided by the party, Marxism-Leninism and the Soviet system.

When Gorbachev became a full member of the Politburo, its average age was seventy – which made him stand out among his colleagues as little more than a schoolboy. Not only did he belong to a different generation from theirs; in outlook and culture he was in many respects closer to members of the intelligentsia who were looking for a new path for the country. An additional link with the intelligentsia came from his wife, Raisa, who had done pioneering work as a sociologist. Intellectuals were naturally delighted that someone who was so obviously 'one of them' had reached the top; but if they needed him as patron, he had an equal need of their 'new thinking'. For he had entered the central leadership at the very time when the country's economic problems were becoming acute – 1978, on one scholar's reckoning, was the precise moment when Soviet economic growth ceased altogether.[6] Radical, though feasible, solutions were badly needed, and only intellectuals of the loyal opposition were likely to come up with them.

During the first half of the 1980s, intellectuals bombarded Gorbachev with ideas which provided the basic material out of which the perestroika programme would take shape. As he recalled, his safe became 'clogged' with reform proposals.[7] At his first meeting with the economist and sociologist Tatyana Zaslavskaya, Gorbachev astonished her by responding to her criticisms with an 'If only I could'.[8] Moving between the two utterly different worlds of an elderly and conservative Politburo and the radical intelligentsia, he had of course to be extremely wary – not for nothing did he keep the reform proposals in his safe. How much of the radicals' ideas he had accepted at this stage is unknown. He had, however, clearly accepted the underlying proposition of the 'new thinking': that there had to be reform of the system rather than simply within it, that political change was the essential precondition of economic regeneration.

Gorbachev's colleagues had, however, chosen him to be a competent and vigorous manager rather than a radical reformer, and at the beginning he behaved much as they expected. The emphasis during his early months was on accelerating economic growth, and his proposals had much of the flavour of Andropov. While he had few natural allies at the top, he did of course have the power of patronage, which he used to build a younger and more vigorous team. Andrei Gromyko was removed after a twenty-eight-year stint as foreign minister and replaced by a close friend in Eduard Shevardnadze, while the octogenarian premier, Nikolai Tikhonov, gave way to a dynamic former industrial manager, Nikolai Ryzhkov. Yet the newly promoted were not necessarily committed reformers, and one of them, Yegor Ligachev, emerged during 1986 as the standard-bearer of those who opposed real reform. There were sweeping changes in the Central Committee after the twenty-seventh Party Congress in February 1986, but despite them this remained a bulwark of resistance to reform right through until 1990. In the Politburo, Gorbachev's position was helped by the early removal of two rivals, Viktor Grishin and Grigorii Romanov; here too, however, Gorbachev lived on a knife-edge. In time he would find support elsewhere to compensate for lack of it at the party's apex, but in 1985–6 he was in no position to mobilize any countervailing forces. The trouble was that reshuffling office-holders would never solve his problem because the new men (and occasionally women) would be chosen from the self-same party apparatus, and the party apparatus was inherently conservative.

1985 and 1986 were in fact to be the grey years of perestroika. The idea itself was floated. There were increasing references to the need for 'glasnost' (openness) and 'socialist democracy'. But how high a mountain Gorbachev had to climb became all too clear at the twenty-seventh Party Congress in 1986. He made a mutedly radical speech to the delegates, and Boris Yeltsin, the recently appointed first secretary of the Moscow city party organization, made an unambiguously radical one; but these were solitary figures amidst a legion of fiercely traditional conservatives who managed to make the congress yet another, though as it turned out the last, high mass of the old communism.

Chernobyl revealed just how little had so far changed. On 26 April 1986 a reactor at this nuclear plant not far from Kiev exploded, and the result was the world's worst nuclear disaster. The immediate response showed the system at its secretive and dishonest worst. True to the Soviet tradition of not admitting disasters, for the first three days there was no official acknowledgement at all of what had happened. Even when the accident was admitted, it was presented as nothing more than a 'mishap'. The minister in charge directed heroic fire-fighting efforts, but he was reluctant to evacuate people. Panic would be a worse evil than radiation, and after a while he even issued a secret decree forbidding doctors to cite radiation as a cause of death. So children played in radioactive dust, people ate contaminated vegetables, and in Kiev the May Day parade went ahead as planned. The government acted in fact as if Soviet citizens were children who were incapable of responding rationally to unpleasant and disturbing information; therefore they had to be kept in the dark.

But a disaster so enormous and with such horrifying potential consequences simply could not be hushed up: within a month, the explosion was getting wide coverage in the media and the message was filtering through that, judged by their performance in this instance, the authorities by no means 'knew best'. The report of the official enquiry in July pinned blame for the disaster solely on the irresponsibility of six senior officials. Many people had, however, by now decided that this and the many other disasters of Soviet life were far from accidental. Irresponsible behaviour was widespread at all levels because this was a society without openness and without public accountability – the very deficiencies Gorbachev had tried with little success to highlight at the twenty-seventh Congress. The way to avert another Chernobyl was not to pillory engineers who had bent the rules under intolerable pressure from above; it was to stop the irresponsible exercise of power at all levels.

Beginning as a defeat for glasnost, the Chernobyl disaster soon gave it an enormous boost. Against this dreadful backdrop, the case for open and uninhibited discussion of things that mattered was far harder to resist. The press became less respectful and cautious; and on 30 May a huge rock concert was held in Moscow to help the Chernobyl victims. Rock in Moscow – and to help the victims of a *Soviet* disaster! Gorbachev himself capitalized on the emotions aroused to push his case. Already he had made it plain that perestroika implied far more than tinkering with the economy. And in the summer of 1986 he raised the stakes higher still – perestroika would be nothing less, he argued, than a revolution in 'social relationships, the political system, the spiritual-ideological sphere, the style and methods of work by the party and all our cadres'. This revolution, moreover, was only just beginning: the more it advanced, the more complex its tasks would become and the more 'the huge scale and scope of the work ahead of us' would be revealed.[9]

But a rolling revolution with unforeseeable consequences was the last thing most of his colleagues wanted. Led by Yegor Ligachev, the conservatives stiffened their resistance to this General Secretary who looked like going far beyond the mandate they had given him. Any hopes Gorbachev may have had of achieving a consensus for reform among the ruling élite had clearly been mistaken. He had underestimated his colleagues' insecurity and their innate conservatism; he had also in all probability not guessed how much his own opinions would be radicalized once he had the General Secretary's overview.

On 15 December 1986, Gorbachev phoned Andrei Sakharov in Gorky and told him that he would be released. Soon afterwards, some hundred other leading dissidents were allowed home. The freeing of the dissidents flashed a signal reminiscent of Alexander II's amnestying of the Decembrists. Here once more was a ruler who was serious about reform and wanted a reconciliation with 'society', and in both cases the very gesture gave added impetus to the reform process. The parallel was not complete, however. The Decembrists, though broken and harmless old men, had been made to live in safe isolation from the capitals. No such constraints were placed upon the frail but still determined and active Sakharov. From now until his death in December 1989, he would be a thorn in the government's side; but his freedom was something Gorbachev had to put up with in order to win and retain support that was indispensable to perestroika's success.

The conflict with his colleagues had come to a head in the autumn and early winter of 1986 over the business of the next Central Committee plenum. Gorbachev wanted to put democratization high on the agenda, turning it from a side issue into the main theme of perestroika. His opponents resisted, and three times the date of the plenum had to be postponed. The clash of interests was now unconcealed: what was at stake was oligarchic power itself. On the face of it, Gorbachev's chances of success were slim. The Soviet oligarchy had by now become formidably well entrenched; indeed, there were those in the West who argued that oligarchy was the natural type of government in Russia and that in a less obvious form it had existed not just since 1917 but for centuries.[10] A less determined and less skilful General Secretary would have backed down at this stage and made do with cosmetic changes that would not have alarmed his colleagues. And beyond the very serious doubt as to whether he could prevail, a still larger question loomed – were the Soviet people yet ready for a real say in their own affairs? This was a question that Russian rulers had been asking on and off since Alexander I; and all who asked it had sooner or later replied in the negative.

3

The short answer to the question was in fact 'yes' and 'no'. Geographical and social islands of modernity (Moscow and Leningrad, the urban middle class) were lapped by a broad sea of more or less untouched traditionalism. So far the islands had not applied any irresistible pressure for democracy. They were large enough to encourage any would-be democratizer to go ahead; the surrounding seas were, however, a daunting reminder of the difficulties which would confront him.

Democracy's prospects were, on the face of it, not so very different from what they had been in 1917: then, too, would-be liberal or democratic islands had bobbed precariously upon a traditionalist sea. The islands had, however, become somewhat different in size and in nature. More than a third of the population were now 'middle class' at least in the sense of not being manual workers or peasants. By 1987, 43 per cent of employees worked in the 'services', i.e. the white-collar sector, and there were no less than twenty-one million graduates. The members of this motley semibourgeoisie with its engineers, administrators and intellectuals were no longer automatically damned in ordinary people's eyes as anti-popular and anti-Russian. But in one respect, the late-Soviet middle class did appreciably less well than its predecessor. Tsarism's middle class had at least been property-owning and had had ample opportunity to get rich; its Soviet counterpart, by contrast, lacked not only civil liberties but economic freedom as well, and given the chance its members would certainly press hard for both. Their rejection of communism and all its works was likely to be categorical. What was not so certain was how they would react if democratization threatened their economic self-interest – by creating instability, for instance; and should that happen it seemed likely that many would go for some authoritarian, though less than totalitarian, form of government that offered firm protection for private enterprise.

Outside these large-ish and relatively hopeful 'islands', the would-be democratizer faced a formidable challenge. Centuries of rule by tsars and communists had provided the worst possible schooling for democracy. People had had it instilled into them that the state embodied certain absolute and indisputable truths and that their rulers unfailingly knew what was best for them. Political questions had been treated as if they were questions in mathematics: answers were either right or wrong, different solutions could not be equally valid, and the rulers' solutions were by definition the correct ones. As it happened, rulers often changed their minds about the solution, even committed glaring volte-faces, yet this had done very little to undermine the habit of seeing solutions as either fundamentally correct or absolutely erroneous.

As a result, there was no tolerant, give-and-take discussion of public affairs, no belief in the virtues of compromise, and little or no acceptance that differing opinions might actually produce better policies. What was missing, too – and this was more surprising – was that agreed framework of values and beliefs which, in the West, underpinned the clash of opinions and stopped it going to extremes. The rulers had of course tried hard to impose such a framework in the form of Marxism–Leninism. The danger, however, was that once the party relaxed its grip, the new breed of politicians would fall out utterly and there would be no common core of agreed beliefs to moderate and limit the divisions among them.

A people taught to think that its rulers' truths were absolute had also been taught to think of itself as forming a single, united and indivisible whole. The Western habit of seeing the community as so many individuals and groups jostling and vying with one another beneath a broad national umbrella was almost wholly unfamiliar. Age-old insecurity, reinforced by ideology, had, as we have seen, made Russians put solidarity first. And the authorities had of course encouraged the tendency to look askance at anyone who wanted to break ranks: such people were splitters who were jeopardizing the wellbeing of everyone else by putting first what they mistakenly took to be their own best interests. Andropov had underlined this point as recently as 1983, and what he said then might in essence have come from any spokesman for tsarism.

For all that, the rulers' claims to represent the national will were now hardly taken seriously. Belief in the ruler-as-god had died with or shortly after Stalin. What had replaced it, however, was not a healthy scepticism which saw politicians as no better and no worse than anyone else but a corrosive cynicism: politics was a dirty business and those who practised it were inevitably self-seeking and corrupt. People protested about the system in various ways. They grumbled about the bosses; they increasingly made jokes about them (imagine joking under Stalin!); and they cut corners, cheated and shirked responsibility for matters which had, after all, been decided for rather than by them. Yet few outside the intelligentsia questioned whether such a system made for sensible policies or desirable outcomes, and few seemed to sense any link between a declining economy and a political system that concentrated all power in very few hands, denied ordinary people even the illusion of involvement in decision-taking, and so stifled in them any sense of responsibility for getting things done.

What remained, however, amidst the cynicism and the destroyed illusions, was the idea of socialism itself, which had somehow survived the party's gross exploitation of it. There was still a widespread commitment to the idea of a socialist society, whatever exactly that meant: and what it meant above all was a society free from the evils people associated with capitalism. Inflation, unemployment, bourgeois domination of society, a wide gulf between the classes, and little or no welfare provision for the poor – these were seen by most as inseparable from the free enterprise system. Capitalism was identified with greed and inequality, and few people realized that it might actually raise living standards for everyone or that the inevitable inequalities of capitalist society might be compensated by the general gain of liberty. As a result, there was little eagerness to move towards any economic system that departed radically from traditional egalitarianism and collectivism. The feeling that communal solidarity had to be protected was crucial. This made the task of creating a multi-party political system difficult; it also put huge obstacles in the way of private enterprise. Liberal politics and liberal economics had the fatal flaw for very many Russians that they were inherently competitive rather than co-operative – they seemed to set person in opposition to person. The Slavophiles' claims that Russians instinctively recoiled from the atomized, 'Gesellschaft' society of the West were to a remarkable degree still applicable three-quarters of a century after the downfall of tsarism.

For all these reasons, there was no question of a rapid transition to Western-style democracy. Gorbachev's immediate aim had to be democratization, and his ultimate aim was democratic socialism rather than liberal-capitalist democracy. From the summer of 1986, he described perestroika as a revolution, but what he wanted was a democratizing *evolution* which built on and where necessary modified the fundamentals of the Soviet system, in particular its planned economy and its welfare provision.

Even cautious democratization would, however, run up against popular attitudes. Most people were unprepared for it and likely to be at best luke-warm towards it. As a result, the chief strategist and tactician of the reform would also have a vital teaching role to perform. 'Today', Gorbachev wrote in 1987, 'it is as if we are going through a school of democracy again. We are learning. We still lack political culture. We do not even have the patience to hear out our friends.' Yet he was optimistic: 'All this is sure to pass. We will master this science, too.'[11] Russians were, after all, educated and intelligent: they would surely respond to the good sense of his arguments. Like any wise teacher, however, he would not push his pupils too hard; he would try to make the new 'science' blend with what was familiar from Russian and Soviet tradition; and he would keep the socialist and Leninist objectives of the reform very much to the fore.

4

His immediate task was of course to defeat the Politburo irreconcilables. 'Democracy', he announced at the January 1987 Central Committee plenum, 'is not simply a slogan but the essence of perestroika.'[12] That was precisely what his opponents had not wanted to have said in public. Before, democratism had been no more than a side-issue; now, in the teeth of fierce opposition, Gorbachev had thrust it to the top of the reform agenda. Moreover, any lingering illusions that this might be mere word-spinning were dispelled when he pointed out that democracy implied contested elections.

Democratization and contested elections were potentially fatal for the oligarchs; and once these ideas had been released with the stamp of approval they could hardly be called back. Why then did Gorbachev's opponents let him go public at this stage with ideas that were so dangerous to them? Why did they submit when they could surely have forced him out? Partly because there was no credible alternative: this politician of all the talents towered above any conceivable rival. A still greater deterrent, however, was that an anti-Gorbachev coup would have provoked widespread protests and perhaps even worse than that. What was certain was that Gorbachev could not have been got rid of as easily as Khrushchev. By 1964, Khrushchev had become unpopular at all levels and people had readily enough dismissed him as a capricious buffoon and an incompetent. Gorbachev, by contrast, was more popular than any leader since Stalin. Not only did he have a fervent grass-roots following; he had strong support from an appreciable minority of the ruling class as well. And if his opponents had ousted him, how would they have justified it? On the democracy issue, he had in effect called the party's bluff. For seventy years it had preached democracy; now he was practising it, and that made it difficult for those who prided themselves on the purity of their principles to cry 'Foul!'

However, in March 1988 Ligachev and the diehards finally made a stand. Taking advantage of Gorbachev's temporary absence, they engineered the publication in *Sovetskaya Rossiya* ('Soviet Russia') of a neo-Stalinist manifesto written by an unknown Leningrad lecturer, Nina Andreeva. The manifesto seemed to be a clarion call to all opponents of democratization, and its publication in a major newspaper created consternation among Gorbachev's supporters. Since there was no official rebuttal, many assumed that the whole reforming project was about to be scrapped. The gains made since 1985 had not been institutionalized or entrenched in any way; they hung on the slender thread of Gorbachev's leadership, and that thread was now, it seemed, in danger of being snapped. Many of perestroika's vocal supporters as a result suddenly fell silent. But the worst did not in fact happen. Gorbachev returned, and before long a magisterial rebuke to the neo-Stalinists, written by his ally Alexander Yakovlev, was published in *Pravda*. The reformers then pressed ahead hard, determined to consolidate their victory and make it irreversible, and the outcome was the mould-breaking nineteenth Party Conference of June–July 1988.

This was the first party conference (as opposed to congress) since the war, and it was the first party assembly of any kind for more than fifty years in which the prearranged pattern was allowed to be disrupted by spontaneity. To the public's astonishment, some delegates seemed to be speaking their own minds. There was even a slanging-match between Ligachev and Boris Yeltsin, who the previous autumn had been disgraced and removed as first secretary of the Moscow city party organization and now demanded to be rehabilitated. It was, however, Gorbachev, as chairman and impresario, who gave the proceedings their different quality. He had already implied that so-called Soviet democracy was not up to much; now he exposed it as a sham, condemning outright 'the proclamation of democratic principles in words and authoritarianism in reality, incantations about democracy from the tribune but voluntarism and subjectivism in practice'.[13] A year later he would go even further and denounce the previous system as a 'despotism', but this for the moment was quite strong enough and it must have shocked many in the audience.

The CPSU would keep its vanguard role and would dominate the new democratic politics; nevertheless, it would have to change fundamentally. By controlling all aspects of life, it had 'literally swaddled society' in a way Lenin had never intended. Now the party would withdraw to a purely strategic role, leaving day-to-day management of the nation's affairs to popularly elected institutions. Rather than try to breathe life into the existing institutions, however, Gorbachev proposed entirely new ones, and these came into existence in 1989. The Supreme Soviet would be replaced by a new supreme governing body, the Congress of People's Deputies, with 2,250 deputies. This unwieldy assembly would meet only once or twice a year but would elect from among its deputies a much smaller legislature of some 450 members, which would be called by the old name of Supreme Soviet. The revamped Supreme Soviet would have 'lively and demanding' sessions; formalism would be reduced to a minimum, and ministers would even have to answer deputies' questions. In his pedagogic role, Gorbachev pointed out to the delegates that debate was a good thing, while lack of agreement, he insisted, was 'a normal phenomenon of the democratic process'.[14] It says a lot about the task he faced that this elementary truth had to be stated! The Supreme Soviet he had created would in fact be what the Soviet Union had never had before – and what Lenin for one would have abhorred: a full-time working parliament rather than an occasional rubber-stamp. Its members would be professional politicians instead of workers temporarily released from factory and farm, and they would be elected under a system that went some way towards providing competition between candidates – though not of course between parties.

In addition, the Congress would elect a new chief executive of state: the Chairman of the Supreme Soviet of the USSR. This new post, which Gorbachev clearly intended for himself, marked a radical breach with Soviet tradition. From now on, the chief executive would no longer be the General Secretary, appointed by and answerable to the highest organs of the party: instead, he would be appointed by the legislature, which in turn would be elected in relatively free conditions by the general population. True, the great majority of deputies would be communists. True, too, as long as the party kept its privileged position, the Chairman would be answerable to it as well and in particular to its policy-making organ, the Politburo. Moreover, the fact that Gorbachev continued as General Secretary would limit his room for manoeuvre as Chairman. Nevertheless, a start had been made in the direction of taking executive power away from the party's exclusive control. Another move in the same direction was the creation of a Committee of Constitutional Review, whose members would act as impartial arbitrators of constitutional issues. This was unprecedented in Soviet experience: a party that was infallible and armed with the one true science had no need, after all, to be judged by arbitrators who claimed to stand outside it. But Gorbachev was beginning to use the language of Western constitutionalism; and behind this there lay a quiet transformation of basic beliefs, values and attitudes.

Communism and the 'new Soviet person' were now heard of very little; the reformers instead set themselves the less grandiose goals of a 'new society' and a 'qualitatively new condition of socialism'. But the most startling of Gorbachev's innovations was 'pluralism', which from 1988 became one of the catchwords of perestroika. By traditional Soviet standards, the idea was blatantly heretical. This after all was a society in which a party holding a monopoly of power claimed to have a monopoly of truth and the support of a monolithically united population. Anyone who suggested that diversity of opinion might be a good thing had been condemned – but here was a

General Secretary seeming to do just that. Admittedly, Gorbachev covered himself by putting 'socialist' before 'pluralism' (he would, however, drop the adjective in 1990); and admittedly he was calling for pluralism of opinions rather than, as yet, of political parties. The first, however, pointed clearly enough towards the second. Either the party was infallible or it was not. If it was not, as Gorbachev now suggested, then the case for its monopoly very largely lapsed.

Not only did Gorbachev say shocking things; by the standards of his predecessors, he acted rather shockingly. They had been remote and awesome, and the one who had failed to act suitably had got sacked. Being ordinarily human was quite inappropriate for someone who was supposed to be not only himself but an embodiment. When the Soviet leader spoke, it was the party with its Marxist–Leninist science, its heroic traditions and its lofty mission that spoke through him; and since the collective will was embodied in the party, the entire nation spoke through him as well. No wonder he could not be quirky or undignified or simply sniffle with a cold. A leadership which handed down its policies as if they were engraved on Mosaic tablets had to be awesome, ritualistic and aloof, and admitting human quirks and weaknesses was out of the question. From the outset, however, Gorbachev acted very differently. Not since Peter the Great stripped away the religious mystique from tsardom had any Russian ruler so dramatically brought the leadership down to earth. Whereas his predecessors had been 'stone-faced sphinxes',[15] he readily showed his emotions, rubbed shoulders to the extent of risking 'oxygen-poisoning' (or so some of his colleagues feared), and made a point of listening to those he mixed with. He was so determinedly 'ordinary' that he refused to let image-makers delete the ugly birthmark on his forehead, and he even encouraged his wife to share the limelight with him, quite contrary to Kremlin tradition.

All of this pointed towards a new kind of politics: indeed, towards the very beginning of politics as practised elsewhere. Politics became a marketplace in which people set up their stalls and tried to sell their policies and their personalities to would-be buyers. True, so far there was only one stallholder in this particular marketplace. Gorbachev nevertheless behaved as if he had rivals, trying to sell himself by arguing his case and getting people to engage with him. It was hard at first to get a dialogue going, let alone the cut and thrust of debate. But he was an able teacher in what he had himself called 'the school of democracy'. He was maybe even too able for his own good; and it was not long before people started answering back and even casting eyes at rival stallholders.

In March 1989, the elections to the new supreme governing body, the Congress of People's Deputies, showed how much the new politics had taken root. There had been nothing remotely similar since the elections to the Constituent Assembly, and the event created such excitement that a closer parallel might be with the elections to the First Duma in 1906. Not that the party had given up its tricks. While competitive elections were allowed, the electoral system was tilted strongly in favour of those who had the support of local party bosses. Nominations of candidates were controlled by election commissions, which the bosses dominated, and numerous conservatives got nominated unopposed as a result. Moreover, 750 out of the 2,250 seats were set aside for public organizations, among them the CPSU. These attempts at perverting the democratic process infuriated many electors, however, and some fifty conservative candidates, including one member of the Politburo (Yurii Solovev of Leningrad), in the event suffered the humiliation of defeat at the polls.

The Congress which emerged from this mixture of gerrymandering and genuine democracy was the most highly educated and the most independent legislature in Soviet history. Token representatives, such as factory hands and milkmaids, had all but disappeared; the deputies were overwhelmingly male professionals. Almost 90 per cent were party members, yet the result of democratizing while keeping the party's monopoly intact was that party membership was now no guarantee whatever of loyalty to the leadership. The party had by now in fact become a broad church divided into warring sects of traditionalists, Gorbachevian centrists and radicals. The radicals, who wanted an outright liberal-democratic Russia, were a small minority of no more than 300 but included some of the most eloquent and impressive members, among them Boris Yeltsin and Andrei Sakharov. Yeltsin had seemed politically dead in November 1987, but had since made an extraordinary come-back: standing in a constituency that embraced all of Moscow, he had scored a resounding victory over an apparatchik opponent, winning more than five million votes. Sakharov, who had acquired almost saintly status in the eyes of many intellectuals, did not have the same populist touch. He had, however, shown that the apparatus's tricks could be turned against it by obtaining, with some difficulty, one of the seats set aside for the Academy of Sciences.

Gorbachev made the most of the conservatives' discomfiture. The elections had in effect been a referendum on perestroika, he declared, and they had shown how mistaken its opponents had been. The voters not only supported perestroika, they evidently wanted it to go further and faster. Now that millions of people had been unleashed into the social arena (he meant 'freed'), authoritarianism was finished. The party had to stop being aloof, secretive and arbitrary; it would have to argue its case, accept public scrutiny, and submit to the rule of law. What in fact he was asking the party was to stop imposing its will and to become instead what it had never been and its founder had never intended it to be – a democratic political party in the Western style.

The Congress which opened on 25 May 1989 was one of the great achievements of perestroika. Once more after many years the country had a parliament, as people at once called the new body and its offspring, the Supreme Soviet. There were echoes here of the Dumas, but some drew a still more stirring comparison – with the Estates-General, which exactly 200 years before, in May 1789, had met in Versailles and begun redrawing the political landscape of France. Yet thére was an important difference. The Estates-General, like the first two Dumas, had rebelled against the ruler; but in this case it was the ruler who, despite fierce opposition, had master-minded the transformation which had made the parliament possible. And his commitment to an entirely new style of Soviet politics came through on the eve of Congress's opening when he told party deputies that they were free to speak and vote as they wished. The stage was thus set for the liveliest public debate the Soviet Union had ever known.

This first session of the Congress was perhaps Gorbachev's supreme moment. He looked out at a parliament elected in at least semi-democratic conditions which seemed to endorse his policy of a steady evolution towards democratic socialism and a socialist market economy. Around him he heard the cut and thrust of a debate which he had done his best to encourage and at which he himself was so good, and despite strong opposition from tradi-tionalists and radicals he could count on the support of the great majority of deputies. If there was a time when his belief in achieving democratic social-ism by consensus seemed realizable, this was surely it. The parliament, very much his own creation, left him on a pinnacle as the father of Soviet demo-cracy; but pinnacles are not easy to sit on, and his position would turn out to be uncomfortable and increasingly precarious.

5

The new politics were accompanied by an equally innovatory foreign policy, and Gorbachev's triumphs at home were matched, even surpassed, by his successes abroad. By almost single-handed effort, he changed the Cold War into a warm peace based on a close personal relationship with Presidents Reagan and Bush; he allowed the countries of Eastern Europe to go free; and he raised the Iron Curtain and encouraged the peoples of the Soviet Union to emerge from isolation and rejoin the world family of nations. A lesser but nevertheless vital achievement was his staunching of the 'bleeding wound' of the Afghan war. The withdrawal of Soviet troops from Afghanistan was completed by February 1989, and it pointed towards a still more momentous retreat – of Soviet troops from Eastern Europe after almost a half-century of occupation.

Foreign policy was of course inseparable from domestic. The Cold War had been a by-product of the regime's insecurity towards its own subjects and its satellites. The enemy beyond had justified a massive military–security establishment and internal repression. Confrontation between the superpowers had, however, put all mankind at risk. The priority given to defence had crippled the Soviet economy. And the optimistic assumptions underlying the Cold War had been largely dispelled by 1985: economic decline and the American lead in defence technology made it most unlikely that the Soviet Union could come out on top in either military or peaceful competition with the West.

The 'new thinking' made itself felt gradually in foreign policy, as in domestic. At the twenty-seventh Party Congress, Gorbachev still spoke of the 'imperialist threat', but he also emphasized the increasing interdependence of countries and the dangers presented to all by nuclear weapons. By 1988, he was talking about international affairs without Soviet jargon, stressing what united nations irrespective of ideology and making much of the Soviet Union's place in a 'common European home'. Contacts with the West multiplied as the Iron Curtain, now seen as an obstacle rather than a necessary protection, fell away. Foreigners were no longer regarded as suspect, the carriers of a dangerous ideological bacillus; and there was even talk of establishing a right of free exit from the Soviet Union. All this made Gorbachev immensely popular abroad, and as the Cold War petered out waves of 'Gorbymania' engulfed him on his travels. Here was a great statesman, a peacemaker and a liberator: a civilized and charming Russian, a man with a smile and without any hang-ups about the West. *Time* voted him 'man of the year' for 1987, and in 1990 he was awarded the Nobel Prize for Peace.

The very enthusiasm for Gorbachev in the West, however, made many at home wonder whether ending the Cold War was really in the country's interest. The military in particular had obvious reasons for discontent. Until 1985, this had been perhaps the most militarized society on earth. Now, under a leader who had neither military experience nor any obvious penchant for the military, civilian values and priorities were taking over; and one sign of this was that the minister of defence was no longer a full member of the Politburo. Education, health and welfare would get more, while the military would get less; and in the summer of 1989 the government announced that defence spending would be reduced by half by 1995. But Gorbachev did more than cut armaments and military jobs; he struck at the military's pride by letting go of its war booty, the outer empire. This, like the shift of resources, was, however, an inevitable consequence of perestroika. If the West was no longer the enemy, then the Soviet Union no longer needed a buffer of client states. If democracy was good for the Soviet Union, it had to be good for the satellites as well. If the countries of Europe formed a 'common home', then the Berlin Wall stuck out as an intolerable anomaly.

The outer empire simply had to be given up. Not only that; the flip-side of giving it up was that Eastern Europe might well become an ideal laboratory for perestroika. Poland, Hungary, Czechoslovakia and East Germany had far more of the preconditions for socialism than the Soviet Union itself. The first two, moreover, had reformist governments. Where the government was stubbornly obscurantist, as in the last two, Gorbachev could hardly impose democratization; but it seemed likely, even here, that pressure for change from below would sooner or later bring about the conditions that he wanted.

In the event, however, the East European revolutions of 1989 dashed Gorbachev's hopes and instead bore out the worst fears of Soviet traditionalists. By the end of the year, the Communist Party had lost its monopoly in all of the former satellites. Of the two likely flag-ships of democratic socialism, Poland had fallen in the summer to the non-communist government of Tadeusz Mazowiecki, while in Hungary it looked probable that free, multi-party elections scheduled for the spring of 1990 would sweep the reformed Communist Party from power. Czechoslovakia's unyielding rulers had meanwhile been overthrown in the 'velvet revolution' of December 1989, which temporarily at least destroyed both the Communist Party and the chances of democratic socialism in the Eastern European country that had seemed best suited to it. In the special case of East Germany, also, things had worked out badly for Gorbachev. The Berlin Wall and Honecker's repressive government had to go, needless to say. But if that made German reunification unavoidable, Gorbachev hoped at least that the two parts of the country would be linked at first by no more than a loose confederation which allowed East Germany to keep its socialist character. He hoped, too, that the reunified country would stand outside the two military blocs. By the end of 1989, however, the East German regime had collapsed and with it had gone any chance of saving socialism on German soil. In 1990 the country was simply absorbed by its larger and more successful neighbour; and what was especially wounding about this was that territory on which the Red Army had achieved victories that had passed into legend and on which many Soviet troops were still stationed thereby became assimilated into NATO.

After the East German collapse, it was hard to resist the conclusion that the Cold War had finished not with an honourable draw but with outright victory for the West. Given the choice, the Germans had rejected their liberators from the east in favour of their liberators from the west. Most other ex-satellites, too, were engulfed by a fierce anti-Soviet nationalism. The idea of a middle way that combined the best of Soviet-style socialism with the freedoms of the West had suffered a serious setback. It was a depressing augury for the prospects of democratic socialism in the Soviet Union itself. To make matters worse, the misfortunes in Eastern Europe came at a time when the reforms at home were creating serious resistance to Gorbachev and his programme.

6

Gorbachev's attempt at economic 'acceleration', reminiscent as we have seen of Andropov, had good results: the economy grew 5 per cent from

1987 to 1988, and per capita real income increased by 3.5 per cent during the same period. From 1987, he became rather more adventurous in his economics, though by no means as adventurous as in his politics. Traditional Soviet thinking still had an inhibiting effect. He had lingering suspicions of the market as something unsocialist, and he had doubts too about private property, especially private farming. Another deterrent to economic radicalism was lack of precedent; and having neither practical experience nor a theory of how to make the change-over, the reformers understandably moved with caution.

Yet if Gorbachev did not have a clear-cut economic policy from 1987, he did have a distinct economic attitude. His aim was a golden mean between the extremes of capitalism and the old command economy which would give Soviet people the best of both. Central planning and a high level of welfare provision would continue. Collective farming would remain the basis of agriculture, though a law of 1989 allowed land to be leased (not sold) to private farmers and by 1990 several thousand private farms had been set up. While the umbrella of state control would remain, everything would be done to encourage entrepreneurial initiative and to discourage attitudes that inhibited it. Decision-taking would be decentralized to enterprises; small- and medium-scale co-operative businesses would be permitted; and wage-levelling would be replaced by a policy of paying people what their work merited. The outcome would be a market economy with a difference: a socialist market economy which operated for the good of all rather than a capital-owning minority.

The aim of an economic golden mean was inspired in part by Sweden. There may have been some influence in addition from China, where radical economic policies were having impressive results, though the Chinese 'model' would be badly discredited, for democrats, by the repression following violence in Tiananmen Square in June 1989. The chief inspiration was, however, a domestic one – NEP. The circumstances of the 1980s were wholly different from those of the 1920s, yet perestroika spokesmen emphasized the creative potential of NEP and the similarities between it and current policies. And here, if anywhere, encouragement was to be found since NEP had combined state and private enterprise, raised living standards, and done much to reconcile a hostile population to the regime. Could not perestroika achieve something similar?

By 1989, however, the signs were distinctly discouraging: prices were becoming higher and goods scarcer. Eight per cent price inflation in 1988 had reached 10 per cent by the end of 1989. What made price rises especially alarming was that they had been unknown since the war. The prices of basic goods and services – say, a loaf of bread and a Metro ticket – had seemed immutable, and this price stability had given people a sense of security. Shortages, by contrast, were an accepted part of life, but now they were becoming worse. Staples like bread, meat, milk, sugar, cheese and tobacco were hard to find, and there was no longer even the certainty that if you scoured for long enough you would get what you wanted. Not everyone suffered, however. The shortages gave a boost to the black market, and marketeers did well of course. So too, it was thought, did the new breed of entrepreneurs, who were running the co-operatives and charging what seemed exorbitant prices. So did anyone with access to dollars, the green gold that everyone wanted but all too few could get. 'Social justice', a perestroika slogan, in practice seemed to mean increasing social disparities. The go-getting and the criminal flourished, but most people found that their living standards were deteriorating.

The economic reforms made things worse, but at least they were an attempt to grapple with serious difficulties that long predated them. The other domestic problem that by 1989 was causing real worry – rising ethnic tensions – had not, however, figured on the original reform agenda at all. If perestroika had been brought into being by economic sclerosis, it was perestroika itself which seemed to have created the nationalities' problem. The nationalities had after all, with rare exceptions, been submissive since the 1920s, and orthodox and liberal party members alike both complacently assumed that this particular problem had long since been solved. In reality, it had simply been suppressed; and once controls were relaxed, the nationalities started asserting themselves.

In 1988 disturbances erupted in Nagorno-Karabakh, a small, mainly Armenian enclave within Azerbaijan. The Armenian majority wanted the territory to be restored to Armenia, from which Stalin had transferred it in 1923. The government was reluctant to give way, fearing that a concession would encourage demands for other border changes and inflame ethnic tensions generally. But while it refused the Armenians' request, in the age of perestroika it could hardly cow them into submission; and the outcome was a bloody and prolonged conflict between Armenians and Azeris, to which putting the disputed territory under direct Moscow rule, in June 1989, proved no solution at all.

Inter-ethnic conflict at least presented no challenge of principle to the Soviet state; and the Armenians had a particular record of loyalty to Moscow. However, in the Baltic states, Georgia and Moldavia, national movements had sprung up that pointed by implication at least towards complete secession from the Soviet Union. In Georgia, feelings were inflamed in April 1989 when the army killed some twenty nationalist demonstrators in the capital. But it was the Balts, with their memories of national independence less than fifty years before, who led the way. Popular fronts were created in all three Baltic states in 1988, ostensibly on behalf of Gorbachev and a more radical perestroika. By 1989, these popular fronts greatly outnumbered the local Communist Parties. In effect the party had already lost its monopoly in the Baltics; and in December 1989 the Lithuanian party caused outrage in Moscow by breaking away from the CPSU in a desperate attempt to win back a local following. Pre-war independence was openly recalled with nostalgia, and the republics' forceful incorporation into the Soviet Union was denounced. In August 1989, a remarkable protest took place against the secret protocols of the Molotov–Ribbentrop Pact when some two million people formed an unbroken human chain stretching from end to end of the three republics.

Such defiance was encouraged by what was happening in Eastern Europe. If Poland could go free, why not Lithuania? For Gorbachev, however, the outer and inner empires were entirely different cases. If he had to give up the first, he was determined to hold on to the second, and defence of the union became, after socialism, the issue on which he took his firmest stand. In September 1989, the Central Committee came out with a new nationalities' policy which confirmed the right of self-determination and condemned previous violations of Leninist principles. The document made it clear, however, that self-determination should not imply secession, and it rejected separatist nationalism in favour of the development of national self-awareness within the framework of the Union. The Soviet Union, according to the document, would be transformed into a genuine federation with 'a strong centre and strong republics'; in the nationalities area, as in economics, the country would be saved from its problems by consistently applied Leninism. But this offered very little to the many people who had come to see Moscow as an oppressor. What could be done in the face of this gathering disaffection? Traditional force and fraud would violate the perestroika philosophy, yet giving the malcontents their freedom seemed out of the question. All that remained was chicanery, and this was much in evidence in the new law on secession of April 1990, which hedged the right with such difficult conditions that it became in practice a dead letter. There were of course respectable economic and strategic reasons for wanting to save the state from disintegration. When the countries of Western Europe were moving towards closer union, dissolving the Soviet Union seemed a move in entirely the wrong direction. Yet lessons drawn from the integrationist tendency in the West were hardly relevant. The Western countries had come to see the disadvantages of national independence after many years of enjoying it; discontented Soviet peoples not surprisingly saw nothing but benefit in the independence they had been denied. Getting them to accept Moscow-style common sense would be hard, especially if it continued to be dressed up in Leninist language; and by the end of 1989 the inner empire was clearly in jeopardy.

Losing some small republics of the fringe would not anyway have been a disaster. What was indispensable was the Russian heartland, and here perestroika had initially got a warm reception. As the decade drew to a close, however, the mood in Russia, too, became more critical. In the case of the Russian working class , the problem was hardly surprising – the workers were bound to be a difficult constituency for a leader whose reforms would most obviously benefit well-educated professionals. Widening wage differentials harmed the working class; so, too, did quality control, which led to production being rejected and hence to loss of bonuses. An anti-alcohol campaign had also badly strained relations between the leadership and the working class. The new regime was clearly intent upon licking the workers into shape, making them sober, hard-working and productive: but they could hardly be expected to enjoy the experience. In the competitive and entrepreneurial society Gorbachev aimed at, there would be no officially favoured social category, but in reality professionals already held pride of place. Congress membership told its own story: more than three-quarters of the deputies had degrees and only 19 per cent were identified with the working class.

The first stirrings of working-class discontent came in the summer of 1989, when half a million miners in Siberia and Ukraine defied the law and organized the first major strikes since the early 1920s. The miners' action was an early warning that the reform process might slip out of control. Politicians had so far done Gorbachev's bidding; but ordinary workers, once they got a whiff of freedom (and the miners had been galvanized by what they saw and heard from the Congress), would be less easy to manage. The miners' demands were quickly conceded, and the right to strike and to form unofficial unions soon followed; but the strike and its knock-on effects nevertheless accentuated the downturn in the economy. Gorbachev's only consolation was that the miners were not protesting against perestroika as such but rather against living conditions which had become so wretched that they could not even get soap to wash with. And while the miners were indignant, their anger was not directed at him: on the contrary, they still hoped that a more radical perestroika would make things better.

But inevitably people did start seeing a connection between perestroika and the marked worsening in living conditions; and in the autumn of 1989 a grass-roots anti-perestroika movement began, which denounced price rises, the profit motive, and the growing role of the market and demanded a return to traditional Soviet values. This was exactly what Gorbachev's conservative opponents wanted, and they were soon manipulating the movement. The Russian United Workers' Front, the main organ of working-class protest, had a Congress deputy at its head and a clutch of conservative intellectuals as its advisers, while the USSR Peasant Union, which campaigned against agricultural privatization, was run by collective farm directors – the 'red landowners', as perestroika supporters nicknamed them.

There was little danger of the intelligentsia being manipulated in the same way: yet even here, as controls relaxed, support for perestroika became more conditional and attitudes more critical. Intellectuals wanted above all to be involved, and they started setting up 'informal' (i.e. technically illegal) organizations, many with politically sensitive cultural or environmental concerns. By the end of 1987, there were 30,000 of these, and 'informals' would mushroom during 1988. Another sign that the opinions of ordinary people now mattered was that, from 1988, opinion polls began to be published. By 1989, the forbidden issues of the *ancien régime* Soviet Union – crime, drugs, sex, disasters, pollution, social deprivation, etc. –

were being discussed publicly, avidly, and often with a morbid obsessiveness. Whereas in the old days the news had been uniformly rosy, the picture had now become one of almost unrelieved gloom. This country which had prided itself on doing so well managed its affairs more incompetently, or so it seemed, than anywhere else on earth. And who or what was responsible for this roll-call of disaster? What but the Communist Party? The blame could not possibly be put at any other door.

Criticism was inevitable; Gorbachev's only hope was that, after the initial outburst, 'above' and 'below' would manage to get a constructive dialogue going. And he tried to offload some of the blame by going much further than Khrushchev in attacking Stalin and Stalinism. By spring 1988, the Left and Right Oppositions had been rehabilitated, Bukharin's widow had become a celebrity, and Bukharin himself had after a half-century of eclipse been put on a pedestal as a precursor of perestroika. For Khrushchev, the watershed year had been 1934; Gorbachev pushed it back in effect to 1929. That was as far as he could safely go without risking the suggestion that the real turn for the worse had come in October 1917, yet holding the line at 1929 became increasingly difficult. During 1987 many people had been touched to the quick by Tengiz Abuladze's film *Repentance*, released with Gorbachev's personal permission, which portrayed a totalitarian dictator with clear similarities to Stalin. *Repentance* had not only helped erode any remaining attachment to Stalin; for many people, it deepened doubts about the whole Soviet experience. Moreover, long-banished rivals were now coming back into the limelight. In 1988 the Orthodox Church had a lucky anniversary: Vladimir, prince of Kiev, had happened to be baptized in 988, and the Church's subsequent 1,000 years of service to the Russian people, dwarfing what the Communist Party had achieved or was likely to achieve, was marked by exuberant celebrations and the reopening of a number of churches. Another sign that official beliefs were crumbling came that year with the order that all history textbooks should be destroyed. It began to look as if the regime was rethinking principles which till now had been cast in iron. Maybe history would soon be freed from politics altogether and there would be no official line; but for the time being, all was doubt and confusion.

As the scope of freedom widened, criticism of the party cut deeper. From the winter of 1988–9, fierce assaults were launched upon perestroika's fundamental proposition – that the mistakes of the Stalin period were a tragic aberration and that the party had now restored the humane and democratic socialism of Lenin. Belief in the 1920s as the golden age of democratic socialism was a myth – that at least was the thrust of a series of articles by Alexander Tsipko.[16] The distinction between 'bad' Stalinism and 'good' Leninism was invalid since the first had been the inevitable outgrowth of the second. Gorbachev's revisionism, Tsipko suggested, had not gone far enough: it was not just the Stalin years but the whole Soviet experience that had to be rejected.

Tsipko's views were widely applauded. One consequence of the gathering anti-Soviet mood was a cult of the final years of tsarism and of the 'martyr', Nicholas II, whose thin, dignified face became a subject for street artists. The publication during 1989 of two, previously banned, classics added weight to the attack. Vasilii Grossman's *Forever Flowing* portrayed Lenin as the product of 1,000 years of Russian slavery, while the underlying theme of Alexander Solzhenitsyn's *The Gulag Archipelago* was that the horrors of Stalinism had grown directly out of the repressive system implanted in the country by Lenin. A sacred figure no longer, Lenin had now in fact become the butt of angry iconoclasts. The writer Vladimir Soloukhin went so far as to accuse him of genocide against the Russian people;[17] and during 1989 the blasphemous suggestion began to be aired that Lenin should be taken from the mausoleum and given an ordinary burial.

Those who wanted to bury Lenin really wanted to bury Leninism, one of Lenin's supporters rightly enough remarked. And these attacks on the father figure, the party and the whole Soviet experience, elicited a furious rejoinder. By no means all intellectuals took the liberal line; there was a strong phalanx of Russian nationalists, and some were vociferously neo-Stalinist. Curiously, the communists and their nationalist allies became known as the 'right' and liberals and social democrats as the 'left'. The labels were the wrong way round from the Western point of view, but in the Russian context they made perfect sense since the communists stood for traditional power and the defence of an establishment, whereas the liberals were challengers to the establishment and would-be innovators. Right and left might loathe one another, but they had one thing of course in common – both rejected the middle. For the right, Gorbachev was not a proper socialist, while for the left he was not a proper democrat, and both dismissed perestroika's claims to embody democratic socialism as utterly bogus. Moreover, these 'extreme' viewpoints were going into the ascendant. As blows rained upon it from either side, democratic socialism was clearly losing the argument.

Perestroika's opponents were united above all by what they opposed. But they did have something positive in common – the cause of Russia. The upsurge of Russian nationalism during the perestroika years was, on the face of it, most surprising. The Soviet Union was, after all, Russia writ large; or so at least it looked to non-Russians. Alone of the Soviet peoples, the Russians were not under the heel of anyone else. Yet they too had their grievances. For the Bolsheviks had, as we have seen, employed a determined internationalism in order to justify their empire, and as a result much that was distinctively Russian had been destroyed. A new 'Soviet' identity had been foisted on Russians, and the very words 'Russia' and 'Russian' had gone into eclipse. Moreover, in some respects the Russians *had* been discriminated against. The other republics had got a great deal of formal autonomy, whereas Russia, as the dominant element, was given very little. Before 1990, there was no separate Russian Communist Party; there was also no separate Russian KGB, Komsomol or Academy of Sciences. Like the other republics, Russia did have its own Supreme Soviet and Council of Ministers, but these were pale shadows and power lay elsewhere.

The non-Russianness of Soviet life had led during the Brezhnev years to a rumble of discontent, mainly from writers, who lamented the loss of church, village, and traditional way of life and feared that modernization might be putting Russian national identity at risk. From 1985, right-wing opponents of Gorbachev tried to mine this vein of discontent. Loss of church and rural tradition might mean little to urban Russians. Yet loss of empire, loss of respect in the eyes of the world, humiliation at the hands of the West – these would surely stir people. Gorbachev, they implied, had come off second-best in his dealings with the Americans: he had given away on-site inspections and disproportionate arms reductions without even getting the Americans to halt their Strategic Defense Initiative (SDI) in return. Even the lifting of the Iron Curtain was a far from unmixed blessing. Western billboards, trade names in Latin characters, McDonalds in Gorky Street, the dollar displacing the rouble, Western experts coming in droves to lecture Soviet people on how to run their own country – was this not Western imperialism in disguise? Many outside the democratic intelligentsia were likely to agree. Soviet people had, after all, had it drummed into them that their country had a mission to save mankind from the evils of the West. Now they were being asked to perform a somersault and act like pupils and suppliants towards a West that apparently had all the answers.

Conservative attempts to manipulate wounded national feelings were natural enough; more surprising was that many democrats too were now taking up the national cause. The democrats' nationalism was of course different from the right-wingers' – it stressed individual rights, was friendly towards small peoples, and saw the empire as the enemy of everyone's liberty, including the Russians'. Such nationalism grew logically out of democracy, yet an eye to the main chance was what turned many democrats into Russian nationalists at this particular moment. Within the Soviet parliament, democrats were a small minority, no more than a vocal pressure-group. But the Russian parliament, due to be elected in March 1990 without any of the 'filters' which had so discriminated against democrats in March 1989, offered them much better prospects. With the charismatic Boris Yeltsin at their head, they might well turn out to be the largest single faction. Given a major voice in the Russian parliament, they would inevitably tilt for *its* rights against those of the parliament in which they were powerless. Gorbachev stood for a democratized Soviet Union; they, adopting an attitude few could have predicted a couple of years earlier, would offer the electorate a fully democratic Russia.

7

The Congress of May–June 1989 had been a supreme achievement for Gorbachev, but it had also been a turning-point. He had set out to teach the nation democracy and his efforts had been given an immense boost by the Congress. No less than 87 per cent of Muscovites had watched the proceedings 'continuously' on television. Across the nation, industrial production dropped by an estimated 20 per cent while the Congress lasted. The political awareness of people changed more during those three weeks, Anatolii Sobchak, later mayor of Leningrad, claimed, than in the preceding fifty years. What stopped people leaving their television sets was the unprecedented openness and the fierce clash of opinions. There were no more forbidden areas, or so it seemed. The party leaders, the military, the KGB, the CPSU, even Lenin himself – all could be savaged.

Where would it end? Not with democracy but with anarchy and bloody repression, or so some friends of democracy feared. It was not only that the obstacles to democracy discussed above still remained to be overcome. New and unforeseen difficulties thrown up by the reform process itself were undermining the stable environment that seemed essential to democratization. Worsening living conditions, for most, were spreading a general sense of insecurity and beginning to breed nostalgia for the old days. Rebellion on the fringe was playing into the hands of conservatives who claimed that the whole reform project had been a mistake. And not only was the multinational state in danger; the decline in respect for the law and a marked rise in violent crime were threatening the fabric of everyday life. An insecure and crime-ridden society was a bad advertisement for democracy and an unpropitious context for it; moreover, in the short term conditions looked likely to get worse rather than better. And in the summer of 1989, certain of Gorbachev's supporters lost their nerve.[18] Reforming across a broad front was impossibly ambitious, they argued; the government should concentrate instead on what mattered most – economic change – and halt the democratization. The problem was that people would never voluntarily accept the sacrifices necessary for building a capitalist economy. They would have to be forced. And the advocates of an interim authoritarianism cited with approval Franco's Spain and, more especially, Pinochet's Chile as examples of regimes which by using strong-armed methods had laid the economic foundations for democracy.

Gorbachev did not in the event suspend parliament, but neither did he set the country on a direct course towards full democracy, and the result was a curiously betwixt-and-between political situation. Parliament continued to reflect a wide spectrum of opinions. Pluralism and competition were now all the vogue. The principles of contested elections, the separation of powers and the independence of the judiciary had been proclaimed and to some extent implemented. The party, it was agreed, was by no means infallible. Yet despite all this and his own commitment to pluralism, Gorbachev still defended the party's monopoly. This was not a matter of principle for him; in principle he had been against the monopoly since 1988. Monopolism, with its right to rule, to define and impose a philosophy of life, and to issue orders with the force of military commands in an arena cleared of alternative voices, was all too clearly incompatible with democratic socialism. The question for Gorbachev was not whether to abolish it but when; and with society unravelling and disruptive tendencies fast increasing, this was decidedly, in his judgement, not the right moment.

But the result of keeping the monopoly was a messy and illogical dual-power situation in which the ruling party vied with parliament. An old regime was dying but had not yet completed its death throes; a new regime was struggling to be born; and representatives of the two, reflecting different traditions and political philosophies, co-existed uneasily. The Politburo vetted parliament's agenda, and all ministerial appointments had to have its approval and that of the Central Committee. The candidates for office had, however, to be approved by parliament as well. Furthermore, they had to run the gauntlet of its permanent committees, which rejected no less than twelve of them. It was a situation replete with delicate ambiguities. When Gorbachev proposed Nikolai Ryzhkov as premier, he referred to 'the real position which the CPSU occupies in our society as a ruling party', but then quickly added that he hoped the choice would reflect as well 'the opinion of our people and of the deputies'.[19] The quandary of the democratizer not yet able or willing to free himself from the undemocratic source of his power deserved some sympathy, and the deputies chose not to embarrass him at this point. Were it to succeed, this would be democracy as Lenin had imagined it: the people and their representatives voluntarily accepting what an élite thought best for them. But the contradiction between a ruling party with monopolistic claims and a popularly elected (and popular) legislature which had almost instantly been recognized as the nation's parliament, was increasingly difficult to gloss over. The issue of ultimate authority was anyway being decided by the democratizing process; and come July, Nikolai Ryzhkov, a more reluctant reformer than Gorbachev, was noting with vexation how parliament was encroaching upon the Politburo's policy-making role. Short of a return to the *ancien régime*, only abolition of the monopoly could remove the glaring contradiction in the political system. Abolition was what public opinion demanded; it was the logical outcome of perestroika; and by the autumn of 1989, defenders of the monopoly on traditionalist grounds had been reduced to a beleaguered rump.

But what exactly would take over the supreme authority of party and Politburo? The obvious answer was parliament. On paper, the Soviet regime was already a parliamentary democracy, and parliament's nominal authority was now becoming something of a reality. Yet parliamentary democracy of the Western type was still a distant prospect. How could this deeply divided Congress and Supreme Soviet possibly provide a basis for the strong government necessary in a time of crisis? Some deputies had a Leninist scorn for 'talking shops' and did not even want to make parliamentary government work, while many of those who did were out-and-out supporters of a liberal-capitalist rather than a socialist path. Furthermore, the disciplined and cohesive political parties which elsewhere underpinned government were completely missing here. The idea of these raggle-taggle assemblies replacing party and Politburo as the ruling power and sustaining a strong government capable of overcoming the crisis was impossible to imagine.

Abolishing the monopoly might therefore result in chaos rather than an orderly transition to democracy. Yet by the end of 1989, any further stonewalling on the issue looked likely to jeopardize the onward movement of the whole reform process. One result of the change, if it were made, would be to reverse the order of importance of Gorbachev's two jobs, as General Secretary and Chairman, and to turn his chairman role into the crucial one. And an obvious solution to the looming problem of authority was to make still more of the chairmanship, converting it into a strong executive presidency. True, until recently Gorbachev had opposed a presidency on the ground that it would concentrate too much power in one person. But by now, not having a strong executive seemed a greater danger to democracy than having one. The very concentration of power made a presidency of the French type what the situation seemed to require; and armed with the idea that the party's role as a force for order and coherence might be taken over in effect by himself as President, Gorbachev came out firmly against the monopoly at the beginning of 1990.

The issue would be decided at the February meeting of the Central Committee, which remained a conservative bastion. For traditionalists, the monopoly was the holy of holies – give way on this and the universe as they knew it would crumble. Gorbachev might argue that the party could still keep its ruling position by winning elections, but that was little consolation to feudal lords who wanted to exercise power as of right. His hand was strengthened, however, by a visiting miners' delegation, whose message – that the party masses demanded change and were fed up with apparatchik control – was splashed across *Pravda*'s front page just before the meeting. Further support came from a 200,000-strong demonstration, the largest spontaneous demonstration in Moscow since revolutionary times, which swept with its anti-party shouts and banners up to the very walls of the Kremlin. Such 'support' was actually a mixed blessing for Gorbachev since many of the protesters wanted to destroy the party rather than revive it. Here was another sign that the forces unleashed since 1987 might in the end engulf him. But the massive show of strength did at least help him achieve his immediate objective. Pressured by the party rank and file on the one hand and the intelligentsia on the other, demoralized, out-argued, and alternatively browbeaten and cajoled by their leader, the guardians of party traditionalism complained bitterly and issued dire warnings but put up no real resistance; and when the resolution renouncing the party's monopoly came to a vote, ironically enough it was only Boris Yeltsin who voted against (on the ground that the reform did not by any means go far enough).

The change, creating a clear-cut divorce between party and nation, was formalized by the Congress of People's Deputies in March. Article 6 of the constitution was amended to put the CPSU on an equal footing with other political organizations, and the chairmanship was replaced by a presidency that would be elected by the people and be completely independent of the party. Gorbachev had, admittedly, decided to keep the party leadership as well, but his opening speech as President made it plain that the presidency came first: as President, he would not act on behalf of 'some separate layer and political tendency' (this description of the party must have burned the ears of true believers!) but instead be 'the representative of the whole nation'.[20] Crucially, as chief executive he would no longer be accountable to the Politburo. This body, which had run the country since Stalin, was now pushed almost casually on to the sidelines. Party affairs narrowly defined would henceforth be its only concern, and for general policy advice the President would look instead to a non-party body, the Presidential Council. But having freed himself from the party, the President took care not to be closely controlled by parliament instead, and on paper at least he would have more power than any Russian ruler since the tsar.

The changes of February/March 1990 were historic, and *Pravda*'s editor for one saw them as amounting to 'literally a revolution [*perevorot*], the completion – the utter completion – of the alteration of the political system'.[21] But that was somewhat overstating the case; in reality, only the first stage of remaking the political system had been completed. The pseudo-democratic façade of power had been stripped away. The party had suffered a bodyblow to its prestige as a result of being demoted. The potential for a pluralistic society and a multi-party political system undoubtedly now existed. Yet some at least of the conditions that had made absolutism possible still remained. The party had lost its right to rule but it had not yet been ousted from its ruling position, and it continued to rule through members steeped in the spirit of monopolism and intolerance who still ran the ministries, industry, the armed forces and the KGB. Yet the party could not rule effectively any more since few people now feared or respected it. The outcome of perestroika's unexpected success was, therefore, not so much a transfer of authority as a progressive breakdown of authority, which the newly installed President had somehow to halt.

Gorbachev's problem was to convert his nominal powers into real ones. His hope of a reinvigorated party pursuing socialism with wholehearted popular support now looked like a pipe-dream. The party was bitterly divided between left and right with a dwindling number of centrists, while the public was becoming disenchanted with both the party and socialism. There was no possibility whatever of this demoralized and wrangling body acting as an instrument of reform. Yet while the party could give him little help, it could still do him great harm: that was why he stayed as General

Secretary. Thus he covered his back; but by failing to break with the discredited CPSU, he threw away the chance of finding support elsewhere and of creating a new democratic basis for his authority. And the danger was that this presidency he had created would turn out to be neither fish nor fowl: neither a traditional fear- and charisma-based Russian executive, nor a new-style executive which people obeyed because they saw the ruler as their freely chosen representative. The President should of course have been elected by universal suffrage. Yet Gorbachev had decided to side-step the popular election laid down in the amended constitution: arguing that the crisis in the country made an electoral campaign inadvisable, he had got his election rushed through by Congress alone, and the deputies had voted him into office by a slightly begrudging 1,329 votes to 495. The democratizer had therefore not been elected democratically to anything. As President, he was simply the choice of Congress deputies, whose prestige would soon sink to rock-bottom; and he had not even braved the hustings to get into Congress, but had instead stepped into one of the places set aside for the CPSU.

The upshot was that Gorbachev had neither a traditional nor a democratic power-base. Many leading figures in the party were now bitterly opposed to him, yet he had failed to build up any new party or following as a counterweight to them. True, at the beginning of 1990 he still had a public approval rating of about 60 per cent. The curve of his popularity was, however, distinctly downwards. Come May Day 1990, he would be driven from the reviewing stand by a hail of abuse; that same month, Boris Yeltsin would overtake him as the country's most popular politician. And plunging popularity was probably the main reason why he had avoided a general election for the presidency. Yet had he been bold enough to go for such an election in March he would almost certainly have won it, even if not by very much. Before long, he would regret having missed the chance, which would never come again, of arming himself with a popular mandate.

On the face of it, Mikhail Gorbachev had never cut a more impressive figure than when he took the oath as President. His achievement within five years had been remarkable: his quiet and subtle revolution from within had dismantled an oligarchic dictatorship which in March 1985 had looked unassailable. The achievement had, however, been more negative than positive; a political and economic system had been taken to pieces but not replaced, and the outcome was a crisis of authority which the presidency was incapable of resolving. Gorbachev had counted on the reform coalition which had gathered around him in the early years proving to be the core of a reinvigorated party. Through this party he would dominate Soviet politics from an expanding centre, winning the support of the great majority for moderate and rational policies. Now, however, the reform coalition was in tatters, consensus had been shattered, and the very idea of peaceful qualitative change through existing structures had come to seem a mirage. His revolution from within had left in its wake a bitterly divided society; a wounded and feuding party; a more or less destroyed ideology; a President whose strategy had collapsed with the collapse of the political centre; a vociferous democratic opposition; and conservatives entrenched in the structures of authority who were determined to fight back for what they had lost. Gorbachev and his fellow reformers had set out to rehabilitate the party and socialism, to restore to Soviet politics the possibilities and the squandered socialist potential of the 1920s; but it began to look as if their reforms had triggered the very system crisis they had wanted to avert.

Notes

1 Mikhail Gorbachev, *Perestroika: New Thinking for Our Country and the World* (London, 1987), p. 50.
2 *Ibid.*, p. 57.
3 *Ibid.*, p. 79.
4 *The Guardian*, 20 June 1990.
5 Zdenek Mlynar, 'Il mio compagno di studi Mikhail Gorbaciov', *L'Unità* (Rome), 9 April 1985.
6 Anders Aslund, *Gorbachev's Struggle for Economic Reform: The Soviet Reform Process 1985–88* (London, 1989), p. 15.
7 *Pravda*, 12 February 1990, p. 1.
8 Tatyana Zaslavskaya, *The Second Socialist Revolution: An Alternative Soviet Strategy* (London, 1990), p. xi.
9 M. S. Gorbachev, *Izbrannye rechi i stati* (6 vols, Moscow 1987–9), vol. IV, p. 37.
10 Notably Edward L. Keenan in 'Muscovite Political Folkways', *Russian Review*, 45, no. 2 (1986), pp. 115–82.
11 Gorbachev, *Perestroika*, p. 82.
12 *Pravda*, 28 January 1987, p. 3.
13 *Pravda*, 29 June 1988, p. 4.
14 *Ibid.*, p. 5.
15 Or so at least someone claimed in a letter to Gorbachev: see his *Perestroika*, p. 70.
16 A. S. Tsipko, 'Istoki stalinizma', *Nauka i zhizn*, 11 (1988), pp. 45–55; 12 (1988), pp. 40–8; 1 (1989), pp. 46–56; 2 (1989), pp. 53–61.
17 Vladimir Soloukhin, *Chitaya Lenina* (Frankfurt am Main, 1989), pp. 42–3; subsequently given Soviet publication in *Rodina*, October 1989.
18 See I. Klyamkin and A. Migranyan, 'Nuzhna "zheleznaya ruka"?', *Literaturnaya gazeta*, 16 August 1989, p. 10.
19 *Pravda*, 8 June 1989, p. 1.
20 *Pravda*, 16 March 1990, p. 2.
21 *Pravda*, 17 March 1990, p. 3.

|11|

Disintegration, 1990–1991

1

The changes of February/March 1990 came as a savage blow to the ruling class, whose members were now threatened with dispossession. The threat galvanized them; and like people under a suspended sentence of execution, they would fight desperately to overturn the sentence. While the ruling class felt endangered by perestroika's radical implications, those who saw themselves as democrats were by contrast becoming seriously alarmed by its half-heartedness. In their eyes, the institutional changes made so far only touched the surface: there could be no secure democracy without economic privatization and the creation of a substantial property-owning class, including a land-owning peasantry. Moreover, unless non-Russians were allowed real self-determination, Russians themselves might soon lose the precarious liberties they had gained.

The key figure in the battle between conservatives and democrats was of course Gorbachev. The enigmatic and increasingly isolated President now resembled someone clinging to a narrow strip of land with the sea advancing on either side of him. There was no democratic-socialist solution to the economic problem. There was also no democratic-socialist solution to the nationalities problem. There were only traditionalist solutions and liberal solutions, and these were poles apart and bound to be deeply divisive. Since the centrist position had very little credibility left, more and more of perestroika's original supporters deserted it. Gorbachev, too, would sooner or later have to jump to left or right.

Neither side liked or trusted him, and he liked neither side. The right saw him as a betrayer, a shifty westernized Machiavel, while the left had been offended by his unwillingness to break decisively with the old order and his party-boss behaviour. Yet both needed him and both had hopes of him. His commitment to socialism and, still more, his determined defence of the union made him potentially usable by the right, while his democratism, humanity and reasonableness gave him common ground with the left. He in turn had a strong antipathy to Yeltsin, but little rapport with Ligachev and even less with the new breed of younger rightists from the military. He was repelled by the capitalist inclinations of many democrats; yet allying with the right might mean renouncing all he had fought for and taking the country back to the cul-de-sac of the early 1980s.

What swung Gorbachev to the left was clear evidence that it was the left which had popular support. By the summer of 1990, he even seemed ready to accept a radical economic policy. The right fought back; but its advance was halted at the twenty-eighth Party Congress, at which Ligachev threw down a challenge to the reformers and was decisively beaten off. Constitutional methods would get the right nowhere. Its members – high-ranking bureaucrats, managers, army and KGB officers – were, after all, an inevitable minority. But if they did not have numbers they had power, especially military power, and in October they used it to blackmail Gorbachev into submission. For the next six months he was in the conservative camp, and during this period all his liberal-minded friends and advisers were sacked or left him. By giving in, he had at least survived in office; he may also have persuaded himself that the right knew best how to save the Union, though he can hardly have thought that after an attempt to coerce the Balts had been made and badly botched in January 1991.

By April 1991, the pressure of public opinion had got the better of his fear of the right, and now he swung back towards the left. The futility of his own centrist strategy was confirmed by the Russian presidential elections in June, when Yeltsin swept to victory and the centrist candidate was crushed. Gorbachev could at least console himself that he had moved, belatedly, in the direction the electorate wanted. But for the right , the implications of the vote were disastrous. After seventy-four years, the Russians had said a resounding 'no' to communism. Gorbachev could perhaps live with the consequences of that; the right could not.

The outcome was the attempted coup of 19–21 August, for which the Baltic violence had already provided a dress rehearsal. The conservatives had tried constitutional methods and failed. They had tried blackmail, and the President had eventually called their bluff. In August 1991 they fell back on the method they understood best – armed force – though like their Bolshevik predecessors they hid it behind constitutional pretences. Gorbachev was indisposed and incapable of exercising his functions, they claimed, and power had passed instead to the Vice-President and a so-called Emergency Committee. The conservatives' attempt could have succeeded, at least in the short term, but they were defeated by the determined resistance of Yeltsin and a relatively small number of democrats, and also by their own incompetence and irresolution. The coup turned out in fact to be a death spasm, a ghostly caricature of the virile and self-confident Bolshevism of 1917: but the shock it created was enough to trigger real revolution.

The August 1991 revolution began as the defence of a reformist ruler against his enemies. Its effect, however, was to change the power balance decisively and to leave Gorbachev at the mercy of those who had saved him. The Soviet Union had some months more to live, but by the end of August the Soviet era was clearly on the way out. For the power of the Soviet 'centre' had been the power of the party-state apparatus, the military and the KGB. But after this revolt, the armed forces command was purged of reactionaries and the KGB was restructured. As for the CPSU, that had come to the end of the road: Gorbachev resigned as General Secretary, its activities were suspended, and in November it was abolished on Russian territory altogether. Deprived of CPSU oxygen, Soviet institutions rapidly withered and their Russian counterparts replaced or marginalized them.

For Gorbachev, the August revolution was an unmitigated disaster: it destroyed the party, threw a deep shadow over socialism, left him humiliatingly dependent upon Yeltsin, and accelerated the disintegration of the Union. The winners were of course the democrats and the man who appeared to be their leader, Boris Yeltsin. They were far from numerous, but their defeat of the coup had made them heroes and for the moment at least embodiments of the national will. They had the advantage, in addition, that with authoritarian solutions discredited and Gorbachev's centrism looking bankrupt, there was no obvious alternative to the ideas and attitudes of the West. Only political and economic individualism, in other words liberal democracy and capitalism, could rescue the country from its miseries.

Yet the democrats' task was appallingly difficult. Unlike in the Baltic states, Poland and Czechoslovakia, there was no nation-wide democratic movement to back them. And like the democratic politicians in Germany after the First World War, they would be undermined by a ruling class which had changed its spots rather than its basic outlook. What they needed was a rapid upsurge of support in the wake of the coup, but despite the euphoric scenes in Moscow this never came. Their following was still relatively small, and it would take successful government to build a larger one. But to govern successfully they would have to agree on a programme, work together effectively, and put through policies that did something for living standards. None of this happened. And the one policy on which most democrats and Yeltsin did agree, economic 'shock therapy', turned opinion against them. It was a 'catch 22' situation. In order to build a democratic and prosperous Russia, they had to demolish the old economic system – yet their policies looked likely to destroy popular good will long before any benefits for the majority had appeared. When Ukraine voted in a referendum for independence, it became clear that attempts to maintain a Soviet state without the CPSU and without socialism were doomed. The Bolsheviks had given the Russian empire a lengthy reprieve, but time had now run out for it. The Soviet Union was finished; and the man who had tried to save the Soviet experiment was going down to defeat.

2

On becoming President, Gorbachev had faced danger from both sides, but the greater threat had seemed to come from the left, which had one invaluable asset – a leader whose popular appeal was about to outstrip his own. Yeltsin and Gorbachev had similar backgrounds: both were peasant boys from distant provinces, both were born in 1931, both had risen through the party apparatus to become first secretaries of their provinces. In character and attitudes, however, they could hardly have been more different. Whereas Gorbachev had left his peasant background far behind and become an urban sophisticate, Yeltsin had stayed close to his peasant origins. He was a rough diamond, moody, impetuous and wildly unpredictable; but while he could be harsh and bullying, he had a warmth, passion and way of engaging ordinary people's emotions that had won him an enormous following. It was a contrast between a supremely rational politician, a virtuoso whose rise to the top had scarcely been marred by a single piece of clumsy footwork, and an emotional and accident-prone gambler who had a streak in him of the rebel against authority and yet had been a tough if popular boss of his province: between a courteous liberal and westernizer and a democrat with something of the roughness and Russianness of the Bolsheviks.

The clash was made worse by personal bitterness. After first treating Yeltsin as an ally, Gorbachev had turned against him and had him thrown out of the leadership in November 1987. Yeltsin neither forgot nor forgave and was determined to have his revenge. His comeback was partly a matter of luck in that it happened to coincide with a rising clamour for justice and democracy. The fact that a campaign against privilege in high places had led to his downfall made this defiant populist an obvious symbol for the discontented. Fighting against the party machine, he had all the appeal of a David struggling against Goliath, and his victory in the March 1989 elections gave him the charisma of a David triumphant.

Intellectuals, however, remained wary of him since he had few obvious democratic credentials. Their natural patron was the civilized, fastidious and eminently rational Gorbachev. Yet in parliament, during the second half of 1989, a partnership nevertheless developed between them and Yeltsin. The brute fact was that they could not do without him. His very experience as an apparatchik was useful since most of them were political virgins. But most important of all, he gave them a potential following among the masses. Without Yeltsin, this largely middle-class democratic opposition looked likely to be hoist with its own democratic petard. With him, the democrats might win a popular majority.

The elections in March 1990 to the Russian Congress of People's Deputies gave the left its opportunity; and in the event candidates associated with 'Democratic Russia', an umbrella organization dedicated to the democrats' cause, won some 350 out of the 1,026 seats. The right did badly, but apparatus candidates, who would probably be loyal to Gorbachev, took about half of the seats. Though that left the democrats well short of a majority, they did at least have a chance of picking up enough support to control the assembly. Moreover, they had done spectacularly well in Moscow and Leningrad. Both cities had returned a majority of democratic deputies, and in simultaneous elections to local councils the democrats had come out on top. Two leading democrats, Gavriil Popov and Anatolii Sobchak, would from now on head democratic administrations in Moscow and Leningrad respectively. The democrats' triumph in the capitals, which had tended always to set the pattern, was a cheering augury of what with luck might soon happen in the rest of the country

The democrats stood for three things: first, naturally enough, complete democratization; second, the introduction of a proper market economy; third, Russian 'sovereignty'. The last did not necessarily imply independence, but it did imply much greater freedom from the centre, and of the three it was much the most threatening for Gorbachev. Democracy did not yet have much general appeal, while marketization was likely to become a positive liability for the democrats. But 'Russian sovereignty' had irresistible patriotic overtones, and if its advocates took control of the Russian Congress they might use it very effectively against him. That was why he had to stop Yeltsin winning the crucial position of Chairman of the Russian Supreme Soviet. But here Gorbachev suffered a serious setback. His attempts to brand Yeltsin as a separatist and an opponent of socialism alienated more deputies than it won over, and on 29 May 1990 Yeltsin was elected Chairman by 531 votes to the 467 for Gorbachev's candidate, Alexander Vlasov. A fortnight later, the Russian Congress issued a Declaration of State Sovereignty with the deputies' almost unanimous approval. This stopped short of announcing Russia's secession from the Union, but it did suggest a very different relationship between Russia and the central power from the one which had existed throughout the Soviet period. From now on, if the Declaration were complied with, Russian laws and the Russian constitution would have precedence over their all-Union equivalents.

By taking control of the Russian parliament and wrapping himself in a nationalist mantle, Yeltsin dealt Gorbachev a serious blow; but his exploits wounded the right as well and spurred its members to want to outdo him. Russian nationalism ought after all to have been their cause, and here was a democrat and a westernizer hijacking it and passing himself off as Russia's champion. Right-wing nationalism crystallized in the demand that Russia should be given its own party organization. Gorbachev was unable to fend the demand off, and the Communist Party of Russia was founded in the Kremlin in June 1990. Here, too, his candidate went down to defeat, and the first secretaryship of the new party was captured, by 1,396 votes to 1,066, by a forthright conservative, Ivan Polozkov. As a result, Gorbachev found himself being squeezed from either size by new organizations of immense potential influence, each of which had held its founding congress to great fanfares and had been captured by an opponent of his centrist strategy.

Of the two challenges, the greater long-term threat came from the democrats, whose congress attracted far more media attention and public sympathy. It was the communists, however, who presented the more immediate threat since their anti-Gorbachev triumph had taken place in the run-up to the twenty-eighth Party Congress. After yielding position after position, the party barons had now taken a stand and were politicking effectively against him. With them on the offensive, Gorbachev seemed in danger of losing control of the party and being ousted as leader, and the twenty-eighth Congress opened in July with counter-revolution in the air. Ligachev led the onslaught with a direct attack on the leadership and its policies and, by implication, on Gorbachev himself. Most of the delegates all too obviously shared his nostalgia for the party's traditions and its lost absolutism. Yet when it came to a vote for the new position of Deputy General Secretary, Ligachev went down to a crushing defeat – by 3,109 votes to 776 – which ended his career as the standard-bearer of the right. Most delegates had accepted, however reluctantly, that they had no alternative to the present leadership and its policies. For Gorbachev, who had offered no concessions, it was another triumph against the odds and it confirmed the impression of him as a political Houdini. His success was, however, seriously clouded just before the end when Yeltsin ostentatiously walked out of the party.

The fact was that Yeltsin could now perfectly well do without the CPSU. His popularity was soaring – by October 1990 he would be the choice of 60 per cent, while Gorbachev's support would have slumped to a mere 21 per cent. Just as the right, gritting its teeth, accepted its dependence on Gorbachev, so he in turn needed Yeltsin, and in the wake of the party congress the two reached an understanding based on a common economic approach. Abandoning the 'socialist market', Gorbachev now spoke out in favour of private enterprise as the motor of economic growth and argued that only the market and private property could underpin democracy. And he appeared to give his backing to a radical new economic programme for a 500-day transition to a market economy. This programme, known after its chief architect as the Shatalin Plan, had strong support from Yeltsin and looked like being the kernel of a left–centre coalition, which, if opinion polls were to be believed, would have had widespread public endorsement.

But for the conservatives, such a coalition was inadmissible; and in October Gorbachev buckled to their demands and suddenly veered away from the new economic programme. The pressure on him had come not only from party traditionalists but from younger men uninhibited by party discipline or customary deference towards the leader, most of them army officers and many from the non-Russian republics. As army men and *pieds-noirs*, they had a triple grievance against Gorbachev. Not only had he brought ruin and humiliation upon the army and given away the outer empire. Now, worst of all, he was in danger of losing the inner empire as well and thus leaving twenty-five million Russians stranded in 'foreign' countries. 'Defence of the Union' was the battle-cry of these hawks, who had formed a vociferous parliamentary grouping called 'Soyuz' ('Union'). And its implications for the Union was what had made the Shatalin Plan anathema to them. For the Plan had accepted the republics' claim to economic sovereignty and given them the right to decide taxes, prices and methods of privatization. The centre's rights would simply be those that the republics delegated to it: which of course made the republics the masters and the central government their dependant. Not surprisingly, Soyuz denounced 'economic separatism' and insisted that in any rejigged relationship between the centre and the republics, ultimate power had to remain with the centre.

On 16 November Colonel Viktor Alksnis, the russified Latvian who led Soyuz, issued a public challenge to the President: unless within thirty days he restored order, a motion of no confidence in him would be put to the Supreme Soviet. It was no empty threat since Soyuz's followers, together with like-minded communists, now had a majority in the Supreme Soviet. And since the constitutional threat was backed by an implied military one, Gorbachev had to take it seriously. He had already gone over to a more cautious economic programme. He went some way towards meeting the demand for a dictatorship by concentrating still more power in the presidency at the expense of parliament and the government. The liberal interior minister, Vadim Bakatin, was replaced by the hardline Boris Pugo. TV and radio were put under a conservative watchdog, Leonid Kravchenko, while *Pravda* began speaking with the tones of the pre-perestroika era. By the end of 1990, all the remaining liberals had gone from Gorbachev's entourage, including his friend Alexander Yakovlev, who had been the chief theorist of the reforms; and apart from Eduard Shevardnadze, who resigned as foreign minister with a bitter tirade in which he predicted imminent dictatorship, most had gone quietly.

But on the vital question of defence of the Union, Gorbachev had failed to buy off the conservatives. A new Union treaty that satisfied the republics yet preserved central domination had been impossible to achieve. Russia, Ukraine and Belorussia demanded that they, rather than the centre, should decide what rights they should have under the new structure, while the Baltic states and Georgia refused to contemplate any new treaty. A particularly sore point for the right was Lithuania, the frontrunner in the secessionist movement, which had actually declared itself independent in March and refused despite intense pressure to back down since.

On 13 January 1991, army and KGB units stormed the Vilnius TV and radio centre, killing fourteen and wounding several hundred people, while loudspeakers announced that power had passed to a so-called Committee of National Salvation. The attempt to solve the Lithuanian problem by violence failed ignominiously, however. Thousands rallied to the defence of the Lithuanian government, which remained safe in a heavily barricaded parliament building, and the Salvation Committee never emerged from the shadows. Similar action in Riga resulted in a similar fiasco. Soon Alksnis was denouncing Gorbachev for having lost his nerve and failed to give the action necessary support. The thuggery by his colleagues had in fact put Gorbachev in an impossible position. He had not wanted or instigated it, yet he was neither able to punish those responsible nor to endorse their action in the ringing tones they would have wanted. His weak-kneed reaction and failure to dissociate himself from the violence made him look like an accomplice or at least a hostage of the right, and it destroyed his last remaining shreds of credibility with democrats. After this, no one could believe in the humane, middle-of-the-road socialism he had once preached so persuasively. You either had to be left or right; and the regime, and Gorbachev seemingly with it, had swung decisively to the right.

Protesting Russian democrats saw clearly that the threat to the Balts' freedom was a threat to their freedom as well. No one sensed this more acutely than Boris Yeltsin. For him, the Vilnius brutality marked the onset of nationwide counter-revolution, and as soon as the news broke he made a dash to the Estonian capital of Tallinn, where he declared Russia's solidarity with the people of the Baltic states and urged Russian soldiers to refuse to repress them.

'I am moving to the right', Gorbachev had told him only the day before, 'because society is moving to the right.' 'You are wrong, Mikhail Sergeievich', Yeltsin replied, 'society is moving to the left, towards democracy.'[1] Who was correct? Large-scale defections from the party, which lost three million members during 1990 alone, seemed to bear out Yeltsin's claim. So, too, did his own soaring popularity. After Vilnius, the conservative media lambasted him as a traitor; but attempts to counter his popularity by rekindling the cult of Lenin, now portrayed by *Pravda* as an almost Christ-like figure, merely showed how desperate the reactionaries were becoming.[2] In March, Gorbachev scored something of a public relations success with a referendum in which 76 per cent of voters said 'yes' to the idea of a renewed Union. Yeltsin, however, managed to blight even this success by tacking on to the referendum the question of whether people wanted a directly elected Russian presidency. Seventy per cent of Russian voters replied that they did. Yeltsin would almost certainly win any Russian presidential contest, and as a President who, unlike Gorbachev, had been popularly elected, he would be more formidable still.

By the end of March 1991, it had come to outright confrontation between the two sides. The right threatened a vote of no confidence in Yeltsin in the forthcoming Russian Congress. Yeltsin replied by calling his supporters to demonstrate in Moscow on the day Congress opened, 28 March, despite a ban on demonstrations in central Moscow which 50,000 troops were on standby to uphold. The resulting showdown was won by the left. A crowd of 100,000 marched on Yeltsin's behalf, calling for Gorbachev's resignation; and to the right's dismay, Gorbachev flinched from using the troops against them. Meanwhile, in the Congress 179 communists, led by Colonel Alexander Rutskoy, had gone over to Yeltsin and so made his position there impregnable.

After the March events, there could be no doubt which side public opinion favoured. There were other reasons also to make Gorbachev rethink. The economy was going from bad to worse: inflation was becoming explosive, unemployment was rising, and production was in sharp decline. In March, the miners in Siberia and Ukraine went on strike again, this time not only in protest against conditions: they were demanding that Gorbachev should go. Their hero now was Yeltsin, and only he had any chance of persuading them back to work. But it was not only the miners who were dealing devastating blows to the economy: so too were Russia and the other defiant republics. Of twenty-three million roubles due to have been paid by republics to the Union budget during the first three months of the year, a mere seven million had been received by the end of March. The government as a result teetered on the brink of financial catastrophe.

Gorbachev's cohabitation with the conservatives had in fact become self-defeating. If the Union and his own career were to be saved, he had to switch over to the republican leaders and the democrats. The new orientation began on 23 April 1991 at Novo-Ogarevo, near Moscow, where he and the leaders of nine republics agreed to draw up a new Union treaty. The details had yet to be worked out, but the '9+1' agreement, as it became known, would evidently give substantial powers to the republics and membership of the revised Union would be voluntary. With this agreement, Gorbachev put the aberration of the winter behind him and returned to the idea of a left–centre coalition, which had come so close to fruition in the summer. The conservatives, he seemed to accept, were nothing but a small, if formidably powerful, interest group. Mired in the past, they had no solutions to the country's problems other than force and fraud. For the architect of perestroika, they were completely unsuitable partners. Yet he remained committed to the Union and to socialism; and saving them from his new allies would be far from easy.

3

The Russian presidential election of 12 June 1991 turned out to be a disaster for all shades of opinion in the party except its most radical fringe. Yeltsin swept to victory with 57 per cent of the vote, overwhelming the representative of moderate conservatism, Nikolai Ryzhkov, who got a mere 17 per cent. The greatest loser was, however, the reformist candidate,

Vadim Bakatin. Had perestroika been going according to plan, the candidate representing the new democratic socialism should have ridden to an easy victory. In fact, Bakatin got a humiliating 3.5 per cent of the vote and came last among the six candidates, trailing even the neo-fascist Zhirinovsky and the Stalinist Makashov. The freest election in Russia since 1917, this had in effect been a referendum on socialism and the CPSU in their old and new versions, and in it the party's standard-bearers had been crushed by a renegade from the party who was promising to build a liberal-democratic Russia on the ruins of the Soviet experiment. For Gorbachev, the outcome could hardly have been worse. He had held up the 1989 elections as a victory for perestroika and the party, and it was perhaps just possible to put such a gloss on the 1990 elections. But in this election the Russians had unquestionably rejected the party and its socialism, and in doing so they had cast the gravest doubt on one of perestroika's underlying assumptions.

Yeltsin moved quickly to capitalize on his victory. On 10 July he was solemnly installed as first President of Russia, with Gorbachev as a politely applauding bystander, in a ceremony whose rituals made the point that after seven decades under Soviet rule, Russia had been reborn. The inhabitants of Russia – and he made it clear that he included all, not merely the 80 per cent of ethnic Russians – would from now on owe their prime loyalty to him as their elected leader; their allegiance to the unelected Soviet leader would be very much a secondary matter. Ten days later, Yeltsin banned political parties from the workplace and thus outlawed the Communist Party cells found in every factory and institution.

Deteriorating living standards continued to erode Gorbachev's already weak negotiating position. Strikes, go-slows and general dislocation were causing a drastic fall in production. The budget deficit was becoming enormous. Inflation, now at 2 or 3 per cent a week, was reaching Latin American levels, thus giving some support to claims that the country had been reduced to a banana republic. The economy seemed in fact to be in free fall, and Gorbachev's popularity plummeted with it. In late July, with his approval rating at 'less than zero', he gave way on the most crucial issue in the negotiations for a new Union treaty – taxation. How much the republics should pay in dues and taxes would be decided by the republics themselves. There would still be a considerable role for the Union government: it would control the armed forces, conduct foreign policy, manage the central budget, and so on. But there was no disguising the fact that the republics, and in particular Russia, would from now on be the senior partner.

Even before this concession, conservatives had been close to desperation. It was bad enough that the new state would be called the Union of Soviet *Sovereign* Republics and thus have no commitment to socialism (which, to make matters worse, was being reinterpreted in the party's new draft programme as if liberty were its first principle). But, more alarming still, membership of the new Union would be genuinely voluntary. Five members of the present Union – the Baltic republics, Georgia and Moldavia – were certain not to join; and since serious doubt had now arisen about Ukraine, the prospect loomed of a Union that embraced little more than Russia and the republics of Central Asia. A first attempt to stop what, for the conservatives, was a quickening slide towards disaster came in June, when Valentin Pavlov, who in January had replaced Ryzhkov as prime minister, made a clumsy attempt to take over some of Gorbachev's powers. In the event Gorbachev fended off the would-be usurper, but did not dismiss or even rebuke him. A month later, leading conservatives, including two generals and three leaders of the future coup, made use of the dyed-in-the-wool *Sovetskaya Rossiya* to publish 'A Word to the People', which fulminated in high-flown language against the disastrous consequences of perestroika. 'Russia, unique and beloved. She calls for your help!' was their final fusillade.[3] But what kind of 'help' were they getting at? It did not need much reading between the lines to see that what they wanted was armed help, yet no charges were brought against them.

The final spur to action came on 2 August, when Gorbachev announced that the new Union treaty would be signed on the 20th. That gave the ringleaders a deadline – they had to act before 20 August. In a sense, they were overreacting. The USSR cabinet of ministers very shortly criticized the treaty for going too far and Yeltsin criticized it for not going far enough, and the chances that it would have provided the basis for a stable decentralized state were therefore negligible. To Soviet grandees who were already bitterly angry about what they saw as Gorbachev's multiple acts of treachery, the treaty nevertheless seemed like a Rubicon – once crossed, their power and privileges, inseparable from the centre's domination of the Union, would be lost irretrievably.

The attempted coup of 19–21 August 1991 should have come as no surprise. The Communist Party had lived by violence and could be expected to die violently. On the eve of the coup, Alexander Yakovlev, who knew his erstwhile colleagues well enough, predicted it. And the *putsch* in the Baltics had given a warning of what would happen sooner or later in the centre. It was not, however, the hawkish colonels of Soyuz who led the way but rather Gorbachev's closest colleagues. The list of the chief conspirators reads like a roll-call of the Soviet establishment: Vladimir Kryuchkov, head of the KGB and mastermind of the conspiracy; Dimitrii Yazov, the defence minister; prime minister Valentin Pavlov; Genadii Yanaev, an undistinguished figure from the official trade union movement whom Gorbachev had imposed in December 1990 on a reluctant Congress as Vice-President, insisting that he needed to have someone beside him whom he could trust; minister of the interior, Boris Pugo; Oleg Baklanov, a key figure in the military-industrial complex; Valerii Boldin, Gorbachev's own chief of staff and factotum. Standing slightly apart but still privy to the conspiracy was Anatolii Lukyanov, Chairman of the Supreme Soviet and a friend of Gorbachev's of forty years' standing.

Gorbachev had trusted them all and had picked most of them. These men were at the very apex of power and collectively represented all its interlocking structures. They did not need to seize power since, subject only to Gorbachev's supreme control, they already had it. Their take-over would be quite different from the Pinochet-type *pronunciamento* that the Soyuz colonels might have tried. Kryuchkov and his junta did not have to resort to anything so demeaning and so risky. They would simply persuade or bully Gorbachev into declaring a state of emergency under powers granted him when he became President. The Supreme Soviet, which faced extinction if the treaty went through, would certainly endorse their action. They would then restore order and sanity in the country with perfect constitutional propriety, using Gorbachev as their instrument.

But here the conspirators made their first mistake. When their emissaries reached Gorbachev at his Crimean holiday villa on 18 August, he proved truculently unco-operative: he would neither declare a state of emergency nor hand over power to his deputy, Yanaev. The people, he lectured the intruders, 'are no longer prepared to put up with your dictatorship or with the loss of everything we have gained in recent years'.[4] They were adventurers and criminals, and the affair would end with civil war and bloodshed. Gorbachev's unexpected obstinacy forced the conspirators back on to the pretence that he was physically unfit, which allowed Yanaev to take over as acting President under Article 127-7 of the constitution. However, they made a rotten job of the deception. When Yanaev announced at a press conference that Gorbachev was 'very tired after all his years in power', no one believed him. There was no supporting medical evidence; and the new rulers' statements had already undermined the medical pretext by making it clear that it was the President's policies, rather than his health, which they regarded as defective. If anyone needed a doctor, it was Yanaev, whose badly shaking hands were caught by the cameras. Yet it is easy to see why the conspirators stuck to their story. These men were insiders, not rebels outside the walls. Their regime had always exercised power behind a façade of constitutional make-believe. Admitting that they were staging a coup would have given the lie to all they stood for. They needed their fib. But they were to pay a high price for it.

Although the new regime was announced at 6 a.m. on 19 August, no tanks moved towards the centre of Moscow until three hours later, and then they moved tentatively, stopping at traffic lights. Internal and external communications were not cut, which allowed the Russian government to transmit orders to the provinces and reporters to tell the world what was happening. Most fatal of all for the plotters, they did not strike ruthlessly at their enemies. They had a list of seventy leading democrats to be arrested at the outset. Tribunals, arrest orders, and concentration camps had been made ready. But in accordance with constitutional propriety, they could not begin the crack-down until the state of emergency had been declared; mass repression, moreover, would have to wait until the Supreme Soviet, not due to meet for a week, had confirmed the emergency. And by the time a KGB arrest squad had reached the dacha of enemy number one, Boris Yeltsin, he and other leading democrats had escaped. By carrying out a coup while trying to pretend that they were doing nothing of the sort, the conspirators finished up with the worst of all worlds.

During the emergency, people were informed, the country would be administered by an Emergency Committee of eight men, among whom were Yanaev, Kryuchkov and Yazov. Political meetings, strikes and demonstrations were forbidden. Newspapers that were likely to resist were suspended, while conservative or pliable ones published the Committee's 'Appeal to the People'. This tugged at much the same emotional chords as the previous month's 'Word'. The country had become ungovernable and was in mortal danger. Extremists were aiming to seize power and break up the Soviet Union. The slide towards a market economy was causing a sharp drop in living standards. A wave of criminality threatened to overwhelm law and order. The Soviet state and its citizens were no longer respected abroad. Avoiding anything Marxist, the authors of the 'Appeal' made a pitch at the traditional desire for security and the traditional dislike of foreigners and native 'adventurers'; and their message was that they would soon restore order, decent living conditions and a country people could be proud of. Moreover, they showed that they were not just men of words by providing a foretaste of the good things to come: articles that had all but disappeared from Moscow shops – coffee, cheese, poultry, and sausage, for instance – suddenly reappeared on the shelves.

Understandably, the conspirators did not expect much resistance. They could count on habitual passivity; and the disillusionment with perestroika and the fierce hostility towards Gorbachev surely favoured them. They were wrong, however, in assuming that people who were disenchanted with perestroika necessarily wanted to go back to the old order. This ignored the immense popularity of Boris Yeltsin, whose response to the failure of perestroika had not been to reject reform but instead to want to go forward rapidly to a market economy and a fully democratized society. And their failure to eliminate Yeltsin at the outset proved to be decisive.

The Russian President had made it to the Russian parliament building, the so-called White House, on the bank of the Moscow river a mile or so from the Kremlin. From there he denounced the coup, declared the Emergency Committee's decisions invalid, and ordered that all Soviet executive bodies were henceforth to obey *him*. He appealed to soldiers not to use their weapons against the people and to civilians to go on strike. 'You can build a throne out of bayonets,' he told the soldiers, 'but you cannot sit on it for long.'[5] And he struck a magnificent pose when he mounted a tank – the picture soon flashed around the world – and, the very spirit of democratic defiance, urged local soviets and ordinary citizens not to yield to the junta.

The coup might well have succeeded, Gorbachev would reflect, a couple of years earlier. But now there was a popularly elected Russian parliament to focus the resistance; there was also a national hero to lead it. This was Yeltsin's finest hour: a born fighter, he unerringly made the right decisions in what must at first have seemed an almost hopeless struggle. And his masterstroke, perhaps influenced by the Lithuanians' successful defiance in January, was the decision to make his stand in the parliament building. Any attack on himself and the deputies and supporters who rapidly gathered around him therefore became an attack on parliament. But not only had Yeltsin made himself the symbol of a beleaguered democracy; worse still for the junta, he had become a symbol of Russia. For what was under siege was a Russian institution which had proclaimed the sovereignty of Russia and was headed by someone who had been chosen by a clear majority of Russian voters. '*Rossiya! Rossiya!*' – 'Russia! Russia!' – chanted the White House's defenders. By making his stand in the Russian parliament, Yeltsin had in fact put the conspirators at an enormous disadvantage. If they attacked, they would expose their constitutionalism as a sham and outrage the democratic instincts of a nation that was beginning to take democracy seriously; they would also underscore Yeltsin's claim that the party had become an anti-Russian organization which was grimly hanging on to power at Russia's expense.

As the stand-off developed, there was a sense of *déjà vu*. Was this not a replay of what had happened in the Senate Square in December 1825? And might it not, if things went well, bring an end to that painfully zigzagging progress towards liberal democracy which had got off to so uncertain a start in 1825? In both cases, liberals or democrats found themselves surrounded and outnumbered by the massed forces of the traditional order. The parallel was especially striking on the night of 20–21 August, when the outlook for those holed up in the White House and expecting a knock-out assault appeared bleak. Yet there were vital differences which suggested that this might indeed be a beginning of the ending of that process begun so long before. Then it was the liberals who had started the action and bungled it; now it was conservatives trying desperately to restore a power-structure that had all but crumbled who had taken the initiative and, as it turned out, misjudged badly. Then the liberals had been so terrified of any popular involvement that they had preferred defeat to the risk of disorder; now the besieged democrats were crying out for popular support, which was all that could save them from the surrounding tanks.

Yeltsin's appeal for a general strike got a positive response from the miners and from his own Sverdlovsk. But support in the provinces was otherwise extremely patchy, and only a handful of local soviets declared against the coup. This wariness was not surprising – provincial Russia was waiting to see what happened in the capitals. In Moscow, things did not initially look at all good for the democrats. The great majority of people turned their backs on the White House drama and carried on with life as normal. Some undoubtedly supported the coup, which across the country had at least 25 per cent support, according to an opinion survey conducted shortly afterwards. Others were either indifferent to what happened or felt that resistance to the Committee was useless: the issue would as always be decided for rather than by the people. By contrast, in Leningrad/St Petersburg (a local poll in June had gone in favour of the old name), the resistance had got off to a more promising start, maybe because the army commander there agreed to keep his troops out of the city. Some 30,000 workers went on strike at the Kirov tractor plant – which tended to disprove the canard that in Russia only the middle class cared about freedom. And on 20 August, a crowd in the 150,000–200,000 range filled Palace Square to hear Mayor Sobchak and others denounce the junta. But in Moscow, too, resistance picked up rapidly; and once it became clear that opposition was far from futile, passive sympathy for the democrats started being converted into active support . By the evening of the 19th, the White House had some 25,000 defenders, at least 5,000 of whom kept vigil overnight. The next day the numbers rose to some 150,000. Though never more than a minority, the resisters were a sizeable and a highly motivated minority. But who exactly were they?

In a nutshell, they were those who cared most about freedom and had most to lose by its extinction. Intellectuals and artists were prominent – a straw poll of White House defenders showed almost half having higher-educational qualifications. The new breed of businessmen took a prominent part also. But above all it was the young who flocked to the White House. Those who were in their early teens when perestroika began, Gorbachev noted, would become 'the most courageous defenders of democracy'.[6] His opinion was confirmed by many people on the spot, including a visiting Radio Liberty official, whose abiding impression was of 'the youth of the vast majority of those who defended democracy on the barricades'.[7] These youngsters had grown up in a society very different from the repressive one of their parents' formative years – they had had pop music and Pepsi and had said and done more or less what they wanted. Playing the music they liked and doing business and even going to church were activities they took for granted. These and other freedoms were, however, threatened by the old men of the Emergency Committee, and it was the threatened destruction of a new and still precarious way of life which sent them to the White House. But if the defence of democracy owed a great deal to boys and young men, it also owed much to women of all ages. Women seem, in fact, to have had a special role in breaking the resolve of the junta's soldiers: and here there was a striking analogy with February 1917. In August, as in February, soldiers were being pushed to the limits of what they could bear by masters making a last-ditch defence of a crumbling and anachronistic order. In both cases, soldiers torn between the demands of duty and those of common sense and humanity were vulnerable to women's pleading. On the night of 20–21 August, when a knockout attack on the White House seemed imminent, some 200 women went towards the advancing tanks with a banner which said 'Soldiers! Don't shoot at mothers!' Elsewhere women gave baskets of fruit to soldiers, and girls climbed on tanks and garlanded their muzzles with flowers. If Yeltsin got through to the soldiers by appealing to their Russian patriotism, the women appealed to their humanity and clearly touched many on the quick.

The conspirators soon realized that the loyalty of officers and troops was doubtful: already on the evening of 19 August, ten tanks had crossed over to the democrats' side, and other likely defections were rumoured. The evening of the next day, Kryuchkov and Yazov withdrew a number of unreliable units, replacing them with hard-bitten and possibly drugged troops from the provinces. Two vital actors were, however, about to change sides. During the night of 20–21 August, the air force chief, General Yevgenii Shaposhnikov, and the head of the paratroops, General Pavel Grachev, hatched a plan of counter-attack should the White House be stormed. Grachev's troops would arrest the junta's ringleaders in the Kremlin; if they resisted, two of Shaposhnikov's bombers would then attack from the air. But the all-out assault on the White House, which everyone expected to be launched by KGB special units that night, never took place. The ringleaders were in the unprecedented, for them, situation of pulling levers and failing to get the response they expected. Spiralling doubt, rumours of defections, even unfavourable weather conditions – all helped weaken their resolve. At 8 a.m. on 21 August, they gave the order for troops to withdraw from the centre. Their implicit admission of defeat provoked scenes of wild jubilation in the streets; while in the Kremlin, the usurper Yanaev drank himself into stupefaction. By the evening of 22 August, most members of the junta were under arrest, and Gorbachev, rescued from his Crimean captivity, was back in Moscow.

Of course, the conspirators could have won had they acted more competently and decisively, just as the Decembrists could have; and if they had won they, like the Decembrists, would have held power for a while. At the start of the coup, most foreign observers assumed that it would succeed, and obituaries of Gorbachev and perestroika were hastily written. But there was nothing fortuitous about the bungling of either set of conspirators. For both, the time proved to be out of joint. Just as the Decembrists took to arms prematurely, so the men of August came too late. This *putsch* of theirs which soon degenerated into farce was a defence of values, institutions and attitudes which a significant minority of Russians now found intolerable, and that minority had been numerous and determined enough to rout them.

4

Counter-revolution turned rapidly into revolution amidst scenes of euphoria reminiscent of February 1917. On 22 August, 150,000 celebrated in front of the White House, in the area now renamed the 'Square of Free Russia', and all around the city pop music and church music, until recently the music of dissent, blared from loudspeakers. But if the victors were happy, they were also bitterly angry at this attempt to shackle them once more. 'Bring the party to trial!' people chanted outside CPSU headquarters, while inside officials hastily shredded documents. By the evening, the crowd had found an object on which to take out its anger: the forty-foot statue of Felix Dzerzhinsky, founder of the Cheka, standing in Lubyanka Square facing the KGB headquarters. Other leading communists were toppled as well, and soon there was an entire mortuary of these fallen demi-gods.

One communist, however, was spared the anger of the crowd – Lenin himself. True, he did not get off entirely unscathed. In Tallinn, Vilnius and elsewhere on the fringe, monuments to him were quickly removed, while the former capital now officially shed his name and became St Petersburg again. Yet in most public places in Russia, the monuments to Lenin were untouched, and queues at the mausoleum if anything increased just after the *putsch*. Lenin, it turned out, was bigger than his party, bigger than Leninism, a true god among the demi-gods, and big enough not to be dragged down with his creations. His survival amidst the debris seemed confirmation that, for all his defects, he had expressed something authentically Russian.

That said, the experiment on which Lenin had launched his country was coming to a humiliating end. The Soviet Union might live on, but the Soviet era was clearly guttering out. In the wake of the coup, there was a spate of suicides. One of the victims, Boris Pugo, was a leading conspirator; but others, it seemed, simply could no longer face life now that everything they had believed in was crumbling. On 22 August, *Pravda* had been suspended. For more than seventy years, this newspaper, so inappropriately called 'Truth', had told Soviet citizens what to think and do. Now they would have to get used to making their own minds up.

'I arrived back', Gorbachev wrote in his memoir of the coup, 'to a different country.'[8] A seventy-four-year detour seemed to have ended. The country went back to the agenda which had been brutally discarded in October 1917, and one sign of that was the red, white and blue flag of the Provisional Government fluttering everywhere. The ending of an era was reflected, too, in the way people addressed one another. True believers still used 'comrade', but most people reverted, except when they wanted to be sarcastic, to the pre-revolutionary 'Mr' and 'Mrs' (*gospodin* and *gospozhha*). Gorbachev had made free with the word 'revolution', yet his changes had amounted to no more than a pre-revolution. The real thing had come out of the blue, been accomplished remarkably quickly, and, apart from the death of three young democrats, had been almost bloodless.

But what kind of revolution had this August revolution been? Above all, it was a revolution against: against the pillars of the old regime, the CPSU and the security apparatus. On 23 August, the Russian Communist Party was suspended by Yeltsin. The following day Gorbachev resigned as CPSU General Secretary. On 29 August he suspended the CPSU itself, froze its assets and had all its buildings sealed. He called, in addition, for the Central Committee to be dissolved and urged democratic-minded communists to set up a new party. Not until 6 November was the CPSU actually banned on Russian territory; but by the end of August, the body which for seven decades had been the mainspring of all activity in the country had in effect been excluded from the political arena. The armed forces and the KGB of course remained, but now they were put into safer hands, reactionaries were purged from them, and the KGB underwent the first of several reorganizations.

The August revolution was also a protest against Gorbachev and his ill-fated middle way, which in the end had alienated almost everyone. A newspaper headline caught the mood: 'Perestroika is over – thank God!' Gorbachev himself now cut a pathetic figure. The conspirator's victim, he had nevertheless inadvertently encouraged them by his ambiguities, and many people suspected him of having been hand in glove with them. On his first day back in Moscow, he restated his belief in Leninist socialism and argued that, despite the coup, the party was still capable of being a force for good. Two days later, after some rough handling by Yeltsin, he accepted the new realities and resigned as General Secretary. That the party had failed him rather than he the party was perhaps academic: his strategy had destroyed the party he believed in and left his own career hanging by a thread.

The August revolution had exposed the hollowness of Soviet power, and it had made Yeltsin and the Russian government unchallengeable. Yeltsin's assumption of supreme political and military power on 19 August had nominally been only temporary. But once the coup had collapsed, it was his decree which dismissed the TV and radio watchdog, and he too who suspended *Pravda* and the other pro-coup newspapers. At the Russian Supreme Soviet on 23 August, he then forced Gorbachev to read aloud the minutes of a meeting of the USSR Cabinet of Ministers at which nearly all the ministers had expressed their support for the coup. With the Cabinet thus discredited, the Russian prime minister, Ivan Silaev, and his colleagues took over the running of the entire country. Yeltsin chose people for the jobs that mattered – crucially, the new ministers of defence and the interior and the new head of the KGB. But he was not content with simply putting his own nominees in key Soviet positions. The coup had in his eyes made the Union treaty due to have been signed on 20 August redundant. The balance of power between the republics and the centre had been changed decisively, and the new balance had to be reflected in a reapportioning of functions that left the Soviet government with little more than a co-ordinating role. And in advance of any new treaty, the Russian government began steadily taking over USSR ministries and leading Soviet institutions.

The relative smoothness of the take-over marked off the August revolution from both 1917 revolutions. True, the party had been cut out of the body politic like an incurable cancer: apart from that, however, the breaches of continuity were little more than formal. This was no February Revolution toppling an incorrigible old regime; instead, a regime that had tried to reform but done too little to satisfy democrats and more than enough to outrage conservatives was simply being superseded. Yet for all that, the August revolution had implications as radical as those of February. Both revolutions had followed a defeat or serious reverses at the hands of a Western power or the West: military, prior to February, economic and ideological, in the run-up to August. Both were targeted at distinctively Russian values and power structures. Those who took control after both saw liberal democracy as the only possible solution to the country's problems, and in both cases Western ideas rapidly filled the vacuum created by the collapse of the previous value system. With communism discredited, socialism tarnished and nationalism at least temporarily held in check by the very fact that the democrats had adopted it, Russia had no alternative after August, or so it seemed, but to establish a fully democratic political system and to underpin it with an economic transformation which created private property and a capitalist economy.

The euphoria of victory created a powerful momentum for change, but the euphoria did not last long and it soon became clear that building democracy on the wasteland left by the collapse of communism would be extremely difficult. The fundamental problem – and here again there was a parallel with 1917 – was that the victors represented no more than a minority, even if a highly vocal, articulate and influential minority. There was no nation-wide democratic movement such as the popular fronts in the Baltic states and Solidarity in Poland, and there were obvious reasons for this. The democrats' slogans were more unfamiliar to Russians than they would have been to Balts or Poles. There was no national oppressor to unite people in a fervent demand for freedom. And among thinking Russians there was by no means a consensus in favour of the democrats: many cultural leaders took a right-wing nationalist position, while some people who did believe in a democratic Russia had hoped to get it from a reformed CPSU right up to the coup. A poll in the summer of 1991 showed only 7 per cent support for the democratic umbrella organization, Democratic Russia. By the autumn, Democratic Russia had 400,000 members; even so, by this reckoning there were fewer declared democrats than employees of the KGB, which in September 1991 still had 488,000 people on its payroll.

True, the coup had attracted no more than minority support despite appealing to the traditional desire for a strong hand and the traditional dislike of the go-getting and the westernized. True, too, the Communist Party and communism seemed to be finally discredited. But post-coup opinion polls showed that many people had still not given up hope of socialism, whatever exactly they meant by it. The polls showed, moreover, great hostility towards capitalism and anything other than small-scale private enterprise; a longing for strong leadership; and much respect for that bastion of Russian conservatism, the Orthodox Church.

This did not mean that Russians could not be won to a more individualistic and libertarian pattern of thinking. The democrats had a clear constituency among the young, the better educated and the better-off. They had high hopes in particular of the emergent business class, even though policies strongly favourable to it had not yet been put in place. But among the masses of Russians who had no inbuilt bias towards them, they would be judged strictly by what they achieved. The crisis which the conspirators had been unable to exploit worsened in the weeks and months following the coup. For most people, living standards continued to deteriorate, while the insecurity caused by economic breakdown was made worse by signs that the Soviet state and even Russia itself might disintegrate. To ask the democrats to solve this multi-faceted crisis was to ask a very great deal of them. Yet, much like the liberals of 1917, they were in a situation where nothing less than successful crisis management could make their victory secure.

5

The democrats' first problem was to decide their policies. That was far from easy. Before the coup, they had been united by their fierce opposition to the Soviet system and their wish to replace it by guaranteed civil liberties, a multi-party political system, and a private-enterprise economy. But once the bogy had been removed such generalities were not enough, and serious splits soon appeared among them.

None denied that major economic reform was essential. Only a market economy could create a reliable constituency for democracy. Only privatization would make a reversion to communism impossible. Only a real boost in living standards could quell the popular demand for a strong hand. A difference of emphasis, however, appeared between liberal democrats and social democrats. The liberals, who were the majority, insisted on radical change, even if this led to short-term hardship; social democrats, by contrast, worried about poverty and unemployment and wanted a slower rate of change and a considerable welfare safety-net. Democrats were divided, too, by the nationalities' issue. They had differing views on how to preserve the Union, if indeed it should be preserved at all; and they fell out acrimoniously over the home-rule aspirations of some of Russia's own constituent republics. In addition, they were unable to decide whether in current conditions a properly democratic state was either possible or desirable. Some defended a strong executive – a 'democratic' case was even made for a Yeltsin dictatorship; others took their stand on democratic principle and condemned the government's authoritarian tendency. Such disagreements thwarted hopes that Democratic Russia might be turned from a framework into a proper political party that united all democrats, and in the months following the coup much of the democrats' energy went into fighting one another.

Even united, however, the democrats would have found it hard to achieve their aims in the face of mounting opposition. Open and raucous opposition came from a 'red-brown' alliance of communists and nationalists, brought together by their commitment to a great-power role for the Soviet or Russian state, their hostility to the West, and their determined defence of the Soviet welfare system. A more quietly effective resistance, however, came from apparatchiks reborn as democrats who had moved over to serve the new regime. These 'partocrats' had indispensable administrative and fixing skills: without them, the machine of government would have come to a halt. But there were other reasons as well why democrats who demanded a purge of apparatchiks – a 'social Nuremberg' – and the creation of a new, untainted administrative class were crying in the wind. Unlike the members of tsarism's ruling class, these people had not stirred up massive popular resentment; and what resentment they had incurred was soon forgotten when it became clear that the ex-apparatchiks were quietly doing their best to undermine the democrats' more radical policies. They were better placed, too, than their counterparts in Eastern Europe, who had been badly compromised by collaborating with Soviet-imposed regimes: any anti-patriotic accusations hurled in Russia had the democrats rather than the apparatchiks as their target. But perhaps the most important reason why apparatchiks slipped so easily into the service of the new regime was that the President of Russia needed them, understood them, and had much in common with them.

Yeltsin ought to have been the democrats' trump card – a popular hero with a majority vote behind him who had fought for democracy at the barricades. Furthermore, he had every reason to be grateful to the democrats, since they had rescued him from the political wilderness, given him a programme, and campaigned passionately for him. Without them, the victories of March 1989, March 1990 and June 1991 would have been impossible. Yet he had remained maddeningly aloof from these loyal supporters. After his election as Chairman of the Russian Supreme Soviet, he had resigned from Democratic Russia on the ground that as Chairman he had to be above parties, and he had not joined any democratic organization since. Nor had he drawn any closer to the democrats as a result of the August revolution; far from rewarding them for their support, he had in fact tended to surround himself with ministers and advisers from the Soviet apparatus.

This stand-offishness looked to many democrats like base ingratitude. Yeltsin had simply used them to get to the top; once there, he was refusing to accept any obligation to them or the policies they stood for. There were, however, sound reasons for Yeltsin's reluctance to tie himself to a political party. By the autumn of 1990, there were more than 300 such parties, yet hardly any of them deserved the name. Only the Communist Party, with fifteen million members at the time of its suspension, had a mass following; the others were minnows by comparison, most of them little more than coteries of Moscow and Petersburg intellectuals. A poll in the summer of 1991 showed 69 per cent of respondents to have no party preferences at all. Worse than that, there was widespread dislike of these proliferating parties; perhaps because 'party' had unavoidable overtones of the CPSU, perhaps because politics were seen as a thoroughly dirty business, but above all because the noisy divisiveness of party politics seemed wasteful and counterproductive, the last thing a country that was falling apart needed. True, back in 1989 the unfamiliar cut and thrust of the newborn Soviet Congress had been greeted with delight. Two years later, however, its prestige had fallen so low that when, in September, Gorbachev persuaded the deputies not to meet any more, this effective disbandment of the Congress was met with hardly any public protest. In keeping his distance from parties, Yeltsin was therefore doing what most people wanted – adopting the role of the strong and independent leader who was determined to rule on behalf of everyone.

Nevertheless, he could not do without the democrats or their policies, and at the end of October he appointed a government with a strong liberal-democratic flavour and announced a new and radical economic programme. Prices would be decontrolled. The budget would be stabilized by slashing subsidies to industry and social spending. Privatization of small and medium-sized enterprises would go ahead. There would be a massive financial boost for private farming. The changes, and especially the unfreezing of prices, would, however, be painful. 'Everyone will find life harder for six months', he warned. 'Then prices will fall and goods will begin to fill the market. By the autumn of 1992 ... the economy will be stabilized and people's lives will gradually get better.'[9]

The 'young Turks' to whom he entrusted the economy had been powerfully influenced by the Reaganite and Thatcherite West and they were determined to smash the old communist economic system. This was a 'kamikaze' government with 'shock therapy' as its slogan. Yet contrary to Yeltsin's promise, it was not everyone who suffered; nor was there any prospect of better times for most around the corner. In this society where inequality had been carefully muffled, the differences began to become glaring. Mercedes and Volvos, cruising past lines of elderly women standing outside Metro stations and trying to hawk items of personal clothing, told their own story. By the end of 1991, 60 per cent of Muscovites were below what was officially regarded as the poverty line. At the hands of democrats committed to Friedmanite economics, Russia began to get a caricature of capitalism, 'wild capitalism' as it became known, which created great inequality and, in the absence of clear legal or moral restraints, a culture of buccaneering and outright criminality. To people struggling to survive, this 'wild capitalism' merely confirmed what their former rulers had drummed into them: that the capitalist economic system was inherently unjust and inhuman. And it was not only from the wilder fringes of the right that the protests came – Vice-President Alexander Rutskoy made rejection of 'shock therapy' one of the main planks in his increasingly bitter opposition to Yeltsin and his westernizing *enfants terribles*. The danger as discontent deepened was that the popular good will won by the democrats in August would be exhausted well before any of the benefits of liberal economics became apparent.

6

Nationalities' policy and the question of the future of the Union created further painful dilemmas for the democrats. Here there was no equivalent of Friedmanite economics to give them a blueprint, and three distinct positions emerged among them: first, a consistently liberal position: not only Union republics but constituent republics of the RSFSR should be allowed independence if they wanted it. Second, a 'Great Russian' position – Union republics that wanted to secede should be allowed and even encouraged to, since many of them were a drain on Russian resources. Russia should, however, firmly assert its right to be recognized as the legal successor to the USSR and the heir to its superpower status, and its constituent republics should not be allowed to secede. Third, a pro-Union position – the Soviet Union should be preserved but restructured in accordance with a new Union treaty, which would grant the republics considerably greater powers than the treaty which the August coup had killed off.

Democratic Russia inclined on the whole to the first position, but the government's young Turks took a strong Great Russian line. Yeltsin, too, had Great Russian instincts. He had once encouraged separatist feelings among the RSFSR's republics; now he made it plain that self-determination for Russia did not entail any such right for its constituent parts. The former defender of the rights of Soviet peoples large and small had become the champion of 'Russia one and indivisible'; and when the small Caucasian republic of Chechenia made a bid for independence, his reaction was to declare a state of emergency there. (The Russian Supreme Soviet, however, promptly annulled the state of emergency, and the Chechen problem would be left to fester until 1994.) This Great Russian face of Yeltsin's was sometimes shown to Union republics as well – most strikingly in late August, when he made a thinly veiled threat that breakaway republics would be punished by having territory taken from them. But on the whole he behaved diplomatically towards the other republics since, unlike his young Turks, he had not yet written the Union off. A reconstituted Soviet Union could still be useful by binding the other republics to Russia, though only on one condition: an absolute minimum of power should be granted to the centre.

The Baltic republics were now lost beyond retrieval – they had established their independence, and won international recognition of it, straightaway after the coup. There seemed little chance, too, of the three Caucasian republics and Moldavia being persuaded to join the new Union. The republics of Central Asia, by contrast, strongly supported a continuing Union. Kirgizia apart, they were ruled by communist bosses in new colours; they had no appreciable democratic or nationalist movements to push the anti-Soviet cause and they were very much dependent upon the centre's economic support. For Russians who wanted to preserve the Union, however, it was the Slav republics of Ukraine and Belorussia that were crucial. Both had been traditionally loyal to Moscow and in both perestroika had been slow to take root. But both, and in particular Ukraine, had caught the nationalist fever. Chernobyl had had a radicalizing effect; so too had the self-assertion of the Russian democrats. Both insisted as a result on having political and economic sovereignty. This did not in itself rule out continued membership of the Union. After the coup, however, the Ukrainian parliament had gone further and issued a declaration of independence, though with an important proviso. The declaration was subject to ratification by a referendum to be held on 1 December 1991.

The Ukrainian referendum gave Gorbachev and Yeltsin a deadline by which they had to put together an acceptable new Union treaty. The Baltics were lost, the Caucasus and Moldavia were most probably lost; but Ukraine might still, it seemed, be held on to. And Ukraine was vital. A Union without it was unthinkable. Gorbachev said so shortly after the coup, and the sentiment would be echoed by Moscow politicians of almost all stripes. More than that, Russia without Ukraine was very hard for most Russians to imagine. How could Russian-speaking Kiev, the cradle of the Russian state and Russian Christianity, be foreign? How could Chekhov's Yalta and the Crimean beaches be foreign?

Economic issues were easier to agree about than political ones, and on 18 October eight republics signed an agreement for economic union. Better still, by mid-November a treaty establishing a Union of Sovereign States (USS) as successor to the USSR seemed to be imminent. This differed appreciably from the treaty forestalled by the August coup, and it left the exact division of powers between the republics and a diminished centre to be decided later. A reception on 25 November at which the agreement for this modest framework would have been signed was, however, called off because of last-minute objections by Yeltsin. The USS should not be a state in its own right, he was insisting, merely a union with a co-ordinating centre. The distinction between a 'confederation' and a 'confederative state' might seem hairsplitting, but for the rival Presidents it was vital. Gorbachev wanted the USS to have the normal functions of a state and to be recognized as a state; Yeltsin was determined to deny him both.

What remained of co-existence between the two men had finally broken down. It had come to an outright conflict between them, with Yeltsin in much the stronger position. And within days of the deadlock, his claim that the Soviet Union was no longer viable as an independent state seemed to have been borne out. On 20 November, the USSR Supreme Soviet failed to muster enough votes to pass the state budget. Two days later, with the USSR facing bankruptcy, Russia took over responsibility for its budget. Soviet officials and military personnel would from now on be paid by Russia. Yeltsin had become the paymaster of the Union, and Gorbachev was powerless to resist him.

The Ukrainian referendum of 1 December 1991 dealt the Union a final blow. Over 90 per cent of voters supported their parliament's declaration of independence, and even in the highly russified Crimea, 54 per cent voted in its favour. If there could be no Union without Ukraine, as Gorbachev had argued, then the Union was indeed finished. For him and for millions of Russians, the collapse of the centuries-old close association of Russia and Ukraine was a calamity. For Yeltsin, however, the result of the referendum had the great advantage that it left Gorbachev without a state and thus removed him from the political arena. The way was now open to create a quite different form of association between the republics, one that was untainted by communism and offered his rival no foothold at all.

The new structure was revealed to an astonished public on 8 December 1991, when Yeltsin, the Ukrainian President Leonid Kravchuk, and Stanislau Shushkevich, Chairman of the Belorussian Supreme Soviet, after a secret meeting signed an agreement which began: 'We, the Republic of Belarus, the Russian Federation (RSFSR), and Ukraine, as founder states of the USSR and signatories to the Union Treaty of 1922 ... state that the USSR as a subject of international law and geopolitical reality is terminating its existence.'[10] In place of the Union whose death sentence their leaders had pronounced, the three states would form a Commonwealth of Independent States, which all republics of the former USSR would be invited to join. The CIS would not be a state and therefore would have no capital, and its co-ordinating centre would not be imperial Moscow but the Belorussian capital of Minsk.

By a strange irony, at the very moment when the Soviet Union was being dissolved, the states of the European Community, meeting in Maastricht, were moving from confederation towards a confederative, if not a federal, state. And Yeltsin managed to see a parallel between the two processes, arguing that the Soviet states, too, were uniting in a new community. In reality, however, the two blocs of countries were moving in quite opposite directions. The words used were revealing. The republican leaders had firmly rejected the term 'union', which the EC would shortly adopt, and had decided instead to call their new association a 'commonwealth' (*sodruzh-estvo*). That of course had quite different echoes – of the talking-shop created by that other great imperial power, Britain, once it had accepted the loss of its empire. True, Yeltsin would have liked a CIS with real substance; ideally, no doubt, he would have discarded the Soviet framework without losing the hegemonic role for Russia which that had legitimized. The Ukrainians, however, were determined to make a reality of their independence, and they were not prepared to put up with a new empire in a democratic guise. They insisted on having their own armed forces of half a million men (while accepting that strategic forces would stay under unified control); and they turned down the one thing that might have given the CIS some substance – a parliamentary assembly.

This attempt by the three leaders to dissolve the Soviet Union was of course completely unconstitutional. On the other hand, it could be argued that Western constitutional norms hardly applied. The state they were dissolving had been set up by flagrantly anti-constitutional means and had flouted democracy throughout. Why then should Yeltsin and his partners feel constrained by the Soviet constitution? Some democrats were nevertheless very uneasy about this deal hatched secretly in the Belorussian forest. However murky its origins, the Soviet regime had in time won acceptance and thus a kind of legitimacy. Whatever his faults, Gorbachev had tried hard to teach people that respect for the rule of law was essential for democracy. Now here was Yeltsin going back to a pernicious Russian tradition whereby the strong did as they pleased and then changed the law accordingly. Gorbachev himself reacted indignantly to the *fait accompli*. He called for the USSR Congress to come out of retirement to arbitrate; he would also have liked a referendum on the issue. For more immediate help, however, he looked to his top military commanders – would they not throw him and the Soviet Union a lifeline? But he was to be disappointed. Yeltsin had cultivated better relations with the military than he had; moreover, as paymaster he had just awarded all military officers a 90 per cent pay rise. Not surprisingly, the military decided that the better prospects for them lay with Yeltsin and his Commonwealth, even though it raised serious doubts about the unity of the armed forces.

Gorbachev's indignation was shared by the leaders of the Central Asian republics and especially by Nursultan Nazarbaev, President of Kazakhstan. The Central Asian leaders had sided with Gorbachev in the post-August power struggle, and the emergence of this 'Slav Commonwealth' was most unwelcome to them. The strong Union with Gorbachev at its head which they had hoped for had now, however, disappeared beyond the horizon. On 12 December, the Russian parliament overwhelmingly ratified the Minsk Agreement and voted to annul the 1922 treaty. The same day the USSR Supreme Soviet acknowledged that it no longer had a role to play. On 13 December, the Central Asian states, accepting the inevitable, decided to apply for membership of the CIS; and on 21 December it was enlarged to include all the Soviet republics, excepting only the Baltic states and Georgia. The CIS had certainly attracted more members than would have stayed within the Union; on that, at least, Yeltsin could congratulate himself.

Gorbachev had already come to terms with the inevitable. He had wanted to put the Soviet state on a new and stronger basis; instead, he was presiding over its dissolution, and on 1 January 1992 it would be formally replaced by the CIS. Even before the end of the year, the Soviet Union had in effect disappeared. On 25 December Gorbachev handed over the ultimate symbol of a modern ruler's power: the briefcase containing nuclear codes. In a farewell TV address he did not hide his regret at having failed to save the Union. As soon as he had finished, the Soviet flag was lowered from the Council of Ministers' building in the Kremlin and replaced by the Russian tricolour. That same day, the RSFSR had been renamed the Russian Federation – or more simply, Russia. Only the red stars on the Kremlim towers and Lenin, still untouched beneath the walls, remained as a reminder of the dying Soviet era.

On 26 December, Gorbachev went to the Kremlin for the last time, only to find his office closed to him – Yeltsin had already taken possession of it. The thin veneer of ceremonial and constitutional propriety could hardly conceal the fact that he had been evicted, just as the CPSU and the Soviet state itself had been evicted. Liberal papers attempted a balanced appraisal of him, but to most people in the street he was simply the principal cause of their miseries. On the day when this final humiliation was heaped upon Gorbachev, the USSR Supreme Soviet met for the final time. But of its several hundred deputies, only two dozen turned up: not enough for a quorum. Those who gathered in the funereal atmosphere were therefore not able to agree to a formal dissolution. The parliament which had got off to so promising a start simply fizzled out, brute reality making a mockery of the constitutional pretences. Soviet power had begun in earnest with an assembly guttering out in the midwinter darkness, and the ending was not dissimilar.

Lenin's experiment, which had aroused the most utopian hopes and yet inflicted appalling calamities upon the country, was being wound up. The Soviet era was following the Petersburg era into the history books, though in this case the rulers had belatedly seen the light and the transition had been managed with very little bloodshed. The name and content of the new era could hardly be guessed at this stage, but it was being born at least under the auspices of democracy. And yet there was little sense of history in the streets as the Soviet Union was expiring. The August explosion of joy was not repeated: far from celebrating, people were so burdened and preoccupied that most of them seemed hardly aware of what was happening. True, there was now more freedom in Russia than ever before apart from those few months in 1917. The subjects of the tsars and the commissars were well on their way to becoming citizens. Yet people were still haunted by the fear that freedom was an ill-omened visitor in whose wake hunger, violence and chaos would stalk the land; and in the dark days of the dying Soviet era, there were not many signs that democratic government, or what passed as it, would rid them of that fear.

Notes

1 John Morrison, *Boris Yeltsin: From Bolshevik to Democrat* (Harmondsworth, 1991), p. 227, citing Reuters, 14 January 1991.
2 For the new cult of Lenin, see especially *Pravda*, 21 January 1991, pp. 1 and 3.
3 *Sovetskaya Rossiya*, 23 July 1991, p. 1.
4 Mikhail Gorbachev, *The August Coup: The Truth and the Lessons* (London, 1991), p. 23.
5 *The Current Digest of the Soviet Press*, 43, no. 32 (11 September 1991), p. 8.
6 Gorbachev, *The August Coup*, p. 31.
7 Iain Elliot, 'Three Days in August', *Report on the USSR*, 3, no. 36 (6 September 1991), p. 67.
8 Gorbachev, *The August Coup*, p. 38.
9 *Report on the USSR*, 3, no. 46 (15 November 1991), p. 2.
10 *The Current Digest of the Soviet Press*, 43, no. 49 (8 January 1992), p. 10.

Conclusion

The fall of the Soviet Union ushered in one of Russia's dark ages. Economic breakdown made living conditions for most people appalling. Violence and criminality of all kinds flourished. Death rates, including the suicide rate, surged. Diseases that seemed to have been wiped out made a come-back. There was a spate of industrial and transport accidents, though the disasters that occurred seemed almost trivial in relation to the nuclear disasters that threatened. Here in fact was a society getting out of control, and underlying its material problems was a moral one. Within a single century, Russia had overthrown not one but two value systems, Christianity and communism, and at the century's end it found itself in a moral no man's land. The post-Soviet nightmare seemed to bear out many of the warnings of earlier Russian conservatives. These were people whom it was tempting to write off as having no natural cohesion, as immature, anarchic, and needing a strong repressive state to integrate them and save them from their self-destructive impulses. In this landscape, Dostoevsky's Grand Inquisitor was an all too relevant figure, offering bread and something to worship in return for the freedom people did not apparently appreciate and could not cope with, and ordering their lives for them as if they were children. It was hard, too, not to recall the prediction of the pessimistic radical Alexander Herzen that Russia would never be liberal, Protestant, or middle of the road.

Hopes that the country might fairly easily make the transition from democratized to democratic politics were quickly dashed. The democrats became intensely unpopular. They were held responsible for the humiliating loss of status and territory which had pushed Russia back to boundaries that resembled those of seventeenth-century Muscovy (although it did still keep a small 'window on the West' around St Petersburg and further south the anomalous Kaliningrad enclave). And their 'shock therapy' was seen as having devastated people's living standards. Yeltsin had promised that prices would fall within six months, yet four-figure inflation roared away throughout 1992. Some friend of the people! Not surprisingly, there was a surge of support for Vladimir Zhirinovsky's fascist-type and grossly misnamed Liberal-Democratic Party, which promised to restore order and avenge the humiliations inflicted upon the country. Not only did support for the democrats fall away. Since a number of deputies deserted the democrats' ranks, Yeltsin found himself without a parliamentary majority and facing fierce opposition from an ill-assorted alliance of patriots, communists and centrists. His confrontation with parliament came to a head in September 1993, when he dissolved the Congress and Supreme Soviet and announced elections for a new legislature. This was drastic action. Nicholas II and Lenin had of course provided precedents for it, though Nicholas, unlike Yeltsin, had at least been within his constitutional rights. Most of the deputies refused to disperse. Moreover, their leaders declared that the President had acted unconstitutionally, as the Constitutional Court confirmed, and that he had therefore forfeited his position. Stalemate developed as both sides appealed for popular support; but the stand-off was transformed on 3 October when some deputies broke out of the blockaded White House and attempted an armed uprising. The army, however, stayed loyal to Yeltsin; and parliament's resistance was finally broken by a sustained bombardment of the White House, which only two years before had become indelibly associated with Yeltsin's own heroic defiance of military might.

The new constitution of December 1993 narrowly got the popular support it needed in a referendum, and it increased the President's powers at the expense of those of parliament. Now he, rather than it, determined the country's basic domestic and foreign policies. In December 1994, Yeltsin took advantage of his enhanced rights to use the strong-armed methods against the rebellious Chechens which he had been prevented by parliament from using in 1991. The Chechen capital, Grozny, was bombarded into rubble, the rebel leader, Dzhokhar Dudaev, was driven into the mountains, a puppet government without local support was set up amidst the ruins, and an undisciplined soldiery was let loose on the civilian population. Parliament and the liberal press protested in vain against behaviour in the worst traditions of Russian imperialism, and there were fears that the assault on this small peripheral republic might prefigure the destruction of liberty at the centre.

The White House and Chechen episodes showed how far the country still had to go before it created a community based on consent. Yeltsin, admittedly under severe provocation in both cases, had acted like an intemperate peasant autocrat and simply bludgeoned his opponents. Yet such actions contradicted much else that he had done and stood for; and his very contradictions, the co-existence within him of the democrat and the imperialist and autocrat, reflected the inevitable contradictions of an end-of-twentieth-century Russia that was struggling to escape its autocratic heritage but in moments of panic or weakness all too easily slipped back into it. The gains made since 1985 remained precarious. The press might be free, yet it still acted as if its freedom existed very much on sufferance. The army was a shrunken and disgruntled version of the Soviet army. The security service was no more than a temporarily neutered KGB. The police seemed to know only how to deal with drunks and rioters.

However, despite economic collapse, loss of empire and widespread demoralization, the gains of the perestroika period held. The dissolution of parliament had been a blow, yet Yeltsin's powers as President under the 1993 constitution fell far short of those Nicholas had had from 1906 and bore no comparison to those of the Soviet leaders. Moreover, the new constitution made a quantum leap forward in relation to previous Russian constitutions. Now, at last, Russia had a constitution in which the rights and freedoms of the citizen were given pride of place, in which these rights were not hedged about by conditions or offset against obligations towards the state, and which was inspired by a spirit of liberal individualism. The events in Chechenia, bloody and atavistic though they were, also provided no evidence of any general regressive tendency. The right denied to the Chechens had been given to the Estonians, Moldavians and other small peoples of the former Union. Even within the Russian Federation, a peaceful accommodation had been reached with the Tatars and other peoples wanting greater independence. Most important of all, the principle of consent as the basis of the civil order had continued to be consolidated at the centre. The belief in a self-regulating society without rulers and ruled had been one of Marxism–Leninism's most beguiling but disastrous myths. The aim has to be the modest one of effectively controlling government rather than the utopian one of eliminating it; and since 1985 the subjects of this previous dictatorship had begun to become citizens in the sense of giving conscious, willing and conditional assent to the rule of those who governed them.

Russia can only be free if a sufficient number of Russians value freedom and accept the necessary limits upon it and the responsibilities that go with it. Freedom requires a generous spirit of give and take, a sense of national unity strong enough to transcend socio-economic differences (and thus hard to achieve when these differences are glaring), and a substratum of shared assumptions about the fundamentals of life. In the aftermath of the Soviet experiment – not something that dropped from the heavens, remember, but the misbegotten offspring of tsarism's distortions – it seemed at times that this was a society so fractured and at war with itself that freedom lay well beyond its immediate reach. There was a rapidly increasing polarization between losers and winners. On the one side was a more or less prostrate majority of victims who had lost not only the modest material security they had known under the Soviet system but also a sense of purpose and identity and were therefore to some degree in shock. On the other was a swelling minority who were singlemindedly getting rich quick, were aggressive, philistine, brazenly showy (foreign cars, mansions in the country, expensive clothes, private schools, Mediterranean holidays) and seemed not to care one jot about those who metaphorically and sometimes literally were lying in the gutter. These *nouveaux riches*, the 'new Russians', were a mockery of that middle class which reformers from Speransky to Gorbachev had hoped for: caring, educated and socially responsible, a class that would underpin free institutions and by precept and personal example win converts to them. Communism, it seemed, was reaching out even from the grave and blighting the chances of a democratic Russia - and what else could one have expected? People had been held in the grip of a repressive and brutal absolutism, and their parents and grandparents had been similarly crushed. Repression had reduced many to a condition of psychological infantilism, ensuring that they were no more capable of coping with freedom when it came than children were of shouldering the responsibilities of adults. At the other extreme, however, were a few strong, talented and ambitious people who had bitterly resented and inwardly resisted the constraints of communism. These had grabbed at freedom with both hands, and once released they were naturally not going to worry about that general good which until recently had justified the shackles that bound them.

While the legacy of communism makes a cohesive and democratic society difficult to achieve, it should nevertheless not be seen as an all-embracing explanation of the country's problems. If many people are prostrate in the Russia of the 1990s, this is not so much because communism has made them unable to stand on their own feet but rather because they have been knocked down by losing their jobs or their material security. These are the victims of the economic disaster precipitated unwittingly by the perestroika reformers and the democrats; and once the economy recovers, as it already shows signs of doing, many will pick themselves up. As for the new Russians, already on some estimates 10 per cent of the population, many will no doubt continue to be aggressive and to flaunt their wealth. But they will not for ever go on reacting against the repression and grim egalitarianism of communism, and sooner rather than later some will realize that social concern is a price worth paying for a stable society.

In relation to the vast expanses of time in which the ancestors of present-day Russians were enslaved, the brief period in which these Russians have been allowed some freedom represents little more than a blink of history's eyelid. We should not expect too much from them too soon. Russia is not and will not in the near future become a Western-type society. Most Russians will for some time to come have to put up with hardships that most of us would find intolerable. We must be prepared for xenophobic eruptions and other forms of irrational and inhuman behaviour. For the Russians, there will be no 'end of history' either in the Marxist sense or in the sense made fashionable recently by Western conservatives who foresee a life without ideological, class or party-political conflicts. In impoverished and divided Russia, the conflicts will be constant and acute. Yet if the democratized framework holds, the opposing elements – the dependants and the predators – may feel their way towards a sense of common purpose, balancing the needs of the community against those of the risk-taking, wealth-producing, creative yet self-serving individual. The 'if' is of course a huge one. There are no guarantees whatever. But it would be a poor friend who did not hope that the Russians of the twenty-first century will have freer and more fulfilled lives than their predecessors', and much in this book gives support to that hope.

Bibliography

What follow are the books and articles in English that I have found most useful in writing this history. I have drawn up separate lists for most chapters, but I have grouped together the titles for the first two chapters and also those for the last two. Books that provide a wide-angled view or are helpful for at least two chapters I have put in the 'General' section; and here each entry is followed by a reference, in brackets, to the chapters for which the book is most relevant.

General

Edward Acton, *Russia* (London, 1986) (1–9).

Vladimir Andrle, *A Social History of Twentieth-Century Russia* (London, 1994) (4–10).

Isaiah Berlin, *Russian Thinkers* (London, 1978) (2–3).

James H. Billington, *The Icon and the Axe: An Interpretive History of Russian Culture* (London, 1966) (1–9).

Jerome Blum, *Lord and Peasant in Russia: From the Ninth to the Nineteenth Century* (Princeton, N.J., 1961) (1–3).

Archie Brown, Michael Kaser and Gerry Smith, eds, *The Cambridge Encyclopedia of Russia and the Former Soviet Union* (Cambridge, 1994) (1–11).

E. H. Carr, *A History of Soviet Russia* (14 vols, London, 1950–78) (5–7).

Michael Cherniavsky, *Tsar and People: Studies in Russian Myths* (New Haven, 1961) (1–4).

Stephen F. Cohen, *Rethinking the Soviet Experience: Politics and History since 1917* (New York, 1985) (5–9).

Paul Dukes, *A History of Russia: Medieval, Modern and Contemporary* (2nd edn, London, 1990) (1–10).

Sheila Fitzpatrick, *The Russian Revolution* (2nd edn, Oxford, 1994) (5–7).

Martin Gilbert, *Atlas of Russian History: From 800 BC to the Present Day* (2nd edn, London, 1993) (1–11).

Neil Harding, *Lenin's Political Thought* (2 vols, London 1977 and 1981) (4–6).

Geoffrey Hosking, *A History of the Soviet Union 1917–1991* (final edn, London, 1992) (5–11).

Jerry F. Hough and Merle Fainsod, *How the Soviet Union is Governed* (Cambridge, Mass., 1979) (5–9).

John Keep, *Last of the Empires: A History of the Soviet Union 1945–1991* (Oxford, 1995) (8–11).

Marvin Lyons, *Russia in Original Photographs 1860–1920* (London, 1977) (3–6).

Mary McAuley, *Soviet Politics 1917–1991* (Oxford, 1992) (5–11).

D. S. Mirsky, *A History of Russian Literature* (New York, 1960) (1–5).

J. P. Nettl, *The Soviet Achievement* (London, 1967) (5–9).

Alec Nove, *An Economic History of the USSR 1917–1991* (London, 1992) (5–11).

Richard Pipes, *The Russian Revolution 1899–1919* (London, 1990) (3–5).

——, *Russia under the Old Regime* (2nd edn, London, 1995) (1–3).

T. H. Rigby, *Communist Party Membership in the USSR, 1917–67* (Princeton, N.J., 1968) (5–9).

——, *The Changing Soviet System: Mono-organisational Socialism from its Origins until Gorbachev's Restructuring* (Aldershot, 1990) (5–10).

Geroid Tanquary Robinson, *Rural Russia under the Old Regime: A History of the Landlord–Peasant World and a Prologue to the Peasant Revolution of 1917* (New York, 1949) (1–4).

Hans Rogger, *Russia in the Age of Modernisation and Revolution 1881–1917* (London, 1983) (3–5).

David Saunders, *Russia in the Age of Reaction and Reform 1801–1881* (London, 1992) (2–3).

Leonard Schapiro, *The Communist Party of the Soviet Union* (2nd edn, London, 1970) (4–9).

Robert Service, *Lenin: A Political Life* (3 vols, London, 1985–92) (4–6).

Hugh Seton–Watson, *The Russian Empire 1801–1917* (Oxford, 1988) (2–4).

Richard Stites, *Russian Popular Culture: Entertainment and Society since 1900* (Cambridge, 1992) (4–10).

Robert C. Tucker, *The Marxian Revolutionary Idea* (London, 1970) (3–6).

Adam B. Ulam, *Russia's Failed Revolutions: From the Decembrists to the Dissidents* (London, 1981) (2–9).

Aryeh L. Unger, *Constitutional Development in the USSR: A Guide to the Soviet Constitutions* (London, 1986) (5–9).

Donald Mackenzie Wallace, *Russia: On the Eve of War and Revolution* (New York, 1961) (2–3).

J. N. Westwood, *Endurance and Endeavour: Russian History 1812–1986* (3rd edn, Oxford, 1987) (2–9).

Karl A. Wittfogel, *Oriental Despotism* (New Haven, 1957) (1–4).

1. Russia at the beginning of the nineteenth century; 2. Unreformed Russia, 1801–1855

G. R. V. Barratt, *Voices in Exile: The Decembrist Memoirs* (Montreal, 1974).

Marquis de Custine, *Russia* (London, 1854).

Robin Edmonds, *Pushkin: The Man and His Age* (London, 1994).

John Gooding, 'The Liberalism of Michael Speransky', *Slavonic and East European Review*, 64, no. 3 (1986), pp. 401–24.

Janet M. Hartley, *Alexander I* (London, 1994).

August von Haxthausen, *Studies on the Interior of Russia*, ed. by S. Frederick Starr (Chicago, 1972).

David Marshall Lang, *The First Russian Radical: Alexander Radishchev* (London, 1959).

W. Bruce Lincoln, *Nicholas I: Emperor and Autocrat of All the Russias* (Bloomington, 1980).

Martin Malia, *Alexander Herzen and the Birth of Russian Socialism 1812–1855* (London, 1961).

Anatole G. Mazour, *The First Russian Revolution 1825: The Decembrist Movement: Its Origins, Development and Significance* (Berkeley, Cal., 1937).

Allan McConnell, *A Russian Philosophe: Alexander Radishchev 1749–1802* (The Hague, 1964).

——, *Tsar Alexander I: Paternalistic Reformer* (New York, 1970).

Roderick E. McGrew, *Paul I of Russia 1754–1801* (Oxford, 1992).

Sidney Monas, *The Third Section: Police and Society in Russia under Nicholas I* (Cambridge, Mass., 1961).

Patrick O'Meara, *K. F. Ryleev: A Political Biography of the Decembrist Poet* (Princeton, N.J., 1984).

Richard Pipes, *Karamzin's Memoir on Ancient and Modern Russia: A Translation and Analysis* (New York, 1966).

Marc Raeff, *Origins of the Russian Intelligentsia: The Eighteenth-Century Nobility* (New York, 1966).

——, *Michael Speransky: Statesman of Imperial Russia 1772–1839* (2nd edn, The Hague, 1969).

——, *Understanding Imperial Russia: State and Society in the Old Regime* (New York, 1984).

Nicholas V. Riasanovsky, *Nicholas I and Official Nationality in Russia 1825–1855* (Berkeley, Cal., 1959).

——, *A Parting of Ways: Government and the Educated Public in Russia 1801–1855* (Oxford, 1976).

P. S. Squire, *The Third Department: The Political Police in the Russia of Nicholas I* (Cambridge, 1968).

Franco Venturi, *Studies in Free Russia* (Chicago, 1982).

Wayne S. Vucinich, ed., *The Peasants in Nineteenth-Century Russia* (Stanford, Cal., 1968).

Andrzej Walicki, *The Slavophile Controversy: History of a Conservative Utopia in Nineteenth-Century Russia* (Oxford, 1975).

Karl Wittfogel, 'Russia and the East: A Comparison and Contrast', in Donald W. Treadgold, ed., *The Development of the USSR* (Seattle, 1964), pp. 323–39.

Richard S. Wortman, *Scenarios of Power: Myth and Ceremony in Russian Monarchy* (vol. I, Princeton, N.J., 1995).

George L. Yaney, *The Systematization of Russian Government: Social Evolution in the Domestic Administration of Imperial Russia 1711–1905* (Urbana, Ill., 1973).

Nicolas Zernov, *Eastern Christendom* (London, 1961).

3. Modernized Russia, 1855–1900

Edward Acton, *Alexander Herzen and the Role of the Intellectual Revolutionary* (Cambridge, 1979).

James H. Billington, *Mikhailovsky and Russian Populism* (Oxford, 1958).

Cyril E. Black, ed., *The Transformation of Russian Society: Aspects of Social Change since 1861* (Cambridge, Mass., 1960).

Edith W. Clowes, Samuel D. Kassow and James L. West, eds, *Between Tsar and People: Educated Society and the Quest for Public Identity in Late Imperial Russia* (Princeton, N.J., 1991).

Ben Ekloff, John Bushnell and Larissa Zakharova, eds, *Russia's Great Reforms, 1855–1881* (Bloomington, 1994).

Terence Emmons, *The Russian Landed Gentry and the Peasant Emancipation of 1861* (Cambridge, 1968).

Terence Emmons and Wayne S. Vucinich, eds, *The Zemstvo in Russia: An Experiment in Local Self-Government* (Cambridge, 1982).

Daniel Field, *The End of Serfdom: Nobility and Bureaucracy in Russia, 1855–1861* (Cambridge, Mass., 1976).

——, *Rebels in the Name of the Tsar* (Boston, 1989).

George Fischer, *Russian Liberalism: From Gentry to Intelligentsia* (Cambridge, Mass., 1958).

Peter Gatrell, *The Tsarist Economy 1850–1917* (London, 1986).

Abbott Gleason, *Young Russia: The Genesis of Russian Radicalism in the 1860s* (Chicago, 1983).

E. Lampert, *Sons Against Fathers: Studies in Russian Radicalism and Revolution* (Oxford, 1965).

Theodore H. von Laue, *Sergei Witte and the Industrialization of Russia* (New York, 1963).

W. Bruce Lincoln, *Nikolai Miliutin: An Enlightened Bureaucrat of the Nineteenth Century* (Newtonville, Mass., 1979).

——, *The Great Reforms: Autocracy, Bureaucracy and the Politics of Change in Imperial Russia* (Dekalb, Ill., 1990).

Derek Offord, *Portraits of Early Russian Liberals: A Study of the Thought of T. N. Granovsky, V. P. Botkin, P. V. Annenkov, A. V. Druzhinin, and K. D. Kavelin* (Cambridge, 1985).

Thomas C. Owen, *Capitalism and Politics in Russia: A Social History of the Moscow Merchants, 1855–1905* (Cambridge, 1981).

Philip Pomper, *The Russian Revolutionary Intelligentsia* (New York, 1971).

——, *Peter Lavrov and the Russian Revolutionary Movement* (Chicago, 1972).

Leonard Schapiro, *Turgenev: His Life and Times* (Oxford, 1978).

——, *Russian Studies*, ed. by Ellen Dahrendorf (London, 1986).

S. Frederick Starr, *Decentralization of Self-Government in Russia, 1830–1870* (Princeton, N.J., 1972).

Franco Venturi, *Roots of Revolution: A History of the Populist and Socialist Movements in Nineteenth-Century Russia* (London, 1960).

Lazar Volin, *A Century of Russian Agriculture: From Alexander II to Khrushchev* (Cambridge, Mass., 1970).

Andrzej Walicki, *The Controversy over Capitalism: Studies in the Social Philosophy of the Russian Populists* (Oxford, 1969).

——, *Legal Philosophies of Russian Liberalism* (Oxford, 1987).

William F. Woehrlin, *Chernyshevski: The Man and the Journalist* (Cambridge, Mass., 1971).

Richard Wortman, *The Development of a Russian Legal Consciousness* (Chicago, 1976).

4. Saving tsarism, 1900–1914

Abraham Ascher, *The Revolution of 1905* (2 vols, Cambridge, 1994).

Terence Emmons, *The Formation of Political Parties and the First National Elections in Russia* (Cambridge, Mass., 1983).

Marc Ferro, *Nicholas II: The Last of the Tsars* (Oxford, 1993).

Klaus Fröhlich, *The Emergence of Russian Constitutionalism 1900–1904* (The Hague, 1981).

Shmuel Galai, *The Liberation Movement in Russia 1900–1905* (Cambridge, 1973).

Leopold H. Haimson, *The Russian Marxists and the Origins of Bolshevism* (Cambridge. Mass., 1955).

——, 'The Problem of Social Stability in Urban Russia, 1905–1917', *Slavic Review*, 23, no. 4 (1964), pp. 619–42, and 24, no. 1, (1965), pp. 1–22.

——, ed., *The Politics of Rural Russia 1905–1914* (Bloomington, 1979).

——, ed., *The Making of Three Russian Revolutionaries* (Cambridge, 1987).

Sidney Harcave, *First Blood: The Russian Revolution of 1905* (London, 1965).

Neil Harding, ed., *Marxism in Russia: Key Documents 1879–1906* (Cambridge, 1983).

Geoffrey A. Hosking, *The Russian Constitutional Experiment: Government and Duma, 1907–1914* (Cambridge, 1973).

George Katkov et al., eds, *Russia Enters the Twentieth Century* (London, 1971).

J. L. H. Keep, *The Rise of Social Democracy in Russia* (Oxford, 1963).

David Lane, *The Roots of Russian Communism* (Assen and London, 1975).

Dominic Lieven, *Russia's Rulers Under the Old Regime* (New Haven, 1989).

——, *Nicholas II: Emperor of All the Russias* (London, 1993).

David A.J. Macey, *Government and Peasant in Russia, 1861–1906: The Pre-history of the Stolypin Reform* (Dekalb, Ill., 1987).

Roberta Thompson Manning, *The Crisis of the Old Order in Russia: Gentry and Government* (Princeton, N.J., 1982).

Robert B. McKean, *St Petersburg between the Revolutions: Workers and Revolutionaries, June 1907–February 1917* (New Haven, 1990).

——, ed., *New Perspectives in Modern Russian History* (London, 1992).

Paul Milyoukov, *Russia and Its Crisis* (New York, 1962).

Maureen Perrie, *The Agrarian Policy of the Russian Socialist-Revolutionary Party: From its Origins through the Revolution of 1905–07* (Cambridge, 1976).

Richard Pipes, *Struve* (2 vols, Cambridge, Mass., 1970 and 1980).

Don C. Rawson, *Russian Rightists and the Revolution of 1905* (Cambridge, 1995).

Alfred J. Rieber, *Merchants and Entrepreneurs in Imperial Russia* (Chapel Hill, 1982).

Thomas Riha, *A Russian European: Paul Miliukov in Russian Politics* (Notre Dame, 1969).

Hans Rogger, *Jewish Policies and Right-wing Politics in Imperial Russia* (London, 1986).

Walter Sablinsky, *The Road to Bloody Sunday* (Princeton, N.J., 1976).

Teodor Shanin, *Russia as a 'Developing Society'* (London, 1985).

___ , *Russia, 1905–07: Revolution as a Moment of Truth* (London, 1986).

Theofanis Stavrou, ed., *Russia under the Last Tsar* (Minneapolis, 1969).

Marc Szeftel, *The Russian Constitution of April 23 1906: Political Institutions of the Duma Monarchy* (Brussels, 1976).

Charls E. Timberlake, ed., *Essays on Russian Liberalism* (Columbia, Mo., 1972).

Donald W. Treadgold, *Lenin and His Rivals: The Struggle for Russia's Future, 1898–1906* (London, 1955).

Andrew M. Verner, *The Crisis of Russian Autocracy: Nicholas II and the 1905 Revolution* (Princeton, N.J., 1990).

Judith E. Zimmerman, 'Russian Liberal Theory 1900–1917', *Canadian–American Slavic Studies,* 4, no. I (1980), pp. 1–20.

5. Dual power and the Bolsheviks, 1914–1917

Edward Acton, *Rethinking the Russian Revolution* (London, 1990).

W. H. Chamberlin, *The Russian Revolution* (2 vols, London, 1935).

Paul Dukes, *October and the World: Perspectives on the Russian Revolution* (London, 1979).

John Dunn, *Modern Revolutions* (2nd edn, Cambridge, 1989).

Marc Ferro, *The Russian Revolution of February 1917* (London, 1972).

——, *October 1917: A Social History of the October Revolution* (London, 1980).

Michael T. Florinsky, *The End of the Russian Empire* (New Haven, 1931).

Ziva Galili, *The Menshevik Leaders in the Russian Revolution: Social Realities and Political Strategies* (Princeton, N.J., 1989).

Graeme Gill, *Peasants and Government in the Russian Revolution* (London, 1979).

Tsuyoshi Hasegawa, *The February Revolution: Petrograd 1917* (Seattle, 1981).

George Katkov, *Russia 1917: The February Revolution* (London, 1967).

John Keep, *The Russian Revolution: A Study in Mass Mobilization* (London, 1976).

Alexander Kerensky, *The Kerensky Memoirs: Russia and History's Turning Point* (London, 1966).

Diane Koenker, *Moscow Workers and the 1917 Revolution* (Princeton, N.J., 1981).

V. I. Lenin, *The State and Revolution,* ed. and tr. by Robert Service (London, 1992).

David Mandel, *The Petrograd Workers and the Fall of the Old Regime* (London, 1983).

——, *The Petrograd Workers and the Soviet Seizure of Power* (London, 1984).

Paul Milyukov, *Political Memoirs, 1905–1917* (Ann Arbor, 1967).

Raymond Pearson, *The Russian Moderates and the Crisis of Tsarism, 1914–1917* (London, 1977).

Richard Pipes, ed., *Revolutionary Russia* (Cambridge, Mass., 1968).

Philip Pomper, *Lenin, Trotsky and Stalin: The Intelligentsia and Power* (New York, 1990).

Alexander Rabinowitch, *The Bolsheviks Come to Power: The Revolution of 1917 in Petrograd* (New York, 1976).

Oliver H. Radkey, *The Agrarian Foes of Bolshevism: Promise and Default of the Russian Socialist Revolutionaries, February to October 1917* (New York, 1958).

John Reed, *Ten Days that Shook the World* (Harmondsworth, 1966).

William G. Rosenberg, *Liberals in the Russian Revolution: The Constitutional-Democratic Party, 1917–1921* (Princeton, N.J., 1974).

Leonard Schapiro, *1917: The Russian Revolution and the Origins of Present-Day Communism* (London, 1984).

Robert Service, ed., *Society and Politics in the Russian Revolution* (London, 1992).

Harold Shukman, ed., *The Blackwell Encyclopedia of the Russian Revolution* (Oxford, 1988).

Theda Skocpol, *States and Social Revolutions: A Comparative Analysis of France, Russia and China* (Cambridge, 1979).

S. A. Smith, *Red Petrograd: Revolution in the Factories, 1917–1918* (Cambridge, 1983).

Norman Stone, *The Eastern Front 1914–1917* (London, 1975).

N. N. Sukhanov, *The Russian Revolution 1917: A Personal Record,* ed. and tr. by Joel Carmichael (Oxford, 1955).

Ronald Grigor Suny, 'Towards a Social History of the October Revolution', *American Historical Review,* 88, no. I (1983), pp. 31–52.

Leon Trotsky, *The History of the Russian Revolution* (London, 1965).

Dmitri Volkogonov, *Lenin: Life and Legacy* (London, 1994).

James D. White, *The Russian Revolution 1917–1921: A Short History* (London, 1995).

Allan K. Wildman, *The End of the Russian Imperial Army* (2 vols, Princeton, N.J., 1980 and 1987).

6. The power of the party, 1917–1928

Jane Burbank, *Intelligentsia and Revolution: Russian Views of Bolshevism, 1917–22* (New York, 1986).

E. H. Carr, *The Russian Revolution from Lenin to Stalin, 1917–1929* (London, 1980).

Stephen F. Cohen, *Bukharin and the Bolshevik Revolution: A Political Biography 1888–1938* (London, 1974).

Robert V. Daniels, *The Conscience of the Revolution: Communist Opposition in Soviet Russia* (Cambridge, Mass., 1960).

Isaac Deutscher, *The Prophet Armed: Trotsky, 1921–1929* (London, 1959).

Samuel Farber, *Before Stalin: The Rise and Fall of Soviet Democracy* (Cambridge, 1990).

Orlando Figes, *Peasant Russia, Civil War: The Volga Countryside in Revolution (1917–1921)* (Oxford, 1989).

Sheila Fitzpatrick, *Education and Social Mobility in the Soviet Union, 1921–1934* (Cambridge, 1979).

——, *The Cultural Front: Power and Culture in Revolutionary Russia* (Ithaca, N.Y., 1992).

Sheila Fitzpatrick, Alexander Rabinowitch and Richard Stites, eds, *Russia in the Era of NEP* (Bloomington, 1990).

Isaac Getzler, *Kronstadt, 1917–1921: The Fate of a Soviet Democracy* (Cambridge, 1983).

Graeme Gill, *The Origins of the Stalinist Political System* (Cambridge, 1990).

Camilla Gray, *The Russian Experiment in Art 1863–1922* (London, 1971).

Peter Kenez, *The Birth of the Propaganda State: Soviet Methods of Mass Mobilization, 1917–1929* (Cambridge, 1985).

Diane P. Koenker, William G. Rosenberg and Ronald Grigor Suny, eds, *Party, State and Society in the Russian Civil War* (Bloomington, 1989).

Christel Lane, *The Rites of Rulers: Ritual in Industrial Society – The Soviet Case* (Cambridge, 1981).

Moshe Lewin, *Lenin's Last Struggle* (London, 1969).

——, *The Making of the Soviet System: Essays in the Social History of Interwar Russia* (London, 1985).

Marcel Liebman, *Leninism under Lenin* (London, 1975).

Evan Mawdsley, *The Russian Civil War* (Boston, 1987).

Mary McAuley, *Bread and Justice: State and Society in Petrograd, 1917–1922* (Oxford, 1991).

Boris Pasternak, *Doctor Zhivago* (London, 1958).

Roger Pethybridge, *The Social Prelude to Stalinism* (London, 1974).

——, *One Step Backwards, Two Steps Forward: Soviet Society and Politics under the New Economic Policy* (Oxford, 1990).

Richard Pipes, *The Formation of the Soviet Union: Communism and Nationalism 1917–1923* (Cambridge, Mass., 1964).

——, *Russia under the Bolshevik Regime 1919–1924* (London, 1994).

Oliver H. Radkey, *The Unknown Civil War: A Study of the Green Movement in the Tambov Region, 1920–1921* (Stanford, Cal., 1976).

——, *Russia Goes to the Polls: The Election to the All-Russian Constituent Assembly, 1917* (Ithaca, N.Y., 1989).

Edvard Radzinsky, *The Last Tsar: The Life and Death of Nicholas II* (London, 1992).

T. H. Rigby, *Lenin's Government: Sovnarkom, 1917–1922* (Cambridge, 1979).

Richard Sakwa, *Soviet Communists in Power: A Study of Moscow during the Civil War, 1918–21* (London, 1988).

Leonard Schapiro, *The Origin of the Communist Autocracy: Political Opposition in the Soviet State: First Phase, 1917–1922* (London, 1955).

Victor Serge, *Memoirs of a Revolutionary 1901–1941* (Oxford, 1963).

Robert Service, *The Bolshevik Party in Revolution: A Study in Organisational Change, 1917–1923* (London, 1979).

Lewis H. Siegelbaum, *Soviet State and Society between Revolutions, 1918–1929* (Cambridge, 1992).

Boris Thomson, *The Premature Revolution: Russian Literature and Society, 1917–1946* (London, 1972).

Robert C. Tucker, *Stalin as Revolutionary, 1879–1929* (New York, 1973).

Nina Tumarkin, *Lenin Lives! The Lenin Cult in Soviet Russia* (Cambridge, Mass., 1983).

H. G. Wells, *Russia in the Shadows* (London, 1921).

Stephen White, *The Bolshevik Poster* (New Haven, 1988).

7. Stalinism, 1929–1953

John Barber and Mark Harrison, *The Soviet Home Front, 1941–45* (London, 1991).

Robert Conquest, *The Harvest of Sorrow: Soviet Collectivization and the Terror–Famine* (London, 1986).

——, *The Great Terror: A Reassessment* (London, 1990).

——, *Stalin: Breaker of Nations* (London, 1991).

R. W. Davies, *The Industrialization of Soviet Russia* (3 vols, London, 1980–89).

John Erickson, *The Road to Stalingrad* (London, 1975).

——, *The Road to Berlin* (London, 1983).

Merle Fainsod, *Smolensk under Soviet Rule* (Boston, 1989).

Sheila Fitzpatrick, ed., *Cultural Revolution in Russia, 1928–1931* (Bloomington, 1978).

——, *Stalin's Peasants: Resistance and Survival in the Russian Village after Collectivization* (Oxford, 1994).

J. Arch Getty, *Origins of the Great Purges: The Soviet Communist Party Reconsidered, 1933–1938* (Cambridge, 1985).

J. Arch Getty and Roberta T. Manning, eds, *Stalinist Terror: New Perspectives* (Cambridge, 1993).

Evgenia Ginzburg, *Into the Whirlwind* (Harmondsworth, 1968).

History of the Communist Party of the Soviet Union (Bolsheviks): Short Course (Moscow, 1939).

Hiroaki Kiromiya, *Stalin's Industrial Revolution: Politics and Workers, 1928–1932* (Cambridge, 1988).

Amy Knight, *Beria: Stalin's First Lieutenant* (Princeton, N.J., 1993).

Stephen Kotkin, *Magnetic Mountain: Stalinism as a Civilization* (Berkeley, Cal., 1995).

Moshe Lewin, *Russian Peasants and Soviet Power: A Study of Collectivization* (London, 1968).

Fitzroy Maclean, *Eastern Approaches* (Harmondsworth, 1991).

Nadezhda Mandelstam, *Hope against Hope* (Harmondsworth, 1975).

William O. McCagg, Jr, *Stalin Embattled 1943–48* (Detroit, 1978).

Roy Medvedev, *Let History Judge: The Origins and Consequences of Stalinism* (New York, 1971).

Alec Nove, *Stalinism and After: The Road to Gorbachev* (Boston, 1989).

——, ed., *The Stalin Phenomenon* (London, 1993).

Anatoli Rybakov, *Children of the Arbat* (London, 1988).

Harrison Salisbury, *The Siege of Leningrad* (London, 1969).

Alexander Solzhenitsyn, *The Gulag Archipelago 1918–1956* (3 vols, London 1974–8).

Nikolai Timasheff, *The Great Retreat: The Growth and Decline of Communism in Russia* (New York, 1946).

Robert C. Tucker, *The Soviet Political Mind: Stalinism and Post-Stalin Change* (2nd edn, London, 1972).

——, ed., *Stalinism: Essays in Historical Interpretation* (New York, 1977).

——, *Stalin in Power: The Revolution from Above 1928–1941* (New York, 1990).

Lynn Viola, *The Best Sons of the Fatherland: Workers in the Vanguard of Soviet Collectivization* (Oxford, 1987).

Dmitri Volkogonov, *Stalin: Triumph and Tragedy* (London, 1991).

Chris Ward, *Stalin's Russia* (London, 1993).

Sidney and Beatrice Webb, *Soviet Communism: A New Civilisation* (3rd edn, London, 1944).

8. Khrushchev and communism, 1953–1964

George W. Breslauer, *Khrushchev and Brezhnev as Leaders: Building Authority in Soviet Politics* (London, 1982).

Archie Brown, ed., *Political Leadership in the Soviet Union* (London, 1989).

Vladimir Bukovsky, *To Build a Castle: My Life as a Dissenter* (London, 1978).

Fedor Burlatsky, *Khrushchev and the First Russian Spring* (London, 1991).

Stephen F. Cohen, Alexander Rabinowitch and Robert Sharlet, eds, *The Soviet Union since Stalin* (London, 1980).

Edward Crankshaw, *Khrushchev's Russia* (2nd edn, Harmondsworth, 1962).

——, *Khrushchev: A Biography* (London, 1966).

Milovan Djilas, *The New Class: An Analysis of the Communist System* (London, 1957).

Edith Rogovin Frankel, *Novy Mir: A Case Study in the Politics of Literature, 1952–58* (Cambridge, 1981).

Mark Frankland, *Khrushchev* (Harmondsworth, 1966).

N. Khrushchev, *Khrushchev Remembers,* ed. and tr. by Strode Talbott (2 vols, Harmondsworth, 1977).

Sergei Khrushchev, *Khrushchev on Khrushchev* (Boston, 1990).

O. Kuusinen, ed., *Fundamentals of Marxism–Leninism* (London, 1961).

Wolfgang Leonhard, *The Kremlin since Stalin* (Oxford, 1962).

Carl A. Linden, *Khrushchev and the Soviet Leadership 1957–1964* (Baltimore, 1966).

Martin McCauley, ed., *Khrushchev and Khrushchevism* (London, 1987).

——, *Nikita Sergeievich Khrushchev* (London, 1991).

T. H. Rigby, ed., *The Stalin Dictatorship: Khrushchev's 'Secret Speech' and Other Documents* (Sydney, 1968).

Michael Scammell, *Solzhenitsyn: A Biography* (London, 1985).

Leonard Schapiro, ed., *The USSR and the Future: An Analysis of the New Program of the CPSU* (New York, 1963).

Alexander Solzhenitsyn, *One Day in the Life of Ivan Denisovich* (Harmondsworth, 1963).

——, *The Oak and the Calf: Sketches of Literary Life in the Soviet Union* (London, 1980).

William J. Tompson, *Khrushchev: A Political Life* (London, 1994).

Yevgeny Yevtushenko, *A Precocious Autobiography* (London, 1963).

9. Conservatism, 1964–1985

Andrei Amalrik, *Will the Soviet Union Survive until 1984?* (Harmondsworth, 1980).

Y.V. Andropov, *The Teaching of Karl Marx and Some Questions of Building Socialism in the USSR* (Moscow, 1983).

Seweryn Bialer, *The Soviet Paradox: External Expansion, Internal Decline* (London, 1986).

Archie Brown and Michael Kaser, eds., *The Soviet Union since the Fall of Khrushchev* (2nd edn, London, 1978).
——, *Soviet Policy for the 1980s* (London, 1982).
L. G. Churchward, *Soviet Socialism: Social and Political Essays* (London, 1987).
Stephen F. Cohen, ed., *An End to Silence: Uncensored Opinion in the Soviet Union* (New York, 1982).
John Dornberg, *Brezhnev: The Masks of Power* (London, 1974).
Alfred B. Evans, Jr, 'Developed Socialism in Soviet Ideology', *Soviet Studies,* 29, no. 3 (1977), pp. 409–28.
Marshall I. Goldman, *USSR in Crisis: The Failure of an Economic System* (New York, 1983).
Geoffrey Hosking, *The Awakening of the Soviet Union* (2nd edn, Cambridge, Mass., 1991).
Jerry F. Hough, *Soviet Leadership in Transition* (Washington, D.C., 1980).
Basile Kerblay, *Modern Soviet Society* (London, 1988).
Moshe Lewin, *Political Undercurrents in Soviet Economic Debates: From Bukharin to the Modern Reformers* (London, 1975).
Roy Medvedev, *On Socialist Democracy,* tr. and ed. by Ellen de Kadt, (London, 1975).
——, *On Soviet Dissent: Interviews with Piero Ostellino* (New York, 1980).
Zhores Medvedev, *Andropov: His Life and Death* (Oxford, 1984).
John W. Parker, *Kremlin in Transition,* vol. I: *From Brezhnev to Chernenko* (London, 1991).
Peter Reddaway, ed., *Uncensored Russia: The Human Rights Movement in the Soviet Union* (London, 1972).
Abraham Rothberg, *The Heirs of Stalin: Dissidence and the Soviet Regime 1953–1970* (Ithaca, N.Y., 1972).
Joshua Rubenstein, *Soviet Dissidents: Their Struggle for Human Rights* (London, 1981).
Andrei D. Sakharov, *Sakharov Speaks,* ed. by Harrison E. Salisbury, (London, 1974).
George Saunders, ed., *Samizdat: Voices of the Soviet Opposition* (New York, 1974).
G. Shakhnazarov, *The Destiny of the World: The Socialist Shape of Things to Come* (Moscow, 1979).
Marshall S. Shatz, *Soviet Dissent in Historical Perspective* (Cambridge, 1980).
Aleksandr Solzhenitsyn, *Letter to Soviet Leaders* (London, 1974).
Pekka Sutela, *Economic Thought and Economic Reform in the Soviet Union* (Cambridge, 1991).
Rudolf L. Tökes, ed., *Dissent in the USSR: Politics, Ideology and People* (Baltimore, 1975).

Stephen White, *Political Culture and Soviet Politics* (London, 1979).

10. The success and failure of perestroika, 1985–1990; 11. Disintegration, 1990–1991.

Abel Aganbegyan, *The Challenge: Economics of Perestroika* (London, 1988).

Anders Aslund, *Gorbachev's Struggle for Economic Reform* (2nd edn, London, 1991).

Archie Brown, *The Gorbachev Factor* (Oxford, 1996).

Mary Buckley, *Redefining Russian Society and Polity* (Boulder, 1993).

James Cracraft, ed., *The Soviet Union Today: An Interpretive Guide* (2nd edn, Chicago, 1988).

Alexander Dallin and Gail W. Lapidus, eds, *The Soviet System: From Crisis to Collapse* (2nd edn, Boulder, 1994).

Robert V. Daniels, *The End of the Communist Revolution* (London, 1993).

John B. Dunlop, *The Rise of Russia and the Fall of the Soviet Union* (Princeton, N.J., 1993).

Michael Ellman and Vladimir Kontorovich, eds., *The Disintegration of the Soviet Economic System* (London, 1992).

M. Steven Fish, *Democracy from Scratch: Opposition and Regime in the New Russian Revolution* (Princeton, N.J., 1995).

Graeme Gill, *The Rules of the Communist Party of the Soviet Union* (London, 1988).

Marshall I. Goldman, *What Went Wrong with Perestroika* (New York, 1991).

John Gooding, 'Perestroika and the Russian Revolution of 1991', *Slavonic and East European Review*, 71, no. 2 (1993), pp. 234–56.

Mikhail Gorbachev, *Perestroika: New Thinking for Our Country and the World* (London, 1987).

——, *The August Coup: The Truth and the Lessons* (London, 1991).

Andrei Grachev, *Final Days: The Inside Story of the Collapse of the Soviet Union* (Boulder, 1995).

A. Hewett and Victor H. Winston, eds, *Milestones in Glasnost and Perestroyka* (2 vols, Washington, D.C., 1991).

Geoffrey Hosking, *The Awakening of the Soviet Union* (2nd edn, Cambridge, Mass., 1991).

Geoffrey Hosking, Jonathan Aves and Peter J. S. Duncan, *The Road to Post-Communism: Independent Political Movements in the Soviet Union 1985–1991* (London, 1992).

Eugene Huskey, ed., *Executive Power and Soviet Politics: The Rise and Decline of the Soviet State* (Armonck, N.Y., 1992).

Walter Lacqueur, *The Dream that Failed: Reflections on the Soviet Union* (Oxford, 1995).

David Lane, *Soviet Society under Perestroika* (2nd edn, London, 1992).

Moshe Lewin, *The Gorbachev Phenomenon: A Historical Interpretation* (London, 1988).

Anatol Lieven, *The Baltic Revolution: Estonia, Latvia, Lithuania and the Path to Independence* (New Haven, 1993).

Roy Medvedev and Giuletto Chiesa, *Time of Change: An Insider's View of Russia's Transformation* (London, 1991).

Catherine Merridale and Chris Ward, eds, *Perestroika: The Historical Perspective* (London, 1991).

John Miller, *Mikhail Gorbachev and the End of Soviet Power* (London, 1993).

John Morrison, *Boris Yeltsin: From Bolshevik to Democrat* (Harmondsworth, 1991).

Alec Nove, *Glasnost in Action: Cultural Renaissance in Russia* (Boston, 1989).

David Remnick, *Lenin's Tomb: The Last Days of the Soviet Empire* (London, 1993).

Philip G. Roeder, *Red Sunset: The Failure of Soviet Politics* (Princeton, N.J., 1994).

Angus Roxburgh, *The Second Russian Revolution* (London, 1991).

Amin Saikal and William Maley, eds, *Russia in Search of its Future* (Cambridge, 1995).

Richard Sakwa, *Gorbachev and His Reforms 1985–1990* (Hemel Hempstead, 1990).

——, *Russian Politics and Society* (London, 1993).

Victor Sergeyev and Nikolai Biryukov, *Russia's Road to Democracy* (Aldershot, 1993).

Graham Smith, ed., *The Nationalities' Question in the Soviet Union* (London, 1990).

Hedrick Smith, *The New Russians* (London, 1990).

Jonathan Steele, *Eternal Russia* (2nd edn, London, 1995).

Robert C. Tucker, *Political Culture and Leadership in Soviet Russia: From Lenin to Gorbachev* (Brighton, 1987).

Michael E. Urban, *More Power to the Soviets: The Democratic Revolution in the USSR* (Aldershot, 1990).

Martin Walker, *The Waking Giant: The Soviet Union under Gorbachev* (London, 1986).

Rachel Walker, *Six Years that Shook the World: Perestroika – The Impossible Project* (Manchester, 1993).

Stephen White, *After Gorbachev* (4th edn, Cambridge, 1993).

Stephen White, Graeme Gill and Darrell Slider, *The Politics of Transition: Shaping a Post-Soviet Future* (Cambridge, 1993).

Boris Yeltsin, *Against the Grain: An Autobiography* (London, 1990).

——, *The View from the Kremlin* (London, 1994).

Tatyana Zaslavskaya, *The Second Socialist Revolution: An Alternative Soviet Strategy* (London, 1990).

Index